PRAISE FOR *EV… …IANAGEMENT*

'I was given 30 words to endorse the 30 new case studies that appear in the 12 chapters of the fully updated third edition of my favourite 'go to' textbook. Here's 3: "compelling, comprehensive, compulsory".'
Dr Richard Keith Wright, Senior Lecturer in Sport Events and Entrepreneurship, Auckland University of Technology, New Zealand

'This book provides an excellent insight into the complex and dynamic event planning process which is so crucial for successful event managers. The authors' planning model is developed strategically and contextually through excellently sourced contemporary case studies from around the world.'
Dr Lucy Laville, Course Director, UK Centre for Events Management

'This book is essential reading for anyone wanting to build a career in our amazing events industry. The balance of real-world, contemporary case studies and insight with educational models truly represent the diverse, complex and thrilling world that is event management.'
Tim Collett, Managing Director, WRG, a division of the Creative Engagement Group, UK

'Having employed dozens of students from the exceptional event management course at Leeds Beckett over the past 20+ years, I know that this incredibly detailed book is a conduit to success for future event managers.'
Amanda Edgcumbe, Founder and Director, Powwow Events

PRAISE FOR THE SECOND EDITION

'This book is truer to the real world of event planning and management than any I used while studying or that I've come across in over 20 years of running events.'
Mark Breen, Director, Cuckoo Events and Safe Events (about a previous edition)

'This book is easy to follow for both event professionals and event management students alike – there is something for everyone. The authors have broken down the planning process into bite-size chunks that are easy to digest, and they offer great tips and reminders for anyone responsible for organizing an event.'
Emma Cartmell, CEO, CHS Group (about a previous edition)

Event Planning and Management

Principles, planning and practice

THIRD EDITION

Ruth Dowson, Bernadette Albert
and Dan Lomax

First published in Great Britain and the United States in 2015 by Kogan Page Limited
Second edition 2018
Third edition 2023

2nd Floor, 45 Gee Street
London
EC1V 3RS
United Kingdom
www.koganpage.com

8 W 38th Street, Suite 902
New York, NY 10018
USA

4737/23 Ansari Road
Daryaganj
New Delhi 110002
India

Kogan Page books are printed on paper from sustainable forests.

ISBNs

Hardback 978 1 3986 0712 5
Paperback 978 1 3986 0710 1
Ebook 978 1 3986 0711 8

British Library Cataloguing-in-Publication Data

A CIP record for this book is available from the British Library.

Library of Congress Control Number
2022049113

Typeset by Integra Software Services, Pondicherry
Print production managed by Jellyfish
Printed and bound by CPI Group (UK) Ltd, Croydon, CR0 4YY

To Matt, my rock, with more gratitude and love than ever.
To the new generation:
Aria, Baby Celine, Lilia and Joel, with love from Nanny.
And to the best roomies in the world, Bernie and Dan (family).
RUTH

To Alister my love, you have inspired me to do more, be better, and never settle, thank you for being my number 1 cheerleader.
To Jojo my second love, who reminds me every day that patience is a virtue, that nothing happens before its time, and to never give up.
To Ruth, Dan, and Mel, simply thank you for everything you are, and more.
BERNIE

To Ally and Evie with love for keeping me going,
Ruth and Bernie for sharing the journey
and the students at the UK Centre for Events Management
at Leeds Beckett for their enthusiasm.
DAN

CONTENTS

LIST OF FIGURES AND TABLES

FIGURES

TABLES

FOREWORD

Among the industries most badly affected by the Covid-19 pandemic has been events. In Britain, the Covid-19 lockdowns led to 17.5 per cent of exhibition businesses closing in 2020 alone, and 126,000 job losses during March–August 2020. For two years, anything that involved people gathering in a physical space was impossible, but more positively, as the authors of this important book say, 'we discovered anew the reasons why events are so crucial to society. Events do more than simply bring people together; they help to build social cohesion, and enhance the wellbeing of participants.'

We missed physical events terribly, but this is a resilient and creative industry. The energy that it expends on creating memorable and safe events for others, it also applied to itself during the pandemic. All kinds and sizes of online events were staged, from birthday parties to conferences, to concerts and commemorations. Events helped bring meaning, purpose and an ability to participate to millions. As we recover from the pandemic, the events industry is recovering too, but it won't be the same. The new knowledge, skills and ways of working that were hard-learnt during the pandemic, such as putting on hybrid events and making them more diverse and inclusive, will be taken forward too.

Besides being an industry that can be harnessed for good, events are important economically too. According to Allied Market Research (2022), the industry's value is expected to reach $1,552.9 billion (£1,166.87 billion) by 2028. While it's difficult to be accurate about how many people work in the events industry, it's estimated that prior to the 2020 pandemic, around 80 million people attended 1.5 million conferences and meetings annually, and in the UK, the sector's 25,000 businesses employed some 530,000 people. Facts about the size and nature of the events industry are eye-watering. Pre-pandemic, the business events sector was estimated to be worth £31.2 billion to the UK visitor economy, with conferences and meetings valued at £18.3 billion, exhibitions and trade fairs at £11 billion, incentive travel worth £1.2 billion and corporate outdoor events valued at £0.7 billion. Leisure events were estimated to be worth £38.8 billion in 2019, arts and cultural events £5.6 billion, music events and festivals £23.6 billion and sports events £9.6 billion. It would be a mistake to think the events business is not a serious one: it's back and it will grow.

The definition of an event according to this book is a planned gathering of people that has a purpose, is memorable or special, and is temporary. Events range from the huge (such as an Olympic Games) to the small (such as a training event) and everything in between: cultural celebrations, political summits, private parties, arts and entertainment performances, educational exhibitions and recreational activities. The industry touches every aspect of human life and endeavour, and this book provides a step-by-step guide to them all.

This fully updated third edition of *Event Planning and Management* adds real strength to the CIPR/Kogan Page series *PR in Practice*. Dowson, Albert and Lomax have revised and added lots of new material directly relating to the radical changes the industry has seen during and post-pandemic, but also the latest developments and thinking on the industry now and into the future. The book begins by defining an event and then takes the reader through a useful overview of the kinds of events that fall under different categories, from music festivals to set-piece sporting events. The authors then move on to an overview of the event planning cycle and introduce their own systematic four-stage planning model: concept, detailed planning, on-site and post event. Unfolding this model, the subsequent chapters cover the crucial elements of event management from research and developing the concept to design, content, venue, operations, staffing, marketing and finance. The section on on-site management is detailed and very practical (as is the whole book), with a sobering discussion on site-safety. No one can forget we are in an era where malign actors want to wreak havoc to draw attention to themselves, but safety is not just about the big things – it's a mindset and attitude that has to be part of the DNA thinking of every event planner. Numerous case studies from all around the world and of a variety of events, along with 'events manager hacks', bring the theory to life and illustrate the key points in a lively and informative way. The book offers good practical templates to help with such things as organizing budgets and service level agreements and the authors do not shy away from tackling some of the tougher issues such as when events have to be cancelled.

The last but one chapter looks at evaluating events, both online and in more traditional ways. Again, by using examples and providing advice on how to develop contemporary evaluation, including on sustainability monitoring, the book brings a wealth of knowledge and practical assistance to anyone wanting to create an event. A fascinating last chapter looks to the future. This is not just a wish list for an industry that has taken a battering in recent years, but, based on research, it is a serious look at what has been learnt and what needs to be taken forward, such as different event forms, how to be more inclusive and how collaboration and innovation have to be embedded in ways of working.

There is so much new in this third edition. Apart from the new case studies from around the world and the general update on all aspects of event management, the new planning model is memorable and brings additional clarity to the planning process. Nothing is missed; from the use of big data and analytics to the new technological advances such as virtual and augmented reality, all are included and explained within a book that is very accessible and readable. It is peppered with examples, advice, practical suggestions, templates and tips and has an online resource bank to back it up. It is written by authors who know the events industry inside out and who have a deep understanding borne of many years' experience and observation. It's a must-read for the absolute beginner and for those wanting a career in this exciting industry. For the more experienced and serious event planner, it's a timely reminder and update of all that makes events challenging and rewarding. Keep it on your desk and use it often.

Professor Emeritus Anne Gregory, University of Huddersfield
Series Editor

PREFACE

We were delighted when Kogan Page asked us to develop a new edition of our book. The first edition was published in 2015 and the second in 2018 with Ruth Dowson and David Bassett as co-authors. This third edition has a new team of authors – Ruth Dowson, Bernadette Albert and Dan Lomax – and we are grateful to David Bassett for his sterling efforts in developing the successful first and second editions. We have completely revised the event planning model, using the benefits of teaching using the earlier editions to our students at the UK Centre for Events Management, since 2015. We have also taken into account the new context in which the events industry operates, following the start of the Covid-19 pandemic, which affected the events tourism and hospitality industries around the world, more than most. We are grateful to Kogan Page and our editor, Heather Wood, for their support.

With about 100 years' combined experience in events, as practitioners in different areas of this exciting industry, we have found that rewriting this book has given us another opportunity to share our practical advice, best practice, events manager hacks, checklists and templates to help others plan and manage their events. We have also been able to call on the resources of events industry professionals from around the world, with over 30 new case studies and other contributions. We want our readers to be able to use the book as a 'how to' guide, to make things easier for them whatever their ability or experience, helping them to gain confidence.

The book can be read either from cover to cover, or by starting with a particular chapter for advice on a specific aspect of the events planning process. The structured approach we recommend is not set in stone, but we recognize that in this industry it is easy to forget something very simple that can adversely affect the outcome of your event.

We hope that you enjoy reading our book and that your events will benefit from reading our stories and experiences.

You can download new additional resources for this book at www.koganpage.com/epm

ACKNOWLEDGEMENTS

Thank you to the following individuals without whose contributions and support this book would not have been written.

To Anne Gregory for initially inviting us to write the first edition of this book in 2013, and the team at Kogan Page for their efforts in publishing it.

A *big* thank you to David Bassett, our good friend and former UKCEM roommate, for his amazing foundational contributions to the first and second editions of the book.

To our wonderful colleagues and fantastic students (past and present) at the UK Centre for Events Management for inspiring us. We've learned so much from you over the years, we thought we would return the favour.

To Jeanette and Julie, thank you for allowing us to use your images.

To Belbin Associates, thank you for giving us permissions to reproduce your content.

To each other for being family!

A huge thank you to our amazing case study authors, Events Manager Hack contributors and specialist industry contributors, including:

Prof Victor Afonso, Katie Aldous, Selina Arnall, Felicia Asiedu, Joe Atkinson, Laura Bennett-Whiskens, Ollie Biddle, Sarah Bird, Dr Tim Brown, Prof Ivan Cohen, Tim Collett, Paul Cook, Joe Cosgrove, Dr Ubaldino Couto, Dr Kate Dashper, Karoline Dowson, Carys Duckworth, Serena Ferrari, Elsa Gavinho, Klaudia Gawrysiak, Lisa Ghany, Gemma Gilbert, Dr Susana Filipa Gonçalves, Ana Gonçalves, Becky Goringe, Sasha Green, Ulrike Hitchen, Naomi Hollas, Jenny Homer, Zeeshana Khan, Dasha Kotwani, Dr Ian Lamond, Cláudia Lopes, Rob Madeley, Amy Mullan, Charlie Mussett, Priya Narain, Lori Novell, Chris Powell, Janine Priest, Dr Adrian Richardson, Dr Roxy Robinson, Adrian Segar, Francisco Silva, Diane Thompson, Neil Thompson, Abbie Thornton, Alessandra Valente, Jessica Vandy, Kharmen Wilson.

A big thank you also to those event industry professionals who weren't able – on this occasion – to contribute. We appreciate how busy you all are, and we salute you all.

ACKNOWLEDGMENTS

01

Events – the changing environment

FIGURE 1.1 The Dowson, Albert and Lomax Event Planning Process – the event environment

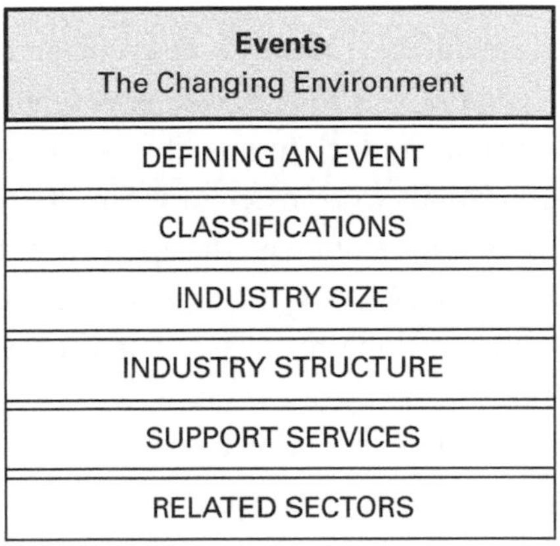

Events The Changing Environment
DEFINING AN EVENT
CLASSIFICATIONS
INDUSTRY SIZE
INDUSTRY STRUCTURE
SUPPORT SERVICES
RELATED SECTORS

In March 2020, the events industry, along with the rest of the world, was just beginning to become aware of the effects of the Covid-19 virus which would become a pandemic that raged across the globe, affecting most countries and resulting in at least six million deaths by March 2022. Along with hospitality and tourism, the events industry closed down for anything that brought people together in a physical space or location. Two years later, we are emerging into what we hope is a post-pandemic era, accompanied by new practices (including regular washing and sanitizing of hands, maintaining social distancing and wearing a face covering) and medical developments in the form of vaccines which have enabled us to meet each other again, even though millions of people are still catching the virus. During the periods of lockdown, in the absence of events, we discovered anew the reasons why events are so crucial to society. Events do more than simply bring people together; they help to build social cohesion and enhance the wellbeing of participants. Throughout history, humans have assembled with ceremony or ritual to achieve and deliver specific results. Today, the events industry is made up of a diverse range of people, and this is reflected in the cultural richness of organizers and audiences. There are many different kinds of events, with different purposes and rich cultural histories that demonstrate how societies celebrate and express relationships, how they mourn losses and acknowledge power, for entertainment, sport and business – and more. Many events are multicultural and inclusive, whether open to the general public or aimed at specific audiences. And even with the same content, or held in the same location, each event is unique.

This chapter explores the origins of the events industry and how it works today in a changing environment. The global events industry size was valued at $1,135.4 billion (£853.16 billion) in 2019 and is expected to reach $1,552.9 billion (£1,166.87 billion) by 2028 (Allied Market Research, 2022). Working in the events industry post-pandemic continues to offer an exciting and often sociable career, with opportunities to specialize in a huge variety of roles. As authors we all have decades of experience as professionals in different areas of the events industry, and we are proud to be part of this resilient sector, which is open to new opportunities as it begins to bounce back. During the pandemic lockdowns, the skills developed in events have enabled many events professionals to transfer to work in other industries and take on different roles, while others have embraced the opportunities offered by the wholesale move to online delivery. The events industry is flexible and creative and offers a bright future to those who are willing to invest their time and energies in learning and gaining new experience.

By the end of this chapter you will be able to:

- give a definition of an event;
- explain the different classifications and categories of events;
- describe the size of the events industry;
- outline the structure of the events industry;
- list the types of events suppliers and support services;
- demonstrate the relationships between events and other closely related industry sectors.

Defining an event

As people involved in the events industry, whether as students or professionals, when we talk about 'an event', we are not talking about natural phenomena, such as earthquakes and storms, but about planned gatherings that bring people together. Smaller gatherings might involve family and friends, work colleagues or work contacts from other businesses. Yet events often bring strangers together, people who might only meet once, on that occasion, and never come across the other participants again. This is often the case when attending larger live events, such as concerts or sporting competitions. The purpose of the gathering will inevitably vary. Sometimes people come together to be entertained, and at other times people gather to be educated. But the important point here is that the gathering is planned and there is a purpose to it. The purpose may be simple or complex, and sometimes the events organizers don't think deeply enough about what the real purpose of an event is, but the first part of our definition is:

> 'An event is a planned gathering with a purpose'

Stop for a moment and think about an event that you have attended. Which event did you immediately think of? A special occasion, such as a birthday party or wedding, or a sports match or a music concert? Maybe you thought of it because it was a particularly enjoyable or emotional experience? You may have been able to share the experience along with your family or close friends. The event may have taken place in an exotic location, or on a gloriously sunny day, or perhaps it was memorable because you learnt something valuable. Whatever the event, it was obviously something important to you, but what made it memorable could be due to any number of factors. This brings us to the second part of our definition:

> 'An event is memorable or special'

Some events last an hour or two, such as a meeting, a concert, or a football match, while others last a day – for example, a wedding or conference. Other events may last a few days – an outdoor festival or industry trade show. Some events might last a few weeks, such as an art exhibition or festive Christmas market. One of the longest events is the World Expo, an international cultural gathering, which lasts for up to six months. The most recent World Expo was in Dubai, and took place from 1 October 2021 to 31 March 2022. (You can read more about this event in Case study 7.3.) The next World Expo is planned for 2025 in Osaka, Japan. But whatever the length of time, all events have a predetermined life cycle with planned start and end dates. This brings us to the third part of our definition:

> 'An event is temporary'

In summary, our definition of an event is 'a temporary planned gathering with a purpose, that is memorable or special'.

The box shows some further definitions and descriptions of an event given by some of the leading events management authors.

FIGURE 1.2 Defining an event

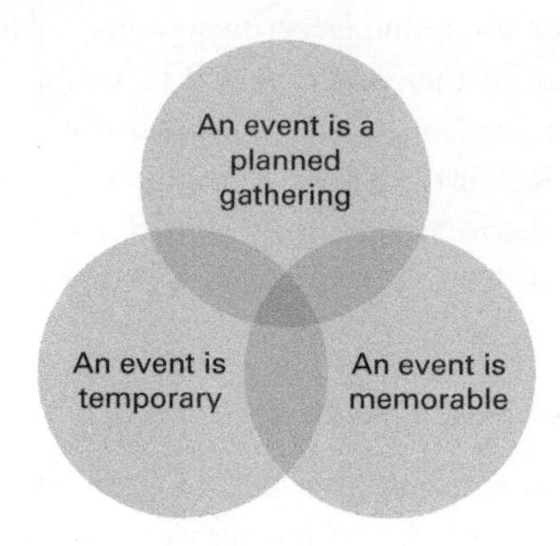

'An experience that has been designed' (Getz and Page, 2020)

'Those non-routine occasions set apart from the normal activity of daily life of a group of people' (Shone and Parry, 2019)

[International events are] 'large-scale events which attract international audiences and media attention and meet a variety of economic objectives for the destinations in which they are hosted' (Ferdinand and Kitchin, 2021)

'Happenings with objectives' (Raj, Walters and Rashid, 2017)

Having seen some other definitions of 'an event', Case Study 1.1 reflects on the question 'What do we mean by events?' and is written from a Critical Event Studies perspective.

CASE STUDY 1.1

The importance of understanding the event-ness of the event

Dr Ian R Lamond, Senior Lecturer and Researcher, UK Centre for Events Management, Leeds Beckett University

Often, when we think about events, words like engaging, exciting, immersive, unique, special, spectacular may come to mind – but how often do we think: what is an event anyway? Our first thought may associate events with celebrations – birthdays, weddings, or something similar. Perhaps our thoughts will drift to some open field festival where we partied hard, or a trade fair where we confirmed that amazing contract. Some may find themselves reflecting on a winning goal at a crucial match, someone receiving their medal for a race run well, lifting high an award for the best single, film, performance, publication and so on. While all these may be considered events, what do they tell us about what the word 'event' names? After all, event is a noun: it names something – a person, place, thing or concept; so, what does it name? Interestingly, that is the nub of the problem – events are processes. They are a set of mixed activities rather than a thing. We need to rethink events as something closer to an adjective or verb. Events need to be understood as ***evental***, in the sense that the processes and activity of politics is better understood as the political.

Processes never occur in a vacuum. They have a relationship with their surroundings, one that is co-creative and mutually co-dependent; they are affected and effected by their situation, as well as affecting and effecting the situation in which they emerge. Consequently, once we have made the move to thinking about events from the perspective of process and activity (i.e. thinking about events from the perspective of them being evental), we have direct access to understanding resource management, contextual sensitivity, and the event's impact/consequence as co-creative and co-dependent. Significantly, those factors cease being something remote, of value to managing an event, to become something central to what makes it an event. To manage those things in a way that lacks thought, examination, reflection, is to distort and fundamentally change the event being envisaged.

How then should we think about events? This will depend on the route that has brought us to this question. The two main pathways appropriate to this book can be drawn under the broad headings of event management and event studies. For both, a key approach is that of narrative deconstruction, though what is meant by that will differ depending on the outcome you are intending. Arguably the outcome of following the event management path encompasses creating a 'successful event' – however you want to define 'success'. For event studies, the output may include obtaining a deeper understanding of the meaning of an event.

Events, as process and activity, are complex; they are layered in multiple and interconnected ways. The interconnected layers constitute the diverse narratives (stories) that are associated with the event. A non-exhaustive list of such narratives of, for example, a trade fair would include those of the traders; technicians; security staff; attendees; marketeers; venue provider; community adjacent to the venue; those producing the stand materials. Of course, the list can go on, and some of you may note that any given item in a list could also be an abridged form of a further list (some people have agents, union reps, their own supply chain networks etc.). The function of event management then becomes the weaving together of diverse narratives to construct one, or a set of, meaningful meta-narratives (higher-level stories) that achieve the desired objectives set for the event. This is one of the key places where event studies fits into the picture.

A critical perspective on the study of the event, whether real, imagined, anticipated, planned or something else, would recognize that any meta-narrative is also one of many possible meta-narratives that can be associated with the event. Not all those meta-narratives will agree with the one intended by the events manager. Some will challenge/contest that narrative, others may be contradictory to it, providing a friction or tension between them and the planned narratives. By investigating those contradictions, tensions and frictions, the implicit presuppositions surrounding the event become clearer. It is possible to identify structures of power, exploitation, prejudice and so on that implicitly or explicitly inform the event's agenda, many of which may have been hidden or obscured in the process of developing and presenting the event itself.

As a critically reflective practitioner, being open to a diverse range of voices, with transparent values and armed with tools that can help unpack some of the richer complexity of events, can provide us with a firm foundation for current and future events planning.

Find out more

Finkel, R, Sharpe, B and Sweeny, M (2019) *Accessibility, Inclusion, and Diversity in Critical Event Studies*, Routledge, Abingdon

Jepson, A S and Walters, T (2021) *Events and Well-Being*, Routledge, Abingdon

Spracklen,. K and Lamond, I R (2016) *Critical Event Studies*, Routledge, Abingdon

Classifications and categories of events

One of the most enjoyable aspects of a career in the events industry is the opportunity to work on a variety of different events. But there are many different types of jobs and specialisms involved in planning and managing events. Below we consider some of the main ways of categorizing or classifying groupings of events.

Classification by event type

Events are most often classified according to their type. So, for example, although a family birthday and wedding might be very different, they can be grouped together as private events. Similarly, a business meeting or trade show can be grouped under the category of business events.

Getz' typology of events is the most commonly used method of categorizing events by type. This classification typology has changed over the years, partly to reflect the influence of the continuing study of events. Table 1.1 shows the six different types of events as categorized by Getz (2020) and includes examples of each type.

If you are planning a career in the events industry, then it's worthwhile gaining experience of different types of events. This could be through volunteering to help at different events, putting on your own events in the local community or even attending different types of events. By getting involved in a variety of events, you will learn new things, try out different types of work and different event roles and make new contacts. The importance of practical skills and experience should not be underestimated in the events industry, along with the connections and networks you make when working (or studying) alongside others.

TABLE 1.1 Getz' typology of events (2020)

Cultural celebrations	Business and trade	Arts and entertainment
– Festivals, heritage commemorations – Carnivals, Mardi Gras – Religious rites – Pilgrimage – Parades	– Meetings, conventions – Fairs, exhibitions – Markets – Corporate events – Educational and scientific congresses	– Scheduled concerts, shows, theatre – Art exhibits – Installations and temporary art – Awards ceremonies
Political and state	**Private events**	**Sport and recreation**
– Summits – Royal spectacles – VIP visits – Military (tattoos) – Political congresses	– Rites of passage – Parties – Reunions – Weddings	– League play, championships – One-off meets, tours – Fun events – Sport festivals

Classification by event size and impact

Some types of events attract huge crowds as well as massive television audiences and social media followings, while for other events the headcounts are much smaller. Some events can make a big difference to people's lives and will live long in the memory, whereas other events have relatively little impact.

A mega event, such as the Olympic Games or the FIFA Football World Cup, will attract viewing figures of billions from around the globe. For example, the Tokyo Olympics in 2021 reached over three billion people. The organizing committees for these events work for years to ensure the success of an event of this size and complexity.

Another way to classify events is through their size and impact. Below we describe and give examples of the four categories of events – local, major, hallmark and mega – identified by Bowdin et al (2012). In light of the changes that have occurred since the Covid-19 pandemic, we have added another classification in this category: virtual events.

LOCAL EVENTS

Examples of local and community-based events include a village fete that brings together members of the local community, or a networking lunch aimed at businesses located in the local community. These events are unlikely to draw a huge attendance or generate a great deal of media interest outside the locality. The amount of time and resources needed to plan an event of this type should also be reasonably limited. Such an event would likely be planned and run by the members of the local community or local businesses.

MAJOR EVENTS

Unlike a local event, major events are likely to attract visitors from outside the local area and region, often in large numbers. Examples of major events for a region include an arts and cultural festival or a national or international business convention. The main purpose for the area hosting such events is to generate increased visitor spend in local shops, restaurants, cafés, hotels and other local businesses. Major events are also likely to attract interest from the media, which in turn aims to bring more visitors to the region.

HALLMARK EVENTS

Hallmark events are those events that become so identified with a particular town, city or region that they become synonymous with that place. An obvious example of a hallmark event is the Wimbledon Tennis Championships. If you were to tell a friend that you were going to Wimbledon they'd probably assume you had tickets to watch the tennis tournament, rather than think you'd be travelling to south-west London. The Glastonbury Festival is another example of a hallmark event although the festival itself is not held in Glastonbury but in nearby Pilton.

MEGA-EVENTS

As the name suggests, mega-events are the largest in terms of their size and impact. Perhaps the best example of a mega-event is the Olympic Games which every four years attracts participants and spectators from all over the world to the host city, as well as commanding TV audiences of billions. For the host city, mega-events have the potential to generate substantial economic gains but the high costs of hosting them can mean huge debts if not managed carefully by the organizing committee and the local events team.

VIRTUAL EVENTS

The pandemic that began in 2020 and which has affected the whole world has had a massive impact on the events industry. As a result of not being allowed to meet together in a physical space for at least 18 months, all opportunities for people to connect through events were transferred online. Even as the pandemic waned, there has continued to be a desire and need to still meet online. It is likely that this trend will continue in the future. Although numbers attending might be smaller than for the biggest events held in a physical space, the combination of broadcast and internet coverage provides future audiences with more options to participate in events they are unable to travel to, and budgets for virtual events are expected to continue to rise year on year. The technological developments in online platforms that have been prompted by the pandemic now allow up to 32,000 online participants on a single virtual event, and access is greater for those streamed on social media.

Other ways of classifying events

Below we look briefly at some other ways of categorizing events.

FREQUENCY

Christmas and New Year celebrations are obvious examples of events that occur annually, although many are spread across several months, from November to January. Business events such as quarterly sales meetings, monthly staff awards and annual prizegiving as well as daily team meetings are also events that can be categorized by their frequency. Music festivals often take place annually, while international sporting events often take place every four years.

GEOGRAPHY

Sporting competitions are a good example of events that can easily be categorized by geography. In sports such as athletics and football, there are World and European Championships, with events occurring every two years. Many countries around the world host both regional and national athletic championships each year. There are also events for international groupings, such as the Commonwealth Games, a multi-sport event for members of the Commonwealth of Nations, a political association with 54 member states that were territories within the former British Empire, covering a geographical area of almost 39 million sq km. In Europe, the annual Eurovision Song Contest includes competitor nations from across the continent of Europe, with other nations able to compete by invitation, including Australia, which has participated since 2015.

SECTOR

There are many different industry sectors, and they all have events. In corporate (or business) events, there are event management professionals and agencies that specialize in developing and delivering events for specific industries, such as the financial services industry or the pharmaceutical industry. This is partly because these industries require specialist knowledge and experience when managing their events, for example when there are specific regulations that impose restrictions on what is or is not allowed. Equally, the sector concept applies to the different types of events, such as festivals, music and entertainment, versus conferencing and exhibitions, or sports events. The events industry offers diverse opportunities in all these areas, and when you are beginning your journey as an events professional it helps to gain experience in as wide a range of events and sectors as possible.

INTERNAL OR EXTERNAL

Examples of internal events include staff team-building events, training, and staff meetings. These events are usually only attended by employees working within a particular organization and are often referred to as 'in-house' events. Large organizations such as the National Health Service in England, with some 1.4 million employees, require lots of events to communicate with their staff about new policy developments. External events, on the other hand, are used by an organization to engage with people from outside the organization. These can include events such as product launches, media events, business-to-business and business-to-consumer exhibitions.

Size of the events industry

With events taking place all around the world, providing any accurate data about the size of the industry is extremely difficult. Table 1.2 shows the host cities and countries for the world's biggest sporting spectacle (the Summer Olympics) and one of the most global political events (the G20 Summit), which demonstrates that events are truly global.

The events industry is fragmented, made up of lots of small companies (often employing only one or two people) operating in the sector. Consequently, it is challenging to calculate the number of companies that exist, or even the number of people employed in the industry. To further complicate matters, there is significant overlap between events organizations and those in other closely related sectors (e.g. tourism, hospitality and sport), which means that categorizing or grouping businesses neatly into a specific sector is almost impossible. The period of the pandemic has caused additional complexity in making calculations about the size of the industry, partly because of the 18-month period during which there were no physical events allowed, and the fact that many people who work in the events industry are employed as freelancers, who were not eligible to be furloughed along with employees. Since 2020, lots of events companies and event venues have unfortunately folded for a range of reasons, including uncertainty and lack of income and cash flow for an extended period.

TABLE 1.2 Host cities and countries for the Summer Olympics and G20 Summit

Summer Olympics	G20 Summit
2020 Tokyo, Japan (moved to 2021)	2021 Rome, Italy
2024 Paris, France	2022 Bali, Indonesia
2028 Los Angeles, USA	2023 Delhi, India
2032 Brisbane, Australia	2025 Brazil (city location to be confirmed)
	2026 South Africa (city location to be confirmed)

Despite the difficulties in obtaining accurate data about the size of the events industry, prior to the pandemic there was a general acknowledgement that the events sector was growing quickly. Unfortunately, the restrictions introduced as part of national and global attempts to reduce the impact of Covid-19 caused a devastating reduction in live events of all kinds. Recent research reports do attempt to provide us with an indication of the size, scale and growth of the industry, so we can compare the emerging situation in 2022 to 2019, prior to the pandemic. The box provides some key statistics regarding changes in the economic value of the events industry.

FACTS AND FIGURES

The British Visits & Events Partnership (BVEP) provides key facts and figures about the value of business events and conferences to the British economy:

In 2019, prior to the pandemic, the business events sector was estimated to be worth £31.2 billion to the UK visitor economy, as shown below:

- Conferences and meetings £18.3 billion
- Exhibitions and trade fairs £11 billion
- Incentive travel £1.2 billion
- Corporate outdoor events £0.7 billion

Leisure events were estimated to be worth £38.8 billion in 2019:

- Arts and cultural events £5.6 billion
- Music events and festivals £23.6 billion
- Sports events £9.6 billion.

Prior to the 2020 pandemic, around 80 million people attended 1.5 million conferences and meetings annually, and in the UK the sector's 25,000 businesses employed some 530,000 people. The Covid-19 lockdowns resulted in the closure of 17.5 per cent of exhibition businesses in 2020 alone, and 126,000 job losses during March–August 2020. While there is evidence of returning demand for events, especially since September 2021, the impact of the pandemic has continued to be felt – for example, because so many weddings were postponed during lockdown periods, the demand for wedding venues has led to the displacement of conferencing and exhibition business, especially while people continue to work from home. International travel disruptions affected inbound events visitors, but recovery is expected by 2025, and in February 2022 most travel restrictions were lifted. While there is uncertainty about what the future of the events industry will look like, there is encouraging news for some areas that are expected to grow, while others will continue to shrink. Sustainability will be an increasingly important factor in the post-pandemic world, with the integration of hybrid events into the calendar, especially in business events, with conferences and exhibitions becoming more experiential to attract people to attend in person. By Q2 2022, CVENT reported that 87 per cent of UK event planners were searching for venues for physical events, while some 38 per cent of business events offered a hybrid option. Some 68 per cent of event planners reported 2022 budgets were increased over 2019 figures.

The impact of Brexit on the UK events industry continues to impose new barriers across the supply chain, with new work restrictions requiring visas for speakers, exhibitors and music touring, along with the requirement for import licences for equipment and other goods.

The Association of Australian Convention Bureaux (AACB) provides statistics to show the importance of international business events to the Australian tourism market. Australia closed its international borders in March 2020, and by December 2021 some 259 international conventions and exhibitions had been cancelled. Many of these events are hosted by locations around the world and so this global rotation means that it may be 5–10 years before these events are able to return to Australia. The pandemic has resulted in the loss of over 700,000 delegate days and $420 million in anticipated revenue from tourism and events businesses from these events alone.

Prior to the pandemic, business events held in Australia attracted 900,000 international delegates a year, while international business event delegate spend was previously $2.7 billion in GDP in total (21 per cent of all international visitor spend). Some 30 per cent of international business event delegates were from Asia, and the business events sector created 22,500 jobs.

Research commissioned by the Events Industry Council (EIC) identified a significant increase in global demand over the previous year by Q3 2021, with over half of companies reporting domestic business travel, and the greatest positive growth in the Middle East, Asia Pacific and North America for hotel room bookings for groups.

Structure of the events industry

The very nature of an event brings people together (as attendees or participants), but it takes a range of individuals and organizations to ensure the smooth running of an event. We group these into three categories:

1. Event clients
2. Event organizers
3. Event suppliers.

Event clients

Event clients are the buyers of events: the people and organizations who hire or employ event organizers to plan, organize and run events on their behalf. Typically, it is corporate companies who have a budget to hire professional event organizers, although private individuals hosting elaborate weddings and parties may also use the expertise of a professional event planner.

Event organizers

Event organizers are professional individuals and groups who plan, organize and run an event on behalf of their clients. An event organizer acts as liaison between their client and suppliers and is ultimately responsible for the smooth running of the event. An event organizer can be tasked with running an event on behalf of their own organization as well as be hired by an external client. For example, in larger companies, certain events such as Annual General Meetings (AGMs) and annual conferences are often run by an in-house event organizer. The potential for problems to arise in running any event means that organizations risk their reputation when they do not use professional events managers.

Event suppliers

Event suppliers make up a wide range of specialist organizations by providing the goods and services needed by the professional event organizer to ensure the success of an event. The larger the event, the greater the need for goods and services, and the more complex the event, the greater the need for increased technical and specialist support, for example sound and lighting engineers or pyrotechnics operators.

Figure 1.3 (although not to scale) represents the relative position and size of the event organizers, suppliers and clients in the industry. At the heart of any event, you will find an event organizer tasked with managing the event on behalf of their client and liaising with various suppliers to ensure the smooth running of the event. In essence their role is to work as an intermediary between their client (or buyer) and the suppliers.

You will notice that each of the boxes in Figure 1.3 is a different size, with the smallest box representing the event organizer who, as already mentioned, is often only one or two people. The event organizer is likely to be setting up a number of events at any one time and dealing with multiple clients, so the box representing the event's clients is larger. The last box, the biggest of all, represents the event suppliers who for any given event (particularly larger and more complex ones) will include a plethora of organizations providing the goods and services needed to make the event happen.

FIGURE 1.3 Key players in the events industry

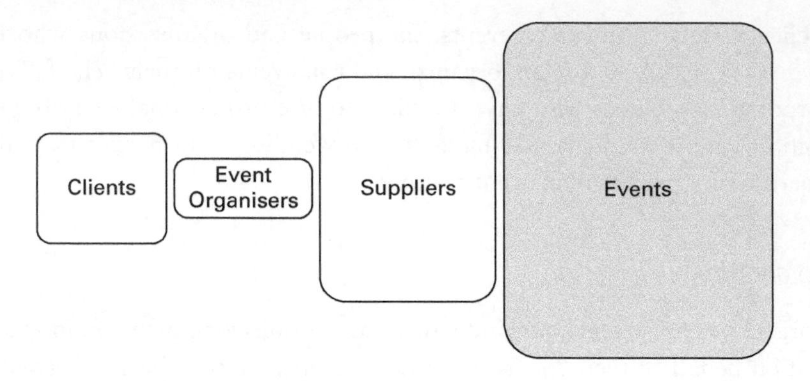

EVENT SUPPLIERS AND SUPPORT SERVICES

The checklist in Table 1.3 contains a list of event suppliers and support services that may be needed to make your event a success. This list can be amended as the equipment, facilities and services required will vary according to the type of event and the activities you have planned.

Case study 1.2 tells the story of the development of a successful international networking group, The Delegate Wranglers, which has provided valuable support to events professionals through the pandemic and beyond.

TABLE 1.3 Checklist of event suppliers and support services

Organizers	**Content**
☐ Professional event organizers	☐ Theming companies
☐ Event management agencies	☐ Guest speakers
☐ Full-service agencies	☐ Workshop facilitators
☐ Event management companies	☐ Artists and performers
☐ Event production companies	**Staff**
☐ Party and event planners	☐ Security
Venue	☐ Stewards
☐ Venue hire	☐ Volunteers
☐ Room hire	☐ Agency staff
☐ Equipment hire	☐ Bar staff
☐ Outside catering	☐ Uniform providers
☐ Toilets and public facilities	
☐ Car parking	
☐ Security	

(continued)

TABLE 1.3 (Continued)

Temporary structures/site	**Food & beverage**
☐ Staging company	☐ Bars
☐ Portable accommodation supplier	☐ Food concessions
☐ Roadway/walkway supplier	☐ Specialist hospitality
☐ Fencing/barrier supplier	☐ Mobile catering
☐ Site vehicle supplier	**Entertainment**
☐ Toilets and public facilities	☐ Local attractions
☐ Waste management	☐ Tour guides
☐ Traffic management	☐ Ticketing agencies
☐ Crowd management	☐ Photographers and video makers
☐ Health and Safety	☐ Music and entertainment
☐ CCTV	☐ Costume hire services
☐ Telecomms	☐ Florists
☐ WiFi	**Audio visual**
☐ RFID / cashless services	☐ Lighting companies
Travel & accommodation	☐ Sound companies
☐ Travel agencies	☐ Multimedia companies
☐ Transport companies	☐ Live streaming companies
☐ Hotel booking agencies	☐ Pyrotechnics operators
☐ Destination marketing organizations (DMOs)	☐ Video companies
☐ Local tourism bodies	☐ Live-streaming services companies
☐ Venue search agencies	

CASE STUDY 1.2

The Delegate Wranglers – international networking

Neil Thompson and Diane Thompson, Founders, The Delegate Wranglers

The Delegate Wranglers (DW) is the daily go-to check-in to positively connect, inspire, educate and provide opportunities for the global events community. Launched in 2014, the community has gone from strength to strength throughout the UK, Europe and overseas. Additional communities have now been launched for the USA and Canada, and for Asia Pacific. In 2020 we became official managed community partners with Facebook and in 2021 we were selected to participate in the Facebook Community Accelerator Programme, which focused on helping leaders harness the power of their community to turn ideas into action. Only 131 participant groups across nine global regions were selected by Facebook from over 500 million groups worldwide.

The group is widely known and respected, offering events professionals the opportunity to connect, gain business, seek opportunities, find jobs, meet up for networking events and ultimately help them to develop their businesses and increase their business network. It is a community that thrives on positivity. The DW has become the pulse of the industry, bringing together buyers and suppliers in a real-time community which has never been available before. It is the largest network of its kind in the UK and has achieved what no other organization has managed: creating a unique community of events professionals – buyers and suppliers – who collaborate and drive millions of pounds of business for the industry every month. This amazing community, for events professionals worldwide, brings all sectors of the industry together under one roof: a safe place they can turn to for business leads, support, advice, guidance and expert knowledge. DWs are connectors – connecting buyers with a problem to suppliers with a solution.

DW is always striving to ensure a community spirit where members work together and support each other. We encourage collaboration, with members working together rather than competing against one another. We have broken down the barriers to make everyone feel part of a special family and not competitors. We have developed strong relationships with members across all sectors: from freelancers to suppliers; from large hotel chains to small independents; large agencies to start-ups; destinations to associations – there is truly something for everyone. All features on the group are developed organically, from identifying a requirement for them by the members online to providing solutions for them. There are lots of free promotional opportunities on the group, such as #supplierhour, #eventhour and #AOBhour plus a Superstar membership which unlocks an additional promotional hour, #superstarhour, and the ability to collect testimonials to prove that the members are genuine, authentic and trusted.

Our aim is to maintain a positive community with like-minded events industry professionals, where business relationships are built upon trust and recommendation. No overtly negative opinions of others are allowed – we would always ask to discuss anything offline. As a rule, there is certainly no room for sarcasm or hostility, rants, nor comments of an aggressive nature on the group, ensuring a community where respect is key and every member is a valued member.

The Delegate Wranglers adapted throughout the pandemic to continue bringing live business leads to the industry, which has seen some sectors booming, while supporting others less fortunate to recover and be there ready for when the restart button was pressed. Covid-19 sharpened our focus on the need to help the DW members and the wider industry, creating new features such as 'DW Live' to help upskill members and DW online socials to enable members to engage with each other during lockdown. We developed a live series of shows every week to bring the community free opportunities to train, upskill and connect with other events professionals, free online socials to bring some fun and let off steam among fellow events professionals, free opportunities for agents to promote themselves through a special agent feature, the same for freelancers, and a free showtime slot for event performers, good news alerts, regular Covid-19 newsletters bringing not only the most up-to-date industry news but also support and opportunities for all.

The Delegate Wranglers has grown to become the industry's most engaged and positive community of events professionals over the past few years (and even more so during the pandemic), guiding, motivating, connecting, supporting, and upskilling over 23,000 events professionals worldwide with the most extraordinary good vibes!

Join us and be a part of the events industry's most engaged and positive community today!

Website: https://thedelegatewranglers.com/join-dw (archived at https://perma.cc/Y3AZ-42GT)
Facebook: www.facebook.com/groups/TheDelegateWranglers (archived at https://perma.cc/H677-MQ3H)

Relationships with other industry sectors

There are many individuals and organizations that would not consider themselves to be part of the events industry but who do in fact spend a significant amount of time planning, organizing, hosting and running events (you may be one of them!). This is because there is significant overlap between the events industry and other closely related sectors such as the tourism, hospitality, marketing, PR and sport industries. There were over 4 million people employed in the events, tourism, hospitality and leisure sectors in the UK in 2019. Unfortunately, these tourism-related industries were among the worst-affected by the pandemic. More than £25 billion of government funding was provided to the UK's tourism, hospitality and leisure industries over the first 18 months of the pandemic. Part of the UK Government's response to the pandemic included making 2022 a year of celebration, with events marking Her Majesty the Queen's Platinum Jubilee (70th anniversary of the accession of Queen Elizabeth II), Unboxed (a six-month celebration of creativity), and hosting the Commonwealth Games in Birmingham.

Tourism

In 2019 the UK tourism industry saw 41 million inbound visits, in addition to almost 100 million domestic overnight visits. Travel was the UK's third-largest service export, and the UK was in the top five countries in the world for inbound visitor spending. But by mid-2021 inbound flight arrivals were down by 90% on 2019 as the sector had completely closed for about eight months in the first year of the pandemic, affecting air, maritime and rail travel, travel agents and related suppliers, accommodation providers, entertainment and visitor attractions. In the UK some 1.7 million people were directly employed in the UK's tourism industry, with tourism directly contributing £75 billion a year to the UK economy, up to 2019.

Tourism is important to the events industry – and vice versa – because large events can attract visitors (e.g. spectators, participants, suppliers and media) from outside a region or country, and often in large numbers. Through the visitors they attract, events can have significant economic benefits for a region, for example more spend from visitors on accommodation, travel, eating and shopping.

In recognition of the economic impact of events, more and more tourism organizations (both local and national) have developed destination-based event tourism strategies to increase the economic benefits of events. The City of Edinburgh, for example, promotes itself as the world's leading festival city, with 12 major annual festivals taking place all year round. Festivals such as the Edinburgh International Festival, the Edinburgh Fringe, the Edinburgh International Film Festival and the Edinburgh Military Tattoo have become a permanent part of the city's identity and help to attract 4.2 million attendees from 70 countries (Edinburgh Festival City Official Website, nd). Hosting an event also plays an important role in enhancing the image of a particular destination, which in turn will help to attract visitors to the region even after the event has finished.

Hospitality

Hospitality is often described as the business of looking after guests and making them feel welcome. A great event organizer understands the importance of being hospitable to those attending the event (e.g. providing a warm and friendly welcome on arrival, or a meal or refreshments in a pleasant environment), and takes pride in the delivery of excellent hospitality. While the concept of hospitality may appear simple, it isn't easy to get right, and can be a common cause for complaints by event participants. It is vital to consider the increasingly diverse needs of event participants, especially in food and drink, with changing dietary preferences (for example, more people are vegetarian or vegan) and the need to recognize and fulfil diverse religious, cultural and health requirements in hospitality settings.

The hospitality sector includes all businesses that provide food, beverages and/or accommodation services. The sector includes restaurants and hotels which often provide the spaces that event organizers need to put on an event. Many private events, such as birthday parties, are held in restaurants, while business conferences often take place in hotels. Hotels also provide accommodation for conference delegates staying overnight.

VIP hospitality is a feature at many large spectator events (in particular, sporting events) and is very attractive to companies looking to entertain clients or potential prospects. At larger events you will find a wide range of hospitality packages to suit a range of budgets and preferences. Typically, VIP treatment at an event involves good-quality food and drink and some of the best seats in the house, as well as being entertained, often with the aim of building or strengthening business relationships.

Like tourism, the hospitality sector was very badly affected by the pandemic restrictions, and uncertainty continued in 2022. In December 2021 economic activity in the food and beverage sector of hospitality fell by 8.1% due to the emergence of the Omicron variant, which led to a wave of cancellations for Christmas festivities and parties. By January 2022, activity in the sector rose by 6.8%, but the Russian invasion of the Ukraine in February 2022 risked further uncertainty, with higher energy prices impacting inflation across Europe.

Marketing

Marketing is all about building relationships with customers. Focusing on building relationships, rather than simply trying to make a quick sale, helps to create long-term relationships with customers – relationships in which the customer keeps buying the product or service and recommending it to others. Events offer a unique opportunity to connect with both current and potential customers, in order to build and nurture relationships and to provide a first-hand sense of a company's brand personality and values.

There are numerous types of events that an organization can host, sponsor or participate in as part of an overall marketing strategy. We give some examples below.

TRADE SHOWS

Trade shows can offer an opportunity to develop relationships between businesses (Business to Business) or to the general public (Business to Consumer). At their most effective, trade shows can be a key part of a company's marketing strategy when it comes to generating quality sales leads. Trade shows and exhibitions tend to be one of the most expensive forms of marketing. In order to ensure the best possible return on investment, an important aspect of trade show marketing is making lead generation more engaging by running contests, competitions and games. Technology has become a major part of trade show displays for innovative exhibitors, helping to attract more attendees to exhibition stands.

CLIENT NETWORKING EVENTS

Engaging clients face-to-face, in a non-sales situation, humanizes your business (ie connecting with people on a personal level). By humanizing your business, you build authentic relationships where clients can be open and honest about any problems they encounter, and you can be honest and realistic about any products you can offer them. Hair and beauty salons regularly host evening events where clients are invited to come along to try free treatments on the night and afterwards offer feedback and suggestions.

CHARITY FUNDRAISING EVENTS

Events can play an important role in how people perceive an organization. A small business owner, for example, who helps a local charity by organizing a fundraising event will establish goodwill by showing people in the community that they are willing to support a cause that's important to them.

EXPERIENTIAL EVENTS

Experiential marketing events, where brands use experiences to connect with consumers, are increasingly popular. Experiential marketing campaigns use live events to engage with customers by giving them an experience they will remember and, importantly, will tell others about. The alcoholic beverages industry was one of the early adopters of experiential marketing, with many big brands creating unique and engaging experiences to connect with customers. The restrictions of the pandemic meant that all events moved online, especially during the periods of lockdown. Now we are emerging from that time, even conferences and meetings are attempting to become more experiential, as people yearn to reconnect.

SPORT

Sport by its very nature involves events and competitions to determine the winners. The very biggest sporting spectacles usually attract spectators and television audiences from around the world, but the world's largest annual participation sports event is the Gothia Cup – The World Youth Cup. This is a week-long youth football tournament held annually in Gothenburg, Sweden, for both boys and girls aged 11–18, with over 1,700 teams from more than 80 nations participating in almost 4,400 matches on 110 pitches. While the Gothia Cup may not attract the same level of attention as other sporting spectacles, it requires careful planning, organizing and running for an event of this size and scale (Gothia Cup Official website, nd). Since 2016, there has been a sister tournament held in China, known as the Gothia Cup China, which has 250 teams participating from 20 nations.

Sporting stadiums are among the largest venues in the world – the largest sporting venue in the world, the Indianapolis Motor Speedway, has a permanent seating capacity for more than 257,000, with additional temporary seating to bring it to a total capacity of 400,000 (World Stadium's Official Website, nd) – and as such, they host some of the world's largest events. Wembley Stadium, the 'home of football' and the second-largest football stadium in Europe, each year hosts major events such as the finals of the football FA Cup and League Cup, as well as international fixtures for the England team, and in 2015 hosted the Rugby World Cup. The stadium also hosts the Rugby League Challenge Cup Final and American football NFL International Series matches. However, there are even more events hosted at the stadium each year that are not related to sport, from major concerts to private events such as weddings and conferences. As with many venues with a specific primary function (such as sports), it is an economic necessity for modern sporting stadia to host non-sporting events, given the costs of building and maintaining the stadium facilities.

Case study 1.3 illustrates the critical decisions that now face event clients and events managers regarding the mode of delivery, considering the options for online and hybrid delivery as well as events taking place in a physical space.

CASE STUDY 1.3

Hybrid events: A reflection on the pandemic and its impact on the long-term event landscape

Dr Tim Brown, Programme Leader Events Management, University of Chester

Nolan (2018, p. 136) prophetically posited that 'the general consensus is that live events cannot be replaced by virtual ones and many of us would only choose to attend a virtual event if a live event were not available'. In early 2020 this is exactly what happened to the events industry when the Covid-19 pandemic resulted in unprecedented closures of numerous industries, including tourism, hospitality, sport and events. The introduction of national 'lockdowns' and a requirement to work from home resulted in business, educational and social activities pivoting online, practically overnight.

Despite the significant negative impact across the events industry, many events professionals identified opportunities for recovery via a pivot from in-person events to online virtual events, particularly in the business events sector, as there was an unprecedented demand for events to continue. As a result, events professionals focused on enhancing the techniques and calibre of virtual events and the supporting platforms, to enhance the consumer experience, and evolve the commercial opportunities of virtual and hybrid events.

Pre-pandemic there was a perceived lack of confidence and skills from both events professionals and consumers in using technology for events, creating barriers for virtual and hybrid event delivery (Sox et al, 2017). It should also be noted that there have been significant technological advancements over the past 20 years benefiting the events industry, but despite this the use of virtual and hybrid events has been slower than predicted. This is due to several key factors. First, the atmosphere, ambience and emotive response of a live event are difficult to replicate online (Getz and Page, 2020). Second, while technology is embedded within our normal lives, there is still a reluctance to use this in place of tried and tested live event experiences. Third, the perceived high costs associated with developing and delivering virtual and hybrid events. Finally, the socialization and networking that live events offer are hard to construct artificially online (Nolan, 2018).

The Covid-19 crisis, however, has resulted in a unique development in people's technological capabilities and confidence, as people have become far more adept at working virtually and utilizing new technologies and platforms in order to work effectively as well as to stay connected socially (Ritcher, 2020). The events industry also capitalized on this crisis and rapidly developed and experimented with new innovations, including: enhancing the calibre of the virtual event platforms, enabling these to integrate with other applications (such as social media, networking apps, and so on); developing practitioner guidance on enhancing the delivery styles and content for virtual events (such as using interview formats for conferences and presentations); and more interactivity for the audience (through live polling, chat functions, and voting). This has resulted in an exceptional growth in virtual events and an appreciation of the benefits that both virtual and hybrid events can provide. As a result of the pandemic the global value of virtual events has increased from an estimated $18.6 billion in 2015 (Raj et al., 2017) to $94 billion in 2020, and is anticipated to grow to over $500 billion by 2028 (Grand View Research, 2022).

The new event landscape

Covid-19 has seen a repositioning within the events world, with the value and potential for virtual and hybrid events being appreciated by numerous event sectors and, more importantly, by consumers, along with the benefits these events offer. For example, virtual and hybrid events: can reach a global audience; are becoming significantly cheaper to develop and deliver than in-person events; virtual events are faster to develop and get to market; they can be interactive and engaging; they can archive and access content post-event; automated functions within the online platforms provide data insights and real-time analytics for events professionals to use; they can be more inclusive and accessible for participants, with subtitling, transcripts, live descriptions, translation and captioning into multiple languages; and finally they are far more sustainable as travel and waste will be reduced by both formats, resulting in a reduction in CO_2 impacts.

Virtual and hybrid events are not without their challenges, however, due to the technical capabilities and initial financial outlay required. And while consumers have increased familiarity with virtual technology, tools and applications, not all events professionals are fully versed in designing and delivering these technically demanding events. With the exception of the business events sector, where more events professionals and venues are proficient in the technical requirements of events, many other event sectors are requiring retraining and upskilling of event staff to ensure they are technically proficient for this future direction of the events industry.

The greatest challenge for virtual, and especially hybrid, events is to ensure that the event experience is not impinged. The technology must therefore be used to support and enhance the experience for those attending in person as well as for those online, to add value to the experience, rather than just for financial gain. Events professionals must design the overall event experience for both virtual and in-person audiences and build in interactivity via appropriate technological platforms and applications to enable the intended event outcome, experience and impact to be realized. The events industry has come a long way in the past few years, but there is still a long way ahead before hybrid events in particular become the standard benchmark for the industry.

References

Getz, D and Page, S J (2020) *Event studies: Theory research and policy for planned events*, 4th edn, Routledge, Oxford

Grand View Research (2022) Virtual Events Market Size, Share and Trends Analysis Report By Event Type (Internal, External, Extended), By Service, By Establishment Size, By End Use, By Region, And Segment Forecasts, 2021–2028 www.grandviewresearch.com/industry-analysis/virtual-events-market (archived at https://perma.cc/RWM6-DWDN)

Nolan, E (2018) *Working with venues for events: A practical guide*, Routledge, London

Raj, R, Walter, P and Rashid, T (2017) *Events management: Principles and practice*, 3rd ed, Sage, London

Ritcher, A (2020) Locked-down digital work, *International Journal of Information Management*, **55**, https://doi.org/10.1016/j.ijinfomgt.2020.102185 (archived at https://perma.cc/7QPN-K4BP)

Sox, C, Kline, S, Crews, T, Strick, S and Campbell, J (2017) Virtual and hybrid meetings: Gaining generational insight from industry experts, *International Journal of Hospitality & Tourism Administration*, **18** (2), 1–38, DOI: 10.1080/15256480.2016.1264904 (archived at https://perma.cc/5XTF-MLAH)

EVENTS MANAGER HACK

'As event organizers the bar is higher than ever before, most events need a virtual component to remain relevant. However, virtual attendance is no substitute to being at an event in-person, the hybrid model to remain attenable needs to offer as much value and opportunity to connect virtually as a live event.'

Selina Arnall, That Event Girl; Social Traders (Australia)

CHAPTER SUMMARY

- The events environment has always been constantly evolving but the Covid-19 pandemic and Brexit have led to significant changes in the sector.
- An event is a temporary planned gathering, with a purpose, that is often a memorable or special occasion for the participants.
- There are many different types of events, and these can be grouped (or classified) according to their type, size and impact, frequency, geography or sector.

- Despite the Covid-19 pandemic causing a complete shutdown of the events industry, planned events have resumed and are taking place again every day all around the world; the events industry has shown that it is a truly global industry that continues to develop.
- The structure of the events industry is complex, with a plethora of organizations and individuals providing the goods and services needed to make an event happen.
- There are significant overlaps between the events industry with other closely related industry sectors such as tourism, hospitality, marketing and sport.

Questions for reflection

1. Reflecting on Case Study 1.1, what do we mean by 'event'?
2. Thinking about events you have attended or worked at, what different types of events can you identify?
3. What event suppliers and event support services have you noticed at events you have attended or worked at?
4. What benefits and disadvantages can you identify for hybrid event delivery?

References

Allied Market Research (2022) Events Industry Size, Share and Statistics | Growth Forecast, 2028 www.alliedmarketresearch.com/events-industry-market (archived at https://perma.cc/4K3E-U7BR)

Association of Australian Convention Bureaux (2021) Australia's border closure results in cancellation of 259 international conventions and exhibitions https://aacb.org.au/mediareleases/Detail/Australia's%20Border%20Closure%20results%20in%20cancellation%20of%20259%20International%20Conventions%20and%20Exhibitions (archived at https://perma.cc/X7AL-UYK9)

Bowdin, G, Allen, J, Harris, R, McDonnell, I and O'Toole, W (2012) *Events Management*, 3rd edn, Elsevier Butterworth-Heinemann, Oxford

British Visits and Event Partnership (2021) The Shape of Events: A report by the Business Visits & Events Partnership, September www.businessvisitsandeventspartnership.com/component/phocadownload/category/10-other?download=446:the-shape-of-events-bvep-report (archived at https://perma.cc/EG6S-DE88)

Events Industry Council (2022) www.eventscouncil.org/ (archived at https://perma.cc/6JZS-WM8V)

Festival City Official Website (nd) [online] www.edinburghfestivalcity.com/the-city (archived at https://perma.cc/G62M-7FHU)

Ferdinand, N and Kitchin, P J (2021) *Events Management: An international approach*, Sage, London

Getz, D and Page, S J (2020) *Event Studies: Theory, research and policy for planned events*, 4th edn, Routledge, London

Gothia Cup Official Website (2022) www.gothiacup.se (archived at https://perma.cc/98HQ-7LGR)

Raj, R, Walters, P and Rashid, T (2017) *Events Management: Principles and practice*, 3rd edn, Sage, London

Shone, A and Parry, B (2019) *Successful Event Management: A practical handbook*, 5th edn, Cengage Learning EMEA, Andover

Wembley Stadium www.wembleystadium.com/Press/Presspack/Stats-and-Facts (archived at https://perma.cc/MLL2-AXPT)

World Stadiums www.worldstadiums.com/

World Stadiums Official Website (ND) www.worldstadiums.com/stadium_menu/stadium_list/100000.shtml

02

The event planning model

FIGURE 2.1 The Dowson, Albert and Lomax Event Planning Process – the planning model

The Event Planning Model
EVENT PLANNING PROCESS
PHASE 1: CONCEPT
PHASE 2: DETAILED PLANNING
PHASE 3: MANAGING ON-SITE
PHASE 4: POST-EVENT

One of the most fundamental parts of staging an event is event planning. Planning an event can engage our creativity and allows us to conceptualize and begin plotting the evolution of our event. It also enables us to visualize and explore using unusual venues, in innovative ways. For many it can be seen as one of the most stimulating parts of developing their event, where organizers get the opportunity to create new and exciting events for attendees to enjoy, in creative spaces, facilitating the transformation of clients' dreams into a reality.

However, planning an event is no easy task; it requires an ability to visualize, conceptualize, forward plan – often without all the information that's needed. For a first-time event, event organizers need to be able to predict, plot and plan a project that has many variables, competing factors, services and moving parts. Getting it right is critical, as effective planning allows the event organizer to deliver high-quality events, which meet objectives in a creative, healthy, safe and enjoyable way, within a specific timeframe and within budget.

The success of the event hinges on how well you, as the event organizer, engage in the planning process and your ability to break down the event into different elements and identify all the sub-aspects of your event. When pulled together, your plans will facilitate the delivery of an exceptional event. The difference between a good events manager and an excellent one is the ability to identify and address not only the macro details (big picture) but also the micro details, from conceptualization to delivery.

Fortunately, the process of planning an event becomes a little easier with experience. This is because planning any event involves a certain amount of repetition, because there are specific key tasks that you will carry out for most events. We call these the essential planning tasks. For example, no matter whether an event planner is tasked with organizing a local village fete or a national sports tournament, many of the essential tasks, such as finding a suitable venue, drawing up a detailed site map, creating a schedule for the event or promoting the event to the target audience, will include the same processes.

For larger, more complex and more elaborate events, relying on experience alone is unwise, and it is critical for even the most experienced of event organizers to adopt a more systematic process for planning and organizing the event elements. Following a structured event planning process will help to guide the event organizer through the different stages of planning an event and make sure that they don't overlook any macro or micro details.

By the end of this chapter, you will be able to:

- explain the value of adopting a systematic approach to event planning;
- describe the four distinct phases of the event planning process;
- follow the event planning process to create a structure for your own event;
- describe the key planning tasks and activities to be carried out at each phase;
- begin your research to develop a robust event concept;
- plan the design of detailed aspects of an event.

Event planning process

As we have already noted, there are certain essential tasks an event organizer will need to carry out for any event. Depending on the size, type and format of an event, an event organizer will prioritize different planning tasks and allocate different amounts of time to these tasks. But the tasks will be carried out in a similar sequence because, for example, it is very difficult to choose a suitable venue or choose a menu until you have a clear idea of what the budget will allow.

Many authors have attempted to outline the specific steps or stages in the event planning process, and we are no different. The Dowson, Albert and Lomax (2022) Event Planning Model includes the tasks considered to be essential when planning

FIGURE 2.2 The Dowson, Albert and Lomax (2022) Event Planning Model

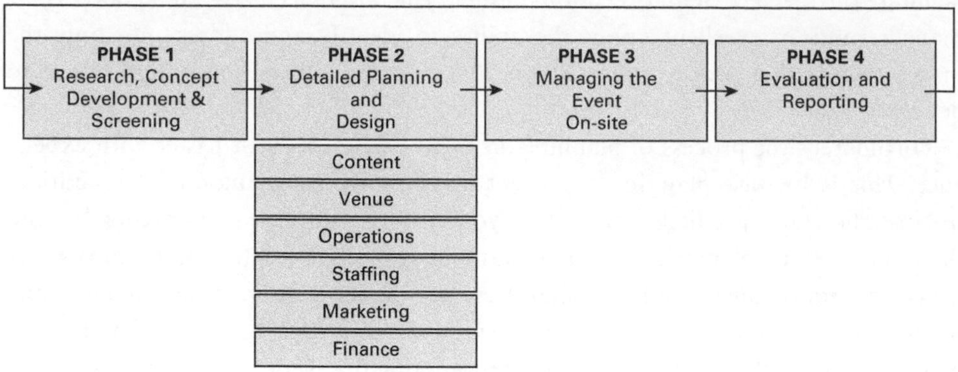

PHASE 1
Research, Concept Development & Screening

PHASE 2
Detailed Planning and Design

Content
Venue
Operations
Staffing
Marketing
Finance

PHASE 3
Managing the Event On-site

PHASE 4
Evaluation and Reporting

an event and these are grouped into four distinct phases. Figure 2.2 includes all that we consider to be the essential planning tasks carried out by an event organizer when putting on an event.

Here we briefly describe each of the four phases of the Dowson, Albert and Lomax (2022) model.

Phase 1: Research, concept development and screening

Research, concept development and screening are all included in the initial phase of the event planning process; this phase provides the groundwork and a strong foundation for the event organizer to plan a successful event. This research should always begin with the identification of the client's mission and values, which will facilitate the development of robust aims and objectives for the event. It is important that these aims and objectives are established early in the process to facilitate your evaluation of the event. Establishing SMART aims and objectives in turn supports the creation of an innovative and relevant event concept which meets and delivers to your client's expectations. The detailed description of this vital phase is found in Chapter 3, but it is important to note that research is required and continues throughout the whole event planning process, underpinning development and delivery for a successful event; for example, reviewing existing suppliers for previous events, layouts and site logistics, health and safety activities. This activity will ensure that you have sourced sufficient information to guide you through the planning phase to the post-event wrap-up.

The research, concept development and screening phase is also about the event organizer getting themselves properly prepared. Within this phase it is necessary for the event organizer to conduct research on previous similar events staged, reviewing any evaluation data for the delivery of those events. It is not always necessary to reinvent the wheel, or change the whole event. This research will often bring to light aspects that have been successfully used in the past. This research may also include looking over previous production schedules, site plans, running orders, types of venues used and evaluation results. All of this will feed into the concept development, the setting of your event objectives and the process of screening what will and will not work. There is always the temptation to rush this stage, but you do so at your peril! Once the detailed planning is under way, an event organizer rarely gets the opportunity to pause and reflect. An experienced event organizer will tell you how important it is that you have taken preparations seriously and pre-empted as many of the potential issues as possible. Within this phase you will be thinking about feasibility as well as research, preliminary concept development and screening, to enable you to review those ideas which may not be suitable or work in this instance. Remember that using existing information and trusted suppliers means that you are making good use of your time and resources and working smarter.

Phase 2: Design and detailed planning

The design and detailed planning phase provides an opportunity to clearly identify the structure of the event, thinking of the what, where, who, how and when various aspects of the event will take place. It often feels like a whirlwind of activity for an event organizer as they race against their timescales to be ready for the big day. With lots to do at this stage (and sometimes not a lot of time to do it), the likelihood is that, certainly for larger events, you will carry out some tasks yourself, while others will be shared within the team and some tasks may require the help of a specialist service provider. Typically, the larger and more elaborate an event, the greater the need for specialist expertise from outside the team (it may be helpful at this point to refer back to the Table 1.3 Checklist: Event suppliers and support services). Within Phase 2, details become critical, and monitoring and tracking the delivery of each aspect of the event ensures that you minimize the margins of error as you move closer to event delivery and managing the event on-site. All these aspects are considered in full in Chapters 4–9. At this point good paperwork is key; the development of your 'Event documentation' or 'Event Manual' is very important, as it will serve as a tool, not only during the planning phase, but it becomes critical for working on-site. Experienced and highly skilled events managers know that, during this phase, ensuring all the details are covered and that communication and documentation are readily available becomes key. It is also very important to ensure that planning information about your event is accessible and available to other members of your team. Any documentation prepared should be written concisely and in a way that others will understand. This is all part of your contingency planning in the event that you or your team members are unavailable and others need to access the event information to run your event.

Phase 3: Managing the event on-site

You have finally reached that moment where you will be managing your event on-site, otherwise known as Event Delivery, at which point all the planning and preparation feeds into the set-up of your event, and your event going live. As an events manager, this is the time you have been waiting for, and whether your event is just for an hour, a day, or a few weeks, you are only as good as the work done in Phase 2. All the planning up to this point has been to ensure that you have created the context for the smooth delivery of your event, but, as many event organizers will state, regardless of how detailed your planning has been, 'Murphy's Law' applies. This is the emergence of aspects that are out of your control, but effective planning in the previous phases can reduce the disruption and stress that this may cause. In the past, your event manual or event documentation became a key part of managing the event on-site, but now that portable devices are available and shared drives are accessible almost anywhere, ensure that you and members of your team have access to the full range of documentation required for managing your event on-site, so that updates and amendments can be communicated in a timely fashion.

At this point, it is prudent to note that the event site functions within three different time divisions, which are referred to as Load in, Event Going Live, and Load out. The success of managing the event on-site hinges on ensuring that you have adequate human and logistical resources, and all the information needed to deliver your event. This includes identifying and assembling an effective and competent team, being able to delegate responsibility, effective communication of information to all stakeholders, and accessing all key supplies, services and other logistical elements that you will now need to coordinate on-site. Chapter 10 considers the detail of planning your event on-site.

Phase 4: Evaluation and reporting

It may seem a little strange to think about planning activities occurring after the event has finished. There are, however, some extremely important actions to be undertaken post-event, and none more so than completing a thorough event evaluation. Indeed, we dedicate an entire chapter to event evaluation later in the book (Chapter 11). Carrying out a thorough event evaluation enables an organizer to assess what worked well and what didn't work well, providing them with useful lessons for planning future events. It also allows event organizers to see whether they have met the event objectives, to assess quality aspects and to reflect on how your practice as an event planner can be improved. Essentially, as an events manager you are as only as good as your last successful event. Evaluation also enables events managers to reflect on best practice and feed in greater innovation and creativity moving forward. It is an essential aspect of the event planning process that can be used as a tool to improve other events.

A CAVEAT

- The value of this model is in its simplicity. There are, however, some important points to note:
  - The planning process diagram should only be used as a guide. The key tasks are not necessarily sequential, and the order will depend upon the type of event as well as how an event organizer prefers to work.
  - There is likely to be overlap between the different phases of the planning life cycle, with tasks under way simultaneously.
  - The amount of time spent on each task will vary depending upon the type, size and nature of the event.

This simple model is unlikely to be detailed enough for larger, more elaborate and more complex events. In this case, a more detailed model could be developed.

Case study 2.1 shows the value of research to define purposeful options to achieve outcomes in New Zealand.

CASE STUDY 2.1

Legacy and impact: the future of business events in Aotearoa New Zealand, April 2022

Jessica Vandy, Founder and Managing Director, The Tenth Letter Consulting, New Zealand

The Tenth Letter is a strategic consulting organization that works in the field of sustainability, legacy, and impact for tourism and events in Aotearoa New Zealand. The Tenth Letter specializes in supporting organizations and destinations with practical solutions for identifying and managing the social, environmental, and economic impacts of events. Director and founder Jessica Vandy has spent the past 18 years working in tourism and events in both Australia and New Zealand.

In 2018, while attending the ICCA Association Meetings Programme conference in Ljubljana, Slovenia, Jessica joined a session on the impact and legacy of business events. This session, hosted by Genevieve Leclerc from Meet4Impact, outlined a set of principles and a conceptual framework in which business events organizers could measure their impact beyond economic output alone.

This session was the catalyst for change.

In 2019, Jessica was tasked with developing Tourism New Zealand's legacy programme: Conference Impact Aotearoa (formerly Enrich New Zealand). The purpose of this programme was to identify, define, monitor and measure the impacts of three international conferences, looking beyond just economic output as the key measure of success.

The three international conferences identified for the programme included the INTECOL (International Ecology) Wetlands conference held in Christchurch in 2021, the International

Working Group for Women and Sport to be held in Auckland in November 2022, and the World Leisure Congress to be held in Dunedin in 2023.

The purpose of the programme was to work in collaboration with each local organizing committee, develop a Theory of Change, and assist them to measure, report, and communicate the key outcomes which resulted in change for their community and wider stakeholder ecosystem. Theory of Change is a methodology commonly used in the field of social impact which demonstrates the cause-and-effect relationship between actions, activities, and outcomes resulting in change.

Each local organizing committee within the Conference Impact Aotearoa programme was tasked with determining an impact goal. The impact goal would represent the change experienced by those benefiting.

For INTECOL Wetlands, the only conference that has occurred since the programme was launched, the impact goal was for New Zealand to be seen as an example of wetlands restoration and management. The theme of the conference was embedded in Mātauranga Māori, traditional indigenous knowledge, and innovative science in wetland research and management.

Through the development of the Theory of Change, the INTECOL committee identified key stakeholders, beneficiaries, activities and actions, indicators and data sources, and some of the intended outcomes which would start to demonstrate the positive societal impacts this conference could have for wetlands management.

Aotearoa New Zealand has lost 90% of its wetlands (approx 2.25 million hectares) since European settlers arrived, posing significant risks to biodiversity. Retaining and protecting existing wetlands, and the subsequent introduction of freshwater environmental reforms, had seen a greater focus and interest from the community on this topic. Aligning the conference theme and impact goal at a time when wetlands management was being communicated more widely was a poignant next step in achieving New Zealand being seen as an example of wetlands restoration and management.

The INTECOL conference was held in October 2021 and the final phase of the project is the continued monitoring, measuring, analysis and reporting of impact from this conference. This will continue to occur in the 12, 24 and 48 months following the conference conclusion. Tourism New Zealand's Conference Impact Aotearoa programme and the three international conference committees have helped to pioneer legacy and impact in Aotearoa New Zealand.

The programme, a first of its kind at the time, has seen the creation of an impact methodology which can be used as a template for attracting future international conference bids. By leveraging these impact projects, international conference organizers will be able to see how Aotearoa New Zealand has been able to demonstrate tangible and measurable social and environmental benefits beyond just the usual economic metrics to demonstrate success.

More and more international associations are seeking out destinations that align strongly with the mission and vision of their organization, as well as being able to demonstrate societal benefits for the communities they represent. By working closely with partners and stakeholders, and using conferences as a mechanism for creating change, Aotearoa New Zealand will continue to establish itself as a competitive destination that is prioritizing the needs and the wellbeing of its people and communities.

As the business events sector rebuilds alongside the international border reopening in May 2022, it will be beneficial for Tourism New Zealand to continue developing their legacy and impact framework, and build further knowledge and capability within the network of destination business events professionals it supports. The past two years have seen an increase in international destinations establishing impact management and measurement programmes including sophisticated tools, resources and methodologies. The future of business events relies on far more than economic measures of success. Business events have a responsibility to demonstrate initiatives and practices that minimize the negative impacts of their activities and amplify the positive.

Since developing the Conference Impact Aotearoa programme for Tourism New Zealand, Jessica now works with local and international destinations and organizations on legacy and impact strategies. She has established international partnerships with Meet4Impact in Montreal and Global Destination Sustainability Movement (GDS) in Spain. She is also a facilitator for the GDS Academy: Impact Management Masterclass, an online training programme for destination professionals wanting to learn the fundamentals of impact management.

Learn more

www.thetenthletter.co.nz (archived at https://perma.cc/4QSN-A8QQ)

Phase 1: Research, concept development and screening

Stakeholder mapping

Even for something that may be as simple as a birthday party, there is usually more than one person to consider when it comes to putting on an event. For most events there are a number of groups interested in the outcome of the event (these are called the stakeholders). A stakeholders can be identified as any individual or organization that has a vested interested in the outcome of the event; these stakeholders may vary in the amount of power and interest they carry, and this can have a significant impact on both the planning and delivery of your event. As the event organizer, it is important to consider what each stakeholder expects you to accomplish, whether they have objectives which are key to them, and how these objectives feed into your planning and delivery. The key stakeholders will also have a major influence on the outcome of the event (ie making it a success or making sure it's unsuccessful), so it is essential to manage stakeholder relationships carefully to ensure that all the important stakeholders are first identified and then managed in a collaborative way.

Preparing the proposal

Potential clients will often shop around to find the most appropriate event organizer to run their event. In this instance, a proposal is commonly prepared by an event organizer in order to persuade the client to hire them. The likelihood is that the client will have invited proposals from several professional event organizers and will ultimately choose which one to hire based on their assessment of the proposal. Therefore, the art of proposal writing is extremely important for a professional event organizer as this can often be how they secure most of their paid work. It is equally important for an in-house event organizer to pull together a convincing proposal that demonstrates the return on investment for their company, to gain the support and financial resources needed to put on the event. While they may not be competing with other event organizers to put on the function, they are competing with other internal departments and projects to secure funding. The return on investment might be not only financial but it could also be how the event will contribute to the company's mission, vision and values.

Perhaps the best-known example of a competitive bidding process to put on an event is in the world of mega sporting events and competitions. Host cities and host nations prepare elaborate and comprehensive bid documents to compete against each other for the right to put on events such as the summer and winter Olympic Games and the FIFA World Cup. The bid procedure involves candidate cities or nations preparing a bid which demonstrates that there is political support and backing from the host region, that the necessary facilities and infrastructure to stage an international event will be in place and, of course, the ability of the host nation to organize the event.

Screening and feasibility

A formal feasibility study is usually carried out for large, complex events, which usually means that the hosting of the event is more costly. With a greater financial investment needed as well as more time and effort to organize the event, the feasibility study focuses on helping to decide whether to proceed with the proposed event.

In determining the feasibility of an event there are two essential questions:

IS THE PROPOSED EVENT THE BEST SOLUTION?

Putting on an event is likely to be one way of achieving the desired objectives, but it isn't necessarily the only solution (or even the best). An important part of the feasibility study is to screen alternative options and solutions for the proposed event. So, for example, if the purpose of a company hosting a staff party is to boost morale – why not just give everybody the day off or use the event budget to pay a bonus to staff? Similarly, if the objective of the event is to raise awareness of new products and services – why not spend the budget on increased advertising and new promotional literature?

IS THE PROPOSED EVENT LIKELY TO SUCCEED?

Some event planners will tell their client that anything is possible when discussing their initial concept for an event. While we admire their optimism, the reality is that there are several crucial factors that will determine whether the event is likely to succeed. For instance, an event organizer will need to consider whether there is sufficient time, finance, resources and support to put on the event, as well as ascertaining whether there is sufficient demand for an event from the intended target audience.

Case study 2.2 explores the processes for beginning the detailed planning in the event design phase, and considers the different perspectives of the client and the event agency, using examples of events in the United Arab Emirates. These elements include the content of the event, the programme, the venue, operational and production aspects, staffing and marketing.

CASE STUDY 2.2

Initial event planning – agency and client-side examples in the United Arab Emirates

Jenny Homer, Experiential Marketing Specialist, luxury automotive brand, UAE; UKCEM Graduate 2015; Winner, The Eventice, 2015

This case study provides two perspectives on the processes for developing and managing an event, from the perspective of the client to the agency working on their behalf.

I joined the Experiential Marketing department, Middle East & Africa in 2021; we still have lots of projects ongoing but the lead time as a client is significantly longer compared to the agency side.

On the client side there are differences in the early planning phase. The process starts a lot earlier. A calendar of events is developed well in advance, with top-line concepts presented to senior management including a business case for budget approval, building in evaluation from the start. The planning client starts with identifying the main objectives, such as: Is this a sales activity? Or for brand awareness? Who benefits from the event? Who is the target audience? Are we collaborating with other departments? Once approved, the internal concept document becomes an agency briefing.

As a client, you rely on the agency for the detailed practical planning, and your main focus is on managing the agency and communicating with key internal stakeholders. On the agency side, you begin with a brief from a client. Much of the time that brief is very detailed, but at the same time lacks complete information. Within the agency team, operational specialists and creatives work with business development to pull the brief apart. To get from brief to concept, the creative team is responsible for developing the overarching creative theme or strategy. Then from an operational perspective, you work with the creative concept to tie the practicalities together. When looking at a venue, you ask: How does the venue complement the product? Is it a venue that attendees have visited before? In the Middle East, there is so much variety that every client wants to be the first to activate in a venue, whether they're the first automotive client or the first luxury jewellery client, so this makes new venues in the UAE very successful. Clients and brands tend to buy into the big creative idea proposed by the successful agency, which can be really challenging from a delivery perspective as occasionally the dream is sold but operationally it is not possible; creativity is very subjective, but creativity always wins.

In the Middle East region, events have much shorter lead times than in Europe; an agency can pitch for an event held one month later, which is tough. Therefore, the event planning process is squashed together and can have less structured timelines.

Once an agency has been awarded the business, the first step in planning is to create a project plan ready for the project kick-off meeting. Some agencies use Excel, which has the ability to turn the project plan into a Gantt chart; you can enter your start dates and end dates, who is responsible for what, automated updates when deadlines have passed and so on. It's good practice to regularly share this with clients so they can track progress and manage their internal deadlines accordingly. The second project planning tool is development of the pitch document into an operational manual. This is detailed enough to show the client what the branded napkins look like, for example, and it triggers decisions such as approvals required. I used to include when an item was approved; and when something needed approving, I added a yellow sticky note box over the top for actioning. This visual approach made it easier and faster for the client to keep track of what needed approving and when. This method also meant that if something happened and someone else needed to take over the project, it was a full A to Z of everything, from when it was a concept through to staffing and traffic management planning. This plan would be on PowerPoint because it's visual and easier to review. In an ideal world you have your master operational presentation and your project plan running in parallel to each other. However, sometimes the project plan gets pushed to the side because you've got less than four weeks until the event. Am I going to spend my time updating this project plan or am I going to use this time to action deliverables? With adequate lead time and enough capacity, you can manage both; however, often in an agency you aren't limited to only one project at a time, but up to six or seven, while also pitching for new business. So as an events manager you must be able to multitask and focus on multiple things at the same time. I used to be a waitress, where you've got seven or eight different tables all at different points of their meal, but you need to be able to keep on top of where they're at in their dining process. Agency life has multiple events, with different things running in parallel, and you have to be able to keep track of it all, from pitches, to planning, to on-site and post-event.

When I first moved to UAE in 2015, Ramadan was much quieter for events; there were very few projects. A lot of people left the country due to the summer heat, and you could walk down the street and not see a single person. Slowly, as Ramadan has been moving earlier in the year and falling into the tourist season, the rules are relaxing. Previously, there was no alcohol or restaurants open until sunset, you couldn't eat out or drink water walking down the street, and no music was allowed – whereas now beach clubs are open, and life continues almost as normal for those not fasting. In terms of business, the UAE mandates that all private and public sector employees work reduced hours during Ramadan, but whether you're fasting or not, everyone works. If you're fasting, you work fewer hours and have the flexibility to start earlier or later in the day. If you're not fasting, the norm is to work two hours less a day. Some employers now have a policy that if you decide to work regular hours, you are provided compensatory leave. A lot of brands integrate events into how Ramadan is practised, for example holding evening events incorporating the launch of a new product with iftar (the first meal after sunset). As Ramadan moves even earlier, I believe it will be more and more like normal times.

Phase 2: Design and detailed planning

The design and detailed planning phase involves a host of different planning activities and tasks. Some tasks will be completed by the event organizer, others might be delegated to a team member, and some tasks may require specialist expertise and support from outside the team.

Each of the essential task areas during Phase 2, as listed in Figure 2.1, is considered briefly in this chapter and discussed in more detail in subsequent chapters. These tasks are not necessarily carried out sequentially, with event organizers all working in their own ways, and the various tasks will require different amounts of time and effort, depending on the nature of the event. There are a range of tools that can help you manage your time and the delivery of the detailed planning, including critical path analysis, project management, and specialist software; These tools can provide support to ensure a structured approach to managing time, logistics and deliverables.

Planning the programme

Having developed a clear idea of who will be attending the event (during the preparation phase), the next step is to create a programme of activities to meet the tastes of the target audience. For example, a music festival organizer will book headline acts that meet the musical tastes of festival-goers, or a charity fundraiser arranging a formal dinner will select a menu that satisfies the culinary tastes and diversity of the guests.

The type of event and its main purpose influences the nature of the programme or event schedule. A team-building event could include activities such as raft-building and orienteering, whereas a staff Christmas party would have a DJ. The location influences the programme of activities. For example, if it is famous for a scenic view, a place of interest or a popular night spot, this may be incorporated into the event programme's social activities.

The event programme is likely to include a combination of formal and informal activities. A wedding service, cutting the ribbon at a shop launch or an opening address from a company owner are considered formal proceedings, whereas informal aspects include social activities (day trips and visits, music and entertainment, dinner, drinks and dancing). The event organizer needs to pull all the various activities together into an event programme (or event schedule) that clearly shows when everything is taking place. There is a temptation to cram in lots of activities but be sure to give attendees the time to relax too, particularly if the event is being held over several days. Chapter 4 discusses planning the event content in detail.

Selecting the location/venue

When choosing the event location (whether it be country, city or town), an important factor is to consider the target audience. An event organizer needs to be confident that enough people will want to attend the event. This involves thinking about how far people are willing to travel and how accessible the location is by car or public transport, the cost of travel to and from the event, and how inclusive the event and space is (discussed in Chapter 7). For example, an invitation to an event in an exotic location is likely to generate a lot of interest from the target audience but only if the time is available and the cost of travel is affordable. You need to be sure that enough people will travel to attend the event.

Once the location has been decided, there may be a vast selection of venues to choose from (particularly in larger towns and cities), including purpose-built convention centres, hotels, sports stadiums, churches, museums, concert halls, universities, theatres, casinos. Outside busier towns and cities, your choice of venue may be more limited, although with a little imagination, even an empty field can be transformed into a glamorous event venue using temporary structures, marquees, tents and staging.

When choosing a venue there are obvious factors to consider: the availability, price and capacity of the venue. Depending upon the type of event there will be other factors to consider, such as proximity to accommodation or availability of car parking. The image of a venue is another factor to consider and whether this fits with the style of a particular event or the expectations of the event attendees. Chapter 5 discusses the key factors in selecting the location and venue.

Planning the site layout

Once you have chosen a venue and the event programme has started to take shape, you can then start to plan the event layout. Wherever the event is taking place (indoors or outdoors), a proper plan of the layout of the venue/site needs to be prepared. This aspect of planning also helps to ensure that you have included all the logistical elements for your event delivery as well as ensuring that you have sufficient space to meet your event objectives but also meet Health and Safety requirements.

One of the first considerations is creating the right environment for the attendees; this does not only refer to the physical environment, but also creating an inclusive space which supports diverse attendees and employees. What is right (or wrong) will depend upon the type of event. For example, the ambience at a classical concert is very different from a rock concert. Despite the difference between classical and rock concerts, there are certain fundamentals that apply when planning the venue/site layout, such as: ensure that attendees can easily enter and exit the event, provide attendees with a focal point (in this case a stage); and ensure that facilities, such as toilets and food and drink outlets, can be easily located and are not too far to walk to.

Another crucial consideration when planning the layout of an event is to ensure the safety of the attendees. Continuing our earlier example, a well-planned concert venue/site will reduce the risk of crowd congestion and crushing as well as the danger posed by temporary structures (e.g. staging, tents, marquees and stalls) and traffic on an event site. Chapter 5 explains the importance of site planning in detail.

Event production and operational planning

Logistics planning is primarily about ensuring the smooth flow and movement of people, supplies and services on to an event site, around the site and finally off the site. It sounds simple, but it is one of the biggest challenges facing an event organizer. The biggest logistical challenge is sometimes before the event is even under way, in planning the operational aspects of the event and event production. For example, a conference organizer attempting to get hundreds of delegates from around the world to attend their event will be involved in making individual and group bookings for transport and accommodation, hotel check-ins and conference registration.

Event logistics planning is concerned not only with the flow and movement of the event attendees but also ensuring that suppliers, contractors and other support services are in the right place at the right time, ahead of the event. For example, a festival organizer has a mammoth task on their hands in getting all the suppliers and contractors on-site before the event begins while getting artists and performers, celebrities, VIPs, and media on- and off-site during the festival.

A good operational event production logistics plan should clearly set out communication details and protocol for staff and key personnel. For a music festival, the plan should include contact details and locations on-site and off-site for stage managers, artist liaisons, artists and performers, in case there is a delay or change of plan.

Case study 2.3 explores the processes for planning the event management for open days at a university.

CASE STUDY 2.3

Planning and managing university open day events

Klaudia Gawrysiak, Student Recruitment Events Officer, Leeds Beckett University; UKCEM Graduate 2019

Leeds Beckett University holds approximately 11 large recruitment events an academic year, alongside smaller events on a weekly and ad hoc basis. The events are organized and run by an internal team of three members of staff. Within the events industry it is standard to have casual workers and support staff to support the event for set-up, for the live event and for breakdown. Leeds Beckett is no different when it comes to a pulsating workforce. The additional staff are divided into three main categories:

- University recruitment staff – these members of staff are taken from the wider recruitment department and are allocated as team leaders around the event.
- Academic and services staff – these members of staff manage the information stands at the events and deliver the course/service-specific talks that run throughout the event.
- Student ambassadors – the students act in two main roles, first as a course ambassador supporting course-specific activity such as lectures, taster sessions and facility tours, and in general roles such as stewarding and registration support.

When managing an event onsite, especially with a complex programme, distribution of responsibility is key to ensuring that all aspects of the event are running smoothly. This enables the events manager to be available throughout the event to troubleshoot in case any issues or emergencies arise. Before the event, a control point is established on each site location, where the events manager will be based.

This management technique works as long as all staff are trained and briefed to a high standard. This includes ensuring that all staff are aware of the activities that are happening on each site, that they are familiar with the layout of the campus, who the team leader is and where they are located, and emergency procedures. One of the key roles given to our team leaders is as building checkers. These staff are put in charge of a collection of buildings and are required to check all rooms being used for any damage or incorrect set-up. They are given a list of set-up requirements for each room and troubleshoot with IT support, porters, or cleaners if anything is found that is not up to the standard needed for the sessions taking place within the room. Student ambassadors ensure that all the information is easily accessible, and that all emergency information, contact information for the ambassador coordinator and the events manager, alongside any other important information, is outlined within their name badge which they collect during their briefing.

When running events with a division of staff responsibilities, communication is a key factor to ensure an event runs smoothly. Putting in place clear communication procedures allows the staff to communicate efficiently. For the recruitment events at Leeds Beckett, radios are the key communication method as they allow staff to communicate between sites. Radios are also given to support teams such as Security and IT Support, as an issue with phone signal and WiFi service in some of the buildings used was identified in previous events. During the staff briefing, radio guidance is given and outlined, such as asking for radio silence if there is an emergency by saying 'Break, Break, Break' and having security on a different channel from the event staff so that they are available to be contacted at any point during the day without interruption from general event queries.

Management of an on-site event also depends on the level of planning that has taken place. In order to allow the appropriate time for the event briefs in the morning, all events are set up the day before. This includes ensuring signage is put up and is correct throughout the buildings, larger outdoor signage is placed correctly, and room signage that outlines the programme of talks to be held in each room around the site is visible for all prospective students and other visitors. Within the planning stages of the event, a briefing pack is created for all team leaders which gives them general information about the event, emergency or support contacts, and duties and tasks that require completing throughout the event.

Recruiting the event team

It may be that an event organizing team is already in place. This is often the case with larger, more complex events where the volume of work requires a team effort. For a private party the event organizing team might be made up of family, friends and neighbours, whereas for a business event, the organizing team might consist of work colleagues, from the same and other departments, as well as people from partner organizations outside the company. Whoever forms the organizing team, it is important to make sure that all agree and are informed of their roles, what and who they will be responsible for, who they will be accountable to, and what and to whom they can delegate. All of this needs to be established early on as, ultimately, the effectiveness of the organizing team can have a significant bearing on the success of the event. The key is to ensure that each member of the team has the role to which they are best suited, have sufficient skills for, and are also able to deliver. Bear in mind that there are several ways to upskill and support your team which will be discussed in Chapter 7.

As the event date draws closer, it is likely that additional team members will be recruited to help with arrangements; these additional staff members can include part-time, fractional workers, freelancers, volunteers and subcontractors. A music festival organizer, for example, will be looking for new recruits to assist with ticketing, wristband exchange, stewarding and security roles. The number of staff needed will depend on the number of event attendees expected, and the size and scale of the event. The complexity of the event will also influence the number of staff required; this can also depend on individual aspects of the event such as health and safety requirements for crowd management and security. An international conference with high-profile guest speakers, each giving presentations simultaneously in different rooms, will typically require a member of staff to be in place in each of the presentation rooms. It is important here that staff are adequately briefed on the day of the event to ensure that all members of the team understand what is expected of them; this is often done through written briefing notes and an effective team briefing and debriefing pre- and post-event. Chapter 7 covers the key human resources and staffing concerns for event planning.

Event marketing

The methods used to promote an event will depend primarily on the target audience and the best ways to reach that audience within the allocated promotional budget. By now, the event organizer should already have a clear idea of the profile of the target participant. The next step in developing an effective marketing plan is to determine the best way to communicate information about the event to the target audience. The event organizer has a variety of marketing tools at their disposal, including sending personal invitations, putting up posters and leaflets about the event or even placing an advert in a newspaper or magazine. But today, most event planners utilize social media platforms, websites and other online forms of digital media to promote their event. In the digital age, it still remains that, generally speaking, the most effective promotional methods are those that communicate directly with the target audience, for example a personal letter of invitation to the event or a telephone call to recommend that people hold the date; however, these tangible invitations are not always possible. Therefore, it is important, when using digital sources, that the communications stand out, are inclusive in how the information is delivered, communicate effectively and do not get lost in the myriad of other digital and online communications in circulation. It should be noted that using only one method of marketing promotion and publicity can be problematic, depending on the target audience and their digital access.

Event promotion can be very costly and, if promotional methods are not chosen wisely, can take up a large portion of the event budget and still not achieve the desired result. In particular, paid advertising on TV, in magazines and through digital media is likely to be very expensive. There is the possibility of free publicity when it comes to promoting an event, with newspapers, magazines, radio, linked industry associations and publications, and television channels all regularly featuring content related to upcoming events. That is, of course, assuming there is a newsworthy story related to the event. It might be, for example, that the event coincides with another high-profile happening or that there will be VIPs attending; these all can be harnessed to communicate your event and message, and opportunities should not be overlooked. Chapter 8 provides details of how to market your event effectively.

Financial planning

Cash flow is the life supply of any organization, with more businesses experiencing difficulties and closing because of cash flow problems than anything else, especially since the start of the pandemic. If an event organizer doesn't have money to pay staff wages, then things are likely to go rapidly downhill. The basic principle of good cash flow management is to make sure that there is more money coming into the business than going out of it. But managing cash flow also requires accurate and up-to-date budgets and that money comes in on time and is consistently managed and reviewed; otherwise, this is where finances can become problematic for some events. For example, at a pay-at-the-door ticketed concert, most of the incoming money will only come through ticket sales on the day of the event. If the event organizer has to pay out money beforehand (e.g. booking artists, advertising the concert), then that could be a large chunk of money going out before any money comes in from ticket sales. Good financial planning involves anticipating any shortfalls in money, allowing the event organizer to make contingency plans for cash flow (e.g. extending credit and payment terms) and managing the financial risk, which can spell the success or failure of your event.

While it would obviously be good for an event organizer to have all the money they need to put on an event, they may need to raise additional funds. Traditionally, events have been quite successful at attracting sponsors. Contra-deals, where, unlike a sponsorship deal, no money exchanges hands, are also commonplace in the events industry; instead, there is a trade of mutually beneficial goods or services. So, for example, an event organizer might borrow some lighting and sound equipment for their event and in exchange will give the supplier on-site promotional and branding opportunities. However, this requires clear benefits for both parties, and should not be used as a means to get free support services that should otherwise be paid for – sound and lighting specialists need to make ends meet too!

Sound financial planning also involves contingency planning (the 'what if...' scenario). For example, what if the event is cancelled, abandoned or postponed? How will this impact on finances? Does the organizer have appropriate insurance to cover actual event costs? How will the organizer manage their financial risk to ensure that it doesn't derail the whole event? Chapter 9 explains the financial aspects of event planning.

Sourcing suppliers and contractors

These is often a need for specialist goods and services (e.g. increased technical support). There are quite literally thousands of specialist suppliers who can provide elements of the goods and services needed by an event organizer, ranging from providing additional staff, to marquee tents and furniture, to flowers and gifts. Indeed, there is a supplier for just about any item or service you could possibly imagine.

For the event organizer, the challenge is in selecting the right suppliers who will provide high-quality, excellent service and support. While there is clearly much to consider when selecting suppliers, there are two simple factors which should always be a high priority. First, it is important to know the past experience of a potential supplier. Have they done this type of work before? Do they have a proven track record? Have they delivered the quantity of service provision you require? In some cases, it might be beneficial to select a new fledgling company, as the supplier will be keen and eager to impress (and, more often than not, cheaper too). However, this may also come with its challenges. Second, it is important to look into the reputation of a potential supplier. In most cases, suppliers who have a good reputation in the industry do so because they are well established and have been in the business for a long time. Where possible, event organizers should stick with suppliers with a proven track record (prior experience) and who come highly recommended for delivering the capacity required and the quality needed. Chapter 9 covers event procurement processes and issues in detail.

Phase 3: Managing the event on-site

Using an effective venue selection strategy, you have selected the destination for your event and taken a systematic approach to finding the venue that will meet all your event requirements. You have thought about safety and security considerations, the image of the location, and ensuring it is in keeping with the client's image and objectives. You have reviewed transport accessibility, travel time, capacity of the venue, reputation, venue cost, and many other aspects of your venue search criteria which will be discussed in Chapter 5. You have planned your layout, have all your logistics and service suppliers contracted and ready to support the delivery of your event. You are now ready to manage your event on-site. Bear in mind that one of the key operational requirements of managing the on-site logistics for your event is ensuring that the movement of people, equipment, goods and services are delivered safely on time and to the right location.

This is where good planning and documentation make the difference, and it becomes evident that this phase of the event is critical in your successful event delivery. It is often thought that event delivery does not start until the attendees arrive on-site at your event venue, but good events managers will tell you that delivering the event or going live is often the easiest part of this process if well planned, and everyone and everything should be exactly where it needs to be on time. Getting all aspects of the site ready for delivery in the load-in phase becomes one of the most detail-driven and time-consuming aspects of your event delivery and getting it wrong can have dire consequences, including high cost implications.

Regardless of the size of the event, the levels of coordination and scheduling required are what Phase 2 is for, with the use of tools like critical path analysis to determine what needs to arrive first, second, third and so on; for example, trackway (surfacing for vehicles to drive on at greenfield sites) needs to arrive before staging and temporary demountable structures. Tables, chairs and tablecloths need to be laid out at a banquet prior to flower arrangements or centrepieces arriving. However, when the paper activity is then a physical activity it is important that all members of the event team work together to maintain site safety, manage delivery traffic and subcontractors and service suppliers, and oversee the whole load-in operation.

Once this is done, your event then goes live: attendees arrive on-site and you deliver your event (Phase 3). This aspect of your event is driven by the provision of elements such as crowd management, safety and security, medical and welfare services, hygiene and cleanliness, and risk assessments. When using outdoor sites, adverse weather conditions also become a factor that needs to be monitored.

When your event is over, you have arrived at your event load-out, which is your load-in completed in reverse order. Again, safety of the team left on-site is still of very high importance, and ensuring that you leave the venue in the contractual condition to avoid any fines or charges is important. Remember, your on-site management is not complete until the last light is switched off and your last team member has left the building.

Phase 4: Post-event: evaluation and reporting

To make your event as successful as possible, it is important that certain key tasks are carried out after the event. Although each of these activities will be carried out post-event, it is sensible to begin planning them in advance.

Evaluation

An evaluation after the event allows the event organizer to find out at the most basic level if they achieved their intended aims and objectives. A proper event evaluation will also help the organizer to assess what worked well and what didn't work well, providing them with useful lessons for planning future events. Evaluation can also be a good way of showing others (e.g. clients, sponsors and partners) that the event was a success, which can ultimately help to justify future events.

An important part of the evaluation will involve finding out the event attendees' opinions of their experience of the event delivery, services and infrastructure. One of the myths about evaluation is that it is extremely complicated and time-consuming, but it doesn't have to be. For example, creating an evaluation survey is an easy way to gather valuable feedback from attendees (e.g. What did they most enjoy? What did they least enjoy?). The types of questions used in the survey are important and should be linked to the intended aims and objectives. For an event such as a conference or seminar, where there is an educational purpose, it will be important to ascertain not just what attendees most enjoyed but also what the attendees have learnt and how they will change what they do because of this learning. In this instance, it can be more beneficial to give attendees a survey sometime after the conference or seminar (ie after they have been able to put some of their learning into practice) to find out their opinion.

As well as finding out the opinions of the event attendees, a proper event evaluation will take into account the opinions of the event participants (e.g. performers, artists, speakers) and also the event organizing team, as well as the thoughts of key suppliers, contractors and partner organizations. This leads us on to the importance of planning a proper event debrief.

Debrief

An important part of the post-event evaluation is a debrief meeting with key individuals from the event organizing team as well as key suppliers and partner organizations. The debrief meeting is an important part of the overall event evaluation as it looks at the event from the perspective of those experts involved in the delivery of the event. The very nature of the events industry means that immediately after an event most of the event organizing team as well as the wider team (suppliers, contractors and so on) will head off in separate directions, most likely en route to their next event. With this in mind, it is a good idea to carry out some sort of debrief immediately after the event while everyone is still on site – this is often referred to as a hot debrief.

In addition, scheduling a debrief meeting not too long after the event is also important. A cold debrief gives everybody time for reflection and allows enough time for the evaluation data gathered from the attendees to be processed. While scheduling a cold debrief with busy events professionals after the event has finished can prove extremely problematic, don't underestimate the importance of gaining valuable feedback from the experts. The reality is that not everything will have gone to plan. There will be things that worked well but there will also be things that could have gone better. It is important to learn lessons from the 'experts' to improve the event for next time, all of which feeds into the Phase 1 research process.

Follow-up

Event follow-up often involves sending out a personal communication to event participants (e.g. a thank you for their involvement). It can also involve sending out promotional materials that you did not give out at the event (e.g. sending a heavy brochure to an interested client) as well as distributing invites and information about upcoming events. It is also important at this time to thank the delivery team and any key and critical service suppliers and volunteers, as this supports the continuation and building of good relationships. It is easy to bombard people with mail-outs and emails, so be sure to plan your follow-up campaign carefully to avoid this.

A final word on the event planning process...

There is no one right way when it comes to the step-by-step process for planning and organizing an event. That is to say – it's unlikely an event organizer will carry out the essential tasks in the same sequence that we've presented them. Indeed, nor is it likely that two event organizers will carry out the essential tasks in exactly the same sequence or dedicate the same amount of time to each task. This is perfectly acceptable because the unique nature of an event means that no two events are the same, which in turn means the process of planning an event is never quite the same. However, for larger, more complex events it is essential that an event organizer adopts a more systematic approach to planning and organizing the event. Imagine, for a moment, trying to plan a week-long international trade show with more than 5,000 delegates attending from all around the world, using only the simple four-phase model we presented at the beginning of the chapter (refer to Figure 2.1). No matter how experienced and talented an organizer you might be, the reality is that relying on such a basic model means that you're bound to forget or overlook something important. In this situation, even the most experienced event organizer will adopt a more systematic approach to planning the event.

EVENTS MANAGER HACK

All roads cannot lead to you. The quickest way to make the best events manager incompetent is to bombard them with tasks and push their hours into the red for days on end. Delegate. Push back. 'I work more hours than you' is a silly game. Don't play it.

Charlie Mussett, Freelance Event Operations Manager and Safety Consultant; Route Operations Advisor, Queen's Baton Relay, Birmingham 2022

CHAPTER SUMMARY

- The success (or failure) of any event is largely down to what happens long before the day of the event; in other words, how well it is planned.
- Planning any event involves a certain amount of repetition because there are various key activities and tasks that are carried out for most events.
- Prior to the commencement of detailed event planning, it is essential to clarify the event concept, objectives (including stakeholder objectives) and budget as well as considering the feasibility of the event.
- Creating a professional and thorough proposal document is essential to gaining support for an event – whether for an external or internal client.
- The design and detailed planning of an event involves a whole host of different activities, and for larger events it is likely an event organizer will need to delegate certain tasks.
- Post-event activities such as the event evaluation need to be planned well in advance in order to provide useful lessons for future events.
- Developing your own bespoke event planning model can help ensure a standardized, more consistent approach to planning events and will make sure that you don't overlook anything important.

Questions for reflection

1. Discuss why using an event planning model benefits events managers.
2. Why is the research phase so important, and how can it support events managers working smarter and utilizing resources more efficiently?
3. Is there a phase of the model which is most critical to the delivery of your event? Why?

Explore further

See the online resources available at the Kogan Page website for this book, including case studies from previous editions of the book – especially the case study on working together to develop a bespoke event planning model by Ken Brown and Ruth Dowson.

03

Research, concept development and feasibility screening

FIGURE 3.1 The Dowson, Albert and Lomax Event Planning Process – Phase 1

Phase 1 Research, Concept Development & Screening
MISSION, AIMS & OBJECTIVES
INFORMATION GATHERING
CONCEPT DEVELOPMENT
SCREENING & FEASABILITY
STAKEHOLDERS
SIGN-OFF

When planning a new event, as events managers, we don't always start with a blank canvas – the event may have been run before, by us or someone else; we may have run a similar event in the past; or the client may have specific ideas or instructions. This chapter aims to guide you through a tried and tested process that can provide you with a clear rationale for your event, as well as developing a snapshot of how it fits into the surrounding events environment. Even after two years of pandemic it is evident that many events lack structure in planning, with ill-defined or no aims and objectives. The pandemic has also changed the way we think about the medium we use for events. In March 2020 when the first lockdowns were put in place, all events planned to be held in a physical location were cancelled – or moved online. For the next 18 months, the vast majority of events took place virtually, using new and existing online tools (including Skype, Zoom, Microsoft TEAMS) with audio and video facilities, and live-streaming on social media (mostly Facebook, YouTube, Instagram). The development of vaccines, combined with testing practices, social distancing and wearing face coverings, has enabled the reopening of the events industry for corporate events, sports and leisure events and even festivals. There are two major

FIGURE 3.2 Phases of the Dowson, Albert, and Lomax Event Planning Model

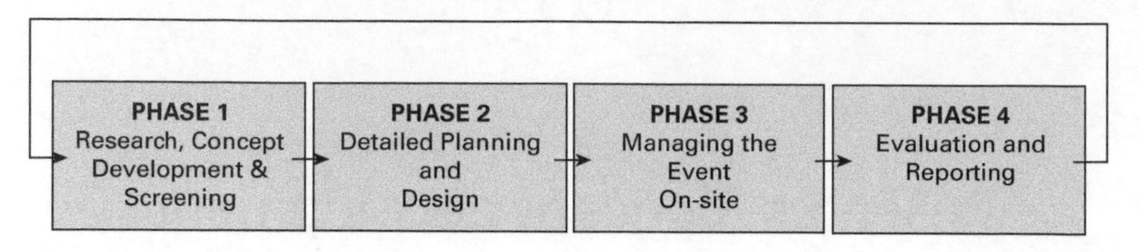

developments that have resulted from this experience, with significant impacts on the events industry now and in the future:

- the rush back to physical event spaces, especially for leisure, sport and music;
- continuing reluctance by significant numbers of people to return to physical event spaces.

The impacts of these important factors will feed into the event planning model throughout the book. The rest of this chapter is based on developing the first phase of the event management process, which is Research, Concept Development and Screening, as shown in Figure 3.2.

By the end of this chapter, you will be able to:

- develop event aims and objectives in line with the client's and your organization's mission and values;
- undertake initial information gathering;
- use a structured approach to develop your event concept;
- apply criteria for screening event ideas to assess their feasibility;
- consult stakeholders about the event concept;
- obtain sign-off for your event concept.

Phase 1: Research, concept development and screening

The first phase in planning an event begins with undertaking research that enables you to create your event concept. This development phase enables you as the event organizer to ensure that you are ready for what lies ahead. Once the detailed planning phase begins, decisions that make changes or lead to the cancellation of the event become expensive, and it is vital for the event organizer to spend adequate time in this phase to become fully prepared to plan, manage and deliver the event.

The rest of this chapter is dedicated to considering a new process that informs the research and development of your event concept and enables you to screen the ideas that are generated. The stages in this process are shown in Figure 5.1, and are explained thoroughly in the rest of the chapter. The research process begins by finding important clues about what is important to the organization.

Mission

The initial stage of the process involves the events manager compiling evidence about the client and their organization, and mapping this data against other stakeholders, in particular against potential event attendees and the events manager's organization.

Many companies and other organizations have identified their mission statement that formally summarizes the organization's purpose (why it exists), values (what principles it holds) and goals (what it wants to achieve). This information can often be found on the organization's website and provides important insights into the organization's culture and values.

WIMBLEDON – THE ALL-ENGLAND LAWN TENNIS CLUB

Example mission statement

'Our Mission is to champion opportunities for all. We use the collective strength of the All-England Club and The Championships to make a positive difference to people's lives.'

Example values statement

'The All-England Lawn Tennis Club is a diverse and inclusive organization which is committed to confronting and eliminating the discrimination of age, disability, gender reassignment, marriage or civil partnership, pregnancy and maternity, race, religion/belief or gender.'

Read more

www.wimbledon.com/en_GB/atoz/about_aeltc.html (archived at https://perma.cc/RFY7-WU9B)

www.wimbledon.com/en_GB/wimbledonfoundation/about_us.html (archived at https://perma.cc/5RP6-DBHS)

Interestingly, neither Wimbledon's mission statement nor values statement mentions tennis, which is what we most strongly associate with Wimbledon. But we can understand from both statements what they see as their purpose, and what is important to them.

This information provides us, as event organizers, with background that can help us to develop an event that supports these statements. This may seem obvious, but unfortunately too many events are created without reference to such vital clues, and often events may be developed in contradiction to the mission and values of the client organization. As an event planner, it would also be useful to check that your own organization's mission statement and values match those of your client – or at least that they are not opposed to them. For example, you wouldn't expect to see a cigarette company sponsoring an event that is raising funds for a cancer charity. Perhaps that's a little too obvious as an example, but the point is one that cannot be overstated. One example is of a cigarette company sponsoring a competition in Asia for a trip to Europe; when searching for appropriately qualified tour leaders, it is vital to ensure that the individuals concerned are open to the use of tobacco. How this message is portrayed is vital; if I am personally opposed to tobacco advertising or its use, I may not be the best person to ask for recommendations. Another example is the hiring of a cathedral for a prosecco festival; some might have a problem with such events being held in a church building, but most would wonder why the organizers were allowed to have topless men working at the event.

These values apply equally to the event and its participants, and as part of this process, we recommend that once you have identified your event concept, you take a broad scan of it to ensure that there is a fit between the client's values and cultural context and those of the event, as well as with other stakeholders, including event participants and organizers.

Case study 3.1 considers how a large and complex international church conference develops its event purpose and objectives to fit with the organization's values and the logistics of taking over a city for five days.

CASE STUDY 3.1

Harnessing a city's capacity: The case of the Kirchentag Conference, Dortmund, Germany

Ulrike Hitchen, Senior Lecturer in German, International and Global Studies, Carnegie School of Education, Leeds Beckett University

The German Protestant Kirchentag was established in 1949, the same year as the Federal Republic of Germany was founded. Processing their experiences of the Third Reich and the Second World War, Protestant Christians and other socially engaged people were looking for a new and independent medium through which to foster a democratic, humanitarian and socially just future within Germany. This convention became known as 'Deutscher Evangelischer Kirchentag' (German Protestant Church Assembly).

Since 1949, the Kirchentag has taken place every two years, over five days, and within different cities across Germany. The convention aims to bring together Christians from various Protestant churches but also individuals and groups from other denominations and faiths, as well as from non-faith backgrounds. Apart from it being a religious event, the Kirchentag sees itself as a platform for social and political debate and change on a diverse range of topics, in which participants engage in discussion and dialogue. The Kirchentag is a multifaceted and inclusive assembly, drawing together various types of Christian worship, meditation, study and music, as well as being a platform for civic debate and dialogue. Each convention is centred around a biblical theme that is of particular social and political relevance.

In June 2019 in a joint interdisciplinary research project with Ruth Dowson, we carried out ethnographic fieldwork at the 37th Kirchentag in the city of Dortmund in northwest Germany. The convention's theme was 'Was für ein Vertrauen' (2 Kings 18.19), translated as 'What confidence is this'. The theme was intentionally made without an exclamation or question mark, in order to maintain ambivalence – with a particular focus on migration, integration and recognition.

Nearly 2,400 diverse events took place at over 220 locations in and near the city centre of Dortmund, as well as in neighbouring towns and cities, making the convention visible throughout. Sites included squares in the city centre, the Dortmund exhibition centre 'Westfalenhallen', many churches, religious, cultural and educational centres, concert and opera houses, schools, theatres, museums, sport centres, Dortmund football stadium, university and even the local zoo. The sheer size and scope of the convention across Dortmund made the event highly visible and accessible throughout the city and wider area.

The Kirchentag was attended by around 121,000 participants from Wednesday 19 to Sunday 23 June 2019. During that time, nearly 21,000 participants stayed free of charge in communal accommodation, which included 17 schools and also sports halls. For each school there were at least 25 volunteers to steward and help. The convention had a festival atmosphere, in which participants brought their own mats and sleeping bags and had breakfast provided by volunteers, mainly from local churches. Schools in Dortmund were closed during the period, adding to the festival atmosphere. In addition, 4,000 participants stayed free of charge in organized private accommodation in Dortmund and in its neighbouring cities and towns.

The Kirchentag aims to be carbon neutral and barrier-free, seeking to be one of the most environmentally friendly large event of its kind. The Dortmund planning committee had followed the concept of 'short distances' ('Konzept der kurzen Wege'), in which most venues should be within walking distance of each other or easily accessible by public transport. With their event entry tickets ('Kombitickets') participants were also entitled to use all forms of public transport in the wider city and some parts of the federal state of North Rhine-Westphalia. This meant that most participants had travelled by train.

On the first night, there were three parallel opening services for approximately 50,000 visitors in three squares in the mainly pedestrianized city centre. The 'Evening of Encounters' ('Abend der Begegnung') is regarded as one of the highlights of the Kirchentag. In Dortmund, it took place across 10 open-air stages, including concerts and cabarets, with hundreds of stalls offering regional culinary specialities. This attracted more than 130,000 people.

The 'Market of Opportunities' ('Markt der Möglichkeiten'), which is always at the heart of the Kirchentag, has over the years developed into a vital meeting place for groups working in the church and in society. This took place in five large exhibition halls of the Dortmund Convention Centre. Eight hundred groups presented their projects, providing information as well as giving opportunities for discussion and building new contacts. It is known as one of the biggest events for networking by civil society initiatives in Germany.

It has been a concept of the Kirchentag to have volunteers help with the running of the event rather than paid staff. Over 4,000 volunteers helped during the convention, mostly young people from church organizations and scout groups, and were easily recognizable by their colourful 'I help' ('Ich helfe') scarves. Without the 'helpers' and stewards as well as numerous other volunteers in planning and organization, the Kirchentag in its diverse form and with its distinct message would not be possible.

Read more

www.kirchentag.org.uk/ktaghist.html (archived at https://perma.cc/X2JY-9F5W)
www.kirchentag.de/ (archived at https://perma.cc/RR4R-6JN2)

Aims and objectives

The initial idea for an event will usually come from the client, and can sometimes be a little vague or ambiguous, so it is an important next step in this first event planning phase to establish clear and measurable event aims (broad goals) and specific objectives that enable the broad aims to be achieved.

Establishing the event aims and objectives

Working with the client to clarify the event concept certainly helps to steer an event organizer in the right direction, but it is first vital to establish the aims and objectives for the event. These elements will guide the event organizer throughout the process of planning and organizing the event.

When establishing the event objectives, it's a good idea to involve not only the client but other key individuals (stakeholders). Any good wedding planner, for example, might tell you how important it is to make sure the mother of the bride is on side with the plans for the big day, but both families can influence who is invited (or who isn't invited!), as well as what happens at the wedding. There are different ways of thinking about the objectives for an event and while there is no magic formula, Figure 3.3 shows some suggestions that will help.

FIGURE 3.3 Establishing the event objectives using the Five Es

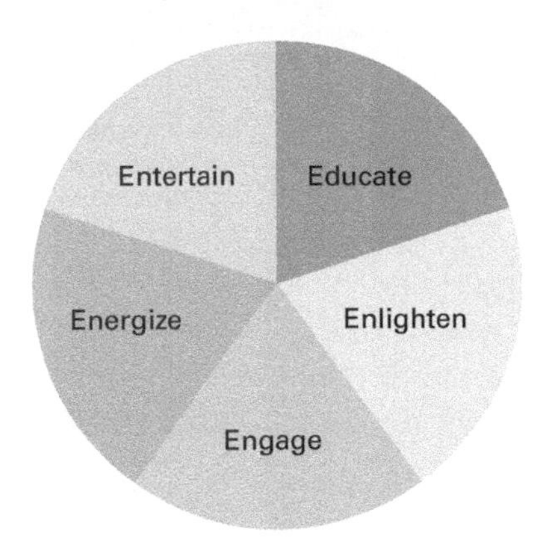

FIVE ES

The Five Es is a simple approach to understanding more easily the emotions that event attendees will experience, which in turn will help the event organizer to establish appropriate and relevant event objectives:

- Educate – training workshops are elements of an event programme that are primarily intended to educate attendees.
- Enlighten – a guest speaker could be invited to speak to event attendees, enlightening them about future issues and trends.
- Engage – motivational speakers can be used to engage attendees.
- Energize – icebreaker activities can be used to energize attendees.
- Entertain – remember to include time for social activities in the event programme for attendees to unwind and to enjoy themselves.

HIERARCHY OF OBJECTIVES

A hierarchy means that different elements are organized in order of importance (in this case the objectives). As an event organizer, you must understand the most important objectives for the client for an event. It is important to prioritize the objectives for an event because there is rarely the luxury of infinite resources (namely time and money) to put on an event and so the event organizer must understand where to focus their time and effort. Figure 3.4 should help you to determine which objectives should be considered as high priority (therefore requiring a great deal of time and effort) and those objectives which are of lower priority.

FIGURE 3.4 Hierarchy of Event Objectives

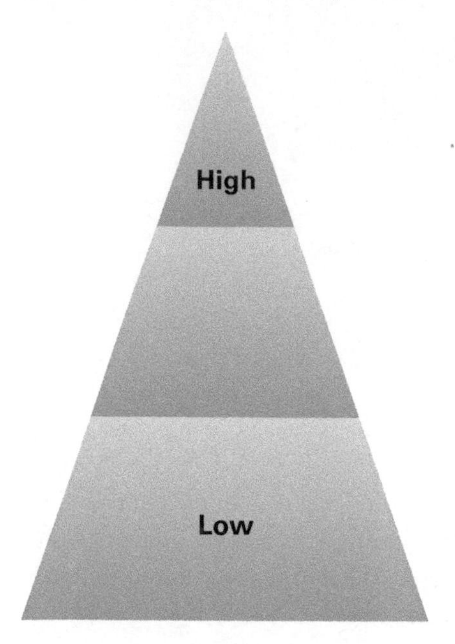

Failure to meet this objective means you are unlikely to be asked to organize another event for this particular client and they might even refuse to pay for the organizing of this event.
This objective may be seen as a 'nice to have' by the client or the client may even be unaware or not care if this particular objective is met.

SMART OBJECTIVES

It is important to ensure that your event objectives are SMART (an acronym for Specific, Measurable, Agreed, Realistic and Time-bound) objectives. SMART is a popular method for developing well-written objectives but in our own experience of working with event clients and event organizers, it is not always used correctly.

- **SPECIFIC** – Objectives should clearly state what you are expected to achieve, using action verbs to describe what has to be done.
- **MEASURABLE** – Objectives should each include a target or milestone so that you can measure whether or not you have achieved them.
- **AGREED** – Objectives provide a definition of success, and it is therefore important that the intended outcomes should be agreed with the client.
- **REALISTIC** – Objectives should be challenging but not unrealistic, taking account of the skills, knowledge and resources of the event team.
- **TIME-BOUND** – Objectives are less likely to be achieved with no time frame tied to the objective-setting process.

For examples of SMART objectives, see www.workfront.com/strategic-planning/goals/smart-goals

LEGACY OBJECTIVES

Finally, when thinking about the event objectives it is easy to focus on the immediate (short-term) outcomes for an event. The Five Es for example (educate, enlighten, engage, energize, entertain) focus on the feelings and emotions that event attendees will experience during or immediately after the event. But the event outcomes can also be much longer term. A term that is often associated with larger events is the event 'legacy', which refers to the lasting benefits or outcomes that result from hosting the event. For example, the legacy objectives associated with hosting a major sporting tournament typically include increasing participation in sport as well as promoting the social and health benefits of playing sport regularly. Indeed, promoting the legacy objectives for a major sporting event has become an important factor in the decision to award a particular event to a host city or nation and is a critical part of the bidding process to win the right to host a major event.

EVENTS MANAGER HACKS

My main objective in events is to delight my attendees. To make it happen, my first task is researching my audience: Who is coming? What do they like? Where do they come from? What are their desires, habits? Gather as much information as you can and from there, draw your event theme and create activities to keep them interested. I assure you that, when the Event is over, they will be asking: 'When will be the next one? ' Listen to their needs, not yours! Success!

Alessandra Valente, Marketing and Events, LATAM, VPA Consulting, Brazil

'Why is this event being held' is the key question to ask before heading off to create the 'perfect' event. Once the event's objectives have been established, you can then effectively brainstorm the event experience. Ask as many questions as you can, especially if you are assisting in conceptualizing the event.

Selina Arnall, Event and Marketing Manager, That Event Girl; Social Traders, Australia

You don't get all of the good without some of the bad. The sooner you accept this, and the sooner you get councils, landowners, venues and transport bodies to accept this, the easier your event planning process will become. Events bring benefits. Events bring disruption. Just make sure the benefits are bigger.

Charlie Mussett, Freelance Events Manager and Safety Consultant; Route Operations Advisor, Queen's Baton Relay, Birmingham 2022

Initial information gathering

The third stage of the event development process to gather a range of information and data that will help you to shape the event concept to meet your event aim and objectives. This involves identifying and analysing new and emerging trends, as well as assessing the internal situation within your client's organization.

Research – identifying new trends

A key part of undertaking the research that is relevant for your event is identifying new trends that might have an impact (positive or negative) on the events you are planning. We have seen from the impacts of the pandemic that nobody can say with certainty what the future holds. But it is unlikely that the future – especially now – is going to be very like the past and, therefore, it is vital to understand trends and likely influences on future events. This part of the research process involves regular environmental scanning (otherwise known as horizon scanning or trendspotting). You could think of it as a form of early-warning system that enables event planners to see potential threats and so avoid any nasty surprises. It is very easy to think about trendspotting in terms of preparing for the worst, but the likelihood is that emerging trends and developments may equally impact favourably on an event, and you should be prepared to capitalize on the opportunities presented. When you are beginning the planning process for a new event, you can use a range of tools to help you to identify different trends, both in the events industry and in the wider external environment.

If done properly, trendspotting by scanning the external environment can help an event organizer to answer such questions as: What are we doing at our events today that will probably no longer work in the future? What types of event are heading for obsolescence? What plan do we have in place to make the most of innovative and exciting opportunities? How does this event need to be different now, compared to before the pandemic? If you feel like you have a good handle on such questions, then you may already be a skilled scanner. If, however, the thought of scanning for emerging trends and developments seems a little daunting (as it does to most of us), below we provide suggestions of what to look for to give you a good idea of the most important trends, as well as some tools to help you to scan the horizon thoroughly.

MACRO TRENDS

First, start with those trends that are impacting on everyone (one way or another), so inevitably they are going to have some sort of an impact on you – we call these the macro (or mega) trends. These are the global phenomena that make headline news every day – trends such as global population growth, resource scarcity, global sustainability, climate change, pandemics, new variants, or advancements in technology. Mega-trends are easy to spot because they are happening already and, because these trends have built up such a momentum, we can be fairly sure that they are likely to continue well into the future. While mega-trends are probably already very familiar to you, the challenge is to put these into some sort of context by considering how these could impact (both well and badly) on the events that you are working on in the future.

MICRO TRENDS

As well as looking at the mega-trends, it is important for event planners to keep a close eye on new trends and developments specifically within the events industry. These industry-specific movements and shifts are typically referred to as micro trends. For event planners, a sound understanding of the industry situation as a whole is imperative to avoid their competitors overtaking them or, more worryingly, taking their event attendees!

External and internal analysis tools

Carrying out a PESTEL analysis will help you to determine how various types (or categories) of factors are likely to influence the future wellbeing of your event. The importance of each category of factors will vary and the same external factors will influence different events in different ways. Important questions to ask yourself are:

- What are the key **political** factors affecting the industry?
- What are the important **economic** factors?
- What **social** trends are most important?
- What **technological** innovations are occurring now?
- What are the **environmental** considerations?
- What current and impending **legislation** may affect the industry?

To understand further what PESTEL is and for tips on how to carry out a PESTEL analysis, visit https://strategiccoffee.chriscfox.com/2012/10/how-to-do-pest-analysis.html

Once you have completed the PESTEL research, there is another tool to help clarify and summarize the results. PESTEL analysis enables you to take a structured view of the external factors that could impact on your event, or on your client's (or your) organization. SWOT analysis stands for Strengths, Weaknesses, Opportunities and Threats – see www.mindtools.com/pages/article/newTMC_05.htm. SWOT examines the internal and external aspects of an organization: Strengths and Weaknesses apply to the internal aspects and Opportunities and Threats apply to the external context that you have identified earlier using PESTEL.

To help you to undertake this external analysis, events professionals can develop their own list of go-to information sources to stay informed and updated on what is happening within the industry. Below we have provided a suggested list of what we consider to be the most appropriate sources. However, it's up to you to choose the best sources to use, depending on the type of work you do and the types of events you are involved in. As we've already said, if you keep a close eye on new trends and developments specifically in your industry, then you make it more difficult for competitors to steal a march on you. Once you have undertaken this process to start your research for your event, you need to update it on a regular basis (say every 2–3 months), and whenever something happens that can affect the situation.

Sources of information for news and developments in events

INDUSTRY MAGAZINES

Most industry magazines are published monthly, and each will take a special focus on an area or topic that is particularly timely and relevant to readers. Mash Media, for example, are one of the UK's leading publishers for the events industry, with monthly publications including *Access All Areas*, *Conference News*, *Conference and Meetings World* and *Exhibition World*. For more information see www.mashmedia.net/

INDUSTRY SHOWS AND CONFERENCES

Attending trade shows and conferences is a great way to learn about emerging industry trends and provides great opportunities to network and discuss these developments with industry peers. International Confex, for example, is the UK's leading exhibition for the meetings and events industry and has been running for around 40 years. For more information see www.international-confex.com/

FACE-TO-FACE NETWORKING

Proactively networking with industry suppliers, customers and even competitors will help you to stay informed about current developments and trends.

ONLINE NETWORKING

Social media networks, such as LinkedIn and Twitter, are a great way to connect and get the latest updates from individuals and organizations in the industry. LinkedIn also provides access to a range of groups and networks for events professionals. In addition, there are alumni networks for graduates that provide connections for new jobs and business opportunities, as well as professional networks such as The Delegate Wranglers – see the case study in Chapter 1 and online at https://thedelegatewranglers.com/.

MEMBERSHIP ORGANIZATIONS

Joining a membership organization can help to keep you informed through regular updates such as newsletters and provides networking opportunities. Meeting Professionals International (MPI), for example, is one of the leading membership organizations for meetings professionals around the world, see www.mpi.org/. There are similar organizations for different sectors within the events industry.

MARKET INTELLIGENCE REPORTS

Publishers of market intelligence reports cover a range of sub-sectors of the events industry, including conferences and meetings, weddings and private parties, live music events and so on. Mintel, for example, is one of the UK's best-known producers of market intelligence information, see www.mintel.com/.

If you are unsure about which are the best sources of information to keep up with news and developments for your industry sector, then ask a colleague whose opinion you value and respect. You could also ask them for recommendations of whom to follow on Twitter or which LinkedIn groups to join, as well as the industry conferences they think are the best to attend.

For some events – but especially for meetings – there is now a logical decision to be made in choosing the appropriate mode for each event – whether it should be held virtually, in a physical event space, or as a hybrid event with some participants joining online. (See Chapter 4 for a section by Paul Cook of Planet Planit with more detail on virtual and hybrid events.)

When planning an event, it is important to be clear about why the event is needed – what its purpose is – and to create an event structure and content to achieve that purpose. In the past, too many events were delivered without thinking about this vital aspect. The pandemic has provided us as professionals in the events industry with the opportunity to start afresh, and take a logical, structured approach to event research and development.

Case study 3.2 considers how technology can bring the customers, planners and venues together to show a much greater range of options early on in the planning process.

CASE STUDY 3.2

Supporting wedding venues – WedPro and Wedding Method conversion software by WeddingDates

Carys Duckworth, UK Sales Executive, WeddingDates; UKCEM Graduate, 2009

WeddingDates' suite of products addresses challenges facing wedding venues across the full engaged couple sales journey:

- WeddingDates Directory matches couples in their search for the perfect wedding venue, with hotels and venues.

- WedPro drives sales leads and conversions for venues, and nurtures the Venue/Couple relationship, providing insights and reporting for venues at every stage of the relationship with engaged couples.
- The Wedding Method package uses digital marketing tools and personalization to drive venues' return on investment

WeddingDates provides services to reduce administration, freeing up venue teams to be more customer-facing. Conversion rates from initial enquiry are high, by encouraging couples to view the venue. WeddingDates nurture the enquiry through to a booking, with consistent regular communication throughout the sales pipeline, supporting the customer experience with clear built-in next steps and following up from the booking stage through to the couple's first wedding anniversary. The focus is on personalization with personal touches such as handwritten notes, whilst meeting couples' expectations for 24/7 information and fast response, when the venue sales teams have their own priorities and constraints.

WeddingDates produce in-depth reports on the UK Wedding Industry. The 2022 Report surveyed 1,200 engaged individuals in the United Kingdom to provide data on key drivers in hotel and venue wedding sales in the £10 billion UK Wedding market, identifying key Wedding Industry changes, providing analysis on where couples book their ceremonies and receptions; total wedding budgets and spend per guest; and factors behind planning or delaying weddings. This information enables wedding venues to discover what couples look for in: hotels and other wedding venues; virtual tours compared to in-person experiences; and trending wedding items. It enables wedding venues to improve their communications with greater personalization when communicating with engaged couples, providing information on key timings for enquiry responses and provides tips to enable venues to connect more effectively with prospective clients (engaged couples).

The 2022 wedding industry report evidenced a new sense of positivity for hospitality and events, with a wedding boom in 2022, despite the undeniable challenges the industry faced over the previous two years. Founder and CEO of WeddingDates, Ciara Crossan, observes that, "Despite the pandemic, we've seen an unprecedented number of venue enquiries at WeddingDates in the past 12 months, up by a remarkable 12% on the previous year. My hope is that this data helps wedding businesses to capitalize on the opportunities, and contribute to a very successful 2022."

While 98% of 2022 respondents identified themselves as brides, for the first time, a percentage of survey takers chose not to identify as binary. Millennials continue to make up the bulk of engaged couples, on par with the UK's average age of 31 at first marriage. Couples adjusting to Covid reality chose to take the pandemic plunge, with a stampede of engagements driving wedding demand in 2022. Fewer couples are putting off engagement, and engaged couples have largely stopped waiting for the pandemic to be 'over' in order to have their big day.

Church weddings are still in decline. In the 2017 survey, nearly 30% of couples were choosing to marry in a house of worship, but that number is now 20%, while in 2021 68% of couples chose to have the ceremony in their reception venue.

Of those couples who have booked a venue in 2022, 28% chose a hotel, in decline for the last two years. Country House and Exclusive Use venues are the next most popular, together representing 38% of bookings. The biggest rises, however, are in castles and barns as people continue to seek something different for their big day, and 2% chose to wed at home.

In 2022, factors important in selecting wedding venue were, in order: Venue, Location, Food, Quality, Overall Value, One Wedding Per Day, Outdoor Space, Accommodation on Site, Venue Décor, Civil Ceremony Licence, Reputation, Cancellation Policy, Wedding Coordinator, Covid Safety.

The Wedding Method

In the era of digital relationships, venues have to work harder than ever to book showrounds. Standing out in a crowded, highly-competitive market requires a more personal approach. Couples used to visit 9 venues; now they visit three venues or fewer. The Wedding Method is an award-winning marketing system that delivers high-quality enquiries, more viewing appointments, and personalized, time-saving automation of the sales cycle to just one venue per area. 33% of couples want to book the first showround online, a 24% increase from 2021. The Wedding Method includes online booking for showrounds, creation of hand-written notes and personalized website links for every couple. WedPro is WeddingDates' management software for wedding venue sales teams, designed to help generate, capture and close wedding sales leads.

Learn more

www.getwedpro.com (archived at https://perma.cc/P75K-3XDB)

Concept development

The initial idea for an event will usually come from the client and can sometimes be a little vague or ambiguous. For example, a client may approach an event organizer to 'put on a huge event' which is held 'somewhere amazing' with 'lots of fun activities' taking place during the event. While this sounds like a great client to work for (already thinking of big ideas for their event), as an events professional it is important to work with the client to develop a clearer concept of the event from the outset. The clearer the initial concept of the event, the less likely the event organizer will spend time, effort and resources (including money) focusing on the wrong things. It is equally important that the client has both a clear and realistic idea of the event so that they are not ultimately disappointed that the event did not meet their initial ideas or expectations. Figure 3.5 summarizes the questions to ask when developing the event concept, using the Five Ws model.

FIGURE 3.5 Developing the event concept using the Five Ws

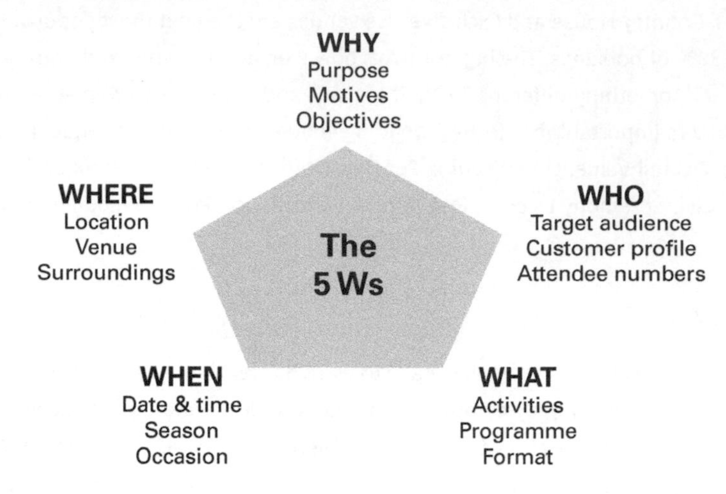

A simple but effective way of conceptualizing an event is to use the 5Ws:

- **WHY** are you putting on the event?
- **WHO** is coming to the event?
- **WHAT** is happening at the event?
- **WHEN** is the event taking place?
- **WHERE** is the event taking place?

Having worked with your client to develop a clearer idea of the event concept (the who, what, where, when and why of your event), it is a good idea to condense this into a one-page event brief. This one-page brief, containing all the important information, can easily be shared with members of your event organizing team as well as any external suppliers and contractors to help give them a clearer picture of the event that your client has in mind. However, it is at this stage that we suggest you begin to generate as many ideas and perspectives as possible – not worrying too much about practical considerations and feasibility, as this comes in a later stage. It's important to do this in as diverse a group as possible, to enable space for different individuals to express their own ideas. The Divergent/Convergent model, which can be found on the Divergent Thinking website (https://divergentthinking.design/why-divergent-thinking), shows a process that helps you to undertake research into a range of alternative events and concepts, combined with research on the client and audience.In developing an event concept, we might begin with a question or problem, which could be 'what does our event look like?' or 'what do potential event attendees want from an event?' Normally, we would consider all the constraints that might impact on the problem, to come up with a solution. But with divergent/convergent

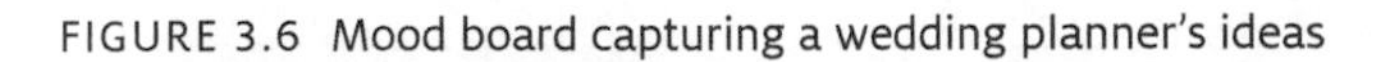

FIGURE 3.6 Mood board capturing a wedding planner's ideas

Photographs courtesy of: Jeanette Sunderland (Netty's Cakes www.nettyscakes.co.uk/) and Julie Armitage (Picture Perfect www.pictureperfectphotographyuk.co.uk/)

thinking, we are encouraged to think more creatively, outside the box, in a non-linear way, disregarding any limitations to produce a much wider range of potential solutions. Once this activity is completed, convergent thinking enables us to screen the ideas for feasibility, which is discussed in the next stage of the process.

Developing the event concept is often an enjoyable part of the planning process, with the opportunity for the event organizer (as well as the client) to explore new and different ways of doing things. Even those of us who might not consider ourselves to be a creative person can still enjoy the process of generating new ideas. Creating a concept or mood board for your event is one approach to enable you to create new suggestions. Mood boards are collages of items such as photographs, clippings, drawings and fabrics which are created to capture or convey the concept of the event. The client can view the mood board and decide whether or not they like the main ideas the board represents. Figure 3.6 shows an example of a mood board capturing a wedding planner's ideas for using black and white polka dots for a wedding theme.

It isn't always easy to develop new and innovative ideas for your events. A more structured approach to building on an initial idea to develop creative options for an event is to use the SCAMPER model, which was created by Bob Eberle – see https://slidemodel.com/scamper-technique/. The SCAMPER model is an effective way to build on initial ideas and combine them for more innovative approaches. SCAMPER is an acronym for Substitute, Combine, Adapt, Modify/Magnify,

Purpose, Eliminate/Minify, Rearrange/Reverse. For each initial idea, SCAMPER provides a list of questions to ask, to help you develop new options. For example, what could you SUBSTITUTE within the initial event idea? How could you combine the initial event idea with other event ideas? How can the event idea be adapted to a different use or context? How could the event idea be modified, or used for a different purpose? What would the event look like with some aspects removed or reduced? What would happen if the event was rearranged?

As an example, applying the SCAMPER technique to a charity client, if the original idea was a coffee morning fundraiser, the SCAMPER technique could generate an event idea that combined a bake sale and the TV show 'Great British Bake-Off'. Another example could use clothes donated to a charity shop for a fashion show only using 'pre-loved' clothes which are then sold to the fashion show audience. (Thanks to UKCEM students Holly Glasby-Hemmings and Iona Taylor for their great ideas using the SCAMPER technique.)

Screening and feasibility

Using the SCAMPER technique will help you to generate lots of creative ideas for your event concept. But the second part of the Divergent/Convergent model will help you to screen out those ideas that aren't appropriate or won't work – enabling you to work on a smaller number of ideas. At this stage it's important to identify the constraints that still exist and that may impact on the ideas you have developed; these include finances, time, operational aspects and marketing. As part of the research you undertake, developing a range of different event ideas, you will also need to ensure that these ideas fit with the client and with the intended audience. This includes mapping the event idea against their values and organizational aims.

Financing your event

Even the most creative and resourceful event organizer is going to incur costs putting on an event. There are examples of events, most notably charitable fundraisers, where financial goodwill and donations from charitable supporters mean that no financial commitment is needed to deliver the event. But it costs money to hire venues, book rooms, feed guests and entertain people at an event.

It is vital for an event organizer to know how much money the client is prepared to spend. If you don't know this, you are likely to find yourself spending time, effort and resources planning and organizing what is not realistic within the financial resources you have. For example, there is no point visiting possible locations and venues only to discover that these would swallow up the entire client budget. Both the event organizer and the client are likely to end up feeling frustrated.

It is important for an event organizer to discuss and agree with their client exactly what is, and is not, included in the budget. For instance, is the budget expected to cover transport and accommodation for guests? Is it expected to cover the cost of an open bar in the evening, or to cover the cost of attendees bringing their partners or spouses to the event?

Other screening factors

There is a range of other important factors that should be considered in order to screen your remaining event concepts to identify their feasibility. These factors include the following:

- **Time:** Is there time in which to organize everything that is needed for the event? An example where the lack of time caused an event failure was the Fyre Festival in Great Exuma, Bahamas in 2017, where the initial venue was cancelled by the owner leaving less than six weeks in which to build a festival site on an island with few natural resources and inadequate physical and specialist event resources. Many event organizers underestimate the time needed to organize an event, and this is often exacerbated when problems inevitably arise. A common response is to throw more resources at these problems, to overcome the time constraints, but this frequently impacts adversely on financial aspects.
- **Event operations:** Do you have access to all the event resources required to deliver the operational aspects of the event? These resources include people with the skills and experience to deliver an event on-site, technical equipment, location, as well as resources to ensure the event content can be delivered.
- **Marketing:** Do you have marketing expertise and resources in the relevant media needed to promote the event? It's not just a matter of setting up social media accounts or printing off leaflets and posters. A successful event needs a clear and detailed event marketing plan, agreed well in advance, that takes account of external changes as well as resources available.
- **Health and Safety:** Are you up to date with what is required to ensure that Health and Safety measures are in place to protect event participants? This includes staff, traders, speakers, as well as paying guests. Even when legal requirements change and are less restrictive, events managers still need to ensure that all participants are kept safe from Covid-19 or any other risk factor.
- **Fit with client aims and objectives:** Have you checked that the event concept fits with the organizational mission and values of the client, of your own organization and of the potential attendees?

EVENTS MANAGER HACK

'The client isn't always right. Trust your experience and be prepared to tell them when things just won't work. Your event experience often outweighs their unrealistic expectations.'

Gareth Brooke, PMP Recruitment

Stakeholders

A key task is to map your event stakeholders. There are obvious groupings, such as the client and the attendees, but a wider list could include sponsors and suppliers, the local community and local government, advertisers and media, travel and accommodation providers. Each different event type of event can have different stakeholders, and it is important to write down a comprehensive list, not only of the different stakeholder groups for your event, but also of your specific contacts within each grouping. Then, when problems or issues with your event arise, these become your go-to contacts – pick up the phone and call or message them, rather than send an email, for a timelier response.

Work out the hierarchy of stakeholders. Which are more influential? Who do you need to consult to make changes, and who needs to be advised? You might complete a version of Mendelow's Stakeholder Power/Interest Matrix. When you do this, remember to make a note of the reasons for your choices. A simple version is provided on this link: www.mindtools.com/pages/article/newPPM_07.htm. And then make sure you keep the relevant stakeholders consulted and informed throughout the project.

For example, a large event such as a music festival will have a long list of stakeholders with an interest in what is happening, and an influence on making the festival a success. In Figure 3.7, we have grouped the different stakeholders as to whether they are from inside the client's organization (internal) or from outside the client's organization (external).

Different stakeholders will have different priorities for the same event, and it is not unusual for the interests of stakeholders to conflict with each other. A good question to ask is: How would each of the stakeholders like to see the largest portion of the budget spent? For stakeholders for a music festival, attendees will be delighted if the organizers 'blow' the biggest part of the budget by booking headline artists and performers, or upgrading camping, car parking or the food and drink area. The artists and performers would like to see the largest part of the budget spent on booking fees, with well-presented and well-stocked dressing rooms and other backstage

FIGURE 3.7 Internal and external stakeholders for a music festival

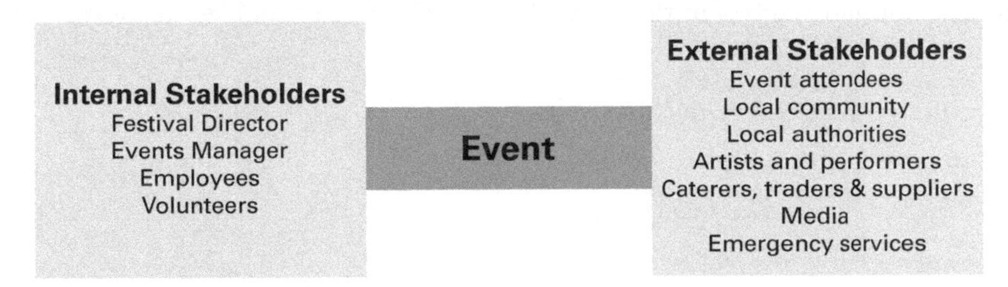

facilities. The local community might want to see a portion of the budget allocated to upgrading facilities and amenities in the local area, or keeping the noise disruption to a minimum.

For an event organizer, keeping all of the various internal and external stakeholders satisfied is not always easy. In fact, it isn't always possible. As an event organizer, the key to putting on a successful event is being able to prioritize stakeholders (who are the most important) and to make sure that nobody significant gets upset or overlooked.

A helpful model for prioritizing (mapping) stakeholders is the Power and Interest Matrix shown in Figure 3.8.

FIGURE 3.8 Mendelow's Stakeholder Power and Interest Matrix

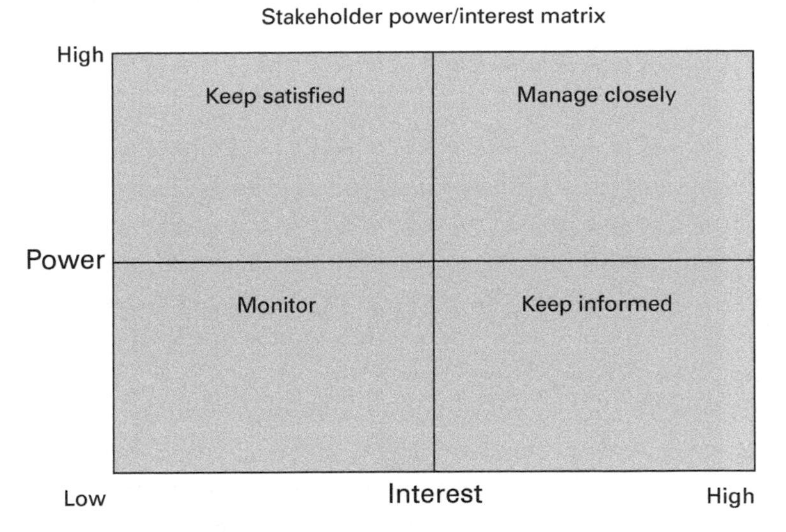

SOURCE Adapted from Mendelow (1991)

This Power and Interest Matrix model groups each of the stakeholders based on their power and interest in the event. It allocates the stakeholders to one of four quadrants/categories:

- Promoters (high power/high interest)
- Latents (high power/low interest)
- Defenders (low power/high interest)
- Apathetics (low power/low interest).

Depending on the category, the model suggests different strategies for the proper communication approach to each category of stakeholders. Stakeholders with high power and low interest need to be kept satisfied. Those with low interest and low power should only be monitored with minimum effort. A stakeholder with low power and high interest in the event should be kept informed and finally the high power, high interest stakeholders should be closely monitored and informed.

Once the various stakeholders have been mapped and prioritized using the Power and Interest Matrix then a plan can be devised for a proper communications strategy for each stakeholder, for example manage closely, keep informed. Going back once again to the example of a music festival, if the festival organizers do not properly communicate and collaborate with the local community (including the local authority) then they are likely to find that, once detailed planning is under way, the objections to hosting the event begin and, in the worst-case scenario, may mean they are not granted a licence or the permission needed to put on the festival.

Sign-off

Once you have completed all these tasks, you need to get sign-off for your event concept and more detailed ideas, as well as the all-important budget. This may be done through a formal approval process within your own organization or the client's – and whatever you do, don't make firm plans or purchases until you have a signed-off contract! Many events will require a written proposal to gain approval.

You should do everything possible to improve the quality of your proposal writing as this is how you and your organization will secure business. The cheapest way to do this is simply to make time to review it. Proposal writing is a critical skill and there are some excellent courses and workshops that you can attend to upskill yourself. These vary from short online instructional courses to more comprehensive training programmes delivered by professional bid-writers. You should also always ask the recipients for feedback on your proposals (especially for proposals that are unsuccessful). Sending a polite email that says, 'May I ask why my proposal was unsuccessful?' can help you to reflect and improve your skills and go on to win the next bid proposal.

The proposal itself could be anything from a simple one-pager to a detailed report or even a verbal presentation (referred to as a pitch). Whatever the form of the proposal, the purpose is the same: to sell your event concept (why, where, when, what and who) to a potential client and to sell yourself as a professional event organizer with the right skills and experience to stage the event. A checklist of what should be included in a proposal for a potential client is outlined below.

EVENT PROPOSAL TEMPLATE

Event details

- Event title
- Reasons for the event
- Objectives of the event
- Brief description of the event
- Event organizer details (including awards and accolades)
- Key members of the organizing team (including skills and experience)

Event concept

Why is the event happening?

- Purpose
- Goals and objectives
- Key messages

Who is the event for?

- Target audience
- Profile (e.g. demographics)
- Estimate of numbers

What will happen at the event?

- Main activities
- Event programme
- Event format (e.g. reception, dinner, concert, lecture)

When and **Where** is the event taking place?

- Date and time
- Preferred location, surroundings

Event implementation (making it happen)

- Physical resource (venue, equipment, technology)
- Financial resource (budget, cash flow, roi)
- Human resource (staff, volunteers, suppliers, contractors)

Other considerations

- Promotion and publicity
- Sponsorship
- Health and Safety
- Security
- Contingency plan

When you finally have obtained approval for your brilliant and creative event concept, with a budget that provides all the resources you will need to make the event happen, you are ready to move on to the next phase in the event management and planning process – detailed planning of key aspects of the event – content, location and venue, operational aspects, staffing, marketing and finance – and these are discussed in detail in the following chapters.

CHAPTER SUMMARY

- To plan an event well, follow a tried and tested process that enables you to develop a creative event to match your client's needs.
- Initial research for the event begins by finding out information about what is important to your client and checking that it matches what is important to your own organization and to the potential event participants.
- Events professionals should regularly consult industry publications, shows and conferences, networking events and other sources of information to help keep them informed and updated on what is happening within the industry that can influence and inspire the events they develop.
- Developing successful events concepts requires you to generate lots of different ideas. These then need to be reviewed against any constraints, such as time and budget.

- Map the different stakeholder groups and work to what needs to be done to keep them happy with the work you are doing.
- Make sure you get your event budget and concept signed off – before you go ahead!

Questions for reflection

1. How would you begin research for your next event?
2. Identify the key stakeholders for a specific event.
3. How could you use the event planning model to improve the way you plan your next event?

Explore further

Mendelow, A. L. (1981) Environmental Scanning--The Impact of the Stakeholder Concept, ICIS 1981 Proceedings, 20 https://aisel.aisnet.org/icis1981/20 (archived at https://perma.cc/K639-KYGQ)
www.bizbash.com/ (archived at https://perma.cc/SJ2K-AEFT)
www.connectmeetings.com/corporate (archived at https://perma.cc/N4G5-5FXE)
www.eventbrite.co.uk/blog/ (archived at https://perma.cc/7PAA-JAVQ)
www.eventindustrynews.com/ (archived at https://perma.cc/5SCZ-A57T)
www.eventmarketer.com/ (archived at https://perma.cc/GY2W-57U6)
www.mashmedia.net/ (archived at https://perma.cc/5CDV-RPAE)
https://standoutmagazine.co.uk/ (archived at https://perma.cc/GL6Z-N7QT)
www.themaineventmagazine.co.uk/ (archived at https://perma.cc/82QJ-QMUW)

04

Developing your events programme and content

FIGURE 4.1 The Dowson, Albert and Lomax Event Planning Process – Phase 2 detailed planning and design

PHASE 2 Detailed Planning and Design
Content
EVENT ELEMENTS
THE EVENT EXPERIENCE
IMMERSION
THEME
PROGRAMME
VIRTUAL EVENTS

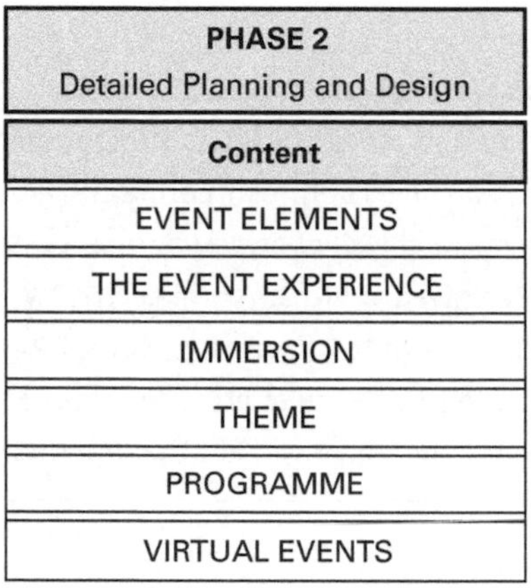

The previous chapter discussed the process by which a client's aims and objectives for staging an event can be interpreted and developed into an appropriate event concept. Central to this process is to consider the type of event (see Chapter 1), the requirements and expectations of the audience and the practicalities of time, finance and operational deliverability. Following these initial decisions, it is important to consider the details of what is going to make up the content of the event and how an event can be delivered in the most appropriate way to meet the needs of both client and audience.

This involves: an understanding of the different elements that make up an event programme; how they can be linked together with a consistent theme; how each activity can be made as rich and engaging as possible, and how a well-planned, evolving programme of activities can take the audience through various states of activity from the beginning to the end of the event. Given that one aspect of our definition of events from Chapter 1 is that 'events are special or memorable', it becomes essential for an event designer not simply to present content in a competent manner, but to blend elements together to create an experience that stands out from an attendee's everyday life.

By the end of this chapter you will be able to:

- apply the different event elements to your planning;
- build in event elements that focus on the event experience;
- understand how to develop an event that immerses participants;
- consider creative theming options;
- develop a relevant event programme;
- understand how to integrate virtual elements in your event.

Chapter 1 identified a range of generic event 'types' that can be used as starting points for developing ideas for event content:

- Conferences, seminars, workshops
- Exhibitions
- Launches
- Parties and corporate hospitality

The event concept generation discussed in Chapter 3 can involve the combining or development of these basic ideas into more individualized or appropriate forms, as can the creation of hybrid or virtual event concepts. The important factor is that each event concept is tailored to the aims and objectives of the client and the expectations of the specific audience, and the events manager should look to combine the most appropriate parts to build a bespoke event experience for their audience.

EVENTS MANAGER HACK

Content is the lifeblood of events; it's the reason the majority of events take place. When building the content for your event it is imperative to know your audience and your objectives. What are your trying to get your audience to think, feel and do as a result of engaging with your content?

Tim Collett, Managing Director, WRG, a Division of The Creative Engagement Group; UKCEM Graduate 2002

Event elements

All events involve the combination of several recognizable constituent parts, or **elements**, to create a specific experience for the attendee. It is the job of the event designer to both identify the most important elements to focus on and then to combine them in a meaningful and creative manner. The choice of elements is closely linked to the expectations of the audience and their cost, although effective event designers can find creative ways to deliver on audience expectations by adapting or developing how event elements are incorporated into their event design to match their budget. As the acceptance of virtual elements in events increases, events designers will have new opportunities to innovate and develop new 'normals' into events, such as incorporating online speakers or audiences into hybrid forms. The challenge and the opportunity of this is for the event designer to understand which event elements are really required 'in person' to deliver the audience experience, and which may be adaptable or best delivered in new more virtual forms.

In addition to specific content related to the event type, for example speakers at a conference, there are five event elements that an event designer can incorporate into the experience they create for their audience.

Venue

Venues are a crucial part of any event design and act as the canvas on which all other aspects of the event are conceived, and their selection and use will be covered in depth in Chapter 5.

Food & Beverage (F&B)

Food and drink is a central part of events, both as a basic requirement for sustenance and as an important part of the wider cultural expectations around how hospitality and welcome are shown by hosts to guests. Moreover, food is experienced by all those attending, and all guests will have expectations as to what they, or the event, should be providing. This may relate to dietary requirements based on health, medical or religious grounds, and while the minimum expectation is for the event to provide options that cover the diets of all expected attendees, the events manager should also consider the wider choices around what appropriate menus might be, dependent on the type and theme of the event.

Depending on the length and type of the event you should consider offering drinks (and snacks) throughout the event. This may include simple things such as ensuring water is available throughout as well as providing hot drinks and break times.

Alcohol at events is an issue that needs to be considered carefully. It can be an important part of celebration and leisure aspects of events, but it is important to note that many do not drink, again for health, medical or religious reasons. As well as excluding many guests, events that become dominated by alcohol can have significant issues with behaviour and other negative outcomes.

As well as being a good opportunity to demonstrate the event host's hospitality, food and drink can also be a significant part of an event budget. As such the expectations of the audience need to be carefully considered as to the level of service, the type of service (e.g. buffet vs formal meal), and an expectation of payment (e.g. providing a free bar) as an important part of controlling event costs.

EVENTS MANAGER HACK

Ask venues to label food; you will always need this for dietary requirements.

Lori Novell, Event Project Manager, The Outlook Creative Group

Hospitality

Hospitality refers to all aspects of the event related to attendees' wellbeing, beyond their food and drink. This can include their welcome, including greeting and information, as well as accommodation (at the event or before/after it) and any special access or opportunities. It is common for events managers to sell enhanced hospitality packages that upgrade certain aspects of the event experience for a higher ticket price and thus to generate significant extra income. As an example, the top hospitality package offered by independent company Steanbow for the 2022 Glastonbury Festival, including luxury glamping, hot-tubs and VIP bar and restaurant, as well as VIP tickets, cost £12,750 + VAT for two people.

Entertainment

Referring to the 5Es of event objectives from Chapter 3 we can see that Entertain and Energize are both important goals of the event designer. Entertainment at events can be both central to the event experience, such as a musician at a concert, or part of a wider part of the event offering. In the former instance, entertainment is scheduled as an important part of the event programme, often towards the end of the event as activity becomes more social. Alternatively, entertainment can be used to change the atmosphere of an event, for instance using music or games, either in conjunction with other elements or as breaks between more focused segments of the event.

Event entertainment will often require significant technical production input, including sound and lighting equipment, as well as a well-thought-through stage setup and design. Recent developments in sound/audio-visual technology are enabling the quality of event experience to be heard and seen more accurately throughout the venue, enhancing the quality of the event content and providing event designers the opportunity to engage audiences in exciting new ways.

Special effects and décor

In addition to more human-centric ways of engaging the audience, event designers can use a range of lighting, special effects and decoration to enliven the event venue and create a unique atmosphere. Ambient lighting is particularly important as it is a very powerful tool for affecting the mood of attendees. Bright lighting encourages active engagement, while dimmer lighting may lead to a more relaxed atmosphere or allow parts of the event space (e.g. a stage performance or speaker) to be highlighted with focused spotlights. The event designer should beware of the lighting and atmosphere getting overly calm, particularly after mealtimes, as some attendees may become 'too relaxed'.

Venue decoration, with drapes, table decoration, projection and props is an important way to visually enact the event design and is an important way of transforming a venue. As well as visually reinforcing the event theme, this has the important role of differentiating how the event venue feels, compared to when other events occur there. At small business events this may be as simple as ensuring there is relevant signage and colour schemes, but can be taken in very creative directions at larger and more culturally focused events such as Expos, parties or music festivals.

Creative use of special effects can also be used to create excitement or wonder, which sticks in the minds of attendees and becomes memorable moments. Outdoors, fireworks have long fulfilled this role and often form part of a crescendo or climax to an event, while more recently, video projection, lighting displays and even drones have become a means of creating a wow factor.

Case study 4.1 tells the story of a family company that runs Indian cultural events in Moscow, Russia.

CASE STUDY 4.1

Indian cultural events in Russia

Dasha Kotwani, Events Manager, The Indian National Cultural Centre, (SITA), Moscow

The Indian National Cultural Centre (SITA) is a non-profit organization with the mission to honour and promote India's beautiful culture and heritage to local Russians, foreigners and Indians in Russia.

Over the past 15 years, SITA has organized various events which have contributed to the building and growth of friendship and relationships between India and Russia. One of the most popular festivals, known as India Day, has gathered 1.5 million attendees during their three-day event.

The India Day festival started as a small open-air event that turned into the largest international festival in Russia. The festival is held annually in the month of August at a local park in Moscow, Russia and is celebrated to honour India's Independence Day. Entrance to the festival is free for all and includes many zones, including

- **Indian Bazaar Zone –** More than 120 stalls selling Indian food, textiles, organic cosmetics, henna, jewellery etc.
- **Relax Zone –** Yoga, meditation and Ayurveda classes for all ages.
- **Cultural Zone –** Represents the best of India and Russia through dance programmes, live music and even fashion shows.
- **Wedding Zone –** One of the most popular things Indians are known for is their weddings. Over 10 Russian couples daily get married as per Vedic traditional rituals.
- **Dance Masterclass Zone –** A zone where all styles of Indian dance forms (from classical to Bollywood) are shown, step by step, for everyone to practise.
- **Indian Films Zone –** An open-air cinema where attendees get the chance to watch the best that Bollywood has to offer.
- **Chess Zone –** India is known for the game of chess and in this zone, children and adults from both India and Russia compete to win.

The highlight of the festival is the Rath Yatra, known as the chariot festival. Over 5 tons of fruit are distributed to the public and the attendees get the chance to move the chariot through the park. The process is accompanied by religious songs and dances by devotees dressed in Indian national clothes. The festival is supported by the Ministry of Culture of the Russian Federation, the Moscow government and Indian Embassy of Russia.

The India Day festival is known for being an escape from reality, a chance for attendees to forget about all their worries and feel as if they have travelled to mini-India for three days.

Due to a high demand for Indian events after the India Day festival, SITA has become the sole organizer of all Indian cultural events in Russia, including events such as International Yoga Day, Holi Mela (festival of colours), Diwali Mela (Festival of lights) and Ganesh Festival.

Read more

http://indiaday.ru/ (archived at https://perma.cc/2KSQ-RDFG)
http://sitarussia.ru/ (archived at https://perma.cc/6ENG-N575)

The event experience

If events need to be 'special or memorable', it is the central role of the event designer to blend the event elements together in such a way that the experience of attending the event is felt as 'different' from what would be seen as routine. The concept of value in providing individualized 'experiences' over simple services has developed since the late 20th century and can be traced back to the concept of hedonic consumption first suggested by Holbrook and Hirschman (1982). Central to these ideas is the importance of understanding the wider social and psychological factors that link to both an experience's uniqueness and how it is remembered.

Pine and Gilmore (1999) provided a very widely followed interpretation of why it is important to consider experiences as a concept, rather than looking at how a service is delivered. This was based mainly on the idea that what customers want (and are prepared to pay for) is individualized, unique moments that respond to their individual needs or desires. By seeking to involve the individual in some way, the experience encourages them to develop, and to have some emotional or intellectual response as a result.

They suggested five rules for experience design to help deliver this:

- Make the experience as immersive as possible.
- Theme the experience.
- Provide 'indelible' impressions by creating stand-out and memorable moments.
- Eliminate negative cues – remove all elements that detract from the theme and the experience.
- Mix in memorabilia – take-away items that will act to remind and refresh the memory after the event. This may seem somewhat out of date in a world looking to reduce waste and consumption. A more modern approach might be to allow moments that are good for capturing and sharing on social media.

In addition to Pine and Gilmore's ideas based on creating individualized experiences and escape from a perceived normality, there has also been much written about the importance of creating a sense of community or belonging at events.

Anderton (2019) suggests that an experience that is 'special and memorable' is based on a combination of four factors, all of which the event designer needs to consider:

- Freedom – the event feels different from everyday life.
- Belonging – the event gives the attendee a sense of community.
- Authenticity – the content provided is novel, relevant, real, or fantastical.
- Transcendence – derived from the three above, the attendee has moments of insight or pleasure either individually or as part of a group or crowd.

By considering attendees' engagement with an event, both as individuals and as part of a community, the event designer can start to blend elements in such a way that the event becomes an emotional experience. Well-designed events challenge attendees to invest effort in their participation in, and understanding of, what is unfolding, forming new memories resulting in some form of change from the emotional journey they have experienced.

Case study 4.2 expresses the powerful emotional aspects of developing a family funeral. Cultural and religious events can often have stricter requirements, and these were impacted during the pandemic. This case study tells the personal story of a British Muslim family bereaved during the Covid-19 pandemic in 2021 and how some of the issues they faced were overcome.

CASE STUDY 4.2

Organizing a Muslim funeral during Covid-19

Zeeshana Khan

An Islamic funeral (or 'Janazah') is a well-oiled machine, but I had no idea how difficult it was until I had to plan one.

My eldest brother Shahbaz was a casualty of the Covid-19 pandemic, and the organization of his funeral started hours before he died in hospital. It was a frenetic process from day 0, from trying to frantically source an Imam who felt comfortable enough to come into a live Covid-19 ward to give him his last rites, to trying to figure out when would be the best day to have him buried.

Janazah-planning is a community effort, but we weren't subscribed to our local death committee, so we had to do it ourselves. Organization is normally left to the male relatives, but trauma responses being what they are, I won the 'suck it up and grieve later' lottery and took over the organization from my elder brother.

I gave myself 48 hours to plan the Janazah, so every second counted. Within the first few hours, I registered my brother's death, obtained the burial card (so that his body could be released quickly) and ordered his burial plot from our local cemetery.

The Janazah consists of three parts.

Preparation of the body

Preparation of the body involves a 'Ghusl' (ritual washing) by male family members, followed by shrouding. Since Shahbaz's death was Covid-related, the biggest challenges were (a) finding a Covid-trained Islamic funeral director, and (b) willing volunteers who would then have to isolate for 10 days afterwards. Disappointingly, nobody offered to help, and even our local mosque refused to offer their on-site Ghusl facilities, which made a (normally simple) process a logistical nightmare. After 12 hours of non-stop phone calls to dozens of people, we found an Islamic centre in a different town run by a group of young Muslims, disheartened by the rigidity of the more well-established mosques. The kindness and generosity of these strangers allowed Shahbaz to have his Ghusl done in the loving arms of his little brother, and a host of eager young volunteers (in full PPE). Everything was Covid safe and nothing was rushed; Shahbaz got the full ritual, and not the stripped-down version that other facilities were offering during these times. The Kaffan (shroud) was donated by a family friend, as we didn't have time to buy one. After washing, Shahbaz was laid on top of three white sheets and shrouded in the prescribed way. Once he was laid in his coffin, the casket had to be sealed immediately, due to Covid risks. A 'Chadr' (sheet) displaying prayers was laid on top of the coffin, and stayed on it until burial. This, too, was donated by the same family friend, and will be used for all future funerals within our family.

Funeral prayers and burial

Organizing the 'Salat-al-janazah' (funeral prayers) at our local mosque was the only instance where I, a woman, was unable to speak directly to the elders of the mosque, so I got a male member of the mosque to speak to the committee on our behalf. Shahbaz's Janazah was held on the holiest day of the week: a Friday. The remaining male family members joined my brother at the mosque, and most of the worshippers stayed after their Friday prayers, to join in the Salat-al-Janazah. There was no time to notify everyone of his death, so the turnout was modest, and social distancing was maintained. The Al-Dafin (burial) took place in the Islamic section of our local cemetery, where the graves all lie perpendicular to Mecca. The final official prayers were said, the coffin was lowered, and the grave re-filled by friends and family. For the safety of everyone, we heavily discouraged anyone from coming near our family (as we technically had to isolate for 10 days), so it was surreal not being hugged and consoled by anyone, but in a weird way, it allowed our emotions stay in check. We covered the grave in flowers and contemplated silently.

Post-Janazah/Mourning

Our mourning period was an introvert's dream. No mourners were allowed to visit, so I didn't have to arrange any catering or speak to anyone. We settled on a small 'Khatam' with our immediate family, but with the power of video calls, our family in Pakistan had a more traditional ceremony on our behalf.

Months on, I look back and I'm grateful for the distraction of those crazy few days. It was a crash course in facilitating the grief of my loved ones, and as hard as it was, I'd do it again in a heartbeat. I miss my big brother so much... I don't think I'll ever recover fully, but this entire process taught me that religion or not, the funeral process is as much for the living as it is for the deceased.

Find out more

www.sherazam.co.uk/muslim-funeral-director-uk/ (archived at https://perma.cc/9E8Z-DDSE)
www.memorialplanning.com/resources/religious-funerals-guide/islamic-funeral-guide (archived at https://perma.cc/6DNX-YCU3)

Immersion

One important way to encourage attendees to engage with what is happening, and thus to make their experience more memorable, is by creating a sense of immersion in what is going on. This involves finding a means to focus them on what is happening in the present moment, forget what is going more broadly in their lives and surroundings, and enter a more focused state of mind.

Toft-Nielson (2014) suggests three useful approaches that can be adopted to increase the immersive nature of an event experience:

Imaginative immersion

The attendee is brought into a story or creative endeavour and becomes interested in the unfolding narrative of what is happening to them.

Challenge-based immersion

The event, or some element of it, will lead the attendee into trying to achieve some goal or engage in some competitive activity. In seeking to solve the problem or win the game they will have to focus their attention, leading to a sense of dislocation and concentration.

Sensory immersion

By altering a space's physical environment, the event designer can make it feel different from usual. By engaging as many senses as possible, the event designer can strengthen the authenticity of this reimagining of a space and make the sense of immersion greater. Considering what the appropriate smells and sounds of the altered space might be, or what music might be appropriate, are very powerful tools in encouraging an emotional response, as they bypass more critical mental processes. When attendees enter and inhabit this enhanced space, they then re-evaluate their normal behaviour and try to understand and inhabit the new world in which they find themselves.

This reimagining of a space can be very powerful, and building multiple immersive techniques together can significantly reinforce the immersion felt by the attendee. There are many new technological developments that support indoor and outdoor venues and event organizers in creating an immersive space, such as German sound company d&b audiotechnik (www.dbaudio.com/worship).

Theming

An important step in the interaction between an event and its attendees and the development of imaginative immersion is to establish the meaning, message or story of the event. This communication should also seek to build connections between the attendees themselves, helping them understand that they are all following the same story or looking for the same meaning. As identified by Pine and Gilmore (1999), a helpful way of establishing this shared understanding is to identify a theme for the event.

Themes can take several forms.

Overlaid story theme

The most recognizable form of theming is where an event adopts a recognizable story or cultural language and creates a fantasy world for its attendees to inhabit (e.g. James Bond, the 1920s, a music festival). The theme allows the participants to use the common language and stereotype that it invokes to quickly develop both a sense of freedom/escape and also a common bond of belonging with all the other attendees. It is then the job of the designer to maintain the authenticity of the fantasy through appropriate content (this is where eliminating negative cues comes in) and then hope that the heightened sense of freedom and community, and a good sense of timing (see Programming), will create an atmosphere where experiences will be more intense and thus more memorable. This type of theming can be very effective with a good choice or story/culture and appropriate attention to detail, but can also be so overpowering that any other important messages the event is trying to convey get drowned out. It will often be found in celebration-style events, especially where attendees may lack more intense shared cultural bonds, such as in office or student parties.

Topic theme

A more restrained approach to theming is commonly adopted by business events and conferences where a single idea or problem is adopted for a particular event. While this doesn't provide the sense of fantasy and escape, it does focus the discussion and mental connections between attendees. The event designer here is much more focused on attracting speakers with specific knowledge and experiences to share and creating a community of knowledge. The main theme can be subdivided into relevant streams, creating groups of individuals with shared interests and developing deeper, more authentic discussion.

Visual theming

Even in the absence of a dominant story or topic, event designers can develop a sense of sensory immersion and visual coherence at an event by adopting recognizable and repeated design elements. Most obviously this can involve adopting a colour palette for the event, with lighting and decoration, as well as signage, being used to create spaces within the venue that feel connected and unique to the event itself. Colours themselves can have effect on mood and atmosphere (yellow is bright and energetic, reds and oranges warm and reassuring, while greens are calmer, and blues and purples are cool and tranquil), although colours can also be used to mirror any existing branding related to the event. A good general rule of thumb is to limit the use of different colours and consider colours that either complement or contrast with each other. More broadly, the use of designs and logos associated with the event can be added to create a branded space, although, as with colour, repetition of a limited number of designs is more powerful than lots of competing images and ideas.

Programming

Events occur over time. As well as simply being a series of structured activities that occur in a predetermined order, events can also be viewed as a journey through which the attendees progress. One of the most important tasks of the event designer is to develop a structure to how the activities link and build that allows the mental and imaginative aspects of the event to develop, while at the same time being aware of the physical, emotional and social needs of the attendees. This process of developing an event running order that flows appropriately is called programming.

Events managers understand that attendees take time and some effort to move from their everyday world into the world of the event. They will usually structure activities such that the expectations of engagement with and immersion in the event content become more intense as the event develops. The level of an audience's engagement and immersion is often referred to as the 'energy'. In a simple event this can be represented visually as in Figure 4.1.

Within this simple model of event programming there are five important phases to consider.

FIGURE 4.2 Graph of event energy over time

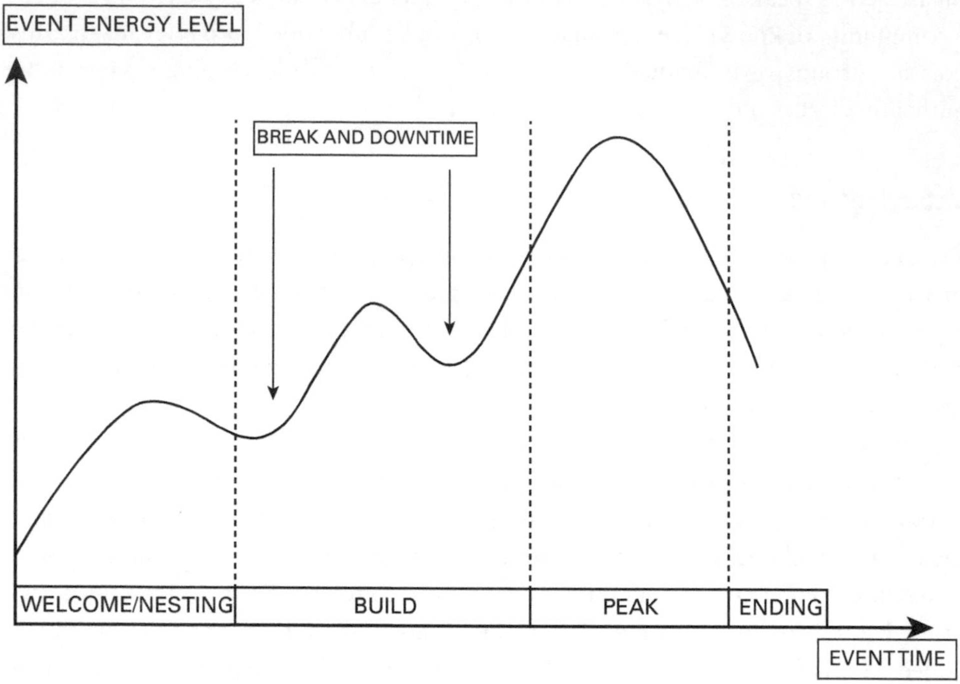

EVENT ENERGY LEVEL
BREAK AND DOWNTIME
WELCOME/NESTING | BUILD | PEAK | ENDING
EVENT TIME

Welcome

When attendees first arrive at an event they are still concerned with the practicalities of their arrival (their journey or accessing the appropriate program link if online) as well as having to consider lots of practical aspects of the event, such as ticket checking and basic orientation. It is important for the events manager to allow time and provide helpful support at this stage, and empathy is important. The events manager and event staff may know what is going on, but it takes time for newly arrived attendees to get their bearings.

Once the practicalities of arrival have been dealt with, it will still take time for attendees to start to understand what their environment is like and how they can engage with it. Carù and Cova (2006) call this the 'Nesting stage' and suggest that attendees will seek out familiarity, whether people they know or engaging in familiar routines such as getting a drink. Events managers should seek to support this while at the same time starting to bring them into the world of the event that will be developing. As suggested above, this can be done through the decoration and adaptation of the environment (remember the power of multiple senses here), as well as through more active means such as icebreakers or inductions at conferences.

Build

Once the attendees start to understand and feel more comfortable in the event space, the events manager should allow them to begin to explore and deepen their immersion. This is an intermediate phase that Carù and Cova (2006) call the 'Investigation stage' and may involve both the physical exploration of the event space as well as a greater mental interpretation of the story of meaning associated with the event. At this stage the events manager should allow as much freedom as possible for attendees to explore and for them to find their own path into and through the event. Immediately confining a guest to a seat or small area will limit their engagement with the event and act to shut down their imagination rather than encourage it. As this stage of the event progresses, the events manager can encourage more active engagement. Audiences may investigate and gain confidence at different rates, so managing a build phase can again require events managers and performers alike to be empathetic as to how their attendees are settling.

At this point, initial activities and content will start to take place. It is important to hold back the most exciting elements of the activity, partly to give the event a dynamic and allow it to build to some sort of finale, and partly to give the audience time to become more and more immersed in what is going on. In evening events and shows this will take the form of warm-up acts, but other event types will have slightly different dynamics.

Peak moment(s)

Once audience members have explored and become comfortable in their environment and understood the new rules of the event space, they enter a final phase which Carù and Cova (2006) call the 'Stamping stage'. They are now in a place where they will engage fully with their environment, become immersed in the meaning and be eager to become an active part of what is going on, in a process called co-creation. For conferences and meetings this will involve them in becoming part of the discussion, while at celebratory events it can be more physical, involving dancing, cheering and singing. This co-creation becomes infectious and reinforces community feelings, leading to a heightened emotional stage and, crucially, strong memory formation. In this phase the events manager should be using all their event elements (performance, sound, lighting) and immersive techniques that they have been holding back in order to get the maximum response. If there has been some story or meaning unfolding, this moment will also reflect the dénouement.

Ending

At some point the event will have to end and attendees will return to their 'normal' existence. This does not happen instantaneously, and events managers should consider a clear and well-understood conclusion to what has happened. This can be an overt announcement or thank-you for those who have been involved, but can also include many visual prompts that signal a clear change in mood and expectation. This can involve a change in lighting (brighter if it has been dark, darker if it has been bright), a change in music style or silence. The events manager should also consider the practicalities of attendees leaving an event and where they will go. It can take some time for attendees to come out of the enhanced mood you have developed and again an empathetic approach should be taken, although the needs of event staff wanting to finish and move into the breakdown and load-out phases of the event need to be considered too.

Downtime and mealtimes

Events that take place over more than a few hours need to factor in the physical and emotional needs of attendees. The concentration and mental exertion required by attendees to build and reach full immersion can be sustained for a couple of hours (think of a play, concert or football match), but if the event is to last longer, attendees will need to take breaks. These breaks can be a powerful tool for events managers when programming, as attendees will use them to reflect on and discuss what has been happening, deepening their understanding and strengthening the message of the event. For many events the social aspect is central, and giving over time for attendees to engage with each other without interference will be an important part of the experience.

In addition to downtime the events manager needs to consider the physical needs of the attendees. If they become hungry, thirsty (or need to go to the toilet), it will become increasingly hard to engage them with the content you have planned. Consider the cultural expectations of food and meal timings and consider how you might allow attendees to access sustenance outside of set times. It is a good idea to link mealtimes and downtime together so that attendees can eat/drink and discuss what has been happening.

Following breaks, and particularly after food, it important to understand that the mood and energy level of the event will have dropped significantly. The events manager will have to repeat the process of building engagement with and immersion in what is happening. If people are digesting a meal, this is a process that cannot be rushed.

Case study 4.3 demonstrates creative ways to engage participants in conferences and meetings.

CASE STUDY 4.3

A workshop on participant-driven and participation-rich meeting design: The American Heart Association

Adrian Segar, Founder, Conferences That Work, USA

How do you teach people who aren't meetings professionals to design and facilitate better meetings?

The American Heart Association (AHA) is devoted to saving people from heart disease and stroke – the two leading causes of death in the world. Each year, the AHA holds eight large scientific conferences, and the association leadership wanted to improve the quality of their meetings. So, in January 2020 I designed and facilitated a two-day workshop to teach participant-driven and participation-rich meeting design and facilitation to 150 cardiologists responsible for creating and running AHA conferences.

I have people **do** things in my workshops because I've found that experiential learning is the most powerful kind of learning. I introduce what we're going to do, lead participants through the exercise, debrief when needed, and repeat this cycle with appropriate breaks.

In 5½ hours, spread over two days, I introduced the following core tools for experiential learning in a group of peers:

- **Small group work** allows every person present to actively participate in and influence what happens at a meeting. Its simplest form, **pair share**, creates short one-on-one conversations between attendees, with each given equal time to respond to a question. I ran numerous pair shares during this workshop, the first on: 'What's your biggest challenge to improving your conference?'
- **Human spectrograms** (also called **body voting**) have participants arrange themselves in the room to reflect their answer to a question. They provide an efficient way to uncover group information that is of interest to its members. Everyone can see who's in specified groups and meet people who are similar to them. During the AHA workshop, we turned the room into a geographic map to allow people to discover who lived near them. Participants lined up by their years of experience as cardiologists, and we then used the line to create small groups each containing a range of experience. Most participants had more than one professional role, so we created triangular spectrograms to view the mix of education/clinical/research, and the research cardiologists explored their mix of population/clinical/basic work.
- Participants also experienced **The Three Questions** – in my opinion, the best way to open a conference designed for active learning, connection and engagement. Each attendee in turn shared their answers to the following three questions (there are no wrong answers) with their group:
  - How did I get here?
  - What do I want to happen?
  - What experience or expertise do I have that might be of interest to others?

- Through their answers, people shared their relevant past, present and desired future with other participants. Group members made individual connections. Common interests and topics for later discussion emerged.
- **Fishbowl** is a simple set of rules that make it easy to facilitate a large group discussion. AHA participants used a fishbowl to discuss a topic near to their hearts: 'What is the best heart-healthy diet?' We began with a human spectrogram that uncovered participants' opinions of plant-based versus omnivore diets, followed by a lively fishbowl discussion.
- We spent workshop time exploring issues of specific interest to the AHA participants. Some of the topics covered included: how to hold better poster sessions, crowdsourcing topics for meeting sessions, using a buddy system for first-time attendee support, and the best ways to follow up presentations in more depth. I also employed **Wants and Offers**, a flip chart and sticky note technique, to help AHA speciality conference organizers request and share presenter resources from their professional networks.
- The workshop included two short presentations on key meeting design concepts:
  - *The conference arc*: the essential structure of participant-driven and participation-rich meetings; and
  - Six reasons to change our conferences:
    1. Traditional sessions provide no connections around content.
    2. Lectures are a terrible way to learn.
    3. The availability of online content.
    4. Professionals now learn predominantly socially, not in the classroom.
    5. Today, everyone has expertise and experience to share.
    6. Most pre-scheduled sessions don't address actual attendee wants and needs.
- Finally, I ran a **Group Spective**, a session that gives attendees time to collectively take stock. I used **Plus/Delta**: a review tool that enables participants to quickly identify what went well at an event and the development of new initiatives and improvements. This closing session built community around a shared experience, and provided valuable feedback on future events to meeting stakeholders.

Teaching people how to design and facilitate better meetings is perhaps the most powerful way for us to improve the quality and effectiveness of our events. The techniques I've outlined are simple and transformative but rarely used. I hope they become better known and more widely practised.

Find out more

www.conferencesthatwork.com (archived at https://perma.cc/6T8X-42M8)

EXPERT PERSPECTIVE: A WHISTLE STOP LOOK AT VIRTUAL AND HYBRID EVENTS

Paul Cook

In addition to in-person events, it is critical that virtual and hybrid events are also considered as suitable formats for clients. The default of in-person events has been eradicated by the impact of Covid-19. The virus created a strong need for virtual events as well as opening opportunities for the hybrid model.

Even though virtual and hybrid events were in existence before Covid, they were in the minority as not being a serious offering. That has now changed. Let's investigate them further and highlight areas to reflect on.

A virtual event

A virtual event has no physical venue for attendees to go to. The clue is in the name. Everything is online. All attendees are online, as are the speakers, sponsors and exhibitors. A virtual event or meeting may also be referred to as an online event, a webinar or a remote event.

A hybrid event

A hybrid event is a combination of an in-person event and a virtual event. Hence the name, hybrid. With an in-person event, people travel to the venue. With a virtual event, people attend via a web-link. With a hybrid event, people have a choice in how they wish to attend. They can do so in person, or they can do so virtually.

A hybrid event can be any size from large to small. It can be based in one physical venue, or it can have several physical locations. The configuration of the hybrid event should always be determined by what will satisfy the organizational objectives, but the key point is that with a hybrid event, there are two audiences. One is 'in-person' and one is 'virtual'.

Key benefits of virtual and hybrid events

Increasing income (sales)

You can go beyond the confines of a physical venue. You can open dialogue with virtual delegates. This is an effective way to start to develop future income.

Encouraging inclusivity

There will be some delegates who would not have been able to travel to your event. Now they don't have to, as they can join virtually.

Extending brand engagement

You can invite many more people to participate in your event.

Reducing carbon emissions

If sustainability is important, virtual and hybrid events need be included within strategy planning discussions.

An event tech platform is not production

Regardless of whether it is a hybrid or a virtual event, tech will be involved. There are numerous event tech platforms for planners to look at. These platforms can help them with all sorts of challenges, such as delegate registration, data capture, uploading sponsors information and so on. What the platform will not do, however, is produce the content of the event. This will be carried out by a production company. They will capture the content and then stream it to the attendees.

It could be that the attendees see the content via a TV screen on the event tech platform, but this is not always the situation. Understanding that a tech platform and production of content are different is essential.

Trust the technology

Technology has always been a key component of event success, regardless of which event format was chosen. However, with virtual and hybrid events there is more technology to consider. The challenge for events professionals is that they cannot understand it all. It is impossible; there is too much of it. While planners may be reluctant to relinquish their control, they simply must. They must trust the technology companies. The same applies to speakers, sponsors and stakeholders; they too need to trust the tech. Companies that work in the tech space every day know the short cuts, the quick fixes and more besides. It is time to trust them.

Rehearsals

Rehearsals are especially critical for virtual and hybrid events. Take any professional sport and you know that the players have a critical need for practice and training. They need to know what to do in all sorts of situations. They want and need to be prepared. It is the same with the military, the theatre and healthcare to name but a few. And so it is in the world of events. There is a need to rehearse and there is no excuse for not doing so.

With virtual and hybrid events there is greater complexity to take care of. Rehearsals have to happen. And it is important that you can differentiate between a ‘run-through’ and a rehearsal. While clients and event producers use these terms interchangeably, they are not. They are two quite different things. And it’s essential you understand the difference.

A 'run-through' is where the producer talks through what will happen. The producer may have asked for all speakers and the client to be on the call, or the focus may be on a specific session. But in a 'run-through' they discuss what will happen. That's it. There is no action. There is no practice.

To illustrate a 'run-through', let's use the example of a panel discussion. In this, the introduction of the speakers would be clarified. Who is introducing them, do they appear individually one by one, how much time is set aside for Q&A and so on? You get the idea.

A rehearsal on the other hand is practising as though LIVE. In our panel example, a rehearsal is the time for action. The 'run-through' has given information on how everything will work. Now it is time to see if it does. And the important thing to remember here is that rehearsals are intended to find the things that work, as well as those that do not work. Rehearsals enable course correction, which is crucial.

Virtual and hybrid events provide greater choice

The range of virtual and hybrid events is vast. For example, conferences, product launches and exhibitions are immediate examples that come to mind.

The choice offered by different event formats is very positive. If delegates can choose how they want to consume event content, the more in control they will feel, which adds to their sense of mental wellbeing. Without virtual or hybrid events, their only option would have been to have attended an in-person event.

These events help promote a healthier mind, which is another benefit. This time it is a benefit for the individual.

When virtual and hybrid events offer benefits for organizations, benefits for delegates and open up possibilities for future organizational growth, they need to be offered by events professionals. Not to do so would be a missed opportunity.

Reference

www.planetplanit.biz/ (archived at https://perma.cc/6XEF-DL8E)

Virtual event design considerations

While virtual and online events pose a challenge in the development of fully immersive event experiences, they also provide interesting new ways of engaging audiences. Reviewing the approaches already explained, it makes sense that the conception of online events needs to focus on the approaches most likely to work, rather than simply trying to re-create pre-existing ideas of what events should be.

Immersion

Clearly, one of the biggest differences for online events compared to live events is the reduced sensory immersion. Not only can the events manager not deploy the power of smell, touch or a 360° visual experience, but they also must compete with a myriad of distractions that online attendees are subject to. The implication is that, in the absence of VR technology that can partially replicate this, designers of online events need to use other means to generate immersion to a greater extent. Creative events need to be much more focused on the place of the attendee within a story or their role in producing content rather than just absorbing it. Alternatively, or in addition to, the use of challenge-based immersion requires the focus and attention of the attendees which will draw them more into the world of the event and out of that of their immediate surroundings. This could take the form of actual games (even having events within gaming environments), or more simply involve more moments in meetings and online conferences involving polls, activities and challenges. The important message is that if online attendees feel external to the proceedings, the more likely they are to drift away and feel the event as just one small aspect of their experience in that moment.

Theming

The ideas of theming still hold for online events, but the event designer needs to think of ideas that will translate easily into spaces that themselves are minimally themed. It is not possible to rely on the theatrics or props, costumes and decoration when all you have is a computer or phone screen. Possibly one of the major issues linked to visual theming is the similarity of the visual look of online platforms. A good question to ask is how the screen image can be harmonized within the event online environment. Consider presenters' screen backgrounds and adopt agreed colour palettes where platforms allow. For hybrid events where some elements are on screen (such as speakers being broadcast into live spaces), consider how the speakers' screens can be made to look and feel like the live space they are becoming part of.

Programme

One of the most important considerations for online or hybrid events is to accept that, if immersion is less intense, then the expectation of attention from the audience should also be less. The stages outlined above (welcome, build, peak, ending, plus downtime) are all still relevant, but the length of time allowed for each stage, and the event itself, will also be shorter. This is supported, as it has become clear that the mental processes required to engage in the artificial world of online spaces through screens are greater than in a live setting, meaning that attendees will become tired, and thus less engaged, much quicker. Consider shorter sessions, more regular breaks, both out of the event entirely (i.e. off screen) and in social chat areas, as social engagement is an important tool for creating an active engagement with what is happening on screen. It is also sensible to make good use of technology to vary and limit the size of groups, as anything over the number of faces acceptable on a screen (six or nine) becomes impersonal and a barrier to active engagement.

CHAPTER SUMMARY

- Making any event memorable requires an events manager to combine the available event elements to create a unique event experience for the event attendee.
- Actively engaging attendees can be achieved by creating immersive experiences using a combination of imaginative, challenge-based and sensory immersion techniques.
- Theming the event is an important means of using common story, meaning or visual tools to communicate with, and create shared meanings for, your attendees.
- Events should have a pre-planned programme of content that manages the level of engagement and energy and allows attendees time to orientate and establish themselves at an event before building to memorable peak moments.
- Online and virtual events need to consider how to engage and immerse audiences on their own terms rather than simply replicating existing event concepts and plans.

Questions for reflection

1. What are the key components of designing event content?
2. What support could you get in developing content for a business event?
3. What steps could you take to integrate hybrid elements into the design of event content?

References

Carù, A and Cova, B (2006) How to facilitate immersion in a consumption experience: Appropriation operations and service elements. *Journal of Consumer Behaviour: An International Research Review*, 5(1), 4–14

Pine, J and Gilmore, J H (1999) *The Experience Economy: Work is theatre and every business a stage*, Harvard Business Press, Boston, MA

Toft-Nielsen, C. (2014) Worlds at play: Space and player experience in fantasy computer games, *Nordicom Review*, *35*(s1), 237–50

Explore further

d&b audiotechnik https://youtu.be/k_K1oIDHv1M (archived at https://perma.cc/9V47-FL6P) The WHY-Series. Soundscape: A return to reality – future-proofing

05

Venue selection and site planning essentials

FIGURE 5.1 The Dowson, Albert and Lomax Event Planning Process – event venues

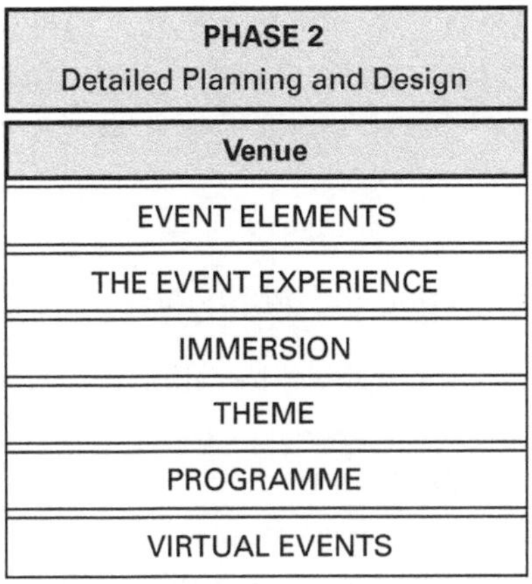

PHASE 2
Detailed Planning and Design

Venue

EVENT ELEMENTS

THE EVENT EXPERIENCE

IMMERSION

THEME

PROGRAMME

VIRTUAL EVENTS

This chapter reflects the importance of selecting an appropriate destination for an event, which may be a continent or region in the world, a specific country or a region within a country. The actual location (which may be a town, a city or a rural locality) is the next priority, followed by choosing the venue for the event. This decision-making process is a vital part of the event planning process and contributes to the delivery and success of the event itself. The chapter explains the process for selecting a venue and discusses potential issues, with advice on how to resolve problems. Once the venue has been selected, the chapter concludes with a detailed section advising on how to work with the venue team to ensure a smooth event delivery. By the end of this chapter, you will be able to:

- select the destination;
- develop a venue selection process;
- plan and undertake venue site visits;

- plan event/venue communication;
- plan an effective site layout for your event;
- design and produce a site map for your event.

Selecting the destination

Destination marketing organizations (DMOs) and venue search agencies are on hand to help in the search for a location or venue. DMOs may operate on behalf of a country, region or city, to promote the benefits of a specific geographic area, and may provide resources to support you in bringing your event to that destination, including a list of venues from within their membership. For example, in the UK, the Business Visits & Events Partnership (BVEP) represents government agencies, trade and professional organizations, to promote Britain's business visits and events sector (www.businessvistsandeventspartnership.com). Meanwhile, the 'Yorkshire' website promotes 'God's own county' to encourage visitors and events to the region (https://www.yorkshire.com/).

Factors to consider when selecting the destination

When selecting your event's geographical location, there are key aspects to consider.

SAFETY AND SECURITY CONSIDERATIONS

The environment in which we live today means that nowhere is immune from threats to the security and safety of members of the public, including event participants and staff. For some destinations, it is worthwhile considering their appropriateness in light of this: think about what are the no-go places for your event participants, as well as identifying the practicalities of travelling to less secure destinations. In 2022, there were still significant threats across the UK and elsewhere, so whatever your location and venue, this is an important factor to consider. Include safety and security aspects as part of your risk assessment for the event and remember that different places may have cultural practices and beliefs that might affect your participants' behaviour, so it's important to make them aware of any cultural sensitivities, whatever location you choose. Although we might perceive some destinations as being more dangerous than others, the reality that is experience tells us that such perceptions do not always reflect reality. An important aspect to bear in mind is 'what do attendees need to know?', from practical arrangements to cautionary advice.

THE IMAGE OF THE LOCATION AS IT RELATES TO THE CLIENT ORGANIZATION AND TO THE EVENT

Many events managers spend their time seeking out the most amazing and wonderful locations – yet, perhaps surprisingly, some events are better held in less exotic locations. In this era when corporate governance is increasingly important, there may be valid reasons why you don't want to draw attention to your event, or to your client. Remember the images from the opening ceremony of the London 2012 Olympics – when the corporate guests stayed away from embarrassment about having the best seats in the house? While in Brazil in 2016, concerns about political unrest and economic recession were given as reasons for empty seats in Rio's Olympic stadium? Yet by staying away from the London Olympics, corporate hospitality VIP ticketholders drew attention to themselves, while the person in the street railed at the Olympic organizers because there were visibly empty stands.

It's no longer just the public sector that wishes to be seen to be obtaining value for money – the influence of the Freedom of Information Act has its impact here. More and more companies are considering the views of their stakeholders when selecting event venues and taking decisions that fit with the corporate values they publicly espouse; increasingly, they are based on a reaction to: 'What would this look like as a story in the *Daily Mail*?' On the other hand, the most important factor may be to wow your client and attendees with an exciting and unusual location or venue. And it's also about what image the location or venue appears to have – despite any cost implications. So if it's a five-star luxury hotel, it could be less important that you got it for a bargain, as internal messages about being thrifty can be undermined by the political impact of the image your decision portrays in the media and internally within your organization. All too often, venues can be selected (and particularly by non-professionals with decision-making responsibilities in events) as a vanity decision, such as a charity selecting an international conference centre for its local event, at exorbitant cost, when more appropriate and cheaper options are available.

ACCESS BY PUBLIC TRANSPORT AND ROAD

For an event to work, it's important to consider whether you want the event to be easily reached, or out of the way. So, if your event is for a global audience that requires an atmosphere of calm and tranquillity, there's no point looking at venues in the area surrounding a major airport, however convenient that seems. Instead, you need to research venues far from traffic and noise, where participants can wander around, undisturbed. Understanding the purpose of the event is vital even at this point. Make sure you're clear about that purpose and identify what you want to achieve and what kind of environment and atmosphere you want to create. And here, transport links are vital, especially for one-day events where participants may be travelling for several hours to reach the venue. The last thing you want is for them to arrive frazzled and stressed, so it helps to choose a venue that is easy to reach. Public transport links are also important considerations for event sustainability, and you can encourage car-sharing if groups are coming from the same direction.

TRAVEL TIME FOR POTENTIAL PARTICIPANTS

In the UK, a 'central location' for an event is often considered to be London, especially because of the excellent rail and air links into the capital. However, it's important to work out where your event participants are coming from and reconsider any 'southern-centric' views you may have. The time it takes for residents and visitors to travel across London once they have arrived in the capital can often make other locations, such as Birmingham, easier to get to, especially for a large group of people. Alternatively, if your event attendees are travelling from across a wide area, it may be worthwhile considering holding several smaller events in different geographic regions.

Case study 5.1 explains how an events management company in the Caribbean island of Trinidad and Tobago supported a non-profit organization. This cause-related event was used to create awareness, educate, and advocate for disability rights. By extension the event attracts visitors and promotes the island as a destination, making the most of its historical background.

CASE STUDY 5.1

Trinidad and Tobago – Changing society through events: Buddy Walk® – Disability Rights Event – Down Syndrome Family Network

Lisa J Ghany, Director Xceptional Events Ltd, Trinidad and Tobago; UKCEM Graduate, 2006

Trinidad and Tobago is an island metropolis with a population of just over 1.4 million people welcoming 141 international tourist arrivals in 2020, according to data published by the World Tourist Organization (UNWTO). Nestled in the southern Caribbean, Trinidad and Tobago is best known for its annual carnival; as the country where the steelpan, the only musical instrument invented in the 20th century was created; and as the birthplace of and home to many sporting heroes, including Brian Lara, Dwight Yorke and Olympic Gold Medallist Hasley Crawford. A short trip via the ferry or plane will take you to Tobago where the beaches, lush tropical rain forest and coral reefs will make you feel as though you are in paradise. It is a country of great warmth and hospitality where events are a natural extension of the life of its people. The islands are packed full of organic community events born out of historical traditions and culture and business events that support the corporate nature of the islands' oil and gas economy. Trinidad has become the meeting place for corporate events and Tobago a place of rest, relaxation and rejuvenation for many, both at home and abroad.

Located in the capital city of Port of Spain, Xceptional Events Limited, established in 2008, has produced many signature events for a variety of clients over the years. In 2012, we had a unique opportunity to become part of a social movement for change on our islands with regards to disability rights and, in particular, for persons with Down Syndrome and their families. Working for non-profit organizations requires heart and passion, as by extension you become an advocate for the cause. The client, the Down Syndrome Family Network (DSFN), was formed by a group of parents who were searching for a better quality of life for their children, and for inclusion and awareness. At the time there was little information available locally, a person with a disability was looked at in a negative way, and the subject of disability was viewed with shame and guilt in many areas of society.

As an affiliate of the National Down Syndrome Society the DSFN acquired all the necessary permissions to host the Buddywalk in Trinidad and Tobago. The idea to incorporate fun events that were inclusive, educational and that celebrated the person with the disability was at the heart of the campaign. The Buddywalk event promotes the inclusion and acceptance of persons with Down syndrome in their communities by getting the community involved.

Xceptional Events was primarily responsible for all aspects of event management. Specific duties included:

- research into Down Syndrome and Disability events;
- design of the event;
- risk management assessment;
- legal requirements, permits, permissions;
- set up of a pre-registration online system;
- volunteer management;
- design and production of medals, shirts, and other collateral material;
- venue set up and dismantle;
- entertainment;
- sponsorship;
- VIP protocol;
- media relations;
- gap analysis.

The Buddywalk has over the past 10 years grown from 250 persons walking for the cause in 2012 to over 1,500 people in 2019. Sponsor involvement has gone from 5 companies in 2012 to over 25 companies taking part in 2019. All event costs are covered through sponsorss contributions. Media coverage is national, with radio, TV and electronic press covering the event on prime-time news programmes. A parallel social media campaign ensured that awareness included the global online community on Facebook, Instagram and YouTube. In addition, local entertainment celebrities play an integral part in the after-walk party. The Buddywalk stage has hosted Soca superstars Farmer Nappy, Destra Garcia, Sherwyn Winchester, Nailah Blackman and the father–son Steelpan duo of Dane and self-advocate

Daniel Gulston. In 2020 and 2021, the Buddywalk was held as a virtual event due to Covid-19 and garnered support throughout the country.

The Buddywalk has become a household name and has created awareness for persons with disabilities. It has by extension created a platform for more conversations about disability rights and inclusion in our country. It has given persons with Down Syndrome their own signature event in the community. By extension, within the past 10 years, we have seen awareness converted into action, which has resulted in Trinidad and Tobago ratifying the UN convention on the Rights of Persons with Disabilities and a National Policy on Persons with Disabilities in 2018. Events like the Buddywalk are an important catalyst for awareness, education and advocacy and can create real change and a better quality of life for persons with disabilities.

References

www.worldometers.info/world-population/trinidad-and-tobago-population/ (archived at https://perma.cc/N6CP-868H)

www.statista.com/statistics/816523/trinidad-and-tobago-number-of-tourist-arrivals/ (archived at https://perma.cc/5ZS3-3WUE)

www.facebook.com/dsfamilynetwork/ (archived at https://perma.cc/W6LQ-SK9P)

www.ndss.org/play/national-buddy-walk-program/ (archived at https://perma.cc/US7M-A5YT)

http://www.social.gov.tt/wp-content/uploads/2020/10/National-Policy-of-Persons-with-Disabailities-April-25-2019-1.pdf (archived at https://perma.cc/T2C3-7YXR)

https://visittrinidad.tt/ (archived at https://perma.cc/M8YV-BDLF)

www.visittobago.gov.tt/ (archived at https://perma.cc/8DHB-SPTF)

Venue selection process

The various aspects of the venue selection process, as covered in the chapter, are shown in Figure 5.2.

The search for an appropriate venue for the event, whether indoors or outdoors, begins with the completion of a briefing document. Part of this process of agreeing a venue search brief is to identify the fit between the overall event objectives and 'must-haves', and the venue selection 'must-haves', which could include:

- geographical location;
- transportation links;
- image, style, or reputation of the venue or location and fit with corporate culture;
- type of venue;
- venue atmosphere;

FIGURE 5.2 The venue selection process

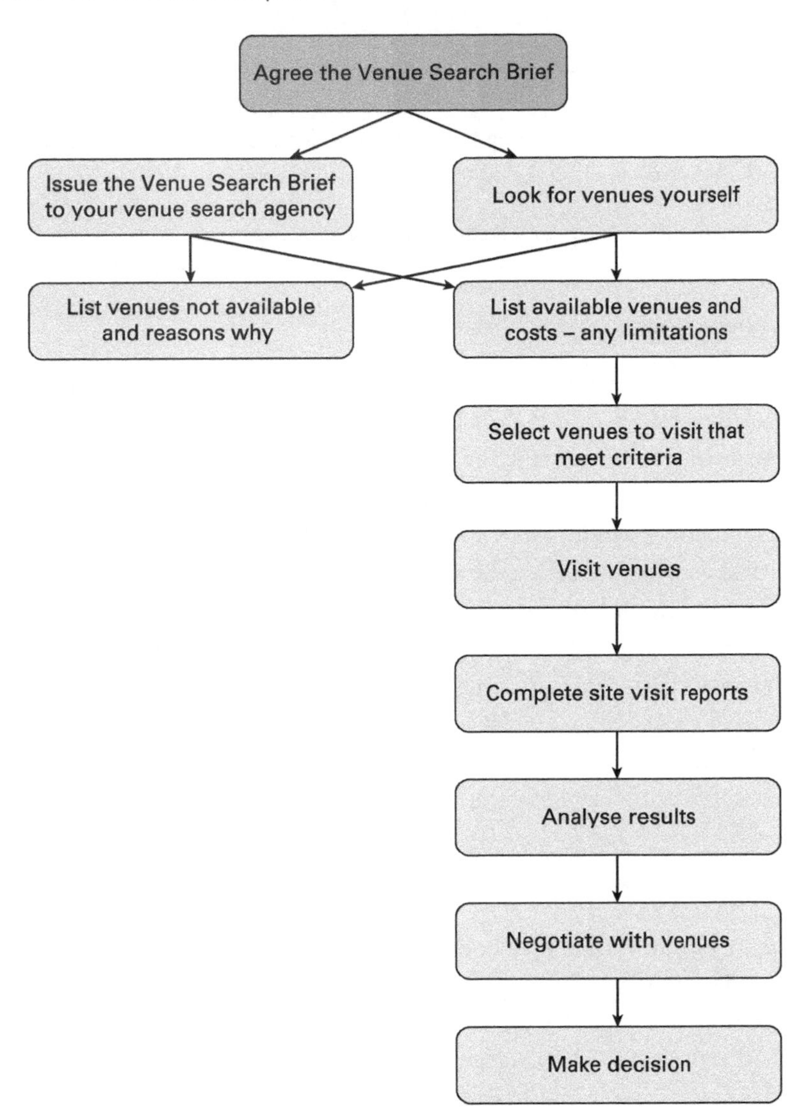

- relative size of the venue compared to your event;
- room capacities and layout;
- suitable facilities available on-site or potential to bring them in, including technology and accessibility;
- cost/value for money;
- proximity, quality, and cost of accommodation (for the event team and for delegates).

EVENTS MANAGER HACK

The MVP (Most Valuable Player) of an event is the venue and location. It is just as important as the event itself! The venue needs to complement the event objectives, concept and your budget; striking this balance is key to a successful event. All the intricate planning cannot make up for a less than ideal venue.

Selina Arnall, Event and Marketing Manager, That Event Girl; Social Traders, Australia

Different venue types

The range of venues is wider today than ever before, as organizations seek to maximize their income by hiring out their facilities when they are not being used for their primary purpose. So no longer is the only consideration which hotel or conference centre to use for your event – the world is your oyster. You could end up holding your event outdoors or indoors, in a field, in a public park, on a boat, in a church or a castle, a museum or sports stadium, in a university or even in a hospital or an aircraft hangar (with built-in aircraft). All these are potential venues and they will all be vying to provide you with event space. Remember, for outdoor venues, you will need to provide all the infrastructure that more traditional venues already have, from toilets to electricity, lighting and rubbish disposal, as well as temporary demountable structures. Case study 5.2 shows how one 'unusual venue' meets the challenge of integrating events within its day-to-day operations.

Venue search and selection

When choosing your venue, it is important to start with a series of questions that help you to identify the suitability of a range of possible venues for deeper consideration. A template of these key questions is provided in Figure 5.3, to match to your own needs in order to develop a clear venue search brief. It can be used as a starting point for the venue search, to be tailored to your organization, to your client and to your event. You might use the brief to help you to find a venue yourself, or you could issue it to a venue search agency to undertake this task on your behalf. This template is based around a corporate event but could be adapted for any event.

Alongside the venue search brief is a list of standard requirements, which you can adapt to those of your organization and its internal processes, policies and regulations (such as the attitude towards paying for alcohol with company funds). An example of some standard requirements is shown in Figure 5.4 for a similar corporate event following on from Figure 5.3. Each client will have their own requirements for the style and size of their event. We recommend that these aspects are discussed and agreed with the client when taking the brief, or in the early planning stages. The importance of ensuring that the rooms and facilities fit the needs of the event as well as the client cannot be overstated.

Specific criteria for venue selection

Creating a unique event may involve the use of an iconic venue, or a modern, historical or more traditional venue. It may mean the client has exclusive access, or shares with other groups. But the venue needs to have appropriate facilities and access to technology required by the client, whether these are in place as a matter of course or whether you need to bring them in. However, it's all too easy to get carried away by your own views and aspirations, rather than looking objectively at criteria. One company had a client who expressed a wish to hold the next event in a castle. The event company researched the options but they soon concluded that a castle really wasn't a suitable venue for this event; and they realized that the organizer just wanted to spend some time in a castle. So they arranged a trip for the client to stay in a castle and booked the event into a more appropriate venue. (Consider the ethical aspects of such actions!) But two-way communication with the client is key to understanding their event requirements and developing an accurate and realistic brief to enable you to find the venue of their dreams.

Case study 5.2 explains how a modern sports stadium, the MKM Stadium Hull, can be utilized for a wide range of different events.

FIGURE 5.3 Venue search brief template

EVENT VENUE SEARCH BRIEF				
To: Venue Search Agency				
Completed by: **Date:**			**Team:**	
Title of event(s):			**Event Owner:**	
Budget holder, team and contact details:				
Budget:	**Total budget:**	**Venue budget:**	**B&B budget (per person):**	**DB&B rate (per person):**
Cost code:				
Event Details				
Number of events: (National, regional or local)				
Proposed date(s): Please provide a number of options				
Event location(s): **NON-HOTEL VENUES ONLY**				
Event timings: Start & finish times – include full programme				
Estimated number of delegates per session:				

(continued)

FIGURE 5.3 (Continued)

<table>
<tr><td colspan="4">Events Requirements</td></tr>
<tr><td>Main room:</td><td colspan="2">Capacity:</td><td>Layout: Cabaret as standard</td></tr>
<tr><td>Breakout rooms:</td><td>No. of rooms:</td><td>Capacities:</td><td>Layout: Cabaret as standard</td></tr>
<tr><td>Exhibition area:</td><td colspan="3">No. of stands (based on 3 x 2m):</td></tr>
<tr><td colspan="4">Accommodation
[Please include quote for accommodation with any non-residential conference venues]</td></tr>
<tr><td colspan="4">All rooms are non-smoking, double rooms for single occupancy</td></tr>
<tr><td colspan="2">B&B accommodation required befor event(s)</td><td>Date:</td><td>Qty:</td></tr>
<tr><td colspan="2">B&B accommodation required during event(s)</td><td>Date:</td><td>Qty:</td></tr>
<tr><td colspan="4">• Please note that if delegates are on a B&B rate, there is a £XX.00 allocation for food & drink (no alcohol). Any additional charges are to be directed to the individual.
• If DB&B accommodation is required, dinner and/or breakfast may be taken in restaurant or by room service. Additional charge for room service should go to the main account.
• Please ensure all charges are routed correctly prior to delegate arrival at the hotel.</td></tr>
<tr><td colspan="4">Catering Requirements
[Please confirm in the response to this brief that these are provided, and the cost]</td></tr>
<tr><td>Breaks:</td><td colspan="3">Normal provision of tea, coffee and biscuits, on arrival, mid-morning and mid-afternoon (3 servings) including:
• Selection of decaffeinated drinks, fruit teas, hot water, cold water and orange juice
• Fresh fruit (especially bananas)</td></tr>
<tr><td rowspan="2">Menus:</td><td colspan="3">We do not have deep fried or fatty foods and the following menus are most appropriate to our events. These are suggested menus and we are open to alternative options from the venue.</td></tr>
<tr><td colspan="3">– Hot meat, fish and vegetarian dishes
– Selection of cheeses
– Selection of cold meats
– Vegetable kebabs
– Baked potatoes
– Selection of salads including: green leaf, bean, tomato basil & mozzarella, coleslaw and celeriac, pasta and rice salads
– Fresh granary rolls / breads
– Light dessert including cheese & biscuits and fresh fruit
– Tea, coffee, water and fruit juice</td></tr>
<tr><td>Lunch:</td><td colspan="3">Preferred choice e.g. Packed lunch, hot food, No of courses etc</td></tr>
<tr><td rowspan="2">Dinner:</td><td>Date:</td><td>Time:</td><td>Venue:</td></tr>
<tr><td colspan="3">Delegates receive an allowance of £20 for their evening meal and should be charged back to the main account. No alcohol is permitted in this evening meal subsidy.</td></tr>
<tr><td>Special dietary requirements:</td><td colspan="3">There must be a wide range of choice for vegetarians. Other special dietary requirements will be communicated with the venue with final numbers or as they arise.</td></tr>
<tr><td colspan="4">Other Requirements
[Please confirm in the response to this brief that these are provided]</td></tr>
<tr><td colspan="4">Disabled access to all areas used by the event</td></tr>
<tr><td colspan="4">As a health-aware organization, we require a No Smoking environment. Signage should indicate No Smoking</td></tr>
<tr><td colspan="4">Car-parking – venue should specify:
• whether car-parking is available on site or nearby
• number of spaces available
• cost
• whether charges can be added to the final invoice</td></tr>
<tr><td colspan="4">No alcohol to be charged to the main account</td></tr>
</table>

FIGURE 5.4 Sample standard requirements

Standard Requirements	**Details**
Financial • Budget Limits • Bill-back • Invoices	Value for money is key Maximum B&B Accommodation Rate London £XX Outside London £XX Maximum DDR Average DDR London £XX £XX – £XX Outside London £XX £XX – £XX To include Dinner, B&B for any speakers/events team and all event costs. No alcohol to be billed back or paid for with company funds. Information required on invoice: – Name of event – Date of event – Contact name (ie Lead Events Manager/Person who made booking) – Venue Search Agency used – Budget Holder's name and address
Sample policy on **Venue Terms & Conditions**	➢ **Value for money is key** ➢ Request setting up credit accounts between budget holder and venue to agree maximum credit limit for invoicing after event ➢ Terms for payment in advance/deposits Venue terms and conditions need to be approved by Finance Manager
Sample Standard Requirement **Catering**	➢ **Healthy Food** Lunches – sample menu (preferred) **We do not have any deep fried or fatty foods and the following menu is most appropriate for our events.** **NB: this is a suggested menu but we would be open to thoughts and comments from venues.** Selection of cheeses Selection of warm and cold meats A fish option Green leaf salads Bean salads Tomato, basil and mozzarella Vegetable kebabs Baked potatoes Coleslaw and celeriac salads Pasta and rice salads Fresh granary rolls and/or breads A light dessert option Cheese and biscuits Fresh fruit Tea and coffee, water and orange juice

(continued)

FIGURE 5.4 (Continued)

	➢ **With Morning Coffee/Afternoon Tea** – selection of decaffeinated drinks/fruit teas, hot water, water, orange juice, and fresh fruit rather than biscuits. Always have a bowl of fresh fruit available. ➢ **Special Dietary Requirements** – offer plenty of choice for vegetarians. Other special requirements will be communicated with the venue as they arise, by the events team. ➢ **Numbers** – identify date final numbers required. Inform us of: maximum numbers in venue; minimum numbers; final number to be charged.
Sample Standard Requirement **Meeting Rooms**	➢ **Layout** – cabaret style as standard. Please check with Event Manager whether 8/10/12 seats per table are required. ➢ **Ambience** – natural light, internal lighting, air-conditioning controls in room, fresh air, windows that open, temperature. ➢ **Security** – lockable room with key provided. ➢ **Noise** – of AV equipment, external – traffic, internal – works ➢ **Cost** – extras, day rate, 24 hour rate, rack rate or deal ➢ **Rooms** – size of room/s, accessibility, number of rooms required – breakout/main room; flexibility ie splitting rooms in half where possible; shape of room/s, location of rooms and proximity to each other; acoustics, sound equipment required, proximity to catering (meals and refreshments); layout of furniture. ➢ **Audio Visual Equipment** – flipchart and pens that work, equipment included as part of the venue costs, e.g. sound system, technical support. In the majority of cases we will use an external provider either venue-sourced or sourced by the events team. ➢ **Catering and Refreshments** – flexibility of timings (in advance and on the day); special dietary requirements; location of refreshments/lunch; drinking water provided in room, adequate supplies, replenished at breaks.

CASE STUDY 5.2

One venue – multiple uses: MKM Stadium, Hull, East Riding of Yorkshire, UK

Kharmen Wilson, Senior Events Executive, University of Leeds

Stadia and sporting venues are typically known for their reputation within the sporting industry, whether that's football, cricket or rugby, to name a few. Stadia are often overlooked by event planners and could possibly be the event industry's best kept secret.

The need for unique and memorable events has grown over the past 20 years, but traditional conferencing spaces are not providing delegates with the space to feel inspired during their team-building days, nor do they provide a unique product that provides those experiential moments we crave at events.

Opening its doors in 2002, the MKM Stadium in Hull is an architecturally impressive, post-modern multi-purpose venue, home to Hull City Football Club and one of Hull's Rugby

League teams, Hull F.C. With a seating capacity of 25,586, the stadium has hosted many major sporting events, as well as large-scale concerts and unusual events such as the travelling action sport stunt show, Nitro Circus. The possibilities of this venue to host non-match-related events are endless: with the technology to cover the pitch safely, it allows the venue to maximize the space for a year-round financial yield.

Located in the city centre of Hull, winner of the 2017 City of Culture bid, the venue is a 10-minute walk from the train station, a perfect central location for commuters. It holds ample parking on-site for match days which can be utilized for events; the car park itself has previously been used as a space to simulate a car crash for delegates to practise saving lives. This example proves there are plenty of opportunities to use sports venues in ways we didn't think possible. In 2017, the venue welcomed Jeff Lynne's ELO tour to Hull. This was a huge logistical operation for the team, involving the build-up of the band's trademark spaceship above the stage, located on the pitch. More recently, the venue adapted its corporate areas to become one of Hull's largest vaccination centres during the Covid-19 pandemic.

As well as events on the pitch, the venue can host events off the pitch. With 10 function rooms, ranging from capacities of 10 to 700, there are flexible options to cater for all types of event requirements, including, but not limited to:

- weddings
- conferences
- exhibitions
- proms
- funerals
- awards dinners
- product launches
- Christmas parties.

The venue offers a full event management service, from initial enquiry through to event delivery. The sales and events team are more than happy to show clients around the venue, discuss event requirements and budget and showcase the fantastic facilities on offer. After the initial meeting, the team will work with their clients to build an event proposal covering all elements of the event: room capacity and layout, AV requirements, room dressing, catering, and special packages for delegates, such as changing rooms and pitch-side tours.

As well as corporate event clients, the venue also offers private event bookings for smaller parties, ranging from christening celebrations and 18th birthday parties to anniversary occasions. It provides flexible low-cost catering options with bar facilities within the function rooms, and of course entertainment and room dressing. It really does offer the full package without breaking the bank.

This special venue is truly one of the most innovative in Yorkshire. It has welcomed thousands of sporting fans, embraced the wins and losses of both home teams over the years and capitalized on the infrastructure's flexibility and the club's reputation to open the venue to hundreds of unique, impactful events. If you are looking for a truly unusual event venue, there is nothing better than having a meeting in a corporate box overlooking the fantastic view of the football pitch, kept in pristine condition all year round.

Find out more

www.wearehullcity.co.uk/stadium/mkm-stadium/ (archived at https://perma.cc/7AEY-TYTJ)
www.wearehullcity.co.uk/stadium/tigers-events/ (archived at https://perma.cc/6GE3-YY2C)
www.hulldailymail.co.uk/whats-on/music-nightlife/review-jeff-lynnes-elo-hulls-156545 (archived at https://perma.cc/MZZ5-6MXW)

EVENTS MANAGER HACKS

Don't get carried away by your own fantasies of hosting an event somewhere you've always dreamed of – save the exotic for your holidays. Keep both feet planted firmly on the ground when it comes to making your choice for the perfect event venue!

Venue search options

Venue search agencies can be very useful to busy events managers in identifying and negotiating with suitable venues. However, they vary hugely in terms of the services they provide, their knowledge of and relationships with venues, the quality of their advice and the amount they charge. This section will unveil the mysteries of how such services are paid for, and what to look out for when selecting an agency to assist you. Alternatively, you may choose to search for a venue yourself, which, despite the obvious benefits of the internet and the many web-based venue-finder sites, can still prove to be a lengthy, tricky and costly process.

Venue search agencies operate on the basis of commission, which is charged to the successful venue. In theory this means that it doesn't cost you (or the client) anything, and a good venue search agency will benefit your client with their knowledge of venues and negotiating clout, which more than covers the cost of finding a venue yourself. Commission can range from 8 to 15 per cent, but venue search agencies can be quite secretive about this aspect of their income. It has to be said that there are some agencies that have negotiated a varying rate with different venues – and it is surprising how much more often those paying the higher 'Gold' rate find themselves on a shortlist of potential venues than those willing to promise a lower 'Bronze' rate. It is also interesting to find that there are some venues that will not countenance working with certain organizations – and it's always worthwhile asking if there are any venues or hotel chains a venue search agency does not have a relationship with.

The process of using a venue search agency requires you to agree a thorough brief to enable them to search on your behalf. (The previous section of this chapter explains how to develop a detailed brief.) What you should not do is to brief more than one agency at the same time, as this leads to confusion and annoys the venues no end. There are different types of venue search agencies, and some are more useful and effective than others. Some agencies have benefited from advances in technology and used the internet to develop a database of venues that can be interrogated to find properties that match a given list of requirements. However, these may be little more than glorified call-centres, whose staff have little actual knowledge of the venues themselves, almost certainly have never visited them, and have no backing or experience to be able to negotiate on your behalf. Finding a good venue search agency is like finding a pearl of great price; they will be experienced negotiators who know not only the venues, but have, over the years, built up good working relationships with venue managers and directors. A key advantage of using a venue search agency is that they will be able to negotiate on your behalf – and by working for multiple clients, their purchasing power is likely to outstrip your own.

Managing the venue search process

Once you have sent your brief to the venue search agency, they will undertake research to find venues that potentially meet your requirements and provide you with a list of possible venues for your event, along with initial prices. These venues should be placed provisionally 'on hold' by the agency on your behalf (on first or second option: second option means that another company has a first option ahead of you), for the dates needed, until you have either rejected or accepted them. It is useful (at least for the purpose of corporate governance, procurement requirements and transparent decision-making), to also keep a list of those venues that do not meet your criteria, for example because they are not available on the dates you require. Flexibility of dates can be a blessing or not, as the agency may randomly pick dates for you rather than providing a whole range, but once dates are firmed up, it may be worthwhile revisiting the list. A useful way of managing this process, which could take from one or two days to several weeks for a complex enquiry, is to use a spreadsheet to track the responses as they come in. This process will also enable you to decide whether a venue meets your criteria or not, list any limitations and support your decisions; a sample layout of the spreadsheet is provided in Table 5.1. At this stage the venue search agency will set up site visits for you at the shortlisted venues.

TABLE 5.1 Venue selection decision matrix

Venue	Venue A	Venue B	Venue C
Location			
Days			
Dates Required			
DDR			
24hr Rate			
Dinner – non-residential			
Explanation			
Room Hire			
Total Cost	£0.00	£0.00	£0.00
Notes			
Meets Criteria			
Savings			
Venue Known			
Min Nos			
Comments			

Case study 5.3 explores managing a Grade II listed venue set in a beautiful Italianate industrial village that was designated a UNESCO World Heritage Site in 2001.

CASE STUDY 5.3

Victoria Hall – the challenges of planning weddings in a historic, charity-run venue

Rebecca Goringe, Wedding and Event Co-ordinator, Victoria Hall, Saltaire, West Yorkshire; UKCEM graduate 2017

For over 150 years, the village of Saltaire has socialized, educated and exercised in the beautiful Victoria Hall. Originally built as a recreation centre for Sir Titus Salt's workers in 1871, the Hall has honoured its initial use and continued to be a hub for community events and celebrations, with weddings now its largest source of revenue. There are many reasons why Victoria Hall is the ideal wedding space – it is unique, impressive and full of character – but it is not without its challenges. Below we explore the challenges and considerations of managing weddings in a charity-run historical venue.

The building has all you would expect of a modern wedding venue: a licence for civil ceremonies, an in-house bar, well-maintained gardens and four beautiful rooms to accommodate ceremonies and receptions. Over the past few years, couples have come under pressure to meet the evolving wedding trends, offering their guests a new wedding experience. As a Grade II listed building, some of these requests, including decorations, entertainment and catering, are not always possible. For example, a brass band wouldn't be permitted in one of our smaller rooms, as it would easily exceed the sound limit; all backdrops (for ceremonies and photo-booths) must be free-standing, as nothing can be affixed to the walls and ceilings; and street food stalls cannot be set up inside because of the catering restrictions. While many couples choose us for our vintage aesthetic and historical significance, the Hall is also hired because of its location, affordability and large room capacity. Not every couple is infatuated with the ornate wallpapering or large Titus Salt portrait. Although regular repair work takes place, the limited and scrutinized budget (as a charity-owned venue) does not allow for 'trendy' updates that would be deemed 'untrendy' in a few years' time. It is vital that couples are aware of our limitations and that we encourage alternative creative ideas that can still give guests the 'wow factor'. Fortunately, tailored marketing and well-maintained wedding directory pages allow the venue to target couples carefully.

As an urban venue in the heart of Saltaire village, there are also considerations for the local residents. Despite having a strict curfew and a limitation on entertainment, fireworks and outside vendors, weddings can still be disruptive to the local community – the late and noisy parties can take place up to three times per week. As a charity-run venue, Victoria Hall is heavily focused on giving back to the community and subsidizes public events and classes to make these more accessible. As a result of delivering these successful events, a number of our wedding clients are from Saltaire. This evidences the positive relationship between the venue and the local residents.

It is not only the event coordinators and managers at Victoria Hall that face challenges from weddings. Suppliers, particularly stylists and caterers, have the difficult task of working within our restrictions. There are limitations on the equipment that can be brought in, the supplies used (tape, staples, nails) and weight/height restrictions. The lack of fitted catering space is one of the biggest challenges for caterers. For this reason, a curated list of recommended suppliers is sent out to couples throughout the customer journey. One benefit of not having an in-house caterer is the flexibility that this offers our couples. They have the freedom to choose suppliers to meet their styles, needs and budget, and as a result, we enjoy seeing a variety of weddings at Victoria Hall.

Despite the challenges mentioned above, Victoria Hall offers transparency, excellent communication and a creative approach to planning weddings, and as such does not encounter many issues with couples or residents. We host a variety of interesting, individual weddings all against the stunning vintage backdrop. Our excellent feedback is testament to our love for weddings, our wonderful couples and our beautiful venue.

Read more

https://saltairevillage.info/ (archived at https://perma.cc/P2VZ-UGPS)
https://victoriahallsaltaire.co.uk/ (archived at https://perma.cc/SZ7F-SSMH)
https://whc.unesco.org/en/list/1028/ (archived at https://perma.cc/97YA-6SNZ)

Venue site visits

Many venues offer familiarization or 'fam' trips, and these may be coordinated by a DMO; however, such visits are usually made on the basis of building a general awareness, rather than having a specific event in mind. In contrast, once you have an actual event, undertaking site visits of potential venues is vital, even if you have been to the venue before on a fam trip. This is because you will see the venue with new eyes and be able to walk through the event as you inspect the venue. Figure 5.5 provides a form with a template for undertaking a site visit, which has been developed mainly for conferences and has been used for hundreds of venues.

FIGURE 5.5 Site visit template

SITE VISIT CHECKLIST	
Venue:	**Date of visit:**
Event title:	**Event date:**
Site visited by:	**Contact:**
Address:	**Tel:** **Fax:** **Email:** **Web:**
Location	
Proximity to motorway network:	Proximity to rail network:
Nearest tube station: Taxi: _____mins Walk: _____mins Bus: _____mins	Nearest rail station: Taxi: _____mins Walk: _____mins Bus: _____mins
Main Room	
Location and proximity from main room: ➤ Registration: ➤ Catering area:	Maximum capacities / layouts Theatre style: _____ Cabaret: – Based on 6 around each table: _____ – Based on 8 around each table: _____ – Based on 10 around each table: _____
Number of Syndicate Rooms: Comments: Maximum capacities:	Syndicate 1: Theatre: _____ Cabaret: _____ Syndicate 2: Theatre: _____ Cabaret: _____ Syndicate 3: Theatre: _____ Cabaret: _____ Syndicate 4: Theatre: _____ Cabaret: _____
Remember to request a copy of the venue's capacity chart in electronic format if not available online ☐	
Stage included in venue hire? ☐ Yes, already installed Cost of hire: £_____ ☐ Yes, can be installed Cost of hire: £_____ ☐ No	Basic AV included in venue hire? ☐ Yes, already installed Cost of hire: £ ☐ Yes, can be installed Cost of hire: £ ☐ No If included, please list items:

(continued)

FIGURE 5.5 (Continued)

Does room have good acoustics? Yes ☐ No ☐ Does room require PA system? Yes ☐ No ☐ PA included in venue hire? ☐ Yes, already installed Cost of hire: £_____ ☐ Yes, can be installed Cost of hire: £_____ ☐ No	Is the room soundproof? ☐ Noise levels: ➢ Air-conditioning: Noisy ☐ Acceptable ☐ None ☐ ➢ Roads: Noisy ☐ Acceptable ☐ None ☐ ➢ Interconnecting doors: Noisy ☐ Acceptable ☐ None ☐ ➢ Kitchen: Noisy ☐ Acceptable ☐ None ☐ ➢ Comments:
Temperature controls located in room? Yes ☐ No ☐ Comments:	Natural light in rooms? Yes ☐ No ☐ Comments:
Is the room lockable? Yes ☐ No ☐ Comments:	Cloakroom available? Yes ☐ No ☐ If so, cost of hire: £_____
Bedrooms	
On-site accommodation: Yes ☐ No ☐ Nearest hotel if not on-site:	No of Bedrooms:
Viewed standard double bedroom? Yes ☐ No ☐	Comments:
Free upgrades to organizers? Yes ☐ No ☐	If so, how many?
Disabled Facilities	
Disabled access throughout venue? Yes ☐ No ☐	Number of disabled bedrooms:_____
Hearing loops provided? ☐ Yes, already installed Cost of hire: £_____ ☐ Yes, can be installed Cost of hire: £_____ ☐ No	Disabled toilets: Yes ☐ No ☐ Disabled car-parking: Yes ☐ No ☐
Catering	
Dietary requirements – can venue cater for special dietary requirements such as: Halal ☐ Kosher ☐ Diabetes ☐ Other ☐ Comments:	
Remember to request a copy of the venue's menus and check regarding healthy food ☐	
Car-Parking	
On-site ☐ Off-site ☐	Number of spaces available:
Name of external car park:	Location:
Proximity to venue:	Cost to delegates:
If public parking, does venue receive preferential rates: Yes ☐ No ☐	If cost, is bill back available:
Health & Safety	
What day is the fire alarm test?	
Non-smoking site Yes ☐ No ☐ All ash trays should be removed and signage should indicate *'No Smoking'*	

The format of this template can be adapted to fit different events and includes a question about fire alarm frequency after one experience in a hotel when the night-time fire alarm turned out to be a regular occurrence, due to a faulty boiler. This form should be completed for every site visit and provides a valuable source of information for future use, as well as providing a rationale for venue selection decisions.

> EVENTS MANAGER HACKS
>
> There's no substitute for a physical inspection of the venue to identify the constraints and opportunities it holds for your event: and one note about toilets –always inspect them!

Analysing venue search results and negotiations

Having undertaken site visits and completed the report for each venue, this information is combined with the previous data gathered to enable you to reduce your shortlist, ask any outstanding questions and have the venue search agency negotiate any specific requirements, special rates or terms and conditions on your behalf. You may wish to include a request for references from a client with similar needs to your own. Once you have made your decision –with or without further input from the venue search agency –the agency will ensure you receive contracts and manage any problems or additional requests you might have with your selected venue.

Communication with the venue

Once you have chosen your venue, remember event attendees will require directions and a range of other information about the venue and its facilities. The venue will also require information about the event attendees, including their names, contact details and the dates they are staying, along with any special requirements such as access or dietary restrictions (e.g. allergies). The template in Figure 5.6 identifies the type of information you will need to provide to event attendees about the venue.

WORKING WITH VENUE OPERATIONS

Once you have agreed on your chosen venue, the hard work begins. Having a structured approach to informing the venue of your needs as they change (they will, inevitably) will help you to control the budget and keep your client happy. Figure 5.7 provides a draft event function sheet that can be used to inform the venue of specific and detailed requirements for your event.

FIGURE 5.6 Venue information template

Venue Name		
Image of venue		
Full address including postcode:		
Telephone number:		
Fax number:		
Email address:		
Web address:		
Facilities:		
Disabled access:		
Directions:	**Air**	
	Rail	
	Underground Metro	
	Road	
Route planner:		
Helpful hints:		
Parking:	**Number of spaces**	
	Charges	
Local taxi number:		
Please note that the above information has been taken directly from the venue. While we have checked this and provided additional information where available, we are not responsible for errors on the part of the venue or online route planners.		
Maps:		
Additional Information:		

The process of organizing a successful event requires regular contact and communication with venue staff. At first this will be with sales staff who may promise you the earth, but operational staff will tell you that it's not that simple. The key to building a good working relationship with a venue is communication, including venue visits, phone calls and supplying detailed information in a timely manner. And make sure you give feedback to staff during and after the event, so problems that arise can be easily and immediately addressed, rather than leaving them with a complaint once you have left the premises. Chapter 4 provides more detail about developing the content and structure of the event.

FIGURE 5.7 Function sheet template

<table>
<tr><td colspan="6">EVENT FUNCTION SHEET</td></tr>
<tr><td colspan="6"><<EVENT TITLE>>
<<DATE>>
<<VENUE, LOCATION>></td></tr>
<tr><td colspan="3">Pre-event contact (Events Team):</td><td colspan="3">On-site contact (Events Team):</td></tr>
<tr><td colspan="3">Tel:
Mobile:
Fax:
Email:</td><td colspan="3">Mobile:</td></tr>
<tr><td colspan="3">Venue event coordinator pre-event:
Tel:
Mobile:
Fax:
Email:</td><td colspan="3">Venue operational manager on-site:
Mobile:</td></tr>
<tr><td colspan="3">Signage:</td><td colspan="3">Meeting room name:</td></tr>
<tr><td colspan="6">Pre-event set-up</td></tr>
<tr><td rowspan="2">Activity</td><td rowspan="2">Timings</td><td rowspan="2">Location / Room(s)</td><td rowspan="2">Set-up and venue responsibilities</td><td colspan="2">Numbers</td></tr>
<tr><td>Confirmed</td><td>Set</td></tr>
<tr><td></td><td></td><td></td><td></td><td></td><td></td></tr>
<tr><td colspan="6">Venue AV Requirements</td></tr>
<tr><td colspan="2">Equipment</td><td>Location / Room(s)</td><td>Set-up and venue responsibilities</td><td>Number</td><td>Agreed Cost</td></tr>
<tr><td colspan="2">LCD Projector</td><td></td><td></td><td></td><td></td></tr>
<tr><td colspan="2">Flip Chart</td><td></td><td></td><td></td><td></td></tr>
<tr><td colspan="2">Overhead Projector</td><td></td><td></td><td></td><td></td></tr>
<tr><td colspan="2">Screen</td><td></td><td></td><td></td><td></td></tr>
<tr><td colspan="6">Event</td></tr>
<tr><td rowspan="2">Activity</td><td rowspan="2">Timings</td><td rowspan="2">Location / Room(s)</td><td rowspan="2">Set-up and venue responsibilities</td><td colspan="2">Numbers</td></tr>
<tr><td>Confirmed</td><td>Set</td></tr>
<tr><td>Registration</td><td></td><td></td><td></td><td></td><td></td></tr>
<tr><td>Morning sessions</td><td></td><td></td><td></td><td></td><td></td></tr>
<tr><td>Mid-morning refreshments</td><td></td><td></td><td></td><td></td><td></td></tr>
<tr><td>Sessions</td><td></td><td></td><td></td><td></td><td></td></tr>
<tr><td>Lunch</td><td></td><td></td><td></td><td></td><td></td></tr>
<tr><td>Sessions</td><td></td><td></td><td></td><td></td><td></td></tr>
<tr><td>Mid-afternoon refreshments</td><td></td><td></td><td></td><td></td><td></td></tr>
<tr><td>Sessions</td><td></td><td></td><td></td><td></td><td></td></tr>
<tr><td>Close</td><td></td><td></td><td></td><td></td><td></td></tr>
</table>

(continued)

FIGURE 5.7 (Contnued)

DIETARY AND SPECIAL REQUIREMENTS	
Dietary Requirements	
Option	**Number**
Vegetarian:	
Vegan:	
Halal:	
Kosher:	
Other:	
Special Requirements:	
Requirement	**Number**
ROOMING LIST	
Name	**Special Requirement**
Other Requirements:	
Billing Instructions:	
Authorized Signatory for main account:	
No. of Bedrooms Contracted/Required:	
Minimum Numbers:	

Planning the site layout

Once an appropriate venue has been identified, the events manager will need to plan how to use the space to ensure that it is used in the best possible way to deliver a safe and effective event. A poorly planned layout can lead to problems with both the experience of the event attendees and effective operational management of the event. For example, gala dinner guests are unlikely to be impressed if there isn't enough space for them to sit comfortably to enjoy their meal or see the evening's entertainment. Equally, while music-festival-goers may enjoy the buzz of busy crowds, an overcrowded festival site can become unsafe, with potential risks to public safety.

When considering an appropriate layout for an event site the three most important considerations are:

- Space
- Movement
- Atmosphere.

Space

The first consideration when planning an effective layout for an event venue is to ensure that there is enough space for all the planned activities to take place in a comfortable and safe manner. The number of attendees that an event space can safely accommodate is referred to as the **capacity**. This an important number to know, as it will determine the number of people that can attend, and thus the number of tickets that can be sold or invites sent, which will have serious consequences for operations, catering and budget. Capacity should be determined for the event as a whole, but for more complex events should also be known for all individual rooms, areas or zones, to ensure individual parts of an event venue are safe and comfortable for attendees.

ESTIMATING CAPACITY OF COMMON ROOM LAYOUTS

The capacity of event spaces, particularly those with seating, can be determined through the creation of detailed-scale site plans that allow the events manager to see where all appropriate furniture and resources will be located. Before this level of work is done though, it is possible to use an estimation process to get a rough idea of capacity based on different common room and furniture layouts. This is very useful when assessing whether a space might be appropriate for the event requirements at an early stage of planning or venue choice. For venues that host events regularly it is likely that this information will be available on request or on the venue website, but there are also rules of thumb that can be used. In this case the events manager should calculate the usable floor area of the room/space and divide this by the space required by each attendee (including chairs and furniture) for that layout.

COMMON ROOM LAYOUTS

- **Theatre style** – Rows of chairs facing front/stage, best suited to large formal events
  - Estimated space required – 2 square metres per person (Price, 2004)
- **Cabaret or banquet style** – Guests seated at large round tables (usually 6–10 per table). Cabaret style includes a stage or similar focal point, best suited for more informal meeting events where discussion is encouraged, or for dining.
  - Estimated space required – 4 square metres per person (Price, 2004)
- **Boardroom style** – Large rectangular or U-shaped table with participants seated round the outside, best suited for smaller formal meetings.
  - Estimated space required – 8–12 square metres per person (Price, 2004)

Events where the crowd are standing or moving are harder to plot and will experience a variety of crowd densities. Managing these is a central part of crowd management (see Chapter 6). For the purposes of estimating a safe amount of space for standing crowds when planning a site layout, The Purple Guide to Health, Safety and Welfare at Music and Other Events suggests providing a minimum of 0.5 square metres of space per person across an event site. More space may need to be provided depending on the required atmosphere, activities, or audience profile of the event.

Regardless of the type of event you are planning, it's important to understand how much space will be required for all the different aspects and activities of the event. Specific types of events inevitably have different additional requirements. If you're planning a business conference, space must be allowed for meeting rooms and hospitality areas, whereas if you're planning an outdoor festival site, allocating sufficient space for camping and car parking is essential. As well as allocating space for public areas, it is necessary to allocate space for 'back of house' areas, including:

- administration/offices
- dressing rooms, green rooms and staff catering facilities
- equipment storage
- media facilities.

Movement

In addition to ensuring that the event venue is large enough to accommodate the required activities and resources, it is important to consider and plan for how attendees will enter, move around, and exit event spaces. This movement of people is often referred to as ICE, an acronym for INGRESS (entry), CIRCULATION (moving around the venue) and EGRESS (leaving the venue). How these activities are managed will covered in Chapter 6, but the event planner will need to ensure that adequate space is provided around these key locations.

Entrances should have adequate space for queues to form and for staff to perform appropriate ticket, registration and security checks. Upon entrance there should be adequate space immediately inside the venue to allow newly arrived attendees to orientate themselves, before they move into the main event space or find their seats.

Within the venue there need to be adequate space and gangways to allow attendees to move between different spaces. Larger events should consider signed paths and routes with open assembly points at junctions, and defined zones to help orientation and avoid congestion within the venue at peak moments of movement. Even smaller events will need to allow attendees and staff space to move between seats, hospitality/bars and toilets and should consider clear paths through seating areas.

Exits, including emergency exits, are an important part of venue safety and evacuation requirements and ensuring they are accessible and kept clear throughout the event duration is a crucial party of safety planning.

Atmosphere

When planning an effective layout, it is important to ensure that different parts of the event experience do not interfere with each other and that attendees are able to see and hear what is going on appropriately. Common issues occur when quiet and loud event elements are located too close to each other, for example if a talk or discussion is interrupted by loud music or raised voices from a nearby bar or hospitality area, and the events manager should consider the sensory impact of elements as well as their space requirements. It is also important that all attendees can see and hear what is happening at the event and that the sight design allows for direct lines of sight to a stage or focal point. If significant distance is involved, video screens and public address systems are crucial to ensure that all attendees are given the opportunity to experience the event as planned.

Designing the site layout

Having understood the space and resource requirements, the next task is to design the layout of the event site. This should be done 'to scale' to ensure that plans match the event space, and that there are no surprises when it comes to building and setting up the space, as this is already a pressured-enough time, without having to redesign elements to make them fit with reality because of lazy planning earlier on. Detailed-scale site design will also allow for an accurate capacity to be calculated, particularly for seated events, as the estimates arrived at earlier on can be replaced with accurate numbers based on actual items of furniture on a scale map.

Step 1: Obtain a detailed plan of the site

This is easy enough to do for most indoor venues. The venue team can usually provide a detailed plan of the layout (e.g. dimensions, capacities, entrances/exits, fixed points) or you can often find a plan on the website. For instance, the venue plans for Halls 1 and 2 at the Yorkshire Event Centre are available for event organizers to download from their website, should these be needed.

It can be more difficult to obtain a plan for an outdoor site. For a site that is frequently used for events, we recommend contacting the landowners or local authorities, to find out if a detailed plan of the site is already available to help design the layout of your event, although dimensions can always be determined using OS or Google maps, in conjunction with a site visit with an appropriate measuring device.

Step 2: Determine the layout of the event

Determining the layout of the event involves deciding where best to position all the activities and attractions as well as the facilities, services, equipment and infrastructure. This can be one of the most difficult tasks for an event organizer, especially for larger, more elaborate events with a wide range of activities taking place.

Developing the design of your event layout will require you to investigate different options and test out your ideas. This is easily done, either by printing off a large map of the site and cutting out ('to scale') icons (the old-fashioned methods are sometimes still the best!) or using simple computer programs that allow shapes to be moved around (PowerPoint works well). Free online tools such as www.floorplanner.com are typically used to design the floor plan of your home but are perfectly adequate for designing the layout of a smaller event site.

Each event will have its own requirements, but the following points should be considered – although even the order that you follow may change, according to the specific type, nature and location of the event:

- **Determine the best position for the central feature of the event.** Once you've decided on the best location for the main activity or attraction, the other activities and attractions can be positioned around this. Be prepared to move things around – it's an iterative process.
- **Situate complementary activities and attractions next to one another:** for example, food and drink stalls generally work well alongside one another, whereas food stalls and toilets don't go so well together!
- **Avoid concentrating too many popular activities in one area.** This will inevitably lead to crowd build-up and congestion and the associated risks to public safety.
- **Site medical and welfare facilities in a prominent position.** First-aid tents and lost and found meeting points need to be positioned where they can be easily located.
- **Allocate prime space for VIPs, corporate guests and media partners.** VIP tickets and hospitality packages are sold at a premium to ensure the best views of the action. Journalists and media organizations require a good view of proceedings as they unfold.
- **Ensure the correct and safe positioning of any technical equipment.** Sound and lighting equipment must be positioned appropriately in order for people to hear and see what is happening at the event.
- **Maintain a visibility distance between front and back of house areas.** Equipment storage, staff offices and crew catering should be kept out of sight and out of reach.

- **Make the event accessible to everyone.** The layout should be designed to allow people with mobility problems, sight or hearing impairments or other special needs to enjoy the activities and attractions.

Step 3: Seek feedback on the proposed layout

Once you've created a proposed layout for the event it is a good idea to share this with other key stakeholders. The venue manager will have first-hand experience of what works and what doesn't in the venue; similarly, suppliers and contractors (particularly those with previous experience of having worked at the event site) can help you avoid any obvious pitfalls. It's always a sensible idea to share the proposed layout with your client to ensure it meets their expectations.

Producing a map of the site

The main (master) site map for an event can end up being very complicated as it will contain lots of detail relating to structures, furniture, power, lighting, pathways, entrances/exits and other important operational considerations. For complex and large events it may be appropriate to use CAD (computer aided design) software to ensure that the master site plan remains comprehensible, although smaller or simpler events may only need more basic hand-drawn or sketch plans. To make master site plans comprehensible they should include:

- a clear key and legend explaining all symbols and colours used on the map;
- the scale of the map;
- the orientation of the map (for outdoor maps it is common to indicate which way is north);
- a grid, with the map divided into boxes. By annotating the grid (a, b, c etc on one axis, 1, 2, 3 etc on the other), it becomes easy to reference and communicate the position of specific elements on a large map.

The master site plan is a crucial tool in the planning of the event site and shows how all the different aspects of the event interact with each other; however, for many groups interested in the event, it contains far more information that they need, or want, to know. As a result, a range of maps should be produced for different groups; these maps can be simplified so that they include only the information that is needed.

EVENTS MANAGER HACK

As a general rule, a site map should always include a comprehensive list of the symbols used on the map. Using universal symbols helps to make it easier for people to read the map and find their way.

IMAGE 5.1 Universal symbols

Audience maps

The purpose of a site map for the audience is to help people to find their way around and identify where key locations are in relation to one another. It is even possible to render the layout of the site in simple shapes, to simplify it further. Consider how audiences will access the map and produce digital versions that can be included in event apps or websites, as well as physical copies that can printed as posters/signs and displayed at prominent locations around the event (remembering to make them waterproof if the event is outside!). See Table 5.2.

Staff and contractor maps

It's easy to think about a site map being only for the event attendees, but staff, suppliers and contractors will also need a map of the site to find their way. Indeed, the first people to use the map will be the staff, suppliers and contractors who need to know where to install temporary structures, locate technical equipment and deliver supplies. Maps in this case will need to be more detailed and to scale, although should still omit any information irrelevant to the group using it.

TABLE 5.2 Examples of different types of site maps used by a delegate attending a large conference and exhibition

Format	Purpose
Downloadable location map available online	Help delegates to plan their journey, e.g. How to find the venue How to access car parking Where to enter the building
A4 size colour-coded plan in the conference brochure, displaying the agenda and exhibitor locations	Allow delegates to plan their personal itinerary, e.g. Which speakers and exhibitors to see Where they will be located
Large waterproof display board in the car park	Enable delegates to find their way to the venue, e.g. Locate the entrance Decide if it is within walking distance Locate the shuttle bus or transport links
Large display board inside the entrance	Ensure a smooth arrival for the delegates, e.g. Where to register or collect their badge Where to find the cloakroom, refreshments and toilet facilities
A5 size cooler map in the conference programme	Help delegates to find their way around the venue, e.g. Which way to go Where to find keynote sessions Where to find specific exhibitors

CHAPTER SUMMARY

- The event site and location should be chosen to match the corporate image and culture of your client, as well as meeting your client's event criteria.
- While event organizers are often attracted by a perceived opportunity to create a unique 'wow' factor for their event, subtlety can sometimes be a more appropriate tool. It's unlikely that any venue will be perfect, as all sites have constraints – but they will also provide opportunities.
- The best way to check that a venue is right for your event is to undertake a physical inspection yourself – armed with structured checklists so you can ask the right questions.
- Ensure the site design, including architecture, structures and furniture, leaves sufficient space for attendees to congregate. Remember to consider sightlines to stages or other focal points.

- Consider ICE – movement of attendees onto (ingress), around (circulation) and off (egress) the site.
- The layout of a venue will have an important bearing on the atmosphere and event experience. Audiences should be close enough to enjoy each other's presence without being so close that they feel distracted, uncomfortable or unsafe.
- Trying to fit too much detail on a single site map will only confuse people and it may be a better idea (particularly for larger events taking place across multiple locations) to produce several smaller maps. It is also sensible to produce different site maps for those attending the event and those working at the event.

Questions for reflection

1 Whose needs should you consider when selecting a destination or location for your event?

2 What features of a venue should you look out for during a site visit?

3 How close is too close? How would you determine how much space attendees need at events to feel energized, comfortable and safe?

References

BVEP (Business Visits & Events Partnership) www.businessvisitsandeventspartnership.com (archived at https://perma.cc/ET7A-QEFV)

Freedom of Information Act 2000. How to make a freedom of information (FOI) request www.gov.uk/make-a-freedom-of-information-request (archived at https://perma.cc/NK5K-4LGW); www.legislation.gov.uk/ (archived at https://perma.cc/BC6Z-RFDP)

Yorkshire (2022) www.yorkshire.com/ (archived at https://perma.cc/WP4L-T8YR)

06

Production and operational logistics

FIGURE 6.1 The Dowson, Albert and Lomax Event Planning Process – Event Operations

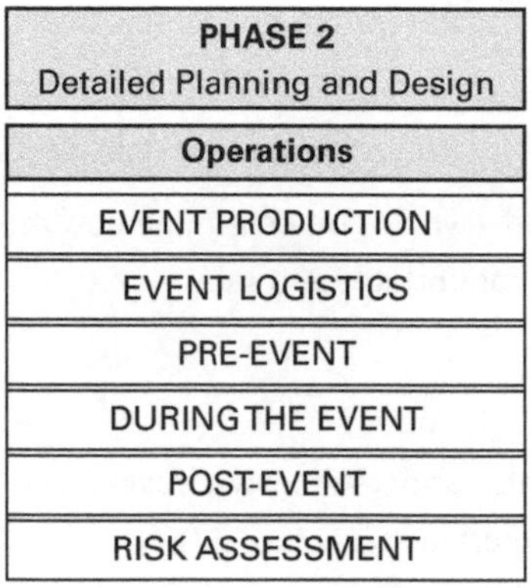

PHASE 2 Detailed Planning and Design
Operations
EVENT PRODUCTION
EVENT LOGISTICS
PRE-EVENT
DURING THE EVENT
POST-EVENT
RISK ASSESSMENT

The core of successful event management is getting the production and logistical operations correct. It is important to note that no matter how much detailed planning you have done, it ultimately feeds into this aspect of your event delivery. To ensure the high-quality production and safe and smooth running of an event, it is important to develop a thorough plan for managing on-site logistics. The purpose of site logistics planning is to ensure that all the right elements (people, equipment and goods) are at the right place at the right time. A tell-tale sign of poor production and logistics planning is when long delays occur at an event (e.g. people stuck in traffic jams or standing in long queues). Poor production and logistics planning can also result in more serious safety issues, such as severe traffic congestion and large concentrations of crowds.

As an events manager, the safety of everyone at your event is of the highest importance; this includes attendees, the event staff and volunteers, the wider event team (contractors and suppliers), as well as anybody else in close proximity to the event (e.g. people living and working nearby). The Health and Safety at Work Act 1974 (HASAWA) is the main piece of UK legislation that lays out your legal obligations and the requirements for the provision of health and safety within your event environment. It places a duty on event organizers 'to ensure, so far as is reasonably practicable, the health, safety and welfare' of everyone involved in an event. It is good practice and strongly recommended to undertake risk assessments to help you decide which risks are specific to your event, and what measures are needed to control potential risks.

By the end of this chapter, you will be able to:

- discuss and identify key event production elements for your event;
- develop an awareness of the importance of good logistical management and the impact on the overall event production through the phases of the event;
- develop an understanding of how different phases of the event are tied into your effective event delivery;
- identify logistical challenges and solutions for your event;
- identify broad areas of concern when it comes to health and safety at your event;
- undertake a risk assessment to help you decide which risks are specific to your event.

Event production

Event production is often used interchangeably with event planning; however, within the Dowson, Albert and Lomax (2022) model, event production is the process by which the event is delivered through the live staging and presentation of the event. It includes the delivery of creative aspects of the event using technological, creative and infrastructural design features to deliver the live experience, as well as the management of the people (staff, attendees and performers) on-site. It includes aspects such as crowd management, medical and welfare, sanitary services and provision, F&B, ticketing, access and accreditation, transportation management and parking, security, and provision of power.

Event production also focuses on the delivery of the event programme using sound, lighting and visual elements, such as pyrotechnics, hydraulic and suspension devices, special effects, staging, creative design features and live entertainment. Along with this, other logistical elements are used to facilitate the creation of the atmosphere, mood and experiences required to meet the aims and objectives of your event as well as meeting your clients' goals and needs.

The delivery of this aspect of the event requires not only expert logistical management but also coordination of teams of production crews, technical crews, entertainers, their entourages, and many other factors: the movement of large and often complex equipment, or of performers and people, including attendees, and the increasing use of innovative technology. All of this is supported by how well you have planned prior to your event, as well as the effective planning and delivery of health and safety for the duration of load-in, your event going live, and load-out.

The key pieces of documentation used are the production schedule and your risk assessment. Along with these, other documentation will include sound and lighting specification documents, design construction plans, structural plans for temporary demountable structures, and other logistical features. These documents will support the smooth and safe production of your event. There are lots of working roles during this aspect of the event, so good and experienced human resources and service suppliers and subcontractors are essential for its success.

Crowd control

For an event of any size, it is important to determine the maximum number of people the event site can safely hold. The profile (and dynamics) of the event attendees must also be taken into consideration. There are potential dangers associated with a high-spirited concert or festival crowd, or the genre of performers themselves.

One of the most effective crowd control techniques is the use of temporary fencing and crowd control barriers as well as stewarding and security personnel. If you are anticipating a large number of attendees, barriers that cannot be moved easily will prove to be useful. It is crucial that you choose the right type of barrier (i.e. difficult to topple over) so that it doesn't present greater risks than those it is intended to control. You can also use barriers to create zones which help your stewards and security manage large crowds more effectively.

As introduced in Chapter 5, Ingress (getting in), Circulation (moving around) and Egress (exiting) your event becomes an important part of your crowd management and control strategy. Not everyone will know their way around your event site. It's important to make effective use of signage to give clear directions or to define a clear pathway. Bear in mind that on your event site there may be people with different language abilities and this needs to be considered, particularly when providing information for and during the event of an emergency. Digital signage is very effective because it allows you to make easy alterations or to change details, and it can also provide information in different languages. Sometimes you might consider it worthwhile to use illuminated signage to help people to find their way around (particularly if the event takes place at night). Diverse audiences also may require signage in different languages or using universal visual cues or images that all attendees can interpret. In some instances, having stewards specifically assigned to assist with crowd movement is critical.

Careful attention is needed to ensure public walkways are fit for purpose when it comes to keeping people safe. Walkways should be wide enough for the number of persons expected to use them at any one time, including people with accessibility requirements, and they must be kept free of dangerous obstructions (e.g. trailing wires or equipment). Convergence points (areas where walkways come together) must be carefully managed (or, where possible, avoided). If an event is being held outdoors, footpaths that are suitable for use in adverse weather conditions must be used, for example non-slip rubber mats, or the use of wood chips, to minimize muddy and slippery surfaces. Alternative emergency routes may be required for people who have mobility challenges or use other mobility equipment.

Traffic management

Allowing any vehicle on to a busy event site is fraught with danger. A well-designed site layout will help to reduce the necessity for vehicles to access the site. for example situating a car park for artists and performers behind the main stage, or situating a drop-off-only car park for stall holders within walking distance of their stalls.

Where it is considered necessary to permit vehicular access, it is best practice to do so only at specific times and not during the event itself. There should ideally be traffic marshals on hand to guide vehicles on- and off-site (maintaining a safe speed). Ensure that you have designated parking for people with disabilities which allows them easy access to your venue, but also easy exit. Bear in mind that motorized and non-motorized wheelchairs need wider routes and stable surfaces to move around your event site.

It may also be necessary to control traffic outside the event site (e.g. temporary road closures, designated routes, directional signage) and a comprehensive traffic-management plan should be drawn up and agreed with the relevant authorities (e.g. Highways Department).

Temporary structures

Many events (particularly those held outdoors) require temporary structures such as staging, tents, marquees and stalls. If this is the case, the siting/location and safe installation of such structures needs to be carefully considered. It may be necessary to maintain a safe distance between each of the structures as well as maintaining a safe distance from the crowd (e.g. to reduce the risk of items falling from stages and towers). It is important to think about arrangements to stop unauthorized persons gaining access to temporary structures such as stages and towers, guy wires and under-stage areas. Furthermore, it is extremely important that any temporary structures are not positioned in such a way that they obstruct any of the public walkways/routes or site entrances/exits. Bear in mind that disabled viewing platforms should be positioned to provide clear viewing for disabled attendees without obstructing other attendees.

It is not expected that you understand the technical requirements of the installation of temporary structures, which is why it is important to source a reputable company with experience in delivering to the scale and complexity of your event. Completion certificates are an important part of the installation of these structures. These certificates ensure that the service supplier has installed the equipment or structure according to structural specifications and health and safety requirements. A copy of your completion certificate should be kept with other key event documentation.

Power provision and electrical safety

The provision of power, particularly on greenfield sites, becomes a critical feature for the delivery of your event. Whether it is through using an existing power source or temporary power sources such as generators, it is important to ensure not only that you have sufficient equipment to facilitate your power requirements, but also that you have skilled electrical technicians and service providers to ensure that your power delivery meets your requirements as well as health and safety standards.

The combination of electricity and water can cause death or serious injury – fact! For any event taking place outdoors it is recommended that, whatever the weather forecast, any electrical equipment is weatherproof and installed correctly by a certified electrician. Whether power is provided by three-phase or single-phase power, generators or other power sources, correct and safe installation by certified professionals is key. Even with events being held indoors, it is still important to be mindful of electrical safety. For example, electrical equipment needs to be properly enclosed, warning signs should be clearly displayed and electrical cabling properly secured. An indoor or outdoor event could be cast into darkness with a sudden loss of power (and light), so emergency lighting, as well as backup power, may be needed on-site.

It is important to ensure that your electrical load requirements meet your electrical provision requirements, as overloading can be the cause of electrical fires and other electrical issues. In keeping with sustainability policies and advances, installation of alternative power sources is now something which can be considered, and service providers are also available to support events managers with reducing their carbon footprint. The use of electric cars may require the installation of electrical charging points at greenfield sites, as well as charging points for mobility equipment such as electric wheelchairs.

Adverse weather

The onset of adverse weather conditions can pose an instant danger for anybody attending or working at an outdoor event. Temporary structures, such as stages, fencing and tents, are extremely vulnerable to high winds and water. Extreme wet weather will create slippery conditions under foot and make driving in muddy conditions potentially dangerous. Contingency plans should be in place (pre-event) to deal with the implications of extreme weather conditions. For example, in wet-weather conditions the event could be moved to an alternative indoor venue, specialist matting could be used to stop people from slipping, or other contingencies can be used, such as wood chips laid over potentially muddy paths.

Medical and welfare

The nature of the event, the age of the attendees, the size of audience and the duration of the event will all influence the level of medical and welfare provision needed on-site. The provision of adequate numbers and types of resource (e.g. first aid, ambulances and paramedics) should be based upon published guidance such as the Event Safety Guide (more commonly known as the 'Purple' Guide). Adequate provision should also be made for lost persons, lost and found children, and lost property, and special arrangements should be made to ensure disabled visitors have adequate facilities and services. This includes aspects such as charging points for electric wheelchairs and appropriate sanitary facilities; as part of inclusive practice, multi-faith prayer rooms and gender-neutral toilets are also important parts of your provision in catering for diverse welfare and multi-faith needs.

Indoor venues may already provide many of the required facilities, but an outdoor site is a very different environment. In this case, it is important to seek appropriate support from an established provider of medical and welfare services for outdoor events (e.g. St John's Ambulance, Samaritans). Medical provision for the event should not rely upon the normal provision made by the statutory NHS Ambulance Service for use by the general public (i.e. '999'). Also note that specialist service suppliers can be contracted to provide support in identifying the needs of attendees with any specific needs.

Cleanliness and hygiene

Adequate toilet and handwashing facilities are required for attendees to maintain personal hygiene. The number of toilets needed will depend upon the anticipated attendee crowd numbers as well as the gender of attendees (women require more toilets than men), and gender-neutral toilets will also be required. Adequate provision must also be made for attendees with disabilities. Indoor venues may already have adequate facilities but additional Portaloos may need to be hired for larger events. Toilets, handwashing, baby-changing and possibly shower facilities (e.g. festival campsite) will all need to be hired for an outdoor event. Anybody who has attended an outdoor event knows that maintaining the cleanliness of these facilities can be difficult and so they need to be located to make cleaning straightforward, as well as a maintenance schedule put in place to ensure that sanitary conditions are maintained.

Any catering outlets should be located in areas where there is minimal risk of contamination of food, so ideally, they need to be kept well away from toilets as well as waste/refuse areas. Caterers need to be provided with sufficient food waste disposal, washing facilities and clean water. A power supply for catering equipment (e.g. refrigeration) is also important in order to keep food fresh and edible. Catering providers also need to have up-to-date and the requisite food standard licences and health certificates. HACCP standards are also essential to ensuring that your food provision is of the highest quality and safety provision.

Fire safety

Basic fire prevention begins with separating flammable and combustible materials (including liquids and gases) from a naked flame or spark. Take, for example, a small fire breaking out on a catering stall at an event. Storing gas bottles elsewhere when not in use minimizes the risk of the fire spreading. If a small fire does occur, a variety of fire safety equipment should be available for putting it out (e.g. fire extinguishers for different types of fires, such as CO_2, water, dry powder or foam and fire blankets) and staff should be trained how to use this equipment. In this example, providing appropriate distance between catering stalls would also help to prevent the spread of fire. If, however, the fire does develop, everyone on the event site must be able to escape easily to a place of safety identified in the Health and Safety briefing.

Security

After the shock of events like the horrific explosion outside Ariana Grande's concert at Manchester Arena and the explosion heard during the France vs Germany football match at the Stade de France in Paris, it's more important than ever that event attendees feel confident that they are safe and secure. Security generally becomes more of a concern when planning large-scale events that will attract media attention as well as an audience. Consider, for a moment, the heightened levels of security at major sporting events such as the Olympic Games and World Cup and major political events such as the G20 Summits. Event organizers must work closely with the police force and specialist security firms to determine whether security measures are needed, such as the use of protective barriers to guard against unauthorized access, security searches on entry and the siting of surveillance cameras. It is important, however, to be mindful that there is a fine line between stringent security at an event and actually creating a heightened sense of fear among attendees. An event site littered with security check points, surveillance cameras and security personnel will ultimately make many attendees feel less safe at the event.

Logistics planning for events

Logistics is considered to have originated in the military where the ability to supply troops with weapons, ammunition and rations, before and during the battle, can make the difference between victory and defeat. As Sun Tzu, the Chinese military strategist of 2,500 years ago, famously said, 'Every battle is won before it is even fought.' More recently, logistics planning has been applied to other specialisms, such as organizing large-scale events; in a similar way, the success of events is only as good as the logistic planning and delivery that takes place.

Logistics planning for events requires you to ensure that all the people, equipment and goods (rather than weapons!) are moved to the right place at the right time. In this regard, your production schedule (which includes the delivery and installation of all logistical elements along with key contacts and responsibility for ensuring the element is in place) is one of the most important documents. Think about a live concert performance; it's no good having the staging, sound and lighting equipment, musical instruments, special effects, camera crews and even the crowd in place, if the star performers are nowhere to be seen. Ensuring that competing logistical aspects of your event are carefully planned becomes the difference between the success and failure of your event.

Because of what happens at an event, there are always going to be logistical challenges for events managers to contend with. Certainly, for larger, more complex events which take place over multiple sites (venues or stages), multiple days and involving multiple roles (staff, volunteers and participants, as well as attendees), dealing with the logistical challenges is a key part of the job. Unlike a logistics manager in a generic business operation, there is no second chance for an events manager to get it right. Hence the need for sound logistical planning and implementation, an eye for detail and some creative and innovative problem-solving skills.

Many people regard event logistics as what happens during the event but overlook the importance of what happens pre-event (supply of equipment and arrival of the performers/artists) and post-event (e.g. dismantling of the site and clean-up operation). Logistical planning should concern the whole operation, as shown in Figure 6.2.

FIGURE 6.2 Phases of event logistics

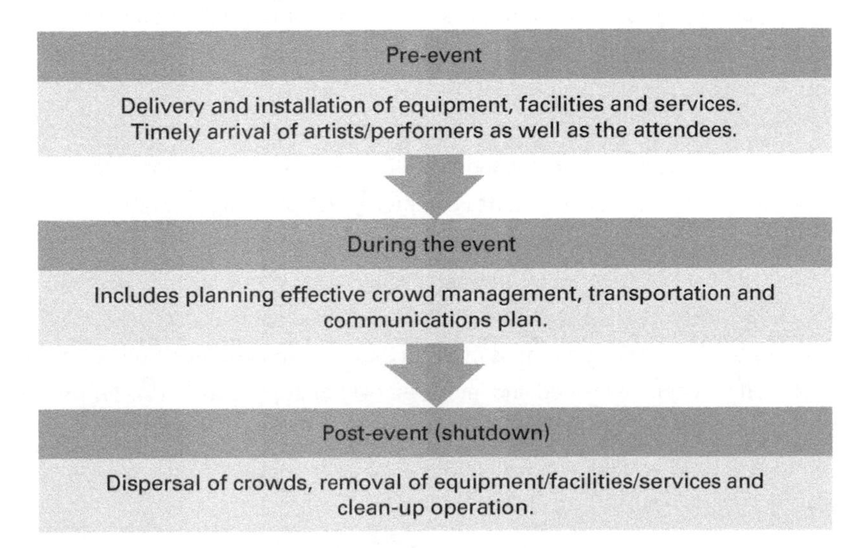

Case study 6.1 highlights the importance of specialist operations personnel who have the right knowledge and skills to deliver venue operations at major sporting events.

CASE STUDY 6.1

Logistics at the Commonwealth Games, Birmingham, 2022

Joe Cosgrove, Cluster Venue Logistics Manager, Birmingham 2022 Commonwealth Games, UKCEM Graduate 2013

The term 'logistics' has been applied for years to all sorts of industries and areas of life. For some people this word will conjure up images of shipping ports, containers, warehouses, and trucks usually accompanied with the tagline 'Right Place, Right Time'. For a relatively small group of others, it paints a slightly different picture, one of hi-vis jackets, steel-toe boots, pallet jacks and sack trolleys accompanied with the mantra 'Right Place, Right Time, Right Vibes'. Venue logistics at the Commonwealth Games is a very niche and specialized area of logistics that offers challenging but exciting experiences and the opportunity to work with some incredible characters.

Major multisport events require years of detailed planning and preparation. The purpose of these events is to celebrate a variety of world-class sporting competitions in numerous venues over a short period of time. An organizing committee (OC) is formed, comprised of multiple functional areas (FAs). It's said that those who work in Games have two main loves in life: sport and acronyms!

Logistics (LOG) forms one of the FAs within the OC. LOG is responsible for filling venues with assets such as furniture, fixtures and equipment (FF&E) and sports equipment. LOG is usually split into two work streams: logistic operations (LOG OPS) and venue logistics (VLOG). LOG OPS deals with temporary supply chains required to facilitate such a massive task. This area of the organization is similar to what most people think of as logistics. LOG OPS, with the help of a third-party logistics (3PL) company, is responsible for the customs and freight requirements for getting this equipment into the country, as well as warehousing and distribution to venues.

VLOG is referred to as the sharp end of the supply chain, or the boots on the ground. It is responsible for receiving FF&E on venue and distributing it to pre-agreed locations for other FAs. This is known as 'bump-in', and requires comprehensive planning, operational skills and knowledge. Bump-in has always presented challenges, and always will; even the most well-planned operation can experience unavoidable setbacks. Venue logistics managers (VLMs) need to be adept at reacting to and resolving issues as soon as they arise.

VLOG utilizes tried and tested methods of event planning and delivery – processes and procedures that have been developed and improved over multiple Games to offer risk-averse solutions to common problems. However, no Games is ever an exact replica of the last. Every host city offers a different experience with new venues, new workforce, new risks and new challenges.

VLOG is a service FA controlling the resource that is used to keep an event running – the 'here to help' FA that utilizes forklifts (FLTs), utility vehicles (UTVs), manual handling equipment (MHE) and crew in order to support other FAs. They are the ones people look to for help in difficult situations and will always be working tirelessly away from the spotlight to find solutions and ensure a smooth-running competition.

LOG and OCs in general are often full of highly experienced individuals who have years of Games experience. As well as this travelling workforce, OCs will always have a considerable labour force from the local area who are taking part in their first Games, bringing a wealth of new knowledge and skills to the organization. Because of their size, OCs have a very specific way of operating, with large FAs reporting into divisional leads who themselves answer to a board of directors and numerous stakeholders. For this reason, integration is one of the key messages that is promoted throughout the organization. It can take some time to onboard and train this new and temporary workforce to follow numerous complex processes and procedures.

Covid-19 has undoubtedly changed the way the world works, with the events industry being one of the hardest hit. Although the majority of events in the world ground to a halt, the Birmingham 2022 Commonwealth Games were deemed too big to fail and the OC began to operate remotely from their kitchens and bedrooms! Few expected this to continue for as long as it did. Planning continued this way for over a year and as more time passed and venues remained closed, employees of the OC became more and more thankful that they managed to remain safe in terms of their employment as well as their health. Although working from the comfort of home seemed a privilege in comparison to a lot of the world's population, it is true that there were difficulties. Site visits could not take place, venues and suppliers were furloughed and integration within the OC was difficult. Recruitment became a challenge as there was a mass exodus of events professionals from the industry. Many moved to permanent careers in other, more stable lines of work and have since remained there, worried that events will suffer further restrictions/lockdowns.

I hope that as restrictions ease and events spring to life again, old colleagues will reignite their love for the challenging and sometimes chaotic world of major multisport events. I also hope that new and enthusiastic events professionals, who may not have heard of the Commonwealth Games and venue logistics, might read this and investigate a career in Games. It is one that has provided me with so much satisfaction, many friends and countless incredible experiences. As long as the Games continue, they will always need event logisticians.

Explore further

www.birmingham2022.com/ (archived at https://perma.cc/56X4-4VK7)
https://birmingham2022.gigroup.com/ (archived at https://perma.cc/MBE7-G4XK)

Pre-event

Sound logistical planning should ensure that all resources are in place for the start of the event, including delivery and installation of equipment, facilities and services; timely arrival of artists and performers; and smooth arrival of attendees.

Delivery and installation of equipment, facilities and services

The delivery and installation of any temporary structures (e.g. staging) is known as the build-up which is followed by the load-in of any equipment, services and goods. Different events involve very different timescales for build-up and load-in – some a matter of hours, some days and others weeks. Indoor venues are likely to include an extra charge for any time needed to set up (which needs to be factored into the budget), so sound logistical planning will help minimize costs.

The general rule is that bulky items (e.g. large temporary structures such as staging and backdrops) are delivered and installed first. Any extensive structural installations will usually arrive on large trucks and trailers and, if an event is being held at a venue close to a built-up area, could cause traffic congestion on nearby roads. To avoid this, build-up may take place during the early hours of the morning. Whatever time of day build-up and load-in occur, it is essential to ensure clear routes for large vehicles to access and exit the site (indoor or outdoor), ensure that access routes into the building are of an adequate size for logistical elements to gain access, also to provide adequate parking, and ensure that local residents are not inconvenienced by noise or other disruptions.

Once the bulky structural installations are in place, the medium-sized items (e.g. tents/marquees and catering outlets on an outdoor site) will be set up, and technical equipment such as sound and lighting can be installed. Finally, smaller items such as furniture (e.g. tables and chairs) and decorative items can be put in place.

Timely arrival of artists and performers

As we discussed in Chapter 4, an event is often made up of a series of activities with a variety of performers, artists, entertainers, speakers, trainers, facilitators and others participating in the event programme. All of these need to arrive on-site prior to the event getting under way or in good time ahead of their participation.

To ensure the timely arrival of artists and performers (we will refer to the plethora of participants as artists and performers for simplicity), it may be necessary to make travel arrangements, to arrange airport transfers, to book accommodation and schedule accommodation pickups on the day of the event. On arrival at the event site, artists and performers may require assistance with unloading, moving and storing equipment and it will also be necessary to organize accreditation passes (e.g.

backstage passes) for them. Don't forget that the artists and performers are the 'stars of the show' and it's very important to ensure they arrive in peak mental and physical condition to put on a great performance. Allocating artist liaisons or an artist welfare team to manage this aspect of your logistics ensures that artists and performers are managed in terms of their timings, welfare, communication, meet and greet, and any additional needs. It also ensures that the event team has someone who can communicate any concerns or issues that may affect the running order to the events manager in a timely fashion. The difference between getting artists/performers/speakers to where they are supposed to be, happy and on time, can mean the difference between the success and failure of your event.

Arrival of attendees

The larger the event in terms of the number of attendees, the bigger the logistical challenge to have everyone arrive at the event on time and safely. For an events manager, there are two main challenges.

DEALING WITH THE LARGE NUMBER OF ATTENDEES

It is not only dealing with the large number of attendees but also the fact that most of them will probably arrive at a similar time (known as a dump of attendees). For example, at a football match, the stadium is often largely empty until 10–15 minutes before kick-off, with most fans arriving in this small window of time. In this case, having the appropriate number of turnstiles (entrances), ticket-sale booths and clear signage as well as a sufficient number of stewards on hand is important to ensure the safe entry of fans (attendees) into the stadium.

It is also advisable to encourage attendees to arrive at different times to ensure a steady flow of attendees (known as a trickle). For instance, at a football match, offering incentives such as pre-kick-off entertainment (e.g. dance or musical performance) or offering promotions on food and beverage (e.g. cheap drinks before kick-off) will help to encourage people to come earlier.

Positioning meet and greeters outside the venue to engage with attendees, answer any questions on access and assist persons looking for specific entrances helps the arrival process. For example, for a large conference registration, having persons report to different zones ensures that congestion and wait time is minimized. An effective way to do this is to have signage and meet or greeters outside who can assist attendees who may need help before they get into the building.

DEALING WITH THE EXTRA TRAFFIC GENERATED BY THE EVENT

For attendees travelling in their own vehicles, good directional information and signage (including information available pre-event) as well as adequate car parking (preferably close to the event) are needed to ensure their timely arrival. By encouraging attendees to use public transport, you will help to cut down on the number of vehicles on the road. Some events managers negotiate reduced fares with local public transport operators, increased bus services, the installation of temporary bus stops close to the event, park and ride facilities, or they provide free shuttle buses from local rail stations.

Certainly, for events generating a large volume of additional vehicles on the roads, a traffic-management plan is essential. This will be drawn up in advance in consultation with the Highways Department and the police, and will include measures such as temporary road closures and diversions, installation of signage and the necessary pedestrian access. This will help to avoid delays for attendees and disruption for the normal day-to-day traffic.

EVENTS MANAGER HACK

I use a visual mapping process: high priority, low priority, high importance, low importance. Then I have different-coloured post-it notes for different projects, and I just start moving tasks around. Eventually, as tasks are completed, they come off the board. I find that much easier to visualize and prioritize than a to-do list.

Jenny Homer, Experiential Marketing Specialist, luxury automotive brand, MEA

During the event

The movement of people (e.g. attendees, staff, artists and performers) and equipment/goods from one place to another during the event is referred to as on-site logistics and involves crowd management, transportation and communications.

Crowd management

Crowd management measures that would typically be implemented during an event include:

- well-positioned and clearly signed entrances and exits to enable easy access to/from the site;
- additional exits to use in case of an emergency;
- use of crowd barriers and fencing to direct crowds and to encourage orderly queues;
- walkways and routes which should be wide enough for all persons, including wheelchair users;

- the provision of on-site transportation for attendees with mobility issues;
- site maps displayed in a suitable format (e.g. on a large display board or on a small leaflet) for attendees to find their way around the event;
- good directional signage both inside and outside the venue;
- appropriate information on signage, for example the event programme (timing and location of activities).

Most indoor venues already have appropriate signage in place, but this isn't always the case with outdoor sites where it is advisable to create a plan especially for event signage. The plan should clearly identify what types of signs are needed (e.g. directional, informational, emergency), where these will be positioned, how signs will be mounted and whether multilingual signs are needed, as well as the use of logos, symbols and colour on signage. Where appropriate it may also be useful to have a public announcement system to announce upcoming activities or any special announcements; this can also be very useful during emergencies or to communicate quickly with attendees, for example the commencement of conference sessions, end of coffee breaks and so on.

Transportation

On a large event site, it may be necessary to put in place a transportation system (e.g. shuttle buses, pick-up and drop-off points) to allow attendees to move around the site. Special arrangements will be needed for any attendees with mobility issues (e.g. very young, elderly, pregnant or disabled) as well as those attendees who are to be given the VIP treatment (e.g. chauffeured buggy service).

The artists and performers may require on-site transportation to move equipment during setup as well as transportation to/from rehearsal areas to changing rooms and performance areas. Media personnel, particularly those with large equipment (e.g. camera crews), may also need transportation to get where they need to be to view proceedings or meet VIPs, performers and artists.

The staff and volunteers working at the event may also require the use of transportation on-site. For example, transport may be needed to help with the restocking of supplies at catering or merchandising stalls, as well as for waste collection and disposal during the event. However, on a busy festival site, large vehicles should not be allowed on-site at certain times of the day.

Where appropriate and possible, having designated on-site transport routes which will be free of pedestrian attendees will help manage the challenges of trying to navigate on-site transport through walking crowds. Bear in mind that anyone who is driving a motorized vehicle on-site should be a licensed driver; even though it may not seem that a golf cart is a standard vehicle, in the event of an accident or incident this will be a key consideration when determining liability.

Communications

An effective communications plan will ensure that appropriate systems are in place to provide information to the attendees as well as for members of the event team to communicate both routinely and in an emergency.

EVENT ATTENDEES

There are several ways of communicating important information to the attendees during an event. Traditional methods include the use of a public address system as well as information boards situated around the event site. New technology has seen the increasing use of digital communications on-site, such as video boards and mobile apps. As a general rule, the more information that can be given to attendees in advance of the event (e.g. a detailed programme of activities as well as an accurate map), the more this will reduce the need for communication during the event.

EVENT TEAM

Effective on-site communications between members of the event team is essential in order to ensure the event runs smoothly. It is important to determine the best communications equipment to use and to establish an effective procedure for communication between team members. It is important that the team is adequately briefed on the expected protocols for communicating as well as the appropriate use and care of the equipment issued. The most suitable communications equipment to use will depend on the size of the site as well as the number of individuals who will be using the apparatus. Each type of equipment has its advantages and disadvantages; for example, walkie-talkie radios may seem a little outdated but mobile phones can encounter challenges with busy networks and poor signal reception in both indoor and outdoor venues, so checks should always be made, rather than relying on the word of the venue managers.

Establishing effective communications procedures will help to ensure all team members are clear about who is the right person to contact in certain situations. For instance, if a problem arises with the projection equipment during a conference, it is important to contact the technical team, or if one of the catering outlets is running short of supplies, the catering manager should be contacted as soon as possible. An effective communications plan will clearly identify who is the right person to contact to ensure decisions are made quickly on-site. This is especially important when it comes to dealing with medical and emergency situations.

Just prior to the event, a walk-round inspection of the site is often carried out to check everything is in place and to spot any potential safety risks or logistical problems. During this walk-round it is also advisable to test that all communications equipment is working properly and that there are no dead zones; in some instances, multiple communication methods may be required to support the communications plan.

Post-event

Once the event is over, the task of shutting down the site begins. There is a tendency to think that the hard work is done when the event is over, but there is still much to do. Any delay in closing the event could mean a delay for the next event coming in (this is certainly the case with popular indoor event spaces), and this will most likely result in a penalty cost or charges, as well as access for load-out vehicles. To a large extent, what takes place post-event will happen in reverse order to what takes place pre-event.

The first logistical challenge is to ensure the smooth dispersal of the event attendees, which can be particularly problematic if all attendees leave en masse (e.g. at the end of a sporting match or concert performance). In this case, event stewards and security personnel will be on hand to assist with the moving crowd. For some events, it may be possible to encourage a staggered dispersal of crowds (in much the same way as a staggered arrival). For example, providing a late bar at an entertainment event or a post-event networking room at a conference is likely to mean some attendees don't leave right away. The journey home is often the lasting impression of an event for the attendees and too often for the wrong reasons – sitting in a long traffic jam trying to exit a festival site, waiting for a long time to board public transport or finding an available taxi can leave your attendees with a lasting memory of your event which may impact their attendance in the future. Sound logistical planning involves thinking carefully about how traffic will exit the site (e.g. opening additional exits) as well as making arrangements for an orderly system for anyone travelling by public transport or taxi. Bear in mind that additional support in terms of stewards and security for traffic management may be needed to ensure that the risk of vehicular accidents is minimized.

Once the event attendees have dispersed, the load-out of equipment and goods begins. Smaller items must be packed up and moved off-site before the breakdown of the larger items (e.g. temporary staging and seating). It is important to ensure supplier and contractor vehicles can access the site easily and it may also be necessary to store some equipment until it can be collected; for example, secure overnight storage may be required for an event finishing late at night, so ensure that you have negotiated this with your venue beforehand and do not assume it will be feasible. When the load-out and breakdown of the site is taking place late at night, it is likely that staff and volunteers are tired, and when people are tired more mistakes happen. Tiredness can pose a risk to personal safety and the safety of others, so it is important to factor this into any risk assessment; it may require you to bring in a load-out team to minimize risk to the live delivery team.

Finally, the clean-up operation can get under way. The site should be left as it was found; penalty charges will be incurred for any damages and unwanted mess (e.g.

posters stuck on walls, balloons on the ceiling), so always confirm what is allowed prior to any installation to avoid any unplanned penalties after the load-out. It is vital to ensure sufficient staff are allocated for the close-down and tidy-up operation to ensure this all happens smoothly without too many disruptions and delays. By this point in most events, the staff are exhausted, so bringing new staff on-site at this point, where possible, is advisable.

Case study 6.2 identifies the issues that hybrid events bring to planning a complex speaker programme for a business event.

CASE STUDY 6.2

Taming the complexity of a hybrid exhibition's speaker programme

Joe Atkinson, Director and Co-founder, Lineup Ninja

Context

As pandemic restrictions eased during 2021, show organizers began experimenting with hybrid event formats that would enable them to continue serving their global audiences, while restarting in-person events to deliver quality networking and satisfy exhibitors' demands. In the exhibition/trade show sector, research conducted by UFI and Explori found that audiences generally thought online events were as good as in-person events for accessing educational content. However, they felt that the networking experience was poor compared to in-person events. Also, exhibitors found it harder to generate or convert leads at online-only shows (UFI/Explori Global Recovery Insight Report).

Event Tech Live

Event Tech Live (ETL) is a trade show dedicated to event technology that takes place in London every November. For their 2021 show, they considered two main hybrid formats: simultaneous and asynchronous online and in-person delivery.

The simultaneous online and in-person format posed some problems: should exhibitors' sales teams try to staff the physical booth while also taking online meetings from the noisy show floor? Doing so could provide a poor experience for both online and in-person meetings while placing a very high demand on the venue's data network. It also ran the risk of making online-only attendees feel like second-class citizens.

The asynchronous online and in-person format means that the same sales teams can attend virtually on the online days and physically on the in-person days. Also, with dedicated online days, there would be less 'class divide' between online and in-person attendees. This was deemed the better option and the ETL team settled on a week-long event: Monday, Tuesday and Friday were online; Wednesday and Thursday were in-person.

Speaker programme challenges

The hybrid approach meant that the ETL team could build a compelling speaker line-up by inviting speakers from around the world. But this – and the asynchronous format – also presented some practical challenges.

Some speakers would only be attending virtually, so their sessions would need to take place on the Monday, Tuesday or Friday. Many of these speakers were also in different time zones, so their sessions needed to be scheduled in slots during the show's opening times, but when they wouldn't be in bed. To complicate this further, several sessions were panel discussions with speakers based in multiple time zones.

Other speakers would only be attending the in-person days, so would only be able to deliver in-person sessions. However, they might be able to pre-record sessions that could be streamed during the online days. Finally, some speakers would be attending both the online and in-person days but might be travelling to the show on the Tuesday afternoon, so unavailable to deliver online sessions at certain times.

These different session delivery modes and sets of speakers' availability constraints created a complex scheduling challenge for the ETL team. This had the potential to become a major headache, had the team tried to manage it with the tools that organizers have traditionally used for this task: spreadsheets.

Any scheduling mistakes could be disappointing for attendees, frustrating for speakers, embarrassing for the organizing team and potentially damaging for the Event Tech Live brand.

Solution

Lineup Ninja is a speaker management platform that ETL had used for the previous three shows. It offers call-for-speakers and speaker invitation workflows, as well as advanced event agenda planning tools.

These tools allow organizers to create session scheduling rules such as 'Sessions where speaker is in category X must take place during time window Y'. The ETL team created categories of speakers such as 'online only', 'in-person only' and so on, and associated them with the relevant days, thus ensuring that all the sessions took place at a time that worked for the speakers and panellists.

The Lineup Ninja team also built a simple, free-to-use tool for organizers to find the best time for a session based on the time zones of the event and the session's speakers/panellists. https://lineup.ninja/tools/

Results

The event was delivered successfully. All sessions ran as scheduled, with the exception of one or two late speaker cancellations due to Covid-19 infections.

> 'Lineup Ninja was a massive help in managing the complexity of a hybrid event agenda. I honestly don't know what we'd have done without it.'

Paul Allott, Event Director, Event Tech Live

Learn more

www.explori.com/blog/the-global-recovery-insights-2021-report-published-the-road-to-recovery (archived at https://perma.cc/LC6F-GMNJ)
https://eventtechlive.com/ (archived at https://perma.cc/TL4D-MRMW)
https://lineup.ninja/ (archived at https://perma.cc/K34F-4LFJ)

Event and public safety

As an event organizer, you are responsible for many things, but none more vitally important than meeting your obligations to provide a safe event.

Sadly, the following examples of tragedies occurring at concerts and festivals since 2010 serve as a stark reminder of the risk to public safety at large events.

FATAL INCIDENTS OCCURRING AT CONCERTS AND MUSIC FESTIVALS SINCE 2010

2021 – Astroworld Festival, Houston Texas, USA

10 killed and over 300 injured during a crowd surge and stampede during the performance of Travis Scott.

2017 – Route 91 Harvest Festival, Las Vegas, USA

A gunman sprayed bullets across a crowd watching fireworks at the end of the festival, killing 58 and injuring 515.

2017 – Ariana Grande Concert, Manchester, UK

A terrorist bomb at Manchester Arena at the end of Arianna Grande's concert killed 22 and injured 59.

2016 – Pulse Nightclub, Orlando, USA

A gunman opened fire in a gay nightclub, killing 49 and wounding 53.

2015 – Eagles of Death Metal Concert, Paris, France

Gunmen fired into the concert crowd at Le Bataclan, killing 130 people.

2015 – Night club fire, Bucharest, Romania

Heavy metal band pyrotechnics sparked a fire in a nightclub, killing 51.

2014 – K-Pop Concert, South Korea

Sixteen people watching an outdoor pop concert fell 20 metres into a concrete shaft, to their deaths.

2011 – Pukkelpop Music Festival, Belgium

Severe storms caused multiple stages to collapse at the festival, leaving four people dead.

2011 – Sugarland Indiana State Fair

Seven people were killed and 58 injured when a gust of wind caused the stage to collapse onto the crowd.

2010 – The Love Parade Festival, Germany

This unticketed free festival drew more than a million people to an area that had capacity for roughly 250,000. More than 500 people were injured, and 21 people died in a crowd crush in the entrance tunnel.

SOURCE Warlaw (nd) and Billboard (2017)

Safety concerns

Events vary tremendously and it is therefore very difficult to provide a definitive list of specific safety concerns. It must be remembered that even though you may be producing and staging the same event, mitigating factors can vary, which requires a suitable and specific risk assessment to be conducted for every event. Varying factors may include number of attendees, weather conditions, performers, staff, layout and so on. Event planners are strongly advised to seek specialist guidance when it comes to health and safety at events. There is more detail about where to find further information and receive guidance and assistance at the end of this chapter.

MAJOR INCIDENTS

For larger events, there should always be a plan in place for dealing with major incidents and emergencies, including terrorism or force majeure. This is known as a major incident plan and covers aspects such as crowd control (e.g. crowd evacuation), traffic management (e.g. access for emergency vehicles), communications (e.g. raising the alarm) and staffing (e.g. what staff should do in the event of an emergency); the emergency services will take over control of all activities in such a situation.

Risk assessment

There will always be risks associated with events (just as there is an element of risk every day when you walk out of your front door). What is important is to put the risk into some sort of context. For example, setting up temporary structures at a large outdoor event site brings a higher degree of risk than setting out tables and chairs at a wedding.

Carrying out a risk assessment will enable you to identify potential risks and decide what measures need to be put in place or what actions need to be taken to reduce the risk.

The UK Health and Safety Executive (HSE) recommends a five-step risk assessment process:

1. Identify the hazards (i.e. anything that can cause harm).
2. Decide who might be harmed and how.
3. Evaluate the risk and decide what needs to be done first (if anything).
4. Record your findings and implement them.
5. Review your risk assessment and update when necessary.

For further information, see the very useful Risk Management section of the Health and Safety Executive (HSE) website at www.hse.gov.uk/risk/index.htm

STEP 1: IDENTIFY THE HAZARDS

The first step of your risk assessment is accurately identifying the potential hazards at the event, a hazard being anything with the capacity to cause harm. A good starting point is to take a tour of the event site to look for any hazards. For large events it will probably help to divide the site into smaller sectors. Bear in mind that you also need to consider the various phases of the event, for example load-in, live event and load-out.

An outdoor festival site, for example, could be divided into the following sectors:

- ticket office;
- wristband exchange;
- car parking;
- main stage;
- main arena;
- arena entrance;

- individual marquees; and
- camping field.

STEP 2: DECIDE WHO MIGHT BE HARMED

The second step involves identifying groups or people at risk of harm. Examples of people at risk on a festival site would include:

- festival-goers;
- employees;
- temporary workers;
- volunteers;
- members of the public;
- contractors;
- suppliers.

You should always pay particular attention to vulnerable people, such as young children, people with disabilities or inexperienced staff, attendees who may not be native speakers. Examples of how people could be harmed on a festival site include:

- cuts and bruises;
- sprains and strains;
- broken and dislocated bones;
- absorbing substances;
- noise injuries;
- burns and scalds;
- crushing or trapping injuries;
- flying or falling objects.

STEP 3: EVALUATE THE RISK

Risk is defined as the likelihood (or probability) of a hazard occurring combined with its severity.

To help evaluate each risk associated with each individual hazard, a scoring system can be used. Often numerical scores are given to the probability or likelihood (L) and severity (S) associated with each hazard and then these scores are multiplied to get a rating for the risk:

$$\text{Risk} = \text{Likelihood} \times \text{Severity}$$

The levels of likelihood and severity are usually categorized into a small number of levels because neither can typically be estimated with accuracy and precision. It is important to be clear as to what the levels or numbers you are using stand for in any risk assessment, as there is no universal system or understanding of what numbers might mean. It is common to see Low–High, Low–Medium–High, 1–3, 1–4 and 1–10 scoring systems used.

An example using a 1–5 system is shown in Table 6.1.

By multiplying the scores for the Likelihood (L) and Severity (S), the risk is given a rating ranging from 1 (no severity and unlikely to happen) to 25 (just waiting to happen with disastrous and widespread results). This is not intended to be a scientific process but helps to determine the level of risks, priority of risks and the urgency to act on them. Again, as with the scoring system, there is no agreed meaning to the numbers or level at which action should be taken, so you should include the risk table (or risk matrix) at the beginning of the risk assessment form.

An example of a simple risk-rating table is shown in Table 6.2.

If a hazard is deemed to carry an unacceptable level of risk, actions must be taken to reduce the risk, by making it either less likely or less severe, or both. These actions are called control measures. Once these have been considered, risk levels should be re-evaluated until the residual risk (risk after the controls have been implemented) is deemed acceptable.

TABLE 6.1 Risk-scoring system

Likelihood (L)	Severity (S)
1 = Remote possibility	1 = Nil
2 = Unlikely	2 = Slight
3 = Possible	3 = Moderate
4 = Highly likely	4 = High
5 = Inevitable	5 = Very high

TABLE 6.2 Risk-rating system

Risk score	Risk rating	Action
1–4	Acceptable	No action required
5–9	Moderate	Reduce risks if reasonably practicable
10–15	High risk	Priority action to be undertaken
16–25	Unacceptable	Action must be taken immediately

STEP 4: RECORD YOUR FINDINGS AND IMPLEMENT THEM

It is important to keep a record of your risk assessment process. This is best done by completing a structured risk assessment form that identifies the definitions of the levels of likelihood and severity you are using and your risk-rating system, and then

FIGURE 6.3 Sample risk assessment form

Wristband Exchange

The wristband exchange procedure takes place under a temporary light weight structure offering protection from the weather, but the structure is open on both sides, providing an easy and highly visible entrance and exit to the main arena.

Probability [P]	Severity [S]
1 = Improbable	1 = Negligible
2 = Remote	2 = Minor
3 = Possible	3 = Severe
4 = Probable	4 = Extreme

→

Risk Level [R]	S1	S2	S3	S4
P1	O	O	O	C
P2	O	O	C	B
P3	O	C	B	A
P4	O	B	A	A

→

Consequences
A = Hazard **must** be eliminated or avoided, work **not** to proceed.
B = Risk **must** be controlled by physical safeguards.
C = Risk **must** be controlled so far as is reasonably practicable.
O = Risk is adequately controlled/insignificant.

Hazard	**Hazard description**	**Risk Evaluation (without controls)**			**Safety Precautions (details of preventative or control measure for hazards)**	**Residual Risk Evaluation (with controls)**		
		P	**S**	**R**		**P**	**S**	**R**
Electric shock		**2**	**4**	**B**	All electrical equipment and wiring to be checked by electrical contractor.	**1**	**4**	**C**
Overcrowding		**2**	**2**	**O**	Fencing to control numbers of visitors entering site. Security guards and stewards assisting in the direction and flow of visitors into site. Effective signage detailing waiting areas and ticket to wristband procedure.	**1**	**2**	**O**
Violence	Confrontation	**3**	**2**	**C**	Security shall be sited in this area with two roaming guards available for back-up if required.	**2**	**2**	**O**
Tripping	Hazards posed to pedestrians in this area (e.g. boggy or slippery areas, other trip obstacles, etc)	**3**	**2**	**C**	Boggy or slippery areas to be cordoned off with tape and/or repaired with wood mulch or gravel. Monitor and remove all trip hazards wherever possible. All wiring to be flown over head or buried.	**1**	**2**	**O**
Weather	Hypothermia, trench foot, sunstroke, dehydration.	**3**	**3**	**B**	Visitors to be informed (via website, tickets, festival documentation) of the importance of bringing appropriate footwear and clothing. Welfare tent to offer free sun cream and water. A limited supply of warm clothing and blankets on site if required.	**2**	**3**	**C**

systematically addresses a full range of hazards and their associated control measures. Not only does this approach lead to a more thorough and thought-through approach, but the risk assessment documents are also good communication tools for showing contractors and staff why actions are being taken. They are also important legal evidence as to the thoroughness of your process, should anything go wrong at your event.

Figure 6.3 shows an example of the risk assessment form for the wristband exchange at the entrance to an outdoor music festival. You should note the inclusion of the risk-scoring system (1–4 in this case) and the risk-rating system (shown as risk level O–C–B–A, and consequences) at the beginning of the document. As can be seen from the first column, the potential hazards identified included electric shock, overcrowding, violence, tripping and adverse weather. The form documents the original risk calculation associated with these hazards, the areas where control measures are required, what the control measures are, and the residual risk showing after their implementation.

Completing risk assessment forms is only the start of the process and it is crucial that the actions you identify actually happen at your event. A well-thought-through plan is useless unless it is put into practice. There have been too many examples of incidents at events that were predicted in risk assessments, but where the control measures suggested never actually materialized.

STEP 5: REVIEW AND UPDATE

Every event is different as venues, audiences, weather and other factors are always changing. Every event needs an individual risk appraisal which should be based both on the specific circumstances and on any information learnt from previous events. As a result, a review of what has happened in the past should feed into risk assessments for future events. Any evaluation of an event (see Chapter 11) should include a review of operational and safety procedures and an assessment of the effectiveness of hazard awareness (Were we right about how likely and severe hazards turned out to be?) and the effectiveness of control measures. Where control measures have been incorrect, risk assessments should be updated to reflect our new knowledge.

A final word on safety...

It is extremely important to emphasize that this book provides only a general overview of the broad safety concerns at events. For anybody involved in planning a larger event or any event involving what might be considered risky activities (e.g. fire walk or fireworks display), it is essential to seek more specific, detailed guidance and assistance as early as possible.

The organizations below will be able to offer specific, detailed guidance on areas such as crowd management, transport and traffic management, medical provision and major incident planning:

Emergency Services: Police, Fire and Rescue, Ambulance Service

Local Authority: Highways Authority (Roads), Health and Safety, Environmental Health

Private Organizations: Health and Safety Consultants, Licensed Security and Traffic-Management Firms.

It is good practice when organizing large outdoor events (e.g. music festivals, open-air concerts, firework displays and street parties) to meet regularly with members from the emergency services, local authority departments and appropriate private organizations (e.g. licensed security firms). Together the individual members of staff from the various organizations will form what is known as the Event Safety Group (ESG) and will meet to give advice to help ensure the safety and welfare of anyone at the event.

The HSE is responsible for the regulation of almost all risks to health and safety arising from work in the UK. The HSE website is an excellent source of advice and there are numerous publications, guides and leaflets available to download (the majority freely available) from www.hse.gov.uk/event-safety/publications.htm

GUIDANCE

- *Managing crowds safely:* A guide for organizers at events and venues
- *Electricity at work:* Safe working practices
- *The safe use of vehicles on construction sites*

HEALTH AND SAFETY REGULATIONS

- *Management of health and safety at work.* Management of Health and Safety at Work Regulations 1999
- *Approved Code of Practice and guidance*
- *Memorandum of guidance on the Electricity at Work Regulations 1989.* Guidance on Regulations HSR25
- *Noise at work:* A brief guide to controlling the risks

LEAFLETS

- *Health and safety made simple.* The basics for your business INDG449
- *Five steps to risk assessment* INDG163
- *Working at heights in the broadcasting and entertainment industries* ETIS6

- *Electrical safety at places of entertainment* GS50
- *Workplace health, safety and welfare.* A short guide for employers
- *Theatrical and stage effects* (including guidance on the planning and management of special effects)

OTHER PUBLICATIONS

- *Guide to safety at sports grounds* (Green Guide) Sports Ground Safety Authority (SGSA)
- *Temporary demountable structures.* Guidance on design, procurement and use (3rd edn) Institution of Structural Engineers
- *Safe use and operation of marquees and temporary demountable fabric structures* (Revised March 2011)
- *Fire safety risk assessment:* Open-air events and venues

CHAPTER SUMMARY

- Event production is key in bringing all of your planning to life and supports you in meeting your clients' objectives. Using a variety of logistics and other elements ranging from audio-visual, creative design and entertainment, you can create lasting and memorable experiences for your attendees.
- The art and science of getting people, infrastructure, goods and services to the right place at the right time and in the right order is what constitutes exceptional logistics management. From load-in to load-out all the preparation and planning leads to this moment, where the coordination of your logistical elements will be the difference between event success and event failure.
- There is nothing more important than ensuring the safety of everybody attending or working at an event and it is extremely important to seek specialist guidance when it comes to health and safety at an event.
- There is always the chance of something going wrong at an event but carrying out a risk assessment will enable an events manager to put measures in place to minimize the risks to public safety.
- The very nature of large events means there are always going to be logistical challenges involved with moving all the people, equipment and goods to where they should be. A sound logistics plan is needed, which should consider the whole operation, including what happens pre- and post-event.

Questions for reflection

1 How important is the planning phase in this aspect of event delivery? What are some of the key event production documents that you need to prepare to facilitate the effective load-in and health and safety on your site?

2 As an events manager you have legal reasons for maintaining site health and safety. What are the other impacts that failing to meet Health and Safety requirements may have on your business or organization?

3 In managing site logistics, what are some of the critical aspects that you must consider to ensure that logistics are delivered on time and to the right location?

References

Billboard (2017) Manchester Arena, Le Bataclan, Route 91 Harvest Festival & More: A timeline of concert tragedies www.billboard.com/articles/news/6762444/paris-shooting-deadliest-concert-shooting-ever-timeline-tragedies (archived at https://perma.cc/ZT64-5QKE)

Warlaw, M (ND) 10 Worst Concert Tragedies. Ultimate Classic Rock http://ultimateclassicrock.com/worst-concert-mishaps-and-tragedies/?trackback=tsmclip (archived at https://perma.cc/LZ4H-Z5PQ)

07

Staffing and human resources in events

FIGURE 7.1 The Dowson, Albert and Lomax Event Planning Process – event staffing

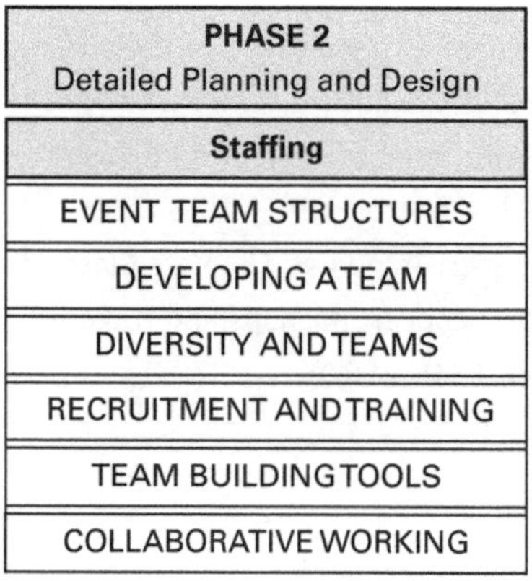

PHASE 2 Detailed Planning and Design
Staffing
EVENT TEAM STRUCTURES
DEVELOPING A TEAM
DIVERSITY AND TEAMS
RECRUITMENT AND TRAINING
TEAM BUILDING TOOLS
COLLABORATIVE WORKING

Building the right events team is key to the success of any event. This is because event delivery is a complex process that requires a range of roles and activities to be integrated and well managed for a successful event outcome. This complex reality of event delivery combines with the pulsating nature of the events organization, which necessitates a much larger group of people to load-in and deliver an event on-site than it does to plan. As a result of this need for rapid expansion of people power, many event organizations have developed a flexibility that includes the capacity to increase in size for on-site delivery of events.

The limitations and benefits of working as a wider team, alongside those outside your own organization, are explored in this chapter, covering models that have proved their worth and identifying drawbacks and opportunities in an industry where groups of individuals, previously unknown to each other, come together to deliver outstanding events. It is important that within this critical process, managers of complex teams understand individual communication preferences and develop processes for managing partners, clients and suppliers. Within this chapter, we explore a range of approaches and develop the concept of 'collaborative working' as it applies in the events industry.

This chapter addresses the core people-related issues facing those who are involved in developing and delivering events. The first aspect we cover is the overall complexity of events and the pulsating nature of organizations in the events industry. This aspect combines the event's core team with a wide variety of contractors, suppliers, freelancers and, often, volunteers, part-time and full-time, who have to work together effectively within a team structure from the inception of the event process. The complexity and pulsating nature of event teams, along with the multiplicity of internal and external staff, make the human resource management of events very different from many other industries. To increase this complexity, it needs to be recognized that organizations are not made up of only standard full-time jobs, but of a combination of core and peripheral staff, part-time, casual, freelancers, volunteers and contracted goods and service suppliers, all of which are brought into the human resource team dependent on the objectives, size and location of the event.

The second element of the chapter details the processes for recruiting and training events staff, providing a range of role descriptions and suggesting useful tools such as EMBOK (Events Management Body of Knowledge), personality instrument MBTI® (Myers–Briggs Type Indicator) and Belbin's team role assessment, which provide benefits to a range of events organizations. Running an event requires the collaborative efforts of a 'team-of-teams approach', often in a short time period. This section considers how teams can function more effectively, not only within the team but across teams – as failing to manage and facilitate effective team functioning can cause significant problems for the delivery of your event which can ultimately lead to event failure. But when it comes to working successfully with a client or suppliers, teamwork and team management are key.

By the end of this chapter, you will understand:

- complex event delivery;
- complex events team structures;
- the pulsating nature of the events workforce;
- staffing levels;
- diversity;
- the Event Management Body of Knowledge;
- role descriptions;
- communication;
- working together, as individuals and organizations;
- collaborative working and developing strategic partnerships.

Complex people concerns in events

The complexity of the people-aspects of events should not be underestimated. The larger the event, the more complex its delivery. The nature of the events organization, or that of the client, impacts upon this complexity, adding layers of internal influence and external regulation. On top of this, the type of event selected can influence the elements that have to be kept in balance, and the type of attendee (such as VIPs) can also add more complexity to the mix. Despite the fact that most people think anyone can run an event, experience shows that most events could be managed more effectively and efficiently if the complex people-aspects of the process were acknowledged and taken into account in planning and delivering the event. The pulsating nature of the events workforce (which requires more people for on-site delivery than are needed to plan an event) is a vital characteristic of this complexity. More recently, more flexible formats for working have added another layer of challenge to the human resource management aspect of events. There are also challenges for organizations required to manage staff working remotely, from different regional or international locations, or dealing with international travel and working with diverse event teams for international offshore event delivery. The diversity which now exists in the sector brings in an added element for consideration which good events managers will always acknowledge and consider effectively.

Complex team structures

Within an event planning structure, there is what can be termed a 'team of teams', also referred to as the 'core team'. These individuals are usually permanent staff, while others are members who are established in the event organization or are part of the core planning group, who have a consistent role within the organization. There are also suppliers, contractors and volunteers, who may serve as part of the repeat human resources used for events; however, it should be noted that these team members, who are considered peripheral team members, are not always necessarily under the direct command of the events manager – a complex mix. Bearing in mind that, in events, just about everything is for hire, the 'Event Site' (formerly known as the 'White Book' and founded by experienced events professionals; https://theeventsite.co.uk/) shows the wide range of potential support services available which need to be integrated within the event delivery team. Management of all aspects of your human resources is important to ensure the smooth running of your event. The complexity of stakeholder relationships within events management, particularly where a functional role in events planning or delivery is outsourced to a third party, underlines the need for taking a structured approach in planning and delivering an event.

There are multiple stakeholder relationships that emerge in an events context. These stakeholders include the client organization, the community context in which the event takes place, the people who attend or participate in the event, suppliers and sponsors, social media and advertising organizations that promote the event, and the teams of staff and/or volunteers who deliver the event. Each stakeholder grouping has a two-way relationship with the event organizer, whether contributing time, skills or resources, and in return, experiences the impacts of the event. All these stakeholders have their own teams, and together comprise the team of teams that delivers a successful event.

The pulsating events workforce

The build-up to events and the post-event breakdown require fewer workers than at the event itself, and this is reflected in Alvin Toffler's 1990 concept of the 'pulsating organization' that changes in size in response to circumstances. Large sports events provide good examples of this feature, such as the Commonwealth Games Birmingham 2022, which necessitated recruiting and training some 13,000 volunteers for the delivery of the games. In 2020 for the Tokyo Olympics 110,000 volunteers were recruited but the games ended up using only 80,000 due to reduced numbers of attendees, but they also noted that they lost over 10,000 of those volunteers who quit due to worsening public opinion of the games due to the Covid-19 pandemic (Reuters.com, 2022).

The reality is that managing an event on the ground requires a much larger workforce than in the planning stages. Particularly for large sporting events, volunteers become a key feature of the event workforce, where the loss of 10,000 volunteers can have dire implications for event delivery. This pulsating nature of organizations in the events industry combines the event's core team with a wide variety of contractors, suppliers, freelancers and volunteers, part-time and full-time, who have to work together effectively within a team structure from a standing start. This makes events very different from many other industries, as events organizations are not often made up of standard full-time permanent jobs.

The phrase 'the gig economy' has its origins in the music sector, but the events industry relies on the flexibility of staff to meet the changing requirements throughout the event planning and delivery processes. Organizations that deliver events are usually working on several events at any one time, which increases the requirement for accurate planning and the development of processes that are adhered to by all events managers for a consistent approach. Chapter 2 explains the development of such processes, but a team approach is vital to gain agreement and consistency in applying such processes. In this regard, difficulties can be encountered if all team members do not follow the agreed process. That's not to say that the process cannot be changed – it would be inappropriate to insist on that, but when a change is agreed by the team, it is necessary that everyone implements it.

In managing a team of people to deliver a series of events, the complexity becomes clear. Not only are people required on-site, but others will be needed back at base to prepare for forthcoming events and to manage communications. Detailed, effectively communicated, and accessible documentation becomes a key feature of ensuring that everyone is on the same page and is aware of their role, authority, responsibilities and what they will be held accountable for.

Prior to an event, a small 'core' team develops, plans and coordinates the structure, style and content of the event, and outsources and procures any support services that are required. These outsourced services may include security and stewarding, temporary demountable structures (e.g. marquees), furniture, toilets, catering, hospitality and bars, technical teams (e.g. audio-visuals – sound and lighting), and may include the use of a venue search agency to source the event location (see Chapter 5). Chapter 1 gives a range of suppliers and support services. Such coordination teams will also liaise with emergency services and local authorities to ensure appropriate cover and planning for emergencies, and develop and deliver marketing, sales and communication plans for the event. (See Chapter 10 on event site management and planning, Chapter 6 on event production and logistics and Chapter 8 on marketing, promotion and publicity). However, these functions may in reality be delivered by separate teams, depending on the size and complexity of the event and the structure of your organization. Events require a much larger team to deliver on-site than is needed to plan the event. Communication is vital within the team, between those who have different responsibilities, and with any suppliers providing outsourced services for the event. Prior to the event, make sure you include the wider team in event briefings and circulation of key event documentation, and make them privy to shared files where information can be accessed.

> EVENTS MANAGER HACK
>
> People make events. Treat them like people, not numbers. Treat them the way you would want to be treated. Brief them well. Share info, but not too much. Want someone to read 8 hours of info? Pay them for it. Travel, food, loos, hot hand wash: they're the basics, not extras.
>
> *Charlie Mussett, Freelance Events Manager and Safety Consultant*

Developing an operational events team

This section focuses on the operational aspects of professional events management teams and outlines the range of event roles, with examples of job descriptions and person specifications that might prove useful. We briefly outline operational processes for recruiting and training events staff and share international models such as EMBOK that can provide benefits to a range of events organizations.

Events roles

In addition to the core event-management team (working alongside any freelancers), a wide range of roles will be required on-site. These additional roles are influenced by the range of support services required, so suppliers of security and stewarding would provide security people and stewards; suppliers of temporary demountable structures, furniture and toilets would need to provide staff to deliver, set up, manage, maintain and break down the equipment provided; suppliers of catering, hospitality, bars and technical teams would need to provide staff to deliver, set up, manage, maintain and break down the equipment, as well as providing trained and qualified technical teams, including staff to prepare and serve food and drinks. Event production roles might also include: stage production management and crew; sponsorship management; artist liaison; photography; media liaison; décor and signage; venue team managers, team leaders and team members; event production; event licensing; health and safety; campsite or accommodation management; security management; box office and wristband control; film crews, including directors, producers, camera operators, researchers and editors; sound engineers, DJ station crews, including DJ station managers, technical supervisors and team members.

EVENTS MANAGER HACK

Ask silly questions, don't assume anything; ask your expert team for help and advice, don't try and do it alone; do versions of event call sheets rather than keep saving over the last version, as you may need to look back at something previously spoken about; keep every email as a backup; don't give timings when letting someone know you'll send something.

Lori Novell, Event Project Manager, The Outlook Creative Group, UK

Case study 7.1 demonstrates the structure for teaching events management students the staffing and human resources aspects of events management in Portugal.

CASE STUDY 7.1

How to work on the essential skills for managing events: The Event Management Learning Model applied in formal higher education in Portugal

Victor Afonso, Susana Filipa Gonçalves, Elsa Gavinho, Ana Gonçalves, Cláudia Lopes, Francisco Silva, Estoril Higher Institute for Tourism and Hotel Studies

The skills needed to manage events have significantly evolved, especially in recent years, showing an increasing need for professionalization to respond to a more competitive market. There is no doubt that formal education can contribute to skills development in this context. The Event Management Learning Model (EMLM) at the Estoril Higher Institute for Tourism and Hotel Studies in Portugal can be a fundamental tool to leverage the events sector, promoting the empowerment of events managers and quality-of-service delivery. EMLM is a student-centric model to promote an environment that allows students to acquire events management skills, which means adapting to ever-changing realities. This model also enables students to gain autonomy by adapting theory to real-context situations and the decision-making process entailed in planning and producing events.

Consisting of five phases, the EMLM follows the planning, production and evaluation of an event, developed by student teams of 4–6 people, guided by teachers specialized in different areas and responsible for different degree subjects.

1. IDEA CAMP: October

- Five-hour creativity workshop
- Preparation (e.g. team's visual identification, necessary material, timetables)
- Appropriate room layout for the creative process and to foster an inviting environment (e.g. inspiring sentences, background music)
- Tasks with limited time for development:
  - Listing ideas
  - Definition of five criteria for idea assessment
  - Clockwise exchange of ideas between teams and assessing the three best ideas of the previous team
  - New exchange between teams + assessing the best idea
- Filling in a poster with pre-given topics
- Poster display and feedback on post-its from students and teachers

2. PROJECT CAMP: December

- Ten-minute team pitch of the project
- Fifteen-minute Q&A

- Guests: Invited lecturers from other courses (e.g. tourism, management, entrepreneurship, marketing); alumni (now events professionals); trade specialists
- This stage allows teams to gather additional feedback on the project

3. EVENT PLANNING: January–May

- Delivery of strategical, tactical and productions plans, considering inputs from project camp
- Communication and decision process with all stakeholders (sponsors, suppliers, partners, media, volunteers, etc)
- Compulsory follow-up meetings with teachers throughout the semester (5–6 meetings/average)
- Tutorial sessions with teachers at teams' request (on-site, online, WhatsApp, etc)
- Delivery of updated strategic and tactical plans (4 weeks before production) and production plan (1 week before production)
- Site inspections
- Contracts
- Licensing
- Rehearsals

4. PRODUCTION: May

- Briefings
- Setting up
- EVENT (monitoring/managing)
- Debriefings
- Disassembly
- Shutdown (communication, payments, receiving, reports, etc)
- All moments under the guidance and supervision of teachers

5. EVALUATION: May/June

- Group report (deeper analysis of every topic of the event)
- Individual activity and analysis in a five-page report (self-evaluation; evaluation of team performance regarding processes, time management, commitment, relationships and leadership; performance of each team member; evaluation of the event from an external perspective)
- 30-minute individual discussions with teachers about the whole learning process

At the Estoril Higher Institute for Tourism and Hotel Studies (ESHTE) in Portugal, the EMLM has been applied in the degree courses for Leisure Management and Tourism Entertainment and in the Master's in Tourism – Strategic Management of Events. Besides being used as a complete process (from phases 1 to 5), it is also possible to apply only phases 1 to 3, with some limitations, mainly regarding the acquisition of some soft skills. Bearing in mind the most relevant skills in event management identified in the scientific literature by academia and events professionals, this model has demonstrated its effectiveness over the years.

Creativity and innovation are among the most relevant skills needed to manage events, both to develop concepts and to find solutions to logistics and production challenges. Therefore, for student teams to create events and find ways to produce them (as there are no a priori resources or budget), they will be compelled to develop proactivity.

During the entire process, the collaborative work, both among the team and between teams (especially in the sharing moments in the classroom), is fundamental to reinforce the learning process and to practise the people management skills necessary to carry out the event's production. Students can constantly work on interpersonal skills, communication, expectations and conflict management. When the production phase arrives, students are exposed to more pressing moments and will have to deal with stress and emotions.

This set of skills is particularly enhanced in events by the time management that the organization of an event imposes. When the date and time of an event are communicated, everything must happen as planned. Thus, attention to detail, multitasking, planning, management and organization are skills developed during the application of the EMLM, especially because events must be implemented during the academic calendar.

On the other hand, for students with no professional background, there is a strong feeling of assuming great responsibilities, even in small and simple events, as they will have to manage and lead a huge number of stakeholders (artists, suppliers, sponsors, audience), but also take risks regarding budget management.

Finally, the practical application of a project in a real context, facing the challenges of the market, with teachers' mentoring and guidance, allows the development of critical thinking, adaptability and persistence, which are fundamental to solving problems and facing unforeseen circumstances, so common in events.

Thus, the application of this model allows students to follow a previously defined and tested (formative) itinerary, with several phases that help them develop the skills needed to be successful events managers. Having been a finalist at the 2018 Hospitality Education Awards (Portugal) and second at the 7th Teaching Innovation & Entrepreneurship Excellence Awards 2021 (International) shows that the EMLM has been subject to continuous improvement. At ESHTE, the teachers who participate in it continue to search for better formats suited to the constant changing reality of the labour market in events, as has happened during the pandemic (hybrid and digital events).

Learn more

https://www.eshte.pt/ (archived at https://perma.cc/Q2BP-R4U7)

Developing role descriptions

When planning an event, you will need to develop role descriptions for each level of position in an events team. At the end of this chapter, generic role descriptions that can be used as a basis for this process are provided. They will need to be tailored to the organization, client and event. A specific job description for a temporary role at a festival may not be as detailed as might be expected.

The following section outlines considerations when scoping the role of an events team:

- Decide the scope of the events team – what events activity the team will support, e.g. management and coordination of key events that provide engagement with internal or external clients and external stakeholders.
- Identify the benefits of events team support e.g. achieve organizational objectives; build new or strengthen existing stakeholder relationships; strengthen client organization's image and build trust with a key stakeholder group; include two-way communication with the target group and support improved effectiveness of the client's activities; and manage risk that could damage the client organization's reputation.
- Key considerations in setting up an events team: that the team has the capacity or potential to expand to deliver the level of events planned; that the client has the financial resources to meet the costs incurred, a realistic budget is available and the budget holder has been identified; that the event objectives have been clearly expressed and approved by the client with appropriate signatory level assigned to the events manager; that there is a clear description of the size, locations and complexity of the event/s; and that there is adequate notice to attract the appropriate audience and deliver a successful event.
- Agreement on the scope of the event team's work, accountability and responsibilities feeds in to the overall evaluation of the event, in terms of whether or not they have been achieved.
- Sample role descriptions for core events management team members are provided with the book's online resources which can be used as they stand, or adapted for your own use.

Diversity and teams

It has long been known that diverse teams are more productive, innovative and creative, and that overall, they improve a business's bottom line. Within events, many event teams will include people from a diverse range of backgrounds, whether in nationality, race/ethnicity, gender, sexuality, disability, neuro-diversity, social class, educational background, gender reassignment, age, or belief systems. Such differences benefit the team immensely, bringing a range of perspectives and ideas that contribute to the success of the event, but some may also involve the need for employing organizations to meet specific requirements to create spaces where diverse individuals are not discriminated against, feel included and are treated equitably. It should be noted that event participants may also share these requirements. In this regard, tools such as the Cultural, Inclusivity and Equity Risk Assessment (CIERA © Albert and Dowson 2022) serve to support event organizers in not only facilitating the functioning of these diverse teams, but also providing appropriate environments for diverse attendees.

It is important for events managers not only to actively recruit team members from diverse backgrounds but also to ensure that they create an environment for team members to be authentic within the work and event environment. Ensuring that the organization's equity, diversity and inclusion expectations are part of your training programme, or providing briefing notes for peripheral workers, serves to facilitate getting the best out of your diverse workforce. Also remember that staff need to be aware of cultural differences and other requirements that come along with diverse groups of people. All organizations should have EDI policies and use tools such as the CIERA to provide inclusive spaces which facilitate a sense of belonging and value for those with diverse backgrounds, getting the most out of every employee.

Case study 7.2 proposes actions that event organizations can take to promote equality and diversity in the events sector, based on its experience in creating and delivering festivals.

CASE STUDY 7.2

Equality and diversity: UK music festivals

Dr Roxy Robinson, Creative Director, From the Fields Ltd

Many companies, including those in the events industry, know that it is a good idea to have a diversity and equality policy. This document is purported to demonstrate a commitment to the Equality Act 2010, which forbids employers from discriminating on the basis of 'protected characteristics' (race, gender, sexuality, disability, maternity, gender reassignment, marriage or civil partnership, religion and age).

While this legislation performs a vital function by tackling discrimination in a range of contexts, the creation of a strategy for diversity is usually approached as a box-ticking exercise. However, history demonstrates that the absence of a strategic approach to diversity can produce glass ceilings and inherently discriminatory company cultures. Despite the increasing levels of media coverage, the reality of discrimination in the workplace remains discernible through persistently poor levels of boardroom diversity. BAME (Black and Minority Ethnic) individuals, for example, make up fewer than 4 per cent of directors of the top 150 FTSE companies in the UK.

For event companies with ambitions of creating a robust diversity strategy that unlocks the potential of the whole workforce, there are many points to consider. For a start, there are both internal and externally facing workforces at play. A music festival workforce, for example, not only includes operational staff (such as stage managers, security, stewards, producers, technicians) but also the front and centre performers on stage. Despite the inclusive veneer of music festivals, the lack of diversity both in the field and on the stage has not gone unnoticed by the British press (see 'Festivals Dominated by Male Acts', June 2017, BBC; 'Music Festivals Continue to Lack Diversity', July 2017, Metro; 'Music Festivals have a Glaring Woman Problem', May 2016, Huffington Post).

This press coverage supports the case for diversifying festivals, not only on principle, but as an important means for protecting a festival's reputation while maintaining industry credibility and good public relations. For festivals, and indeed all organizations, the 'tick-box' approach to diversity has had its day.

From the Fields Ltd

From the Fields Ltd is responsible for the organization of a portfolio of UK festivals, most notably Kendal Calling (Cumbria) and Bluedot (Cheshire). The curation of festival programmes is also provided as a service to external clients, including Bournemouth Borough Council's Arts by the Sea festival. The company ethos is founded on creating exceptional experiences for audiences, via efficiently produced and imaginatively curated events.

With an ambition to foster diversity both on and off the stage, in the first instance From the Fields considers the mix of demographics of its music line-ups in terms of both gender and ethnicity when making bookings. The supply of artists is dominated by white men, particularly in the category of acts that have the ticket-selling clout for performing on the main stage, although efforts are made to balance the line-up where possible. The reality is that there are many practical challenges in achieving this, which come in the form of limited artist availability, prohibitively high fees, and exclusives put down by competitors that limit the ability of suitable artists to perform.

In 2017 From the Fields appointed a consultant to examine its two largest festivals with a view to developing its strategy for diversifying its BAME audiences and workforce. An audience development report was produced which has empowered the company to take steps to further explore practical options for developing BAME audiences and representation within the programme. While the business is still at the beginning of this journey, the key insights from the report are shared here. It is hoped that events students will carry these recommendations into the future as they develop their own practices in the events industry.

Three recommendations

1 Diversify representation

In the digital age, festival marketing has become a visual art, with photography and video acting as critical tools for reaching audiences. This is a point of consensus among event marketing managers. Nevertheless, there is far less awareness around the idea of 'visual barriers'.

Visual barriers are subconscious barriers to participation. These can form when groups are excluded from visual representation in the marketing materials that are deployed to advertise a cultural event. On the flip-side, the visible presence of diversity shown in photography, video and design can act as a self-fulfilling prophecy, because greater representation tends to fuel greater levels of participation. This same principle of diverse representation can be applied to line-ups of music, panel discussions or any public-facing collection of entertainment.

2 Forge partnerships with diversity-led organizations

Limited resource is an issue shared by most festival organizations, making the prospect of sharing workload by partnering with a relevant community group a promising one. Partnerships with organizations that are focused on supporting specific communities or cultural scenes can feed into a range of actions that support audience development.

These include consulting on making your event accessible to audiences via marketing and event design, unlocking pools of talent that might be in your event's locale and embedding diverse content in its programming.

3 Target market

BAME communities are not evenly distributed geographically but tend to cluster around specific locales. These locales are often neglected by festival promoters in terms of their target marketing. The distribution of print flyers and posters, for example, is usually targeted at city-centre locations, with a view to gaining a presence at the busiest bars, clubs and areas with high young professional and student footfall. Expanding out of this remit to include venues, restaurants and community centres in suburban areas with a high BAME population, coupled with the engagement work detailed in point 2, can be a straightforward but powerful way to engage more broadly and raise awareness. The same principle can be applied to targeting across the marketing mix, including digital marketing, radio and magazine advertising, and PR.

Read more

www.bbc.co.uk/news/uk-england-40273193 (archived at https://perma.cc/36CC-3D9N)
http://metro.co.uk/2017/06/19/music-festivals-continue-to-lack-diversity-with-six-in-seven-top-spots-filled-by-all-male-acts-6717937/ (archived at https://perma.cc/SF8V-5WGE)
http://data.huffingtonpost.com/music-festivals (archived at https://perma.cc/FT5D-XPLL)
http://fromthefields.co.uk/ (archived at https://perma.cc/M2WN-CRWZ)
www.kendalcalling.co.uk/ (archived at https://perma.cc/8VGV-YUJL)
www.discoverthebluedot.com/ (archived at https://perma.cc/R2BL-8BFQ)

Recruitment and training

Recruiting and training large numbers of on-site events staff adds to the complexity of team structures, but it is also important to ensure that you recruit the right people for the core team as well. With recruitment for large-scale events that require many volunteers, mainly online methods are used to advertise vacancies and for recruiting, supported by email, social media and online resources for selection and training processes. In addition, multiple face-to-face training sessions might also be held in different geographical locations to enable volunteers to understand their own roles and those of professional paid staff, such as security and stewards, as well as how to respond to specific scenarios.

Increasingly, core events teams require professional skills – specifically, those of events management. As a key supplier of qualified events professionals, the UK Centre for Events Management, which was established at Leeds Beckett University in 1996, has an international teaching and research team with permanent events academics and practitioners. While events management education is now offered at over 70 higher educational establishments, the UK Centre for Events Management was the first to offer pure events management degree-level qualifications and is widely recognized for its innovations in teaching and in placing employability at the heart of its provision. Such educational institutions have strong links with their alumni, and events sector vacancies are often circulated by graduates through their alma mater, whether in addition to or outside of publicly advertised means. As the first European provider of degree-level events management education, the UK Centre for Events Management has the largest network of several thousand graduates working around the world, from the UK to Australia, China, the Middle East and North America.

Online social media sites such as LinkedIn provide useful contacts with educational and professional events networks; in addition, there are professional industry associations and networks, including the following, that may be useful for recruiting events professionals:

Association of British Professional Conference Organizers www.abpco.org/

Association for Conference & Events www.ace-international.co.uk/

Association of Event Organizers www.aeo.org.uk/

Association for Events Management Education www.aeme.org/

Association of Event Venues www.aev.org.uk/

Association of Independent Festivals https://aiforg.com/

Business Visits & Events Partnership www.businessvisitsandeventspartnership.com/

Event Hire Association www.eha.org.uk/

Event & Visual Communication Association www.evcom.org.uk/

Eventia www.eventia.org.uk

Events Supplier and Services Association (ESSA) www.essa.uk.com/

International Association of Exhibitions and Events www.iaee.com

International Congress & Convention Association www.iccaworld.com/

International Special Events Society www.isesuk.org/

Meetings Industry Association www.confpeople.co.uk/about-us/mia

Meetpie.com www.meetpie.com

National Outdoor Events Association www.noea.org.uk/

Society of Event Organizers www.seoevent.co.uk

Society for Incentive Travel Excellence www.siteglobal.com/

The Association of Festival Organisers www.festivalorganisers.org/

The Event Services Association https://new.tesa.org.uk/

For smaller core teams, recruitment may be through formal associations or more informal networks, such as events educational establishments or personal contacts.

EVENTS MANAGER HACK

Never underestimate the power of networking, whether it's somebody you've studied with at Uni, or somebody you've worked with on a project, or within a company, it's always good to stay in touch because you just never know –

Jenny Homer, Experiential Marketing Specialist, luxury automotive brand, Middle East & Africa

The Events Management Body of Knowledge (EMBOK)

In the past, as practitioners, we would have found a tool such as EMBOK extremely valuable, particularly in the area of human resources, covering fundamental HR practices such as training and recruitment, performance management, staffing and organizational structure. The EMBOK is a descriptive summary of the scope and processes of event management, a framework for future development of the event-management profession, and a flexible tool for all industry stakeholders. (www.embok.org/)

Practical implications: staffing levels

If an events team is delivering only one event at a time, or even an event series, that can be challenging enough, but – as is common in the events industry – there may be new events being planned and developed throughout the delivery period. The complex programme of events delivered by one team of five events managers, an events assistant and six freelancers over a five-month period included 43 events, 12 event themes in 15 locations with 7,280 attendees on 84 event days.

In order to provide adequate on-site staffing for managing regular events like this, a rule of thumb is to provide at least one experienced events manager for smaller events up to 100–150 attendees.

However, it should be noted that if some of these events are repeated at different locations around the country, as the team becomes comfortable with the structure and content, it is possible to leave on-site work to one person. Once numbers go above 150, the number of events staff increases, thereby underlining the concept of the pulsating event workforce. Thus, for 500 delegates, 8–10 staff are needed, but this also depends on the complexity of the event.

It must be said that the number of events staff depends on the event – and that size is by no means the only factor to consider. Additional staff might be required depending on the type of event and its complexity, as well as whether there are any logistical or security considerations, such as the attendance of VIPs.

More staff are needed to run a much larger event, such as a festival. At the annual Beat-Herder Festival (beatherder.co.uk/) held on the Lancashire/Yorkshire border, there are up to 10 staff working in the box office alone, dealing solely with accreditation for approximately 2,000 artists and performers, on-site staff such as stewards, stage technical crews and operations managers, commercial traders, press and media and VIP guests – in addition to the separate wristband exchange team for the 12,000 paying festival-goers.

When developing a team to work on your event, selection processes may range from online to word-of-mouth and personal recommendation, but care must be taken to verify that recruits have the required experience – and increasingly, relevant (events) qualifications. Training should include: the event and its background, the role, attendees and their needs, processes to be followed during the event, communication channels, working as a team, and activities that enable the team members to get to know each other.

Wider team of teams: individuals working together

From an outsider's perspective – such as that of an event attendee – the individual does not care whether your team is made up of core members, freelancers or suppliers. To illustrate this, imagine that you visit a supermarket where you're unfamiliar with the layout. You see someone in a uniform, so you ask them for directions to find a specific item. 'Sorry,' they reply, 'I'm on the cleaning team.' You hadn't noticed that their uniform was orange instead of the familiar blue, but what does that matter?

Surely, they know where the item is displayed? As customers, we don't really care which team they're on. They may even work for an outsourced supplier company. And the colour of the uniform is irrelevant. When you're looking for a specific item, you expect the staff in the supermarket to be able to direct you.

Event attendees are just the same – only events are more likely to be made up of people who work for a range of supplier organizations. And taking into account the pulsating nature of events organizations, it's all the more important that each individual involved in delivering the event knows that they need to be able to respond to any question or problem – to understand not only their own role within the scope of the event but also others' roles. The response might even be 'I'll take you to someone who does know', but this example highlights the importance of training and briefing staff who work on any event. Despite the split in responsibilities between different types of event staff, the perception by event attendees is that they are all on the same team. If you run events on a regular basis, perhaps for a specific client, one option is to develop a wider team of people who will work for you regularly: a team that knows how the client prefers to operate, a team that understands each other, as well as understanding the event's purpose and delivery. With such a team it is not only easier and more effective to staff an event, but the event attendees will gain a more consistent, quality experience. Having a larger potential 'temporary' on-site team than is necessary for just one event provides you with the flexibility to service more than one event at a time and takes account of availability as well as skill sets and experience.

Team-building tools

Whether building a team from scratch or bringing together a group of people who have worked with each other in the past, induction and training programmes are vital to ensure the success of the event. Team-building tools also facilitate the building of a psychological and emotional investment with the organization and also with other team members. When individuals work together, a range of factors can influence their interaction and ability to communicate effectively, all of which have a significant impact on the delivery of their roles. Personality and communication preferences add to the complexity of a team. Through the use of an interactive workshop which we developed based on the characteristics of the Myers–Briggs Type Indicator (MBTI®), team members are able to recognize, communicate and navigate work styles and personalities more effectively. Rather than complete the questionnaire, it is possible to explore each of the dimensions using a narrative style related to real examples. Workshop participants take part in activities and discussions within small teams as part of a process in which they get to know each other and learn about their own communication preferences and styles, which essentially leads to more effective teams. In the UK, the MBTI® is administered by Oxford Psychologists Press (you can read more about this at www.opp.com and www.myersbriggs.org). There are many other psychometric instruments that can be used, and our aim is not to promote MBTI® above any other instrument.

The four dimensions of MBTI® are:

- Energy: identifying the individual's focus on the inner or outer world. **Extraverts** gain more energy from being with others, while **introverts** gain more energy from their inner life.
- Gathering information: identifying the individual's preference for gathering information. **Sensing people** gather specific concrete data, while **intuitives** make connections, interpreting and adding meaning.
- Making decisions: identifying the individual's preference when making decisions. **Thinkers** prefer rational logic, while **feelers** base decisions on an emotional level.
- Lifestyle: identifying the individual's focus within the outside world for structure or openness. **Judging** people prefer to live structured lives, using time to make decisions, while **perceivers** prefer to keep their options open to new information and emerging situations, putting off decision-making.

Creatives and logics

While event teams are made up of a range of different people with different personalities, in our work with students at the UK Centre for Events Management, once students have self-assessed for their Myers–Briggs Type Indicator, we noticed that many students seem to describe themselves as 'Creatives' or 'Logics'. Although these terms have not been officially researched, we found that events management students often see themselves as in one group or the other. The success of a team may depend on its diversity – as well as on enabling people with different communication preferences to understand their own and others' communication preferences. Rather than seeing the other type in a negative light, we work with students to frame such difference as positive, adding to the capability of the events team.

EVENTS MANAGER HACK

My tip is an understanding that I've come to, in terms of how people are in events. You're either a creative, or you're an operational, and many creatives aren't very organized. If you're really organized, nine times out of ten, you're not very creative. It's just how it is. And now I know what type of events manager I am. And I can tell you, I have the odd creative day. But some of the stuff that these creatives come up with, I think, 'how do you even think like that, it's wild'. When I look at the stuff that they produce, storytelling and how it ties into the message, and this is what the visuals are going to look like – I'm amazed. But I see the practicalities very clearly.

Jenny Homer, Experiential Marketing Specialist, luxury automotive brand, Middle East & Africa

Companies working together – corporate personality style?

We have also worked in a range of corporate environments, some of which seem to have a strong bias in terms of personality, either as a whole organization or a specific department. While not wanting to overstate the case, actuaries, for example, might tend to be introverted, while marketing colleagues might be more extraverted. Whatever your preference, working in an environment that places more value on one preference than another can be emotionally draining and demotivating; while some people will attempt to 'fit in' to the prevailing context (with different outcomes), others will fight against it. Overall, it is more effective for organizations to encourage and enable an environment that values difference and the range of contributions made possible by diversity, than to deny it and impose compromise or conformity.

Understanding communication preferences

Whatever tool you choose to use, it is always worthwhile first knowing more about yourself, identifying strengths and weaknesses, and then being able to apply that understanding to those you share similarities with, as well as to those different from yourself.

Another popular tool is the Belbin® Team Roles, which can be identified by using a short questionnaire to identify different patterns of behaviour that individuals adhere to and advises that the team should comprise the range of roles available. Table 7.1 shows a summary of the descriptions of the Team Roles identified by Belbin, with benefits and limitations of each type.

TABLE 7.1 Belbin® Team Roles, benefits and limitations

BELBIN Team role type	Contribution	Allowable weaknesses
Plant	Creative, imaginative, free-thinking. Generates ideas and solves difficult problems.	Might ignore incidentals and may be too preoccupied to communicate effectively.
Coordinator	Mature, confident, identifies talent. Clarifies goals. Delegates effectively.	Can be seen as manipulative and might offload their own share of the work.
Monitor evaluator	Sober, strategic and discerning. Sees all options and judges accurately.	Sometimes lacks the drive and ability to inspire others and can be overly critical.
Implementer	Practical, reliable, efficient. Turns ideas into actions and organizes work that needs to be done.	Can be a bit inflexible and slow to respond to new possibilities.
Completer finisher	Painstaking, conscientious, anxious. Searches out errors. Polishes and perfects.	Can be inclined to worry unduly, and reluctant to delegate.
Resource investigator	Outgoing, enthusiastic. Explores opportunities and develops contacts.	Might be over-optimistic and can lose interest once the initial enthusiasm has passed.
Shaper	Challenging, dynamic, thrives on pressure. Has the drive and courage to overcome obstacles.	Can be prone to provocation and may sometimes offend people's feelings.
Teamworker	Cooperative, perceptive and diplomatic. Listens and averts friction.	Can be indecisive in crunch situations and tends to avoid confrontation.
Specialist	Single-minded, self-starting and dedicated. Provide knowledge and skills.	Can only contribute on a narrow front and tends to dwell on the technicalities.

SOURCE Reproduced with kind permission of Belbin – www.belbin.com

Collaborative and partnership working – a new way forward for events in the team of teams

Traditional ways of working have included hierarchies and control methods, but in the current environment some event organizations have developed new ways of working collaboratively in partnership with other organizations – including with their competitors – in order to survive and to thrive. Competition entails the need for a winner and for losers – while collaboration and building alliances can enable successful outcomes, whether for internal or external stakeholders. But such action depends on the structure of your own organization, as well as that of the client and suppliers. The development of such close partnership relationships involves high degrees of teamwork at all levels of the organizations involved, in which individuals are encouraged to contribute across teams, broadening their roles and responsibilities and encouraging contribution. Small businesses will find such flexibility easier than large corporations, but the introduction of such approaches, while complex and challenging to manage, will facilitate the achievement of collaborative advantage for all involved.

Case study 7.3 explains the contribution of health and safety to the overall events team for one of the largest and most complex events in the world.

CASE STUDY 7.3

Health and Safety as part of the Events Team – Expo 2020, Dubai

Amy Mullan, Health and Safety Advisor at UAE Pavilion, Gallowglass Middle East; Health and Safety Manager, Gallowglass Health and Safety LLP; UKCEM Graduate 2021

World Expos take place every five years and last six months; historically Expos are one of the oldest and largest international festivals. The world comes together to share ideas, experiences, and innovatively make plans for future generations. Expo 2020 was hosted by Dubai, UAE and was the first World Expo to be held in the Middle East, Africa and South Asia (MEASA) region. Expo 2020 opened its gates to the world on 1 October 2021: over the six-month period an astonishing 20 million visitors experienced 'The World's Greatest Show'. Visitors had the opportunity to explore the 438-hectare site in which 192 pavilions of countries from around the world provided a unique yet collaborative experience of 'connecting minds and creating the future' – a collaborative power to build a better world and shape the future, with a key focus on sustainability, mobility and opportunity. At the epicentre of Expo 2020 Dubai, on 500 acres stands the UAE Pavilion; it is the largest pavilion at 15064 m^2 across and 27.8 m high. UAE Pavilion is shaped like a falcon in flight and features 28 carbon-fibre wings that can fully open. The pavilion is an immersive multisensory visitor experience that showcased UAE's journey from the ancient roots of UAE culture to its transformation into a unified nation of diverse people. It was an opportunity for locals and visitors from across the globe to be educated on the collective progressive movement at shaping a better future and celebrate 50 years of an Emirati dream.

First and foremost, as HSE Manager of the UAE Pavilion at Expo 2020 Dubai there was a responsibility to manage all aspects of H&S and the environment for all those working or visiting the pavilion. During the initial stage HSE created an event management safety plan (EMSP) which identified any foreseeable risks and allowed for adequate planning and procurement of resources. Ultimately, it involved ensuring that all foreseeable risks were controlled to an acceptable level. During day-to-day operations, UAE Pavilion established and maintained a specific and comprehensive occupational H&S programme inclusive of the management of health, safety and environment constraints, to reduce the likelihood of accidents, injuries and harm to the environment. It also included Covid-19 exposure and possible related issues. All the policies and measures implemented aligned with government and Expo legislation and guidance.

The greatest challenge regarding the health and safety of the UAE Pavilion was the convoluted nature of the building's layout. Despite providing heightened health and safety concerns, the overall risk was controlled through the implementation of additional preventive measures. As example, the venue had five first-aid locations to ensure that efficient first aid could be provided in a timely matter in the case of an emergency. Clear and open channels of communication is a paramount factor to consider in the overall operations of health and safety. EMSP will simply not work if not effectively communicated to all relevant persons within the venue. UAE Pavilion communicated using three key methods: email, radio and WhatsApp. Furthermore, pavilion management held three briefings per day which all functional area leads attended to report any key information. Briefings allowed continuity between shifts, the sharing of clear and concise information and collaborative teamwork. The unison of the UAE Pavilion team was enhanced through the use of technology. A world-class incident management system (We Track) was used daily by all managers to submit their pre-opening checks, log any incidents during operation and build reports. By carrying out tasks on a centralized system, all functional areas were kept up to date with daily operations and scheduled special events in real time. The UAE Pavilion promoted a positive safety culture: H&S was embedded into all aspects of operations across all functional areas. All persons working at the UAE Pavilion followed policies and procedures to ensure their and others' health and welfare was at the highest level.

The UAE Pavilion team worked together by connecting our minds and bringing together our unique specialities as functional area leads to showcase our pavilion to visitors from across the world. It was a very humbling event to be part of, as it provided an opportunity for the nation to come together in a safe and socially distanced manner after 18 months of being so disconnected due to the global pandemic: acting as a platform to reimagine the world of tomorrow. To conclude, a key learning from this project which I will carry on in my career is the importance of being proactive in the management of risk, as it enables all aspects of safety to be covered – a vital element when operating in a dynamic environment.

Learn more

www.bie-paris.org/site/en/about-world-expos (archived at https://perma.cc/BFE5-ZESZ)
www.expo2020dubai.com/en (archived at https://perma.cc/Y4TN-GT4U)
www.expo2025.or.jp/en/ (archived at https://perma.cc/A599-GCBP)

Staffing – events team

Job descriptions

We have developed a range of sample job descriptions which you can download at www.koganpage.com/epm. There are summaries below.

ROLE SUMMARIES

The **events manager** role includes the following responsibilities:

- Lead strategic planning, management and delivery of national and local events.
- Manage external resource sourcing, selection and procurement processes, e.g. venues, AV, personnel.
- Manage events team.
- Lead coordination of event facilitation, administration and technical support requirements.
- Manage event evaluation and initiate improvements.

The **events coordinator** role includes the following responsibilities:

- Coordinate and deliver event management, including venue liaison.
- Coordinate speakers and facilitators.
- Use online events management tool to deliver high-quality event administration.
- Organize exhibitions, communications, e.g. delegate packs, email.
- Provide on-site event management, including managing relationships with external suppliers.
- Maintain requisition and ordering processes.

The **events administrator** role includes the following responsibilities:

- Deliver all aspects of event administration, including delegate bookings, production of delegate packs and delegate resources where required and provide post-event online access to materials.
- Use online events management tool to deliver high-quality event administration.
- Respond to queries; manage team email inbox.
- Organize team travel and accommodation.

FACILITATORS, HOSTS AND OTHER ROLES

For events that require facilitators, it is possible to use in-house staff who are trained and experienced facilitators, thereby reducing the need for a large team of permanent staff and developing internal levels of expertise while retaining funding within the organization. In addition, the events team should include staff who can develop event content. Event hosts can be drawn from relevant in-house staff and key local personnel, from a team of freelance staff, or hired in.

There are many useful networks that can assist you in hiring your team. Examples include: The Delegate Wranglers (www.thedelegatewranglers.com/ – see Case Study 1.2) and NOWIE – the Network of Women in Events (www.thenowie.com/), as well as LinkedIn-based and graduate networks. Blogs are also useful network resources, such as the Events Manager Blog (www.eventmanagerblog.com/about-me/). These networks are not only helpful when hiring a team but also for individual events managers in developing their careers and starting a business. One of our online case studies, contributed by Jody-Ann Rowe, Founder and CEO, The Event Certificate in Canada, illustrates some of the resources that are available to support events managers in using their on-site experience to support their professional development, building their careers and their own businesses.

CHAPTER SUMMARY

- This chapter has explored the unusual nature of the events industry, which requires much larger numbers of staff to deliver an event than it does to develop it.
- It recognizes the reality that many events management teams face multiple event delivery dates and ongoing development of new events in the planning stages. This all adds to the complexity of developing teams that are able to work together successfully, often at short notice, and with little time for introductions.
- The chapter introduces some useful tools, such as Belbin and the Myers–Briggs Type Indicator, which can be used to develop a team approach and offer practical ways of communicating more effectively within a team, enhancing the team's ability to perform.
- It suggests partnership opportunities and provides a range of role descriptions that may be useful when planning your events team.
- Without a team, events don't happen. Developing a collaborative approach in which team members appreciate those who add value in different ways is more likely to lead to a successful event.

Questions for reflection

1. What qualities would you look for in recruiting a member of an events team?
2. How would you go about recruiting new events professionals to work for your organization?
3. How could you widen the diversity of your events team?

References

Belbin (2022) www.belbin.com/ (archived at https://perma.cc/PHP8-34QU)

Belbin (2022) Belbin Team Role Summary Descriptions. www.belbin.com/about/belbin-team-roles (archived at https://perma.cc/7JPZ-53ZY)

MBTI (2022) https://eu.themyersbriggs.com/en/tools/MBTI (archived at https://perma.cc/NYF6-2N4K)

Reuters.com (2022) Olympics: All dressed up with no one to help. www.reuters.com/lifestyle/sports/olympics-all-dressed-up-with-no-one-help-tokyo-volunteers-sit-spectators-2021-07

08

Drawing in the crowds – marketing events

FIGURE 8.1 The Dowson, Albert and Lomax Event Planning Process – marketing events

PHASE 2 Detailed Planning and Design
Marketing
PROMOTIONAL PLAN
TARGET AUDIENCE
SOCIAL MEDIA PLATFORMS
SOCIAL MEDIA CONTENT
TRADITIONAL MEDIA
PROMOTION SCHEDULE

All events require promotional activity. This could be a simple reminder for previous event attendees to hold the date, or it could involve a more sophisticated, prolonged campaign to entice new attendees. A successful promotional campaign generally starts early and then continues to seize upon regular opportunities to generate publicity in the build-up to an event. As a good event organizer knows, when it comes to putting on an event, creating a buzz around an event is crucial to help draw in the crowds.

There are many ways to promote an upcoming event, including campaigns on a variety of social media platforms, television and radio, featured articles in newspapers and magazines, poster displays and leaflet drops, prize draws and competitions. A successful promotional campaign will often make use of multiple methods, but with resource limitations (e.g. money, time and staff), deciding which ways are most effective requires careful consideration.

The most appropriate methods are largely determined by the target audience itself, where different target customers may be best reached using different tools. Before undertaking any promotional activities, it is, therefore, important to find out as much as possible about the intended audience in order to understand the best way to make them aware of the event and attract them to it.

By the end of this chapter, you will be able to:

- develop a promotional plan for your event;
- identify and appeal to your target audience;
- select the right promotional tools for your event;
- use social media to build excitement before, during and even after your event.

Developing a promotional plan

There are many choices regarding how, where, when and to whom to promote your event. While there is no one right way to create a successful promotional strategy, there are practical steps you should take to give focus and direction to your efforts.

Here are five simple steps to follow:

1. Set the objectives.
2. Establish your budget.
3. Define your target audience and tailor your message.
4. Select the best promotional tools.
5. Measure the results.

Like any good plan, there needs to be an element of flexibility, but careful planning helps to ensure that resources (namely money, time and staff) are used effectively.

Setting objectives

The main purpose that promotion serves is to attract an audience for an event. A football match played in an empty stadium is always disappointing and so is a conference with only half the expected number of delegates. Pulling in a crowd is not only good for the atmosphere at an event but is often a critical component that determines financial success where income from attendees is needed to pay for the costs of staging the event.

Promotion is also important for reasons other than attracting a crowd on the day. Possible objectives for event promotions may include the following:

- **Building awareness.** For example, a new event may be largely unknown to the target audiences, which means initial promotional efforts must focus on telling them who you are and what you have to offer.
- **Reinforcing the brand.** For example, a festival organizer might use promotion to help build a strong relationship that can lead to a festival-goer becoming a loyal customer.
- **Providing information.** For example, a conference organizer will want delegates to access any important information before the conference starts, such as arrangements for travel, registration and check-in.

Before beginning any promotional activity, you need to set clear objectives to provide you with focus and direction. Setting objectives will also enable you to measure the effectiveness of your promotional efforts.

Establishing your budget

It's not easy to come up with a realistic budget for your promotional activity. Below are some of the options you can use:

- **Task method:** Perhaps the simplest way to set the budget is add up the costs of the various promotional tasks planned. One thing to keep in mind is that obtaining accurate costings in advance might be challenging.
- **Percentage of sales method:** Here the budget is set at a percentage of the forecasted sales revenue, e.g. allocating 10% of sales revenue to promotion. Clearly this method is only suitable for an event that will generate revenue, e.g. ticket sales.
- **Competitor-oriented method:** The budget set is in line with the promotional budget for other similar events. The rationale being: if you want to remain competitive, you have to spend as much as your competitors. Again, obtaining accurate costings might prove difficult.
- **Incremental budgeting method:** This approach starts with an assumption that a detailed look at last year's budget offers a starting point for estimates for this year.

Defining your target audience and tailoring your message

It's often said that the better we know our target audience – their general age, gender, occupation as well as their motives and desire – the better we're able to communicate with them. But, as an event organizer, we're usually required to communicate with multiple audiences with different expectations, who attend for different reasons and behave in different ways. Therefore, creating an effective promotional campaign requires you to identify and understand the differences between target audiences before responding to them. Audience segmentation enables you to come up with messaging that resonates with your target audience.

Selecting the best promotional tools

This is where you need to decide which promotional tools to employ and to what extent. With so many great social media platforms available, it is easy to see why social media promotion is a key element for success in many campaigns. But traditional promotional activities – such as advertising, press releases, pricing promotions, personal selling and direct mail campaigns – all still have an important role to play in promoting events. No single promotional tool offers a guarantee of success. Each tool has strengths and weaknesses, and budgets are limited. A well-rounded promotional campaign will typically use several different techniques at one time.

The Four Cs is a useful way of assessing the suitability of each element of a proposed promotional campaign (Figure 8.2).

Measuring the results

Understanding how to measure whether your promotional activities are delivering the best possible results can save you time and money and help ensure the success of your event.

FIGURE 8.2 Four Cs of promotional planning

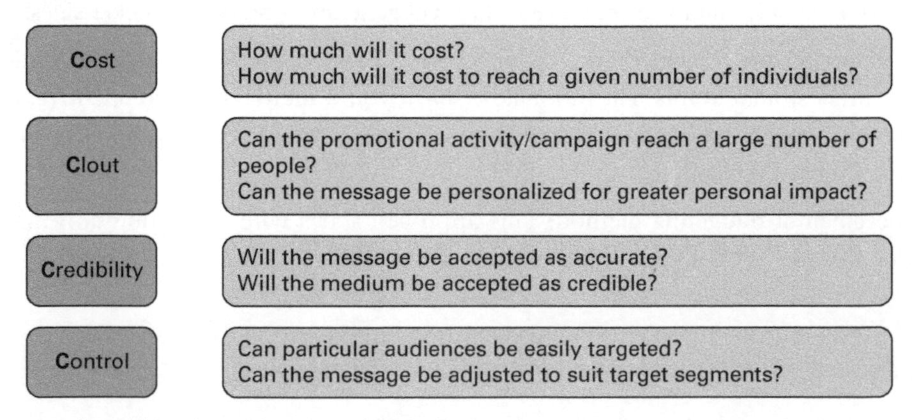

SOURCE Adapted from Chartered Institute of Marketing (2009)

What you measure will vary depending on the type of event, but some of the ways to evaluate your promotional activities include:

- Ticket sales: Tracking the number of tickets sold is one of the simplest ways to deduce that your current promotional strategy is having some sort of positive effect.
- Return on investment (ROI): You can calculate an overall measurement, but a more specific breakdown by each promotional activity – the amount spent on each activity versus the amount of sales each brought in – will tell you exactly which worked, and which fell short.
- Customer feedback: Customer surveys, general customer feedback and social media comments can all reveal what your customers think of your promotional activities and which promotional tools have the greatest impact.
- Competitor response: The actions of your competitors can often be very telling when it comes to the success of your promotional plan. If competitors rush to copy what you've done, the plan is working. If your campaigns go largely ignored, there may be an issue.

Identify and appeal to your target audience

There is always the temptation to jump right in, but before launching your promotional campaign it is essential to define your intended target audience as well as what it is that you want to say to them.

By now, you should already have a good idea of your audience. As we discussed in Chapter 3, developing the event concept (remember the Five Ws) involves thinking carefully about who your event is being aimed at – the target audience. But it can't be emphasized enough: the more you know about your audience the easier it is to come up with promotional messaging that resonates with your target audience and encourages them to attend.

Audience

Perhaps the most common mistake in determining the target audience for an event is thinking too broadly. For example: you've been tasked with organizing a business networking event for new business start-ups, so ask yourself – who is your target audience? Easy, right? It's people who have recently started a new business. But what about people who are *thinking* about starting a business? It's important to be as clear as possible about your audience, because doing so will make it much easier to determine how best to reach them and make the message more appealing to them.

As we have already said, thinking about your target audience as a homogenous group is far too simplistic, as there are likely to be many sub-groups interested in attending your event. Continuing with the example of a networking event for business start-ups, you could split the attendees into different groups based upon factors such as the type of business or size of business, as well as criteria including their motive for setting up a new business or their motive for attending the event.

Breaking down (or segmenting) the target audience into sub-groups makes it much easier to determine how best to reach each group and tailor the message more precisely to them. Two commonly used approaches to segment a target market involve segmenting by demographic and psychographic variables.

DEMOGRAPHIC SEGMENTATION

This involves dividing the target market into sub-groups, thinking about the profile of the attendees based on tangible characteristics such as their age, gender, occupation and so on. This helps an event planner to gain a better understanding of *who* typically attends an event. This method can be particularly useful when an event planner can draw on historical attendance data to determine the audience profile.

When determining the demographic profile of the target audience, it is important to consider the following factors:

- age
- gender
- occupation/profession
- marital status
- family life cycle
- location
- language
- education
- income
- race/ethnicity
- ability/disability

Some of the factors listed might not be particularly important for one type of event but could be extremely important for another. For instance, an event aimed at celebrating the successes of high-flying young businesswomen will be more concerned about the gender and age variables than any others.

PSYCHOGRAPHIC SEGMENTATION

This is the division of the target market according to variables such as their attitudes, interests and values. This helps to gain a better understanding of *why* the target audience chooses to attend an event. This involves detailed analysis and classification of target customers based on criteria such as their attitudes, interests and values to gain more insight into their motives for attending.

Possible motives for attending an event include:

- Experience something new.
- Visit somewhere new.
- Meet key business contacts.
- Find potential customers.
- Spend time with family and friends.
- Meet new friends.
- Excitement and entertainment.
- Rest and relaxation.

Combining psychographic with demographic data significantly improves our understanding of the target audience, giving us a much clearer picture of the typical event attendee – not only *who* they are but *why* they are attending – which improves our ability to target promotional efforts.

Message

Having thought carefully about the target audience for your event, the next step is to determine exactly what it is that you want to tell them about the event (the message). On the face of it, the message you wish to communicate to the intended audience seems straightforward – 'buy a ticket', or better yet, 'buy a ticket today!' And, of course, there is a time and place for hard-hitting messages like this. But care is needed with determining the *right* message – a message that is deemed appealing by the target audience. Sometimes a hard-hitting message (e.g. buy a ticket) might put off a potential customer, and a more subtle message may be needed. In marketing terms, we talk about positioning messages which are designed to communicate something about the brand or image for a particular product (in our case the event itself). So rather than instructing the target audience to buy their ticket, the message might focus on compelling reasons for them to do so, such as, 'this event is the biggest of its kind', 'the best of its kind' or perhaps 'the first of its kind'.

The average person receives hundreds of messages (not all about events) and so each message must work extremely hard to get noticed. No matter how the message is delivered, your target audience will only read those that capture their attention.

Below are some things to think about to help to ensure that your promotional messages are deemed worth reading or listening to by your target audience.

USING DIFFERENT TYPES OF MESSAGE APPEALS

Appeals speak to a person's needs, wants or interests. Three of the most common message appeals include those listed below.

> A helpful exercise to gain a better understanding of your target audience is to create a buyer persona, or description of a typical individual who would represent your target audience. This is a great activity to undertake with other members of the event organizing team. Ask each other questions like: What does our typical attendee look like? What are they wearing? Who are they with? What are they thinking about right now? How did they get here? What are their hobbies? Which social media spaces are they swimming in? What is their number one reason for attending our event? And even, what is their name? You can even create a mood board or portfolio of images, activities and webpages that reflect them. This exercise allows you to 'get under the skin' of your target audience, helping you and the team to learn more about the target audience – and it can be good fun too!
>
> IMAGE 8.1 Who am I?
>
> 
>

Fear Fear appeals focus on the consequences of negative outcomes or missed opportunities. Fear messages are powerful as they tap into basic human evolutionary survival which often seems more pressing to an individual than basic reasons leading to instinctive responses. A common use of fear marketing for events is the Fear Of Missing Out (FOMO), with general messages around the positive experiences that will be missed by not attending. As events get closer, FOMO can be turned directly into sales by stressing limited ticket numbers or the possibility that events will sell out, leading potential attendees to turn their interest in an event into an active decision to purchase a ticket.

Humour Many of the most memorable promotional campaigns (not just for events) tend to be funny. There have certainly been no shortage of laugh-out-loud TV ads over the years, with TV advertising campaigns often relying on humour as way of grabbing and holding the attention of television audiences. When it comes to getting your message across for an upcoming event, good humour can be a great way to capture your audience's attention and build anticipation in the lead-up to an event.

Romance For anyone looking to put a romantic twist on their event (e.g. Valentine's Gala Dinner), using romantic quotes and sayings as well as beautiful images of couples and romantic settings offers a way to connect with their audience on an emotional level, and is therefore likely to form an integral part of their promotional message. There is, however, a fine line between what is considered romantic and what is considered cheesy (the sort of thing that happens in a heartbreakingly bad romcom!) or crude (the sort of thing that happens in a raunchy music video). But before you rule out the benefits of using romantic appeal, stop for a moment and ask yourself: *'What is the most romantic city in the world?'* One city always tops the rest: Paris. Each year, Paris capitalizes on its romantic allure to attract millions of foreign visitors to the city of love. You do have to be careful when using romantic appeal, though; the key is to ensure your message (as well as imagery) is appropriate to your target audience (which can be difficult with such a culturally diverse target audience for many events).

CHOOSING INFLUENTIAL MESSAGE SOURCES

Lots of companies ask influential people to talk about products and services on their behalf. This is because using influencers not only spreads the word about their products to a wider audience but can be more persuasive than messaging straight from the companies themselves. An influencer doesn't necessarily have to be someone famous, but the person does have to be a combination of credible, trustworthy and likeable, in order for his or her messages to be perceived as convincing by audiences.

The first lesson you should learn when engaging with influencers is to listen first. Take the time to get to know them by following them on their most active social media platforms (more about this shortly). But at the same time, it's important you engage with them – leave a comment on their social media posts or updates or blogs as well as promoting (sharing) what they have to say on your own social media.

Remember: this is a two-way street; you can't expect them to share your content for nothing.

There are several options when it comes to choosing an influential person (or source) for your promotional messages. Your task is to identify which source is the most appropriate (i.e. which is most likely to persuade the intended target audience).

Here are some options you might consider:

- your company CEO
- an industry expert
- a successful entrepreneur
- a real customer
- a company employee
- an amateur or professional athlete
- a television or media celebrity
- a film star
- a fictional or cartoon character
- a political, religious or community leader
- a writer, journalist, or blogger.

Event promoters, too, realize that using influencers can help them to grow their reach, generate interest and have a positive effect on attendance for their event.

EVENTS MANAGER HACK

A key component of any pre-event marketing strategy is experimenting with messaging to see what resonates with audiences. This 'growth-hacking' technique is cost-effective, and it highlights areas of high engagement. Experimenting with messaging is also efficient as it displays content that isn't engaging audiences by providing insights into consumer habits.

Abbie Thornton, Events and Marketing Manager, Institute of Water, UK

Speaking your target audience's language

If we can speak a language that matters to our target audience about who they are, their experiences and their interests, we have a much greater chance of capturing and maintaining their attention.

Take a moment to consider which (if any) of the following events you are likely to pay more attention to:

- A party or a bash?
- A concert or a gig?
- A festival or a fete?
- A get-together or a gathering?
- A meeting or an assembly?
- A conference or a convention?
- A celebration or a shindig?

For some of you the words will resonate right away; for others, they won't.

Speaking the language of your target audience (ie carefully choosing the right words and phrases) helps to ensure that your promotional messages are picked up and acted upon.

Using visuals to engage your audience

Creating an effective message isn't only done using words; visual stimulation can also have a powerful impact on the recipient.

Effective graphics and visuals rely on using simple and easily understood images that will stand out clearly in the busy real or online worlds in which they will be seen by potential audiences. Consider using vibrant or contrasting colours, images and typeface that catch people's attention, ensure that information is clear and easily read and that the visual space looks considered and uncluttered.

To achieve this, it is worth following four basic principles of design (Williams 2014):

Contrast – Avoid elements in the design that are merely similar; either have them the same, or very different.

Repetition – Repeat important aspects of a visual design such as colour, shapes, logos, fonts to create a sense of unity.

Alignment – Ensure important elements in a design, particularly type, follows a grid or alignment to make it look clean and considered and allow messages to be read easily.

Proximity – Group items relating to each other, together. This helps organize information and reduce clutter.

Remember to ensure that you have created materials that are accessible for people with visual (colour palettes for neuro-diversity) or hearing impediments (subtitles), or other disabilities, to ensure that you have created an inclusive marketing/advertising strategy that takes into consideration your diverse audience.

Increasingly, social media also rely on video and animation to grab the attention of users and can be a powerful and necessary aspect of online communication.

> EVENTS MANAGER HACK
>
> Create a personalized experience for your target audience by getting to know their unique personas, purchasing habits and motivations to attend events. By tuning your marketing efforts to fit your researched profiles, you can build a relationship with your potential attendees and transform them into a registered attendee.
>
> *Selina Arnall, Event and Marketing Manager, That Event Girl; Social Traders, Australia*

Promotional tools

There are different ways to reach your audience before an event begins. Some methods reach a wider audience, some are more personal; some methods reach the audience immediately while others take a little longer; some are expensive and others reasonably cheap (there's no such thing as free promotion because all promotional activity requires at least an investment of time).

Social media for event promotion

Event promotion and social media go hand-in-hand. People attend events to connect and interact with one another (whether it is family and friends, work colleagues or even total strangers). Likewise, people join social media networks such as Facebook, Instagram, Twitter and LinkedIn to connect and interact with people. It makes perfect sense to use social media to help you create the buzz and attract the right attendees to your event.

A study of 1,335 events professionals found that nearly all respondents (93 per cent) were using social media to promote at least one of their events and almost one-third (32 per cent) were using social media for all of their events (Events Manager Blog, 2018). Indeed, many attendees will look sceptically at an event that isn't using social media, leading to questions about whether an event is outdated compared to other events that are making full use of social media.

The real benefit of social media is the value of connecting, interacting and engaging with event audiences before the event as well as during and after the event (often right up until the next event). Social media provides event organizers with an opportunity to create a community around their event: to converse with attendees, to share ideas with them, to ask for feedback and even to ask for recommendations about how to improve the event (this process is known as co-creation).

A CAVEAT

Before moving on, it's important to acknowledge that the social media landscape is continually evolving. The platforms we consider 'mainstream' today will inevitably date, new platforms emerge and existing platforms create new ways of sharing content. But one thing we're confident of is that event planners will continue to use social media as a vital promotional tool for connecting, interacting and engaging with audiences.

Choosing your social media platforms

With different social media platforms available, one of the easiest mistakes to make is to try to spread your content across every social media platform. Spreading yourself too thinly on social media is counterproductive and it will ultimately hurt your event in the long run. Rather than trying to be active on every social media platform, consider picking two or three social media sites that are closely aligned with your event and are mostly used by your target audience. This will help you become more efficient (saving time and money) and more effective (think quality not quantity) in your social media promotion.

While there are no exact rules, here are three very important factors to consider, ensuring that you focus your promotional efforts in the right places when it comes to social media:

1. **Do your potential attendees spend time there?** It may sound obvious, but you need to find out where your target audience 'hang out' when it comes to social media. It's often a case of making some educated guesses. For example, data show that a much higher percentage of women use Pinterest than men. A wealth of fascinating data about who is using social media is available (the majority is freely available on the internet) to help you choose the right social media platform for your target audience.
2. **Does this platform make sense for the content you are producing?** With social media the most important thing is to share content that will grab your audience's attention and generate interest in your event (more about must-have social media content shortly). A natural extension of this is selecting the best platform(s) to share that content. So, for example, if you want to introduce the guest speakers to your audience by sharing a video bio, YouTube is ideal for you. On the other hand, if you want to share behind-the-scenes photographs from your event,

choose a platform best suited to photo sharing, such as Instagram, while humorous video might be better shared through Tik-Tok.

3 **How are other event planners using social media?** Keeping an eye on your competitors' social media presence can provide valuable insight into where you should be focusing your own efforts. As well as seeing which social media platforms they are using, you can see exactly what content they're posting, how often they're posting and when they're posting. While it would be a mistake to simply copy your competitor's social media activity, if certain social media seem to be working for them (i.e. high levels of engagement with their audience), we would recommend thinking seriously about doing the same – only better!

Social media platforms overview

Below, we look briefly at the different types of social media and what they're used for:

Facebook: Still the most popular social media platform, with many events-focused features such as Events & Groups as well as a well-developed and effective suite of paid promotional and advertising tools. Now seen as more established and used by an older demographic.

Instagram: Visual focused platform dominated by posts and stories featuring strong images and, more recently, video content. Especially popular with millennial and generation Z audiences.

LinkedIn: Unlike most other social platforms, LinkedIn is primarily a career- and business-oriented platform. LinkedIn users are specifically looking for content related to their professional and career development. So, for instance, if your event has anything to do with business networking, it makes perfect sense to establish your presence on LinkedIn. LinkedIn users tend to view their accounts during the working week and during typical working hours (09.00 to 17.00); something to keep in mind when posting event updates on this network.

Twitter: Twitter is a social networking site where users share updates, news, thoughts, opinions in brief 'tweets' (text messages of up to 280 characters). Tweets can also include images and links to web pages as well as links to other tweets. Twitter's 280-character limit means messages have to be short and snappy, making it the ideal platform for real-time updates about your event (e.g. a flash ticket-sale or line-up announcement).

YouTube: The world's biggest video-sharing network is second only to Facebook in terms of users. YouTube is owned by the largest search engine (Google), which means YouTube videos are a great way to increase your event's online search visibility. But there is a hard truth for any event organizer: people don't visit YouTube to learn about your upcoming event. You have to earn your audience's attention by creating the sort of video content they want to watch and share with their family, friends, colleagues and associates.

TikTok: The short-format video platform has grown rapidly since its release in 2016 and, while still most popular with younger age groups, is becoming more common across older demographics too. The platform combines some of the reach of Twitter, using hashtags, with the ability to generate viral content and audience participation

Pinterest: Pinterest, like Instagram, is all about images. Pinterest stands apart by focusing more on being a digital scrapbook which allows users to view, collect, organize and share images that they like from all across the web. The most popular categories (for scrapbookers) include food and drink, fashion, travel, home décor, craft projects and weddings. With women four times more likely to be Pinterest users than men, it provides a powerful platform to gain exposure to female audiences.

Ways to promote your event using social media

Whether you're holding a muddy music festival or a glitzy awards dinner, using social media can be an incredibly useful tool to communicate and engage with your audience.

There is no shortage of options to consider when it comes to using social media. Indeed, one of the best things about using social media is that there are plenty of inexpensive options for event organizers on a tight budget.

We've compiled a list of some of the best ideas that have been given to us on how to use social media before, during and after your event.

BEFORE

Social media is the ideal promotional tool for reaching out to prospective event-goers to get them excited about the upcoming event. Creating enthusiasm before the event not only gives them something to look forward to but will encourage them to promote the event to their friends, family and colleagues.

Consider the following options.

Setting up an event page on Facebook This may seem like an obvious choice. But for many events there is still no better place to start than setting up an event page on Facebook. It's such an easy way to promote your event, too. Simply add an event photo, and then enter your event's name, location and frequency (e.g. occurs once, weekly or monthly). If you've set up the event with an online ticketing provider, you should also include the URL.

Facebook only allows you to send event invitations to your friends. So, if you're trying to maximize the turnout, make sure you share your Facebook event with all of the people involved with your event as well as any relevant influencers who would care about your event (e.g. asking a fashion and lifestyle blogger to promote your fashion show).

Creating a hashtag for your event This will allow users of Twitter, Instagram and TikTok to search for and post relevant content about your event

Hashtags should be short and easy to remember but also unique to avoid confusion with other events. Once you have decided on a hashtag, use it on anything relevant to the event.

Video promotions and teasers Video content absolutely needs to be part of your social media promotion strategy. Over the past few years, most large events have had some type of video content to share on platforms such as YouTube, TikTok and Instagram. But nowadays, when it's so easy to create simple and quick video content, it's vital for smaller events too.

Video is an excellent way to give your attendees an insider look at what your event is all about and what they can expect to see on the day. For example, giving a conference attendee a sneak peek into this year's speaker sessions and workshops; or giving a festival-goer behind-the-scenes footage and interviews with this year's headline act.

Video teasers are a great way of building anticipation and excitement leading up to an event by gradually revealing important news and updates in the days, weeks or months prior to the event. A tried and tested approach for many event organizers is asking speakers, artists and performers (the stars of the show) to pre-record a teaser trailer to reveal what they're most looking forward to and why.

Peer-to-peer advocacy/customer testimonials Peer-to-peer (P2P) advocacy encourages customers to engage other customers by advocating a product or service (in our case an event) to their friends, family or colleagues. For example, a conference organizer will encourage someone who registers to share the conference details with their colleagues and associates. Often some type of incentive is offered for anyone who can provide a referral or get someone else to sign up.

Testimonials come from real people – real customers who have attended your event and are happy to share their comments with others. Personal recommendations from previously satisfied customers are one of the best ways to convince prospective eventgoers to sign up for a ticket. Video testimonials are one of the most trustworthy forms of testimonial because they serve as 'social proof' to potential customers.

Testimonials come from real people. More than anything, you want people's personalities to shine though. The best way to bring personalities to light is by making the testimonials more conversational. People open up more when they feel they are having an everyday conversation. Ask questions designed to make your event attendees feel they are having an everyday conversation, such as:

- If you were to recommend our event to someone, who would it be and why?
- How would your best friend compare our event to others they have attended?
- How likely is it that they will attend our next event?

Create adverts Most social media platforms offer a way to increase your customer base with paid advertising. You can target your adverts to specific types of people, for example anyone working in the IT sector in your geographic area. More about social media advertising later.

DURING

With your event now taking place, this is your chance to maintain the buzz around your event (particularly important for an event running over several days) and to create a sense of FOMO (fear of missing out) among those who didn't attend, so they're more likely to sign up for a ticket to your next event.

Consider the following options:

- **Attendee live posting:** Attendees will be taking and sharing their own photos and video while the event is taking place, with Twitter being a particularly powerful tool for real-time updates. This immediacy is a powerful tool you have at your disposal to engage with your existing audience and to reach out to a wider audience (your audience's audience). A thank-you post is a simple and often overlooked way to show an event attendee how much you appreciate their attending and telling others about your event.
- **Real-time event updates:** Organizers should consider hiring a professional photographer to allow higher-quality photos being posted on social media, particularly Instagram. For many high-profile business events, it's important to retain a corporate brand image and posting high-quality images will allow your event to be represented better. Make sure you check the restrictions that GDPR imposes and obtain relevant permissions from those being photographed.
- **Display social media posts at the event:** As well as broadcasting what is happening beyond the event itself, consider finding a way of showing and sharing posts between attendees at the event. This can be a particularly effective way of generating questions or discussion at conferences and similar events.

- **Behind-the-scenes footage:** Behind-the-scenes footage offers you a chance to share photos and videos of all kinds of important stuff that occurs in the background of a successful event. Whether it's the backstage crew working hard to set up, the hair and make-up artists making performers look beautiful, the chefs hard at work in the kitchen or the transport team moving guests to and from venues, these behind-the-scenes experiences provide opportunities to share the story of the people behind your event.
- **Live video feeds:** Live-streaming your event is a great way to engage online audiences and draw new viewers to your event. Facebook Live and YouTube Live are both popular choices to stream live video content (e.g. keynote presentations and panel debates) to thousands of followers in real time. Since YouTube is designed as a video platform, users come to YouTube with the intention of consuming video content. By contrast, Facebook offers video as an addition to existing social media activities (updates about what you're doing, sharing interesting photos etc), so users have the option to ignore live video in their news feeds entirely.
- **Fun competitions:** A social media competition can be a highly effective form of engaging with your audience. People love it when they can actively get involved with a competition and use their creativity and humour in order to win prizes. Asking competition entrants to share funny (but relevant) photos from the event is one of the simplest competition ideas and proven ways to boost your social media visibility. Make sure you come up with a unique hashtag that reflects your competition and your event and instruct entrants to use this hashtag in their posts to be in with a chance of winning.

EVENTS MANAGER HACK

Hire a professional photographer to take high-quality photos of your event. The quality of the photographer's images will be picked up on by the target audience as an indicator of the quality of your event, so don't scrimp when it comes to hiring a professional. To make sure you have lots of photographs from your event to share on social media, you need to plan ahead and let the photographer know the shots you need from them and how you plan on using these images. If there are key attendees who must be photographed (headline performers, keynote speakers, VIPs, celebrities, competition winners, sponsors), make sure to point them out to the photographer in advance.

Dan Lomax

AFTER

So many events professionals focus on using social media before their event but fail to realize it's a great place to keep the conversation going after the event is over and done with.

Consider the following options:

- **Follow up with pictures and posts:** As soon as your event is over, you should post pictures, share personal highlights and thoughts about how the event went, give shout-outs to everyone who helped make the event happen and so on. This is a great way of capitalizing on the 'freshness' of your event, and it will help to make sure those people who missed out want to be there next time.
- **Get feedback:** Social media can be a great way of getting quick and concise feedback about how the event has gone. This can be deliberate (e.g. sending a post-event survey) or just a review of comments and discussions that have occurred.
- **Video montage:** As mentioned before, creating video content for social media is easy to do and is well received. After your event ends, collate your best video content as well as videos shared by attendees, and compile these into one video montage designed to showcase the best bits from your event. If your video is any good, your attendees will most likely share it with their social networks, giving your event additional exposure and expanding your network even further.
- **Thankyous:** Thank your social media followers and follow them in return if they have participated in creating a buzz around your event (e.g. entering competitions), build your audience base and make sure you respond to any social media messages directed your way.

Case study 8.1 tells the successful story of cultural history museums in Norway developing their customer base by building new brands and making the most of social media.

CASE STUDY 8.1

Using social media and events to promote the Historical Museum and Museum of the Viking Age in Oslo, Norway

Karoline Dowson, Marketing and Events Manager, Historical Museum and Museum of the Viking Age, Oslo, Norway; UKCEM Graduate, 2012

The Historical Museum, known as Historisk Museum, used to be three separate museums that have come together under one umbrella. It's like a treasure chest. In the museum you will find exhibitions about Norwegian history from the Stone Age to the Viking Age and the Middle Ages. You can experience our rich collection of stave church portals, see one of the only two best-preserved Viking helmets in the world, explore Egyptian mummies and take in our ethnographic exhibitions.

The museum has a unique perspective as our archaeological items tell stories from the past, and our ethnographic items give an insight into the world's cultural diversity, comparing historical perspectives to social issues that we face today, through exhibitions, events and social media channels such as Instagram, Facebook and Twitter. It was very important to make the information and stories accessible to people who are not archaeologists or historians. Each historical object holds the key to so many stories, and we continue to find objects with new stories and perspectives all the time. Our social media posts give people access to these stories.

We started a theme on Instagram called Viking Wednesday. Every Wednesday we posted an object and told the story behind it. It's short and sweet, a fun fact about that object and what it tells us about the time the Vikings lived in. It's evolved now, so we just do the Object of the Week, which isn't only about Vikings but could be an object from the Stone Age or the Iron Age.

The effect this has had on our Instagram is that we have grown from having one account covering both museums with 300 followers, to having one account for each museum with a total of 35,000 followers. Just on Instagram. We also have a Facebook account for each of the museums which grew from having a few thousand followers to a total of 80,000 followers on both accounts.

We decided to make the accounts more focused with a small team curating the posts with a very specific target market in mind. This strategy came about because we researched who was actually following us. Were they speaking English or Norwegian? Were they part of the research community or were they ordinary people interested in history? Because we had only 300 followers, we also looked at who we wanted to follow us, who we wanted to attract to come to the museum. We decided that especially on Instagram, we want it to be easily accessible for people to learn about history, archaeology and ethnography in a really easy and fun way. So followers don't have to sit there and read a lot of complicated stuff. Instead, you see a beautiful picture of an object that really captures your attention. And then you can read a fun fact about that object in one minute or less. And that was very popular.

We wanted to capture both the Norwegian audience and the international audience, so we write posts in both English and Norwegian. The text that comes with the picture comes in English first and then Norwegian afterwards.

Events also play a massive role in how we market both the museums. It's about giving people an occasion to come to the museums – it's not just marketing that gives the message 'come and visit our museum'. When we had a new exhibition, it used to be an exclusive closed opening, with very few people. Now it's a much bigger event that's open to the public, because the opening of the exhibition is a marketing tool for the whole museum as well as for the exhibition. We still do exclusive pre-openings for specially invited guests, but the big opening is for everyone.

The people who come and get excited about the new exhibition will go and tell their friends, and it creates a buzz around the exhibition. The biggest exhibition opening we had was for the new Viking Age exhibition VIKINGR, designed by the famous Norwegian architects Snøhetta. We had almost 4,000 people on Facebook showing interest in coming, but we had to cap it off at 500 for reasons of room capacity.

Our events marketing is mainly through Facebook, because it's easier to follow up there; we create an event, then market it through Facebook and Instagram with an advertising and promotions budget. We found that that if people say on Facebook that they're coming, about half actually do, so we launched free ticketing from the Facebook pages which is more effective; once they sign up through a website, that is a lot more binding, and we also send an email a couple of days in advance, saying that if you can't come because we're fully booked, it would be great if you could cancel, which allows other people to come. That works really well; we get a lot of cancellations, then we open up last-minute tickets for more people to come. A lot of our events are fully booked; before the pandemic, we had 80–90 per cent of our events fully booked.

The popularity of our events comes down to us spending a lot of time thinking about how to make the events relevant and accessible, and fun for people to come to.

We've done 'Night at the Museum' for adults and kids; we switch off all the lights in the museum and invite the visitors to come and explore the museum in the dark with a flashlight. When everything around you is dark and you shine a light on one object, that object becomes so much more amazing. We collaborate with local Viking re-enactors and have actors who dress up to help the history come alive. For young adults and students we've done Fake History Night, which is like a pub quiz with a pop-up bar and music. These events are attracting people who wouldn't normally go to museums. We still have specialist lectures, but they aren't offered to the wider audience. We do a series that we called 'Refleks', where an archaeologist and another speaker use information from history and compare it to issues that we're facing today. We started live-streaming these, because so many wanted to come and we could only seat 80 people. We also started a collaboration with NRK, which the biggest radio channel in Norway; they streamed it there, as well as on our website and Facebook page.

There is a very big re-enactment community with the Middle Ages and the Viking Age in Norway, which hosts lots of festivals, family events, battles and the Viking Games. We collaborate with these communities a lot for our events and have even hosted a festival at our museum. For this audience authenticity is vital – getting the clothes and weapons right when they re-create battles and other events – so they often come to the museums as a source.

Marketing the museum using social media and events has highlighted the importance of having clear branding, clear messages, not overcomplicating things, but simplifying things; you get two seconds when people cast an eye over your post. If you don't capture them in two seconds, you've lost them. Social media has really driven the whole branding process of the museum forward.

Explore further

Museum of the Viking Age www.khm.uio.no/english/museum-of-the-viking-age/ (archived at https://perma.cc/Q24V-AQNM)

Historical Museum www.khm.uio.no/english/visit-us/historical-museum/index.html (archived at https://perma.cc/ZEW3-LH2B)

Instagram and Facebook

@VikingtidsMuseet

@HistoriskMuseumOslo

Social media content strategy

Your content strategy focuses on how you can optimize your content for social sharing to increase the reach and visibility of your event on social media.

Here are the two most important questions to ask when devising a content strategy that's right for your event:

- What makes a piece of content share-worthy in the first place?
- How do we make it easy for people to share content?

CONTENT IS CRUCIAL

No matter what social media platform you're using, the most important thing is to create content that adds value for your audience. Essentially, all social networks revolve around content, whether it is pictures, videos, animations or simply words (refer to the checklist below for different forms of social media content that you can share), but only relevant, meaningful content will grab your audience's attention and gain interest in your event.

CHECKLIST: DIFFERENT FORMS OF SOCIAL MEDIA CONTENT

Event updates	Top tips/ life-hacks
Blog post	How-to guides
Webinar	FAQs
Video	Client testimonials
Image gallery	Case studies
Presentation slides	Quotes
Ebook	Competitions
Whitepapers	Limited time offers

Before you start sharing content, think carefully about the type of information that is useful to your audience. Social media users want to receive information that is relevant and appealing, not just 'spam' that clutters up their social media feeds. To create a community around your event, you need to make it worthwhile for someone to follow you. For example, a live entertainment event could use social media to make announcements when a new artist/performer is confirmed or to give attendees a sneak preview of what's happening backstage. If your social media content doesn't provide any value to your audience, they're unlikely to remain part of your community for long.

This brings us to the question of 'How do you add value through social media content?' It's not our intention, in this book, to address this question in detail.

However, we do offer the following set of questions for you to consider when it comes to creating and sharing valuable social media content with your target audience. While this list is by no means exhaustive, if you're unable to tick at least some of the boxes, you probably need to give more thought to the content you're sharing with your target audience.

CREATING AND SHARING VALUABLE SOCIAL MEDIA CONTENT

Is it helpful?	Is it educational?
Is it interesting?	Is it informative?
Is it entertaining?	Is it inspiring?
Is it exciting?	Is it thought-provoking?
Is it funny?	Is it innovative?
Is it clever?	Is it unique?

Part of the etiquette of using social media is not to be too pushy or salesy. If all that you do is sell, sell, sell continuously, it won't be long before your followers are unfollowing you. The golden rule of content marketing is that only 10 per cent of things you share should be self-promotional (e.g. promotions and offers). The good news is that you don't need to create the other 90 per cent of content yourself. As shown below, the majority of the content that you share (60 per cent) can be cherry-picked from trusted third-party sources. So, for example, a conference and exhibition organizer could pick out the best content that is relevant to a particular industry sector as well as sharing interesting content created by the conference speakers or exhibitors. Sharing third-party content is a very effective and much quicker way of engaging with your community without having to create original content yourself.

THE GOLDEN RATIO OF CONTENT MARKETING: 30:60:10 (RALLYVERSE, 2014)

- Thirty per cent of what you share should be first-party content (original content you created).
- Sixty per cent of what you share should be third-party content (cherry-picked from trusted sources).
- Ten per cent of what you share should be calls to action (e.g. promotions and offers to incentivize sales).

Shareability

Even if you have great content, you can't just sit there and expect people to share it. You need to do something if you want others to share your content.

Below we offer some practical tips on getting more shares on social media, but don't neglect the fact that you need to produce great content so that audiences will find it relevant and appealing and will not think twice about sharing it:

- **Asking for shares:** There's nothing wrong with politely and kindly asking your network (e.g. family, friends, colleagues, associates) to share your social content with their network. But only ask if you're willing to do the same favour for them.
- **Tagging users:** Tagging is when you mention someone in a post or comment. When you tag someone in your posts, the person included receives a notification about that post and hopefully will read and share it too.
- **Adding share buttons:** You can add social media sharing buttons to every piece of content you create, making sharing even easier. Putting share buttons at the top of the page is ideal because they're visible and obvious.
- **Using visuals:** Just like we said earlier, people are drawn to visually appealing content, and as a result, posts with photos and videos receive more shares. Remember to check for permissions!

Social media advertising

Having warned against being overly salesy when it comes to using social media to engage with your audience, there are, however, certain situations when directly advertising on social media can go a long way to growing your audience and engagement. You should consider using social media advertising when:

- Your event is new with no established social media community.
- There isn't enough time to create valuable (share-worthy) content before the event.
- There aren't enough people to create and share valuable content.
- Your promotional budget won't stretch to other forms of advertising (social media advertising is relatively inexpensive).

You can advertise on nearly every platform and the process of creating an advert is, in fact, very similar.

This process typically involves the following steps.

STEP 1 – CREATE A SPECIFIC CAMPAIGN

Each platform provides options including things like a website clicks or conversions campaign (i.e. signing up for a ticket), a followers' campaign (i.e. growing your online community) and a post-engagement campaign (i.e. more people reading your content).

STEP 2 – CHOOSE YOUR TARGET AUDIENCE

There are lots of different targeting criteria to choose from. Demographic variables such as age and gender are fairly standard methods to target audiences and tend to work in the same way regardless of the platform. Most platforms offer more niche targeting options. LinkedIn, for example, allows you not only to target users by specific industries but also to limit your target audience to users with specific job titles, job seniority or job skills.

STEP 3 – SET A BUDGET

The two most common methods are setting an average daily budget for your campaign or setting a total budget for each campaign.

> EVENTS MANAGER HACK
>
> Retargeting is a highly effective tool that targets your adverts on Facebook to people who have already visited specific web pages but not others. So, for instance, an event organizer might run a retargeting campaign on Facebook for people who have already visited the event homepage but then didn't sign up for a ticket. Facebook retargeting allows you to follow up with the people who have already shown an interest in your event and to remind them how great your event is and why going to your event is the right decision.
>
> *Dan Lomax*

Traditional media

Before the advent of social media as a promotional tool, event planners were faced with the following choices to communicate with audiences to make them aware of an upcoming event and how it might benefit them:

- advertising
- sales promotion
- personal selling
- media publicity
- direct marketing.

While social media has had a huge impact on the way we promote our events, the traditional promotional techniques listed above still play an important role in drawing in the crowds.

Below are some things to think about to ensure that your overall promotional campaign does not overlook the advantages of traditional promotional tools.

Advertising

Advertising is any paid form of communication designed to influence the target audience. Ultimately, the purpose of an advertising campaign is to generate a positive (or buying) response from the target audience (both existing and potential customers).

Advertising plays a particularly important role in new events, where no previous attendees or event community exists. For example, every summer brings a new crop of music festivals to join the long-established festivals on the UK summer festival scene, and festival organizers must entice people to attend to make their event viable. In this situation, it is usual to set aside a large proportion of the budget (and time) on advertising activities as, essentially, you are starting from scratch.

Advertisements for events can be found in many different places, including:

- national newspapers
- local newspapers
- local what's on guides
- glossy magazines and brochures
- trade magazines and publications
- television commercial breaks
- local radio
- national radio
- cinema screens
- banners on websites
- pop-ups on search engines (e.g. Google ads)
- pop-ups on online videos (e.g. You Tube)
- social media advertising
- billboards, posters, and leaflets
- buses, taxis, and aeroplanes.

The AIDA model originated in the world of advertising and serves as a helpful checklist to aid the production of an effective advertisement:

A: Grab ATTENTION, e.g. with a catch headline or powerful image.

I: Gain INTEREST, e.g. by outlining the benefits of attending.

D: Create DESIRE, e.g. using a time-limited promotional offer.

A: Instigate ACTION, e.g. including a 'click here' button.

Which advertising medium to use largely depends on the target audience (e.g. what TV channels they watch, what social media they are using, what they read, listen to and so on) but also how much you have available to spend on advertising in the promotional budget. The biggest disadvantage of advertising, compared to other promotion avenues, is the cost. Prime-time television advertising is no longer the draw it was, with the availability of subscriber channels, and this has reduced costs from the region of £200,000 per 30 seconds, not including production costs which can be far greater, depending on content. A 30-second advert slot during the last-ever *Friends* episode cost a staggering$2 million – still the most expensive ever in the UK (Day, 2003).

While advertising can often be an expensive promotional method, there are different advertising rates to suit different budgets. Most top magazines and publications for event planners, for instance, will offer full, half, quarter and eighth page advertising rates (see Figure 8.3). Cheaper rates are also available depending on where the advert is positioned in the magazine (front-page adverts are often the most expensive). When it comes to online advertising, running Pay-Per-Click (PPC) campaigns can work well when wanting to keep costs down.

EVENTS MANAGER HACK

Don't underestimate the importance of putting up posters and handing out flyers as low-cost and *effective* ways of advertising your event. When it comes to designing your poster (or flyer), it is easy to get carried away with making it eye-catching. However, don't lose sight of the end goal of your poster: to promote your event. Do not forget to include the *basics*, such as name of the event, date and time of the event, location of the event and where to buy tickets, and remember to double- and triple-check spelling and grammar before sending files to print.

Dan Lomax

FIGURE 8.3 Standard advertising sizes in magazines

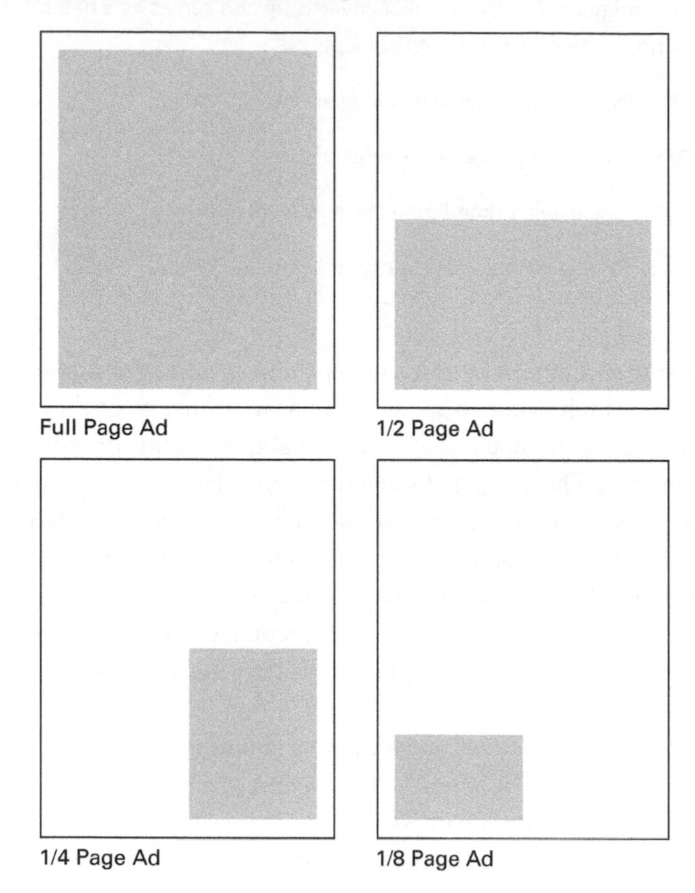

Sales promotion

In order to help event organizers increase ticket sales, a commonly deployed ticketing strategy is offering sales promotions and incentives. Incentives and offers used to sell tickets come in all different shapes and styles. But these are not very different from the promotional offers you find on the high street. We have listed some examples below for you:

- Discounted prices
- Money-off vouchers
- Buy-one-get-one-free (BOGOF)
- Free gifts
- Competition entry
- Loyalty schemes
- VIP packages.

In order to create the desired effect (i.e. a spike in sales) it is also important that any promotion is time-limited. eBay and Groupon are two excellent examples of successful online businesses built on the concept of time-scarcity. It seems that our basic human instinct simply won't allow us to miss out on a great deal, thus creating the urge to act quickly to avoid disappointment.

Sales promotions and offers can be used in different ways, making them an extremely versatile promotional tool. Some promotions may be designed to tempt new customers to give an event a chance, others to reward loyal customers (e.g. by offering early-bird ticket prices for existing customers) and some to give ticket sales a much-needed boost with the event only days away (e.g. last-minute offers). Sales promotions work particularly well when combined with advertising, with the offer (or deal) providing the central message for the advertisement.

Customers taking advantage of sales promotions and offers are generally required to give something in return (surely one good turn deserves another). Typically this will involve handing over their contact details (email, telephone or address) which, of course, means that next time around it is much easier for you to tell them about an upcoming event.

There are, of course, drawbacks to using offers and incentives as a means of promoting an event. Event planners need to be careful not to be seen to give away too much too cheaply. A cheap deal on tickets is certainly not a suitable tactic for a luxury event that offers attendees a touch of glamour, style and sophistication. In this case, a BOGOF offer will only serve to cheapen the event and is more than likely a turn-off for potential event attendees. And, of course, with offers and incentives being time-limited, the effectiveness of any promotion is only short lived. This short-term orientation may sometimes have a negative effect on the long-term future of the event.

EVENTS MANAGER HACK

Approach sponsors and other partner organizations to provide gifts and giveaways for competitions in the build-up to an event. This will help you to generate excitement ahead of the event and is also a great promotional opportunity for sponsors and partner organizations. In return, you could give them some free tickets for their customers. A win–win! (But check GDPR requirements first!)

Personal selling

Personal selling involves person-to-person contact whether it is face-to-face or via a telephone conversation. There are no glossy brochures, no competitions and gimmicks, no publicity stories; just good old-fashioned person-to-person selling (i.e. asking for the business). In a sense, person-to-person selling is what all other promotional activity leads up to, with selling positioned at the sharp end of any promotional activity – the act of moving a potential customer to an existing customer (often referred to as closing the sale).

Personal selling tends to be more prominent in the business-to-business (B2B) events sector where it remains the norm to call potential attendees during business hours to let them know about an event. Personal calls and visits are also commonly used to sign up exhibitors for large trade shows and exhibitions. However, the rise of the *pop-up* phenomenon (there are pop-ups for everything now) has made it trendy to target new audiences in pop-up locations on high streets and in shopping centres, giving a new lease of life to personal selling in the business-to-consumer (B2C) sector.

The *art* of selling is sometimes overlooked by those responsible for promoting an event. Not to put too fine a point on it – without selling, there are no attendees, and without attendees there is no event. An experienced salesperson knows the value of a pre-prepared script to help them deliver a succinct sales message (i.e. why the event is relevant to the person) and also that anticipating customer objections will help prevent them from becoming flustered.

Media publicity

Having a third party publicize your event – newspapers, magazines, radio stations and television channels all run features about upcoming events – gives it more credibility than if the same information was presented in an advert. And, better still, it won't cost you any money!

It all seems too good to be true...

The downside of promotional messages delivered by a third party is that you lose control of the message content. Whoever said that there is 'no such thing as bad publicity' obviously didn't work in events. Bad publicity is hardly likely to encourage someone to purchase a ticket or register to attend an event.

To help ensure favourable media coverage for your event, you need to master the art of the press release. When it comes to writing a press release, you're facing a tough crowd (journalists). Many journalists get a lot of press releases every day. You have to make their job as easy as possible for them. The following checklist gives 10 top tips to keep in mind when preparing your next press release.

CHECKLIST: PREPARING A PRESS RELEASE

- All the important information is included in the first couple of sentences – think Five Ws!
- A catchy headline is used to grab the reader's attention.
- Relevant facts and figures are provided to back up the story.

- Relevant and interesting quotes are used to flesh out the story.
- A clear and prominent 'call to action' (e.g. do you want readers to buy a ticket?).
- Use simple language, keep sentences short and avoid jargon.
- Check the press release for typos and grammatical errors and then check again!
- Photos bring a story to life, so always include one or two high-resolution digital images with your press release.
- Include all of your contact information (name, telephone, mobile, email and postal address).
- Find out the newspaper or magazine's deadline and get the press release done and sent out.

Simply telling your media contacts that an event is happening isn't necessarily newsworthy. All good stories need a hook and it is the particular hook (or angle) that makes the story newsworthy. Different media sources will have different ideas about what is newsworthy. The skill is matching a story (or more precisely the hook of a particular story) with an appropriate media source and subsequently their audience.

The checklist below includes 10 questions to help you determine if your event is newsworthy. If your event ticks one or more of the boxes then we would recommend contacting the media.

CHECKLIST: IS YOUR EVENT NEWSWORTHY?

- Will there be a large number of people attending?
- Will any high-profile individuals be at the event?
- Are there a large number of people participating?
- Is the event happening locally?
- Will the event attract large numbers of tourists?
- Is your event taking place on a memorable date or special occasion?
- Does the event coincide with any other newsworthy events that are happening?
- Is the event in any way considered controversial?
- Does the event offer the opportunity for a human-interest story?
- Will there be an opportunity for good visuals (e.g. pyrotechnics display)?

Direct mail

When planning a promotional campaign for an event it is easy to focus on attracting new attendees, but it is equally important to remind previous eventgoers about the benefits of the event. This is where direct mail (including email) has an important part to play. Direct mail campaigns remain the cornerstone of many events' promotional campaigns, particularly within the corporate events sector. Many of the large corporate shows still rely on direct mail-outs to deliver 'save the date' teaser cards, personalized invitations, complimentary tickets and important updates to generate the largest number of registrations.

By definition, direct mail travels directly doorstep-to-doorstep from the event organizer to the target customer; but perhaps email-to-email is a more accurate description nowadays with an ever-increasing number of email campaigns. Email is a cheaper alternative to direct mail letters, postcards and other promotional items. Not only can online messages be delivered cheaply, but you also benefit from being able to track your campaign successes and failures easily (feedback can include email bounce, open and click-through rates), perfect for honing future campaigns.

There are several factors that all email marketers should consider when creating an email campaign as part of their promotion strategy. The checklist will help you to improve your email marketing success.

CHECKLIST: CREATING A SUCCESSFUL EMAIL CAMPAIGN

- Your event (or company) name must be clearly stated in the domain name, which appears in the 'sender' line of the email.
- Don't use the CC or BCC fields. Personalized emails have a much better open and response rate. Emails using CC or BCC often end up in the 'spam/junk' folder.
- Give your email a professional look by adding your event or company logo.
- Make good use of the top two to four inches of your email, which is the prime reading space.
- Don't overload recipients with too many messages. Keep the body of your message short and scrolling to a minimum.
- Make both images and text clickable. Clickable links should send recipients through to a purpose-built landing page (e.g. registration page) to convert click-throughs.
- Don't send large attachments and images that may clog the recipient's inbox.
- Provide recipients with a clear way to contact you for more information.
- Provide recipients with clear instructions on how to unsubscribe from future mailings.
- Don't forget to test your email campaign before you send it out.

Direct mail is sometimes referred to as database marketing. For many events, a list of past attendees can be easily obtained. To a large degree, the success of a direct mail campaign is reliant on having an up-to-date list. If customer names, addresses and emails are out of date then direct mail is unlikely to prove to be an effective promotional activity. One of the best ways of maintaining an accurate, up-to-date customer contact list is by enticing customers to sign up for discounted tickets, free gifts and competition entries in exchange for their contact information.

Promotional schedule

Timing is one of the most important factors in a successful promotional campaign. Start too soon and people won't be ready to consider attending, start too late and their diary is full.

FIGURE 8.4 Promotion campaign calendar template

Promotion Campaign Calendar												
	Jan	Feb	Mar	Apr	May	Jun	Jul	Aug	Sep	Oct	Nov	Dec
Social Media												
Facebook												
Instagram												
Linked-In												
Twitter												
YouTube												
Tik Tok												
Advertising												
Radio / TV												
Print Media												
Online Media												
Publicity and PR												
Press Releases												
Blog Posts												
Direct Mail and Advertising												
Email Campaign												
Flyer Campaign												
Direct Mail												

Creating a promotion calendar is an effective tool to help you plan and stay on top of your promotional activities. There are different ways to set out the layout of your promotion calendar. Keep it simple. Figure 8.4 provides a simple template to get you started. This can be easily amended to suit your specific needs.

CHAPTER SUMMARY

- All events require some sort of promotional activity to generate a buzz ahead of the event.
- Before launching a promotional campaign, it is essential to determine the intended target audience and exactly what it is you want to say to them.
- Combining psychographic with demographic data will significantly improve your understanding of the target audience, giving you a much clearer picture of the typical attendee and their motives for attending.
- One of the most common mistakes that many event promoters make is to create social media content that is too sales oriented. Your goal is to make sure that your content is share-worthy.
- Using influencers to spread the word about an upcoming event not only helps increase reach and visibility but can also be more persuasive than messaging straight from the event organizing team themselves.
- Social media is increasingly used to promote events, but the more traditional methods (e.g. advertising and direct mail) still have an important role to play.
- The level of promotional activity for an event will vary but drawing up a promotional plan in the lead-up to your event is advisable.

Questions for reflection

1. How can you integrate social media into your event marketing plans?
2. What are the disadvantages of relying on social media for event promotion?
3. How will you research and select the communication channels that fit your event's target market?

References

Chartered Institute of Marketing (2009) www.cim.co.uk/ (archived at https://perma.cc/5B3L-QPSY)

Day, J. (2003) 'Single ad slot in Friends finale costs $2m', *The Guardian*. Tuesday 13 May 2003 www.theguardian.com/media/2003/may/13/broadcasting.advertising (archived at https://perma.cc/PS5Z-REU8)

Rallyverse (2014) www.slideshare.net/Rallyverse/the-golden-ratio-for-social-marketing-part-ii-how-do-marketers-mix-their-content-in-practice (archived at https://perma.cc/WMT6-GQRL)

Williams, R. (2014) *The Non-Designer's Design Book*, 4th edn, Peachpit Press, Berkeley, CA

Explore further

Eventscase Blog (2022) Social media management in the event industry https://eventscase.com/blog/social-media-management-in-the-event-industry (archived at https://perma.cc/48YZ-JKYV)

09

Finance, budgeting and procurement in events

FIGURE 9.1 The Dowson, Albert and Lomax Event Planning Process – event finance

PHASE 2 Detailed Planning and Design
Finance
OUTSOURCING
BUDGETING
FINANCES
INCOME
PURCHASING & PROCUREMENT
FUNDRAISING

If the first task of an event organizer is to identify the objectives for a specific event, it is clear that without a good understanding of the extent and sources of income and details of anticipated expenditure, an event is destined to fail. Whether through sponsorship, ticket sales or advertising, financial resources may be obtained from outside the client organization as well as from within. Resource requirements must be identified at an early stage in the event management process. In this chapter, we explain how this can be achieved, providing examples with relevant and useful tools, techniques and templates.

By the end of this chapter you will understand:

- decision making to provide in-house or outsourced events management elements;
- budgeting and forecasting event finances, cash flow and break-even;
- managing event finances;
- purchasing and procurement of suppliers;
- a range of financial issues that need to be considered in events.

A key aspect of event evaluation includes an analysis of the costs of the event. The more detailed and specific your objectives are in developing the event – including its intended purpose and expected outcomes – the more likely your organization is able to work out whether an event has been worthwhile – and perhaps whether it might be repeated. The financial aspects form part of these important measures. All too often, an event takes root in the mind of an individual, without a realistic assessment of the potential costs and benefits of the activity. This not only includes costs paid out by the event organizer or client company, for example hiring a venue, but it should also include an accurate valuation of less visible internal costs, such as staff time and measuring the negative impact on the organization's brand or reputation if the event fails. Chapter 11 covers evaluation more fully.

Outsourcing

With any event, one of the decisions you will need to make is whether you can or should use the resources you have within your own organization, or whether there are some resources you need to obtain externally. This could include sourcing a venue for the event, sourcing a range of service suppliers (such as audio-visual equipment and technical support), or finding help with creating and managing the event itself, from advance planning to on-the-day delivery. The box describes what outsourcing is and its benefits.

OUTSOURCING

Definition: Outsourcing is the transfer of an organizational function to a third party.

Why outsource?

Cost – outsourcing can be more cost-effective than outright purchasing; this is discussed in more detail in the following sections.

Time – in the tight timescales of events management, combined with the peak of the pulsating nature of events that requires a bigger workforce on-site, there isn't always the luxury of time to deliver all the different aspects within the resources of one company.

Expertise and specialist equipment – supplier companies may provide a range of skills, knowledge, experience and/or specialist equipment and facilities that are not needed within the company on a full-time basis, so buying in these resources as needed makes more efficient use of financial resources.

Risks – bringing in expertise spreads the burden of responsibility and reduces the overall risk to the event. Each supplier is responsible for undertaking risk analysis for their specialist area.

Quality – using specialist resources – whether people or equipment – enables the event management team to deliver a higher-quality event experience.

(With thanks to Simon Bell, UKCEM for inspiration)

If you are participating in or sponsoring someone else's event (such as the Wimbledon Lawn Tennis Championships, for example), you will need to consider how best to use the opportunity to meet your objectives as well as retaining a level of control. It may be easier to purchase corporate hospitality tickets for a well-known event than manage an event of your own, but controlling quality, information and communication is then out of your control, and the resulting experience is no longer unique.

So, in considering the benefits of outsourcing versus delivering an in-house event, it is important to identify the potential costs involved. However, outsourcing an activity does not make the cost problem go away, as considerable time is spent in managing the relationship with the outsourcing provider. Most events organizations will choose to outsource at least some of the services required for an event, and this leads to what can become a complicated web of in-house/outsourced relationships and communication. One option is to retain the majority of the event management process in-house, which may be done by recruiting new staff with relevant events skills and experience. Other resources can then be outsourced to key suppliers.

Outsourcing key suppliers

When outsourcing key event support services, there are potential issues that need to be resolved:

- understanding the organizational procurement and finance processes and policies (including deposits and advance payments, where required), and agreeing processes for confirming variations between the purchase order amount and the final invoice;
- timescales for processing of purchase orders and payment of invoices;
- authority to sign off budgets;
- identifying all the different support services needed to deliver the event, and deciding which can be provided in-house and those that must be outsourced.

A key consideration in outsourcing is whether equipment should be purchased and owned by the organization itself, or hired direct from a supplier. If equipment is to be purchased outright, it is recommended that two sets will be needed, to provide backup and logistical cover for multiple events. Estimating the costs of the two options (purchase or hire, excluding VAT) will help you to make that policy decision.

However, organizations may still choose to hire equipment, despite the likely higher costs, if they lack the appropriate technical support to maintain equipment and deliver a quality service. The likelihood of equipment becoming obsolete should also be considered, as the pace of technological change is inevitable. This shifts the risk of technical obsolescence to the supplier.

The actual cost of in-house delivery can be substantial but is often invisible, as resources (such as staff) can be spread across a range of activities. However, once a professional events team is in place, it can provide support to numerous events. If additional projects emerge, an in-house team can be increased in size to meet the extra capacity as needed. The cost of outsourcing such a capability is likely to be much higher (our own experience is that the cost could be in the region of six times higher to outsource), but outsourcing has the flexibility of enabling costs to be monitored more effectively on an event-by-event basis, as well as providing events expertise that may not be available in-house. Some organizations – particularly in the public sector – have restrictions on allowable headcount, so outsourcing is often used to get round this 'problem'.

There are substantial risks associated with the assumption that anyone can run an event. The stress caused to inexperienced and unqualified individuals, and disruption to organizational workflows, can be devastating, with resulting risks to (individual and organizational) reputation – all with financial implications.

Budgeting

It is unlikely that the events manager will know exactly how many people are due to attend until the day itself, so managing numbers accurately and keeping historical data on booking trends, ticket sales and no-show rates is vital. Even if the event is cancelled, there are still costs involved that need to be recorded and justified.

A 'comments' column in the budget spreadsheet helps to explain the rationale behind any decisions or changes, such as small incidental costs added to each event. Once you have run an event or a series of events, it is worthwhile reviewing all the different types of expenditure and the amounts, so you can amend your spreadsheets for the next time. Make sure you consider whether an item is really a one-off, or whether it is possibly going to recur. Also be aware of the high costs charged by many venues for 'incidentals' such as photocopying.

If an event is part of a series, it is important not only to review the cost of each event, but also to be aware of the overall costs of the event series as a whole. This is because it is very easy for incidentals and new costs to creep in on one event and then continue without challenge, which means that small amounts can add up to become much larger ones (especially incidentals), so accurate records are vital.

EVENTS MANAGER HACKS

An event budget is your friend, not your foe, for it can often provide reasoning behind decisions or changes made during the planning process, which is advantageous when reporting to the event stakeholders. From reporting to evaluating success, your budget is a useful tool to reflect upon and inform future events.

Selina Arnall, Event and Marketing Manager, That Event Girl; Social Traders, Australia

Don't rush building your event budget. Consider every factor of your event and what will be required to deliver it. An accurate budget is the start of your operational plan for your event. A table may cost £5 to hire, but how will it get there and back? Who will put it up and dress it? And how much will all this cost?

Tim Collett, Managing Director, WRG a Division of The Creative Engagement Group; UKCEM Graduate 2002

Table 9.1 shows an example budget for a series of half day workshops.

TABLE 9.1 Budget for an event series

Total budget:	£125,000.00	Based on anticipated numbers of 100 (lunchtime/ afternoon session) + 50 (evening session) × 11 dates		
	Projected	Revised	Actual	
Room hire	£15,664.34	£14,660.82	£14,736.13	
Lunch	£16,435.50	£8,689.94	£8,429.89	Changed finger buffet to brown bag lunch
Staff meal	£0.00	£2,031.25	£1,721.31	
AV	£31,978.70	£32,035.20	£30,675.70	
Teas & coffees	£4,318.50	£3,377.80	£4,340.69	
Staging	£0.00	£555.45	£555.44	
Bed & breakfast	£5,871.80	£4,240.30	£4,163.85	
Speakers' expenses	£0.00	£0.00	£1,014.20	
Courier	£0.00	£0.00	£1,275.79	
Incidentals	£0.00	£1,337.40	£1,596.90	

(continued)

TABLE 9.1 (Continued)

Total budget:	£125,000.00	Based on anticipated numbers of 100 (lunchtime/ afternoon session) + 50 (evening session) × 11 dates		
	Projected	Revised	Actual	
Contingency	£0.00	£0.00	£6124.70	Venue cancellation charges – venues not used
Running total (Net)	**£69,950.34**	**£66928.16**	**£74,634.60**	
Vat @ 20%	£13,990.07	£13,385.63	£14,926.92	
Running total (Gross)	**£83,940.41**	**£80313.79**	**£89,561.52**	
Underspend	£41,059.59	£44,686.21	£35,438.48	

A key challenge in compiling an accurate budget is that for a longer event there will be some people who dip in and out of the event at different times. As a result, you don't want to pay for all the elements of the event for those who aren't attending the whole event.

The example in Table 9.2 shows a complex two-day conference, which has 130 participants (including the events team and speakers) staying overnight at the venue. However, 50 attendees don't stay overnight because they live locally, but they do join the group for dinner, so you are charged the day delegate rate (DDR) plus the cost of dinner for this group. One way of minimizing costs for an event like this is to reduce the number of 24-hour and DDRs booked and add in extras such as room hire and refreshments.

It is well worth the commission they receive from the venue to use the expertise and contacts of a reputable venue search agency. It will negotiate on your behalf to obtain the best financial agreement for your event. Not everyone finds negotiation easy, so using an external company can help you to minimize unnecessary costs. What you save here could be used for another event.

Rather than just accepting the DDR or 24-hour rate quoted, if you have some attendees at your event for part of the time, or as non-residents, consider whether it is worthwhile splitting up the costs into different headings, thereby paying for what you have used, rather than assuming thateveryone is there all the way through an event. For example, many people leave events early – say, if they have a long journey back home – and it is possible to calculate the proportion of teas and coffees you won't need at the end of the day. Table 9.2 shows an example budget for a complex two-day conference.

TABLE 9.2 A complex two-day conference

Event name: Venue			
Dates:			
Total budget:	£70,000.00		
	Unit cost	Qty	Total
Room hire (Suite A)	£2,978.72	1	£2,978.72
Room hire (Suite B)	£4,680.81	1	£4,680.81
Room hire (Suite C)	£1,276.59	1	£1,276.59
24hr rate	£221.27	130	£28,765.10
Day delegate rate	£59.57	50	£2,978.50
Evening dinner	£34.04	50	£1,702.00
Tea & coffee	£3.20	200	£640.00
Tea & coffee	£3.20	40	£128.00
AV	£10,376.00	1	£10,376.00
Contingency			
Running total (Net)			**£53,525.72**
VAT @ 20%			£10,705.14
Running total (Gross)			**£64,230.86**
Over/Under budget			£5,769.14

Budgeting considerations for event cancellation decisions

Many events are cancelled prematurely in an effort to save money, due to low take-up of event places. However, before making any final decision about cancelling an event, it is advisable to consider the full cost implications of such a decision. Whatever the reason for cancelling an event, it is often worthwhile continuing with an event booking, as once a contract is signed, 100 per cent of the invoice will have to be paid out to companies such as the venue and caterers, on the basis of these signed contracts. It is also important to consider the possible negative PR aspects of making cancellations, including the views of potential attendees and media coverage about wasted money, especially in the public sector. A worked example of costings for a cancelled event demonstrates that the actual cost savings are minimal and restricted to certain areas. It should be noted that the AV cost-saving is more due to the kindly nature of the AV supplier, who would have been within their rights to adhere to the contract, or at least charge a cancellation fee.

In reality, once the contract is agreed (not necessarily signed, as verbal agreements can be binding), you are liable for up to the full amount, whether the event goes ahead or not.

But if you do need to consider cancelling your event (due to low take-up, for example), always check the impact on your budget first, as cancellation charges may be higher than you thought (Table 9.3). Consider negotiating with your venue about rearranging your event, as this can be a cheaper option. Also remember that people often buy tickets at the last moment, so study the trends from previous events.

Responsible finances

Planning an event can be a complex process, not just in terms of logistics but in managing the event finances, such as deciding who will pay for what – and in some cases, who is **able** to pay for specific elements. For smaller events, the bill can be handed over to the one client, a simple task. When several organizations collaborate to host an event, their internal politics and circumstances add layers of complexity to the decision-making process, such as policy restrictions, funding limits and corporate governance. Make sure all these elements are clear before you finalize the event's budget.

Managing event finances

It is always useful to be able to provide a logical rationale for each line of expenditure, not only for internal purposes but also for justifying costs to clients. When there are multiple sponsors and a range of stakeholders involved in an event, clear lines of responsibility are even more important for maintaining (or breaking) relationships before, during and after the event.

If one organization has different financial policies or procurement procedures from another, always make sure that you strictly abide by them. It is worthwhile treating all expenditure according to the criteria of the 'strictest' financial guidelines for that project.

TABLE 9.3 Cancelled event – budget

	PROJECTED			ACTUAL		
	Unit cost	Qty	Total	Unit cost	Qty	Total
Room hire	£3,084.38	1	£3,084.38	£3,084.38	1	£3,084.38
Lunch	£8.25	300	£2,475.00	£8.25	300	£2,475.00
AV	£2,839.00	1	£2,839.00	£2,839.00	0	£0.00
T&C	£2.25	300	£675.00	£2.25	150	£337.50
Bed & breakfast	£118.00	5	£590.00	£118.00	0	£0.00
			£9,663.38			**£5,896.88**

> **EVENTS MANAGER HACK**
>
> When negotiating a contract with potential sponsors, make sure you know about any financial restrictions or practices that could impact on the financial aspects of the event.

Income sources

The sources of income for any event are limited. Funding for expenditure comes from three sources: from the client, from sponsorship other than the client, or from ticket sales. Costs can be minimized in various ways before the event, but generated income is what pays the bills afterwards.

The range of sources of income provided by sponsors, ticket sales and exhibitors can be supplemented by advertising income and, for larger events, the sale of media rights.

There are times when the positive impacts of what might be considered an otherwise successful event are overshadowed by disagreements over finances. (This takes the individual calculation of who pays what on the restaurant dinner tab to another level!) In such circumstances the pain is felt for a long time afterwards, and the positive impacts of a successful event may fade once the final financials are known, as the original event partners regret their initial ambitions. Each sponsoring organization may have had many long internal debates as they sought to pay for the event. But it is often the case that partners who end up paying more than they originally bargained for may choose not to do business with the others again.

The complexity of relationships between different stakeholders should be recognized up front in any event planning process, and this is especially true of the financial perspective. In addition, elements of real life may intervene, requiring a total rethink of the plan. Case study 9.1 tells the history of an annual re-enactment event held in London, promoting living history, and the financial challenges it has faced.

CASE STUDY 9.1

The King Charles I Commemorative Parade, London – the financial impacts of public policy on a small community event

Dr Adrian Richardson, Staff Officer, The King's Army of The English Civil War Society; formerly, Principal Lecturer, UKCEM, Leeds Beckett University

Since 1972 The King's Army, an historical re-enactment society of some 600 members, has conducted a parade in central London on the last Sunday in January to commemorate the execution of King Charles I in 1649. Until 2009 the route started outside St James's Palace and several hundred members in authentic military costume marched at funeral pace down The Mall, across Horse Guards Parade and onto Whitehall to parade at the spot of the execution of

King Charles in 1649. The event was very popular with mid-winter tourists, regularly drawing crowds of several thousand at this quiet time of year for the capital's attractions.

Although staged in a very sensitive location in security terms, it was allowed and assisted by the Metropolitan Police, the Royal Parks Department (then part of the Department of Culture, Media and Sport), the Lord Chamberlain's Office at Buckingham Palace, Army Headquarters at Horse Guards and Westminster City Council. The event budget was approximately £2,000, which was met entirely from King's Army members' annual subscriptions. Sponsorship had been sought, but this was of limited success due to Royal Parks' rules which ban leafleting and advertising.

In early 2009, the Metropolitan Police withdrew its direct support, and consequently the English Civil War Society was required to:

- make an Application for Road Closure (£850 at 2009 prices);
- prepare a Road Closure Management Plan (estimated £4,000–6,000);
- arrange for crowd barriers (£400–600);
- engage stewards and a Steward Supervisor (£200–£600);
- hold Public Liability Insurance (in 2009 the King's Army had £5 million of cover, which is now £10 m);
- provide a legal indemnity to Westminster Council – this was problematic as the King's Army is an unincorporated association.

These changes meant that the budget for this event would therefore rise from £2,000 to some £9,500. As a result, the 2010 event was at risk of cancellation, which would have ended a tradition of nearly 40 years. At that time, many small community events in London suffered similar problems where public agencies reduced support or introduced charges reflecting the

IMAGE 9.1 King's Army Parade

impact of recession and then austerity policies in the UK (Webster 2014). Similar issues led to the late cancellation of the Big Green Festival in 2009 due to police concerns (Vidal 2009) and there were licensing issues arising from 2016 incidents (Robson and Clark 2016) that led to the cancellation of the long-running T-in-the-Park festival in Scotland in 2017.

Fortunately for the King's Army and its annual parade, the Royal Parks Department regarded the event as a fixed part of the ceremonial calendar in the capital, so they agreed to permit the event to be staged entirely within their jurisdiction, with the ceremony held each year since 2009 on Horse Guards Parade itself. Royal Parks are no longer a government agency and now function as a charity, and as a result the possibility of charges being levied is currently being considered. Increasing security concerns (the UK risk level for terrorist attack was 'severe' for early 2022) and the matter of Covid-19 have made the event more challenging to organize and run. Although the event could not be held in 2021 when the UK was in lockdown, the King's Army was able to hold a very successful event in January 2022 – the 50th anniversary of the very first parade and the 30th since the author took on its planning and organization.

Read more

The activities of The King's Army and its umbrella organization the English Civil War Society are described here: www.thekingsarmy.org.uk (archived at https://perma.cc/5QQK-JQBE) and www.ecws.org.uk (archived at https://perma.cc/3TQD-NRB6)

For a video of the 2020 event see: www.youtube.com/watch?v=xNGGgfoGIqY&t=5s&ab_channel=BASIL%27SMILITARYBANDS (archived at https://perma.cc/AU3L-KD79)

The 2022 event is described here: www.thekingsarmy.org.uk/whitehall-parade-2022.html (archived at https://perma.cc/L58E-94YN)

Robson, S and Clark, F (2016) *The Daily Record*, Glasgow

Vidal, J (2009) *The Guardian*, London

Webster, E (2014) AIF 6-year Report https://aiforg.com/wp-content/uploads/AIF-Six-Year-Report-2014.pdf (archived at https://perma.cc/28ZV-DBA5)

Cash flow and break-even

A primary reason for the failure of many businesses is lack of cash flowing into the business when it is needed. It is important to ensure that you have enough income to pay the bills as they come in for each event that you manage. To work out the cash flow for an event, first develop an event budget, listing all income and expenditure. In this

EVENTS MANAGER HACK

As a supplier you can check that your client is capable of paying you, using Companies House records (www.companieshouse.gov.uk/toolsToHelp/findCompanyInfo.shtml), before entering into a contractual agreement (or doing any work!). As a client for event services, you can also check the financial background of suppliers.

instance, we have started with an estimated income of £60,000, and included some details for clarity.

A month-by-month cash flow statement can be developed and updated monthly to reflect accurate transaction details. There are examples available in the online resources at www.koganpage.co.uk/ which can provide useful templates that can be adapted for your own use, as well as forming a basis on which to begin a discussion with the client to enable an accurate assessment of the services required and develop a cost.

Case study 9.2 tells the story of a recent events graduate making the most of her learning about event finances to build a company creating vital event supplies – cake!

CASE STUDY 9.2

Baked by Maya

Ivan K Cohen, Ph.D. Associate Professor in Finance and Economics, Richmond University, the American International University in London

Maya became an undergraduate student in 'Creative Events Management' at a university in Cornwall in 2019. One of her passions was to bake: cakes, cupcakes, biscuits and so on. With the onset of the Covid-19 pandemic in 2020 Maya was forced to spend her final year as a student back home in London, learning remotely. The upside to this was that she got to spend a lot more time in her parents' kitchen indulging her passion for baking. Because she liked to post images of her bakes on social media, Maya rapidly discovered there was demand for her baked goods. She set up an account on Etsy (etsy.com) to monetize her creativity.

After graduation in 2021 Maya found herself a full-time job, which limited her time for baking. However, she missed having the time to indulge her creative impulses and decided to branch out and go full-time as a baker. To facilitate the business side, Maya set up a limited company with a registered address for £79.99 +VAT (www.paramountformations.com). This enabled her to issue shares. Maya sold these to family and friends at £100 per £1 share nominal, giving her a small fund of equity capital to develop her business as it expanded. As a limited company 'Baked by Maya Ltd' was able to open a business bank account with a workable overdraft limit.

Originally Baked by Maya offered to provide a variety of cakes, biscuits and other baked goods for individual events, such as family gatherings, parties and so on. She soon found demand for her products from corporate events, primarily through contacts she had made at university and during her full-time job. This increase in demand meant the need to upscale, including finding a more suitable premises than her parents' kitchen. To find new premises required developing a medium-term business plan in order to obtain a small business loan from the bank. Fortunately, Maya knew how to do this having taken such a module during her degree.

While the move to professional premises was not cheap, combined with the need for occasional staff, *some* of these costs were offset by the reduced costs of purchasing ingredients such as flour, sugar and so on in bulk. However, for the first time Maya also needed to account for her own time, paying herself a reasonable salary, although the hope was that in time she would also be able to receive a dividend (share of profits paid to shareholders) as the business grew.

To minimize costs Maya planned to continue marketing via social media, which was almost costless. Combined with word-of-mouth, she was soon able to develop a loyal and regular client base. And while Baked by Maya continued to offer some products through the post via Etsy, the bulk of the company revenues now came from providing for corporate events.

To try to add to their own equity capital, Baked by Maya also hopes to attract funds via sponsorship or, indirectly, through donations of ingredients or packaging from suppliers who would hope to raise their profile in consequence.

Purchasing and procurement

Within events management, organizations rarely have the internal resources to deliver all aspects of the event. As has been said earlier, they often need to outsource (buy in) specialist services, equipment and support from a range of other companies.

Purchasing and procurement terms

- Larger organizations will have specialist functions (even separate departments) to manage the process for outsourcing resources. These may be known as 'purchasing' or 'procurement' teams.
- Purchasing involves the outright acquisition of services, equipment or other goods for monetary payment.
- Procurement includes the acquisition of goods or services in any way, which could include leasing, temporary hire, borrowing or contra-deals (swap).

There are financial implications of corporate and public sector collaboration. Some organizations find it acceptable to provide in-kind services (or contra-deals) to contribute towards a project, but this can complicate the process of drawing up event budgets when a range of different parties are involved, or if they withdraw their support even at an early stage.

The procurement process will depend on the cost of the service being procured, the client and the type of supplier. If there is already a relationship with a potential supplier organization, it may be possible to justify the use of a 'preferred supplier' to the client, perhaps on the basis of previous experience and skills, favourable rates, good working relationships or availability. Alternatively, you may need to obtain several quotes from different companies.

For public sector clients – and increasingly, with private sector clients, as we have said before – transparency is an important factor in procurement, so it may be appropriate to put the business out to tender. For public sector organizations in the European Union there are financial restrictions against which this should be measured (www.ojec.com/Threshholds.aspx). As a rule, it is appropriate to go to tender for projects on which expenditure is less than £118,000/£188,000. The pressures of financial transparency for corporate governance mean that for a service costing about that amount, it would be good practice to issue a tender document. The impact of Brexit means that the EU rules no longer apply to the UK, but there are generally expected to be similar standards in place (unless procuring personal protective equipment (PPE) during a pandemic, in which case it helps to be on good terms with a Member of Parliament or government minister to fast-track approval for your application).

If sustainability is a consideration for the client or for your organization, it might be appropriate to advertise the opportunity locally, to reduce the carbon footprint of the eventual supplier as well as encouraging local businesses. The ITT (invitation to tender) is a formal communication to potential tenderers and can be used to emphasize your own or the client's commitments to current issues such as sustainability and quality, while enabling an equal opportunity to potential suppliers.

Procurement of goods or services for events may be achieved through a range of options:

1. Three quotes: the events manager issues a request for quotes for services, equipment or other goods, to three companies, who will respond with a price and possibly other relevant information, for example delivery date, availability, previous experience. In the public sector, three quotes would be limited to expenditure of up to and around £10,000. Increasingly, private sector companies will use more formal tendering processes for larger purchases owing to the constraints of corporate governance.
2. Tendering process: this is a formal process where the ITT (or invitation to provide a quote) is advertised more formally. In the case of public sector organizations, expenditure above set limits (over £100,000 for event-related purchases, but these

limits vary according to the type of public sector organization) should go through a complex and lengthy official procurement process. There are specific websites (e.g. www.tendersdirect.co.uk) that list the range of tenders currently available. The tendering process is described in detail below.

3 Preferred supplier: once a tender process has been undertaken, an organization may decide to appoint one or more preferred suppliers, with whom they develop an ongoing relationship for supplying specific goods, equipment and services. In smaller companies the process for appointing a preferred supplier may lack the rigour required by public sector and larger organizations, such as using a supplier because your brother-in-law owns it.

Within the tender process, there are four distinct phases:

- **Phase 1: Pre-tender**
  - Set up core team; agree the roles required (e.g. events team, finance, legal); agree the levels of responsibility and areas of expertise required by team members; establish specific objectives for the procurement project.
  - Formulate plan: agree actions, dates, complexity of the tender, the value of the tender.
  - Develop a specification for the required goods, services or equipment and criteria for evaluation, outlining the purpose of the purchase and the shared values required of any potential supplier company.
  - Develop tender documentation: develop and use templates for a common structure; include roles, objectives, instructions to tenderers (examples follow in sections below).
- **Phase 2: The tender**
  - Invitation to tender: examples of documentation are given in the section below.
  - PQQ – for larger procurement processes, there may be an initial stage that involves a pre-qualification questionnaire (PQQ) which enables finance/legal departments to filter out any unsuitable potential suppliers.
  - Initial visit and briefing: this depends on what is being procured. For a venue selection, a site visit is always recommended (see Chapter 5 on location). Particularly for locally based suppliers, the process of managing the ongoing relationship might begin with an initial meeting prior to the selection decision. For larger purchases, there may be the opportunity for potential suppliers to meet and ask questions for clarification about the purchase.
  - Submission of tenders: for legal reasons, in the public sector (and for best practice elsewhere), responses to tenders are kept securely in a locked (or if electronic, password-protected) place, to ensure equal treatment for all submissions.

- **Phase 3: Evaluating the responses**
  - Evaluation of the tender: decide which roles and individuals are required to undertake evaluation (e.g. permanent staff as opposed to contractors). During this process, ensure that professional relationships are maintained, and any bias or prior relationship is acknowledged.
  - Shortlisting: Set up a shortlisting meeting, decide which roles are required to attend.
  - Meeting/interview: if the decision is made to interview potential suppliers, ensure that there are no undue influences on the process.
  - References: feel free to request formal or informal references from organizations with prior experience of working with the supplier. This can range from a set tick-box pro forma to a telephone call.
  - Visit existing sites/customers: if needed you may choose to arrange visits to the supplier's existing customers, but be sure to have a clear purpose for the visit and a means of gathering and giving feedback.
- **Phase 4: Appoint the successful supplier/s**
  - Appoint the preferred supplier: having marked each supplier against specific criteria, add up the scores to compare the ratings. The company that is appointed must be the highest scorer.
  - Negotiate and sign contracts: again, agree the relevant roles with authority to appoint, negotiate and sign contracts.
  - Commence service: this may be the first project of many, or a one-off arrangement, but either way, there needs to be a formal recognition of the start of the relationship.
  - Monitor and evaluate: this may be undertaken by the use of key performance indicators (KPIs), measurable targets, two-way feedback, regular meetings and identified process improvements.
  - Debrief unsuccessful tenderers: this task may be given to the procurement team to ensure a robust process.
  - Ultimately the events management company still maintains overall responsibility for the quality and success of the event and so needs to carefully manage the selection of suppliers and partner organizations. Key to this is having appropriate financial and procurement processes and supporting documentation.

Documentation templates

This documentation for financial management of an event can be built on a solid foundation of openness and transparency, whether internally or between client and supplier. There are example templates available to download with the online resources, which can also provide a useful basis on which to begin a discussion with the client to enable an accurate assessment of the services required and develop a cost.

It is useful to gather the important financial and other relevant information you will need from your client to help you plan the event, and this can form the basis of a Service Level Agreement between your organization and the supplier (or even with the client). The detailed approach helps to identify where responsibility sits, in a clear fashion, so as to avoid assumptions about who is doing what (and the ensuing mistakes). You could adapt it to use with your own suppliers or clients.

Case study 9.3 explains the benefits of using budgeting tools for event businesses.

CASE STUDY 9.3

Technology developments for event management budgeting

Felicia Asiedu, Senior Marketing Manager – Europe, Cvent, UK; Co-founder, Diverse Speaker Bureau

Despite a temporary pause of events at the beginning of 2020, the switch to virtual and hybrid events means the events industry is growing, and event technology teams are increasing their numbers to keep up with the demand. As teams and event complexity grow, event technologists are developing more specialized skill sets.

To be effective in the role, corporate event technologists also need to have visibility into a range of functions within the event department, including budgeting, marketing and reporting, alongside event planning.

Event budgeting in this new era – Excel just won't cut it anymore!

Believe it or not, many pre-pandemic event budgets still lived in Excel sheets manually updated and cobbled together from invoices. These are prone to error and often not as up to date as they should be. With the increased number and complexity of events, event technologists should take advantage of event management software that makes it easier to manage event budgets.

Sophisticated budgeting tools alleviate the pains of tracking funds, recalculating variable costs and monitoring budget surplus. Assuring your budget information is accurately collected results in actionable reporting to demonstrate the ROI of your meetings and seamlessly track savings.

Good event management software enables the following:

- Capture high-level budget estimates per spend category.
- Input or import granular budget line items (rooms, audio-visual, food & beverage, production agency and space, speaker costs, etc) per cost category.

- Track negotiated rates and actual paid against the initial quote to show their return on objectives (Budget vs Actual).
- Design customized budget templates to shortcut the budget creation process and ensure consistency.
- Standardize categories, subcategories, taxes and General Ledger codes to accurately track and report spend across meetings and ensure data integrity.
- Track budget line items in local currencies and establish exchange rates to convert items to a base currency for better reporting.
- Analyse key spend metrics through a robust reporting engine (i.e. aggregate spend by: category, subcategory, event format, vendor, corporate division, geographic location, etc).
- Integrate or transfer your data between event management systems like Cvent and other systems like Concur's Expense module or QuickBooks.

Know your expenses – your expenses help you shape your budget

The explosion of event formats (virtual, in-person, hybrid) has led to a natural increase the use of event technology, production tools and staff. As a result, the cost of running events looks set to rise.

Events remain a great way to engage with customers, partners and prospects. But how to create events that generate the most value for organizations remains a question. How do you price events to entice people to pay the right amount without leaving money on the table?

Although the pandemic has made it more challenging to monetize events, organizations are finding innovative ways to drive value. There are now more opportunities for event planners, technologists and marketers to think beyond ticket sales and recognize the hidden value within their events.

But new models and methods brings some confusion and many questions:

- What kind of registration types should you offer?
- How much should you charge?
- Should you tailor price points for different audiences?
- Can you still make money on free events?
- How can you prove ROI?

To price and ticket your event optimally, you must first define its value – for attendees, sponsors and the organization itself. You can then maximize that value by mapping it to relevant attendee, sponsor and organizational goals. Maximizing value leads to higher ROI for your organization and a more rewarding experience for your audiences.

The procurement process – invitation to tender

Table 9.4 is an example of a template for issuing an ITT for supplying a vox-pop video for use at a conference. It is by no means a perfect example, but the purpose of each section is explained. The potential suppliers should be provided with a written description of the service required – this may be called an 'invitation to tender', a 'brief' or a 'specification'. The more detailed this document is, the more insight the potential supplier will have as to what is required – and a more accurate a costing will be provided in return. However, as events are generally one of a kind, rather than a standard off the shelf, it is possible that these costings will act only as a guide.

There should be a letter with instructions to tenderers with terms and conditions, contractual details and relevant policies, with a response pro forma and timetable for progressing the procurement process.

TABLE 9.4 Template for the event background

AUDIO VISUAL SERVICES (VOXPOP PRODUCTION)	
Event: title, audience	
Venue: venue name & location **Website:** venue website **Please visit the link below for all venue technical specifications should that be necessary:** Venue website link to floorplans	**Event date: date**
Session timings – Date: 09:00–15:30	**Estimated numbers: 450**
Set-up date & time: **Date: 18:00–22:00**	**Return to: Contact details** **Name:** **Email:** **Tel. No.:**
Event background: This conference will be an opportunity to hear how [audience] across England are using [purpose of event] within their roles and how it has benefited them and [other stakeholders]. It will build on the success of the first event which was held on [date]. It will provide delegates with an opportunity to learn more about [organization] and how it will deliver better and safer [purpose], from a [stakeholder] perspective. There will also be an update on the progress which has been achieved over the last 12 months, and an opportunity to see live demonstrations of some [technology] packages. A Q&A panel will provide people with an opportunity to ask questions and provide feedback about their own experiences of using [technology]. An interactive session will demonstrate key areas of the [product]. Speakers at the conference will include [list name/s, role/s and organization/s], who will share their experiences and explain how [product] could have improved their [experience].	

The event background profile in Table 9.4 provides a context for the event and should outline the event's aims and objectives, the target market for the event and the full contact details of the events manager. This section enables potential suppliers to gain an understanding of the level of service required and sets standards that must be achieved to ensure event quality by setting down effective management systems and procedures. The more detail provided about the event, the more accurate a financial quotation will be in response.

Table 9.5 outlines the details of the event and the service required.

TABLE 9.5 Template for the event details and services required

Event details				
Date	**Start time**	**End time**	**Function**	**Room**
01/05/23	09:00	10:00	Registration	Ground floor reception
01/05/23	10:00	11:10	Plenary session	Room A
01/05/23	11:10	11:30	Refreshment break	Lounge B
01/05/23	11:30	12:50	Plenary session	Room A
01/05/23	12:50	13:30	Lunch and exhibition	Lounge B
01/05/23	13:30	15:30	Plenary session	Room A
01/05/23	15:30		Conference close	

Objective of the vox pops

The vox pops will be used to open a [organization] conference which is taking place on [date]; they will be 10 minutes in length. The aim is to capture a range of views from [vox pop subjects] who are now using [products] in their everyday roles. For example [example of product use]; their experiences, and the benefits.

Vox pops	Additional points
The views of [stakeholders] will be gathered using the following sources: [list sources]	• Numbers of days' work anticipated for this piece of work: four • Please note that in order to obtain the information required for the vox pops, extensive travel around the country will be necessary • The vox pops will also need to be produced in the following formats: – DVD – MPEG 1 in 352×288 resolution

Please specify the cost and number of crew, equipment and additional resources needed for this piece of work. This must include editing, both pre- and post-event.

Evidence of similar past video work should be included in your bid for the tender (on DVD or similar).

Please also specify the day rates for crew, equipment and additional resources.

Should you require further information in regard to this tender, please feel free to contact us on xxx xxxx xxxx.

(*continued*)

TABLE 9.5 (Continued)

Eligible companies must meet the following criteria:
Have adequate personal, public and employers' liability insurance
Ensure work is carried out in a safe manner in compliance with the Health & Safety at Work Act 1974
Adopt best-practice procedures and work safely to reduce risk as far as is reasonably practicable
Be prepared to work and liaise with venue Health & Safety officials to ensure adherence to any specific venue requirements
Provide up-to-date risk assessments and method statements to show safe working practice
Ensure staff/technicians are fully trained
All electrical appliances must be PAT tested and certified for safe use
Other requirements:
It is expected that the AV team will be prepared to work unsociable hours in accordance with AV industry habits and the event requirements
The AV director is responsible for members of their team at all times. An assigned technician will be fully responsible while on-site recording the vox pops
Please quote for all above, with all items including options, costed separately

There are three aspects of a specification that will assist potential suppliers reach a better understanding of the service required. These are:

- Specification by function: created within the event planning process, this tells the supplier the purpose of the service – what the service is supposed to do – including resources the supplier should provide for the client, appointing the right person for the right role and completing the project.
- Technical specification: a detailed breakdown of resources, including staff and technical equipment by type, quantity and days needed. It may request additional documentation from the supplier, such as risk assessments, method statements, legal requirements, site maps/floor plans, to assist the tenderer in making the decision.
- Specification by performance: it should include relevant health and safety, ethical, quality and sustainability issues, and address delivery of service, with attention to detail to meet the event's quality standards. Could be stated in terms of performance results and criteria for verifying compliance, such as KPIs. Could identify shared corporate values.

For a fuller description, any specification should include details of the required support service/equipment based on the above three headings. The Purple Guide (www.thepurpleguide.co.uk/) lists all relevant legislation and regulations that can be included in these sections. The guide was written by The Events Industry Forum in consultation with the events industry and the UK Health and Safety Executive. Its aim is to help events organizers to manage health and safety, particularly at large-scale music and similar events.

Costing additional items separately will aid consistency in comparing responses. It is important to agree costing and pricing strategy in advance to ensure value for money and an ability to measure return on investment. Providing a pro forma for responses will aid this clarity.

A process for agreeing changes to the contract should be included to minimize disagreement during and after the event.

Evaluating tender responses

Evaluation criteria can be weighted for relative importance and will enable consistency across different evaluators in selecting potential supplier/s for final negotiations. Sample criteria are listed in Table 9.6.

Below is an example of responses to a tender for AV and vox-pop video that demonstrates the usefulness of a consistent response format. The suppliers are being judged against specific criteria and providing prices against details in an ITT. The different responses from the four companies are compiled within the template to enable a comparison and, ultimately, a decision on the choice of supplier. The responses are split into different sections, listing the equipment, (human) resources, miscellaneous additional costs, discounts and a cost summary.

Once the financial evaluation has taken place, the responses should be rated against the evaluation criteria. These could include a demonstration of an understanding of the requirements, the ability and capacity to meet the event requirements, quality, sustainability and other policies, financial reliability and liquidity of the supplier company, and references.

RESPONDING TO SUPPLIERS WITH THE DECISION

Once the decision has been made, confirmation emails should be sent to the successful and unsuccessful suppliers. Templates are shown in Tables 9.6 and 9.7.

TABLE 9.6 Sample evaluation criteria

Please note that this tender will be evaluated on the following criteria:

- quality
- meeting the specifications
- cost vs budget
- availability
- past experience

TABLE 9.7 Tender responses example

1. EVENT TITLE – DATE – AV TENDER RESPONSES				
Tender ref:				
Item	Supplier A	Supplier B	Supplier C	Supplier D
Laptop	DECLINED	£750.00	DECLINED	£385.00
Wireless remote control		£10.00		Not quoted
LCD projector (main)		£600.00		Only quoted for one – dual screen projection requested £180.00
Projection screen (main)		£92.00		£63.00
Large plasma monitor/screen		£2400.00		£2016.00
Stage set		£1450.00		£1800.00
LCD TFT Floor screen		£100.00		£50.00
VGADA – Signal splitters		Not quoted		Not quoted
Lectern		£80.00		£31.50
PA system		£550.00		£486.50
Radio microphones(lapel)		£250.00		£157.50
Radio microphones (handheld)		£250.00		£157.50
Portable printer for on-site use		£82.00		£45.00
Flipchart stands and paper		£125.00		£52.50
Spare power extension cables		FOC		FOC
Poster display boards		£240.00		£88.00
TOTAL		**£6979.00**		**£5512.50**

2. RESOURCE COSTS	
Company	**Total price**
Supplier A	**DECLINED**
Supplier B	**£2130.00**
Supplier C	**DECLINED**
Supplier D	**£2650.00**
*Double resource costs as only quoted for one day not two	

3. ADDITIONAL COSTS		
Company	**Description**	**Total Price**
Supplier A		DECLINED

(continued)

TABLE 9.7 (Continued)

3. ADDITIONAL COSTS		
Supplier B	£11330.00 included in this cost for vox pops. Additional equipment and transport	£11852.00
Supplier C		DECLINED
Supplier D	£7715.50 included in this cost for vox pops Additional equipment and transport	£10425.10

4. DISCOUNTS			
Company	Discount	Discount %	Total discount
Supplier A			DECLINED
Supplier B		40% equipment 10% set & stage/display boards	£2289.40
Supplier C			DECLINED
Supplier D		30%	£5576.28

5. SUMMARY OF TOTAL COSTS				
DESCRIPTION	Supplier A	Supplier B	Supplier C	Supplier D
EQUIPMENT COSTS	DECLINED	£6979.00	DECLINED	£5512.50
RESOURCE COSTS		£2130.00		£2650.00
ADDITIONAL COSTS		£11852.00		£10425.10
LESS DISCOUNTS		£2289.40		£5576.28
INTERACTIVE SERVICES				
TOTAL COSTS		£18671.60		£18587.60

Evaluated by:

Name	Position	Date
Name	Position	Date

Dear...

Thank you for your AV quote in regards to....

Having considered the various quotes that we received in regard to this event we have decided on this occasion to use another supplier.

If you would like to discuss things further with us please feel free to contact us either by email or telephone.

Thank you once again for taking the time to submit a quote.

Yours sincerely

Events Team
Organization name
Web: www.webaddress.com
Please address event emails to events@organization.uk
Events online: http://eventsonlinesystem.co.uk

Dear [supplier contact]

Thank you for your quote for the above event to be held in [location] this month.

We have reviewed all the quotes and I am pleased to tell you that we would like to appoint [company name] to cover all AV requirements for this event.

We hope that you and your team are still available on less [date]. We will contact you by [date] to go through the finer details. In the meantime if you have any queries please do get in touch with us.

Thank you once again and we look forward to working with you.

Yours sincerely

Events Team
Organization name
Web: www.webaddress.com
Please address event emails to events@organization.uk
Events online: http:// eventsonlinebookingsystem.co.uk

Following this process and using these templates will save time and effort when sourcing suppliers, and enable you to keep financial control more effectively. Further templates are available online.

Fundraising

Many organizations are faced with the challenge of creating and delivering events with little or no budget. For many smaller charities and voluntary organizations, their aim is to raise funds so that they can meet their organizational objectives, so ideas for running events on a shoestring are valuable. With this type of event organizer in mind, we have devised a list of suggestions for fundraising on a budget.

A dozen ideas for saving money on your events:

1 Beg, borrow or charity shop. (Don't steal!) When you've got your list of requirements to deliver your event, find cheaper ways to obtain what you need. Charity shops are a great place to buy all sorts of things – from tablecloths to glassware and crockery (vintage is very on-trend). Try asking your friends, find out what you can borrow, and turn to local online recycling websites (www.freecycle.org/) as well as social media.

2 Use what's included in the venue hire. Try living with the colour of chairs in the room, rather than splashing out on colour-themed chair covers. Use the tablecloths provided.

3 DIY: make your own. Be creative. For a cheap and cheerful wedding reception, buy a bolt of material in the bride's preferred colour (purple), and drape it over the brown curtains of the local village hall. Use the venue's own tablecloths (which had seen better days) and sew your own table covers, which sit on top of the tablecloths, to match the chosen colour scheme. Pre-cook all the food at home and bring in a team of friends to manage the on-site kitchen and wait on tables.

4 Include volunteers in your event staff. We're not by any means recommending that events managers forgo the professionals, but for events on a budget, there are plenty of events management students eager to add volunteering hours to increase their on-site events experience. Contact your local university or college to find out if you can provide some work experience for their events, graphic design, marketing or photography students. And get the professionals in to run the professional events!

5 Avoid peak times. Choose a day or time of year or location that's less popular – you'll find that it's cheaper, too.

6 Go for simpler food options. A brown bag lunch can be healthier (and less sleep-inducing after lunch) than a three-course sit-down meal.

7 Find local sponsors. It's back to 'who do you know?' Visit your friends and the shops on your local high street to ask for donations in kind, or for raffle prizes.

8 Make a budget. Sounds obvious, but make a budget – and stick to it! Don't spend money on things you don't need, double-check numbers are accurate, and control who spends what by making sure different members of the team aren't making spending decisions on their own that mean instead of raising money you end up making a loss.

9 Get quotes. Get more than three quotes (minimum). And haggle. (The professionals call this 'negotiating'!)
10 Use social media to help market your event – but don't rely on it, because it depends who your target audience is.
11 Ask yourself before you buy, 'Do we really need this for our event?'
12 Downsize or rearrange your event rather than cancel. Some venues will be flexible to help keep your booking (but check the terms and conditions of the contract first), so speak to the venue sales team.

In the UK, charities have to abide by the legal and financial constraints imposed by the Charity Commission (www.gov.uk/government/organisations/charity-commission), which also provides guidance and regulations to fundraisers on responsible activities, as well as pointing to other avenues of advice, for example from the Institute of Fundraising (www.institute-of-fundraising.org.uk/home/).

EVENTS MANAGER HACK

Keep track of all spending, it'll save so much time in the reconciliation stage.

Lori Novell, Event Project Manager, The Outlook Creative Group

Case study 9.4 outlines the benefits of a collaborative project between a social enterprise organization and students studying events management.

CASE STUDY 9.4

Wild Rumpus collaboration with Manchester Metropolitan University Event Management students

Janine Priest, Programme Leader and Senior Lecturer, Manchester Metropolitan University; ***Sarah Bird***, Director, Wild Rumpus CIC, UK; ***Katie Aldous***, Talent and Development Manager, Wild Rumpus CIC, UK

Event Management students at Manchester Metropolitan University (MMU) study basic financial management for events as part of their degree programme. This includes topic areas such as budget management, break-even and how break-even point can influence the ticket price for an event, resourcing events and negotiating on costs with suppliers, ensuring adequate cash flow for an event project, and the importance of profitability where making a profit is an intended objective of the event.

With this in mind, second year Event Management students at MMU are assessed with a simulation scenario of planning and costing a one-day family festival. Students are required to design, budget and resource the event, and are invited on a site visit to understand the space they are working with in the simulation task. This type of simulated assessment provides students with a valuable 'practice run' at the financial planning needed for an event. This is an important stepping-stone in their learning journey, as they are required to plan and deliver a 'live' event towards the end of their second year of study.

To help students acquire realistic insights into planning a family festival, industry collaboration is utilized through involvement of event industry professional Katie Aldous, who is Director of Organisational Development and People for Wild Rumpus. Katie's contribution to this project is a guest lecture to the students, to highlight the financial considerations for Wild Rumpus' festival portfolio. The presentation to the students includes key aspects such as desired event outcomes and impact, stakeholder management, costing, cash flow, ticketing and external influences.

Wild Rumpus is a community interest company founded in 2009 initially to run a weekend family camping event, Just So Festival. The aim was to take families outdoors for a creative adventure that would help them connect to nature through high-quality arts and culture. In the first year it attracted an audience of approx. 2,000 and now this award-winning event is capped at 5,000.

As a not-for-profit event the aim was always to break even, so it was established with no initial investment. A budget that allowed for incremental growth was developed and contracts were negotiated to allow for cash flow, with invoices being paid after the event, once ticket money and other earned income had been received.

The budget forecast was developed on a mixed income model, not overly reliant on one income stream (this model has offered extra resilience in recent years when external influences have impacted on the viability of events). Tickets were priced lower than other weekend festivals in the first year to attract people and because it was a family audience, so they were inevitably buying multiple tickets. Under three's were free but children's tickets were charged for as they were 50 per cent of the audience.

The two founding directors established the festival by investing their own time heavily in marketing, PR, fundraising and programming. With a vision for the festival and a very clear picture of the target audience, they built their own website, wrote press releases, designed flyers, wrote blogs, took flyers to places where families spent time and built a strong social media presence.

As families bought tickets the resulting income stream allowed them to buy insurance, hire infrastructure like toilets, skips, staging and audio equipment and to invest in performers.

Other income streams included a grant from Arts Council England, a grant from a local charity, concession income from food traders, bars and glamping, and business sponsorship from companies who wanted to market their brand to a family audience.

Income v Expenditure breakdown:

First year income:

Ticket income 70%

Concessions/Bars/Glamping 10%

Grants 10%
Sponsorship 10%
First year expenditure:
Infrastructure 40%
Programme 35%
Marketing 5%
Staffing 20%

The event has always relied heavily on in-kind support from others. As part of a cultural ecosystem there is a symbiotic relationship with a wide variety of stakeholders, from contractors, media, audiences, funders, volunteers, vendors, artists, community groups, businesses and so on... in order for Wild Rumpus to thrive they need a healthy ecosystem around them.

External influences on income and expenditure fluctuate all the time and the events market can be particularly volatile when working on an annual planning cycle. Expenditure can be impacted by an increase in fuel duty; a change in the VAT rate on tickets; a change of supplier; adverse weather conditions; the insurance market and so on; income can be influenced by competition in the market; shifts in the economic climate; the weather conditions the previous year and so on. It's important for Wild Rumpus to remain flexible and agile in responding to these external influencing factors.

The budget is also heavily influenced by the demographic of the festival-goers. For example, as the entire audience at Just So Festival consists of families, bar sales are dramatically lower than you would find at a festival with a younger demographic.

Wild Rumpus has delivered Just So Festival for over a decade and although the budgets have increased from under £70k in the first year to over £450k by year 10, the percentages haven't changed dramatically.

Wild Rumpus now also produces a range of other festivals and events, education and digital projects as well as artist support programmes from their woodland creation centre in Cheshire.

Key takeaways of the collaborative project

The positive impacts of embedding industry practice into the university-level curriculum are widespread, but most significant is the opportunity for knowledge exchange and the sharing of expert insights through collaborative teaching, providing an overall authentic learning experience. Students have the opportunity to develop their understanding of financial considerations for events and the decision-making process involved. These are essential skills for students to take into the workplace in their future careers within the event industry.

The talent and development programme at Wild Rumpus aims to engage young people in all aspects of their work; being able to talk to students about the community interest financial model was a fantastic opportunity to demonstrate a way of working that is often overlooked. The opportunity to engage and inspire potential entrepreneurs with the message that anything is possible and discussing what measures of success look like for Wild Rumpus was useful in the planning of delivery. Answering questions and being able to share acquired knowledge with the outdoor arts creators and producers of the future was a valued experience that prompted discussion throughout the Wild Rumpus team!

Websites

www.wildrumpus.org.uk (archived at https://perma.cc/8R8W-PD9P)
www.justosfestival.org.uk
www.mmu.ac.uk/study/undergraduate/course/ba-events-management (archived at https://perma.cc/V928-DV8W)

Factors to consider in effective procurement and good financial management for events

The 'AIG effect' was born in 2008, when the American International Group, then sponsors of Manchester United, one of the world's most recognizable football teams, succumbed to the global economic crisis and received $85 billion from the US Federal Reserve (Godwin, 2009). Days later, one of its subsidiaries hosted insurance agents at a luxury California hotel, at a cost of $443,000, and the company was lambasted across the press. The next event it was due to hold was summarily cancelled, beginning a retreat by large corporations from anything remotely luxurious, and sending economic shivers down the spine of the hotel industry around the world, as company after company cancelled their bookings for fear of a press backlash. Years later, questions are still asked of corporations if shareholders – or even onlookers – deem expenditure unwarranted. And it doesn't necessarily mean that a room costs what the rack rate states – many events result in upgraded bedrooms at a fraction of the advertised charge. So – when you run an event – any event – make sure you know why you're running it and how much everything costs. And consider what it would look like if it made it into the press ...

The combination of public sector and commercial involvement indicates a requirement to abide by strict government procurement rules and be sensitive to commercial interests and potential embarrassment in the press.

Factors to consider

For UK public sector bodies, there are significant restrictions on any procurement, and any activity can be subject to requests under the UK's Freedom of Information Act 2000 (FOI) (www.legislation.gov.uk/ukpga/2000/36/contents). In addition, corporate sponsors of specific activities, such as drinks receptions and conference dinners, might pose problems for governance in public sector or charitable organizations. The rule of thumb many public sector organizations operate is: 'would it pass the test of appearing in a national newspaper?' ie would it pass the scrutiny of the harshest critic looking for scandal? Government departments are often subject to negative press articles about events deemed unsuitable by whoever is throwing the first stone, and regularly receive FOI requests from journalists on events-related expenditure.

The Taxpayers Alliance (www.taxpayersalliance.com/), which claims to be 'an independent grassroots campaign for lower taxes', is often the named source of FOI requests, which can, of course, easily be interpreted as 'needless expenditure' by local and national government, and taken out of context.

The 2010 Bribery Act (www.legislation.gov.uk/ukpga/2010/23/contents) recognizes bona fide corporate hospitality or other promotional expenditure as an important part of doing business. However, care (and advice) should be taken when planning such events, whether for public or private sector clients.

When multiple organizations collaborate, higher variable costs that may not be covered by registration or ticket income still need to be paid for by someone; such situations may result in tense negotiations between the key collaborators, to the detriment of their ongoing relationships. This problem is not uncommon and occurs at many events – whether festivals, music gigs, corporate hospitality or even conferences, all can be subject to the idea that 'we have to invite X – but we can't make a charge'. Although music events and festivals often have guest lists, they are not the only ones to face the challenges of long guest or VIP lists and controlling the availability of free tickets can make or break any event. Saying 'no' on the day is not only embarrassing for the guest and the box office crew or registration desk, but it can also ruin customer or client relationships built up over time, in an instant. Another issue that faces many events, and especially large events, is dealing with cash on-site, which requires secure facilities.

The following mini case study shows the importance of measuring financial success in events.

CASE STUDY 9.5

How to measure success: ROI is more than ticket sales

Felicia Asiedu, Senior Market Manager Europe, Cvent, UK; Co-founder, Diverse Speaker Bureau

Many organizations focus on ticket sales as the key driver of ROI, but ticket sales are just one slice of a much larger ROI pie. Cvent has identified five benefits that contribute to event ROI:

- **Direct revenue** – Ticket sales, sponsorships, advertising, merchandise sales, exhibitors, government grants

- **Attributed revenue** – Revenue after the event that was influenced by product demos or interaction with sales staff during the event
- **Attributed sales pipeline** – Leads and opportunities generated at the event that eventually become sales
- **Brand equity** – Attendees' positive experience and impression of the brand as it relates to the event
- **Knowledge exchange** – Information and insight shared between customers, prospects, and the organization

When assessing the full value of your events, you must look at all the benefits they provide to the organization along with the costs. There are many things beyond direct revenue that impact how much money an event will make. It can take time for these to come to fruition, but it's important to include them in ROI.

Structure tickets and prices to deliver the value attendees and sponsors want. Ticket price is not just about calculating costs and adding a profit margin; it's also about how much people want what you're selling. A value-based ticketing strategy finds ways to ensure each buyer's perceived value of the experience equals or exceeds the price they pay.

As we have shown in this chapter, managing finances and procurement processes are not easy tasks for events managers. However, we have included a range of templates in the chapter and online to make this task easier, and we end this chapter with some key points that should be considered:

- Control supplier expenditure by agreed per diem expenses – or cover them yourself (e.g. booking overnight accommodation for on-site staff, including external suppliers).
- Availability and responsibility of staff to sign off against the budget – including from the client side. Make sure you have sign-off from the client for any expenditure you incur, as it may not be possible to claim back unauthorized expenses. Make sure that the staff who are signing off expenditure are authorized to do so.
- Make sure you have the relevant insurances to cover your event, guests, and staff, both on- and off-site.
- Put in place a variation to services agreement as part of the procurement process – to agree changes to the original commission, and costs.
- Agree an advance payments and deposits schedule and check all terms and conditions thoroughly before you sign the contract.
- Agree feedback processes as part of the contract, from your organization to the supplier, and from the supplier to you. Feed back relevant improvements to the client.
- Beware of hidden charges made on the day for last-minute items such as photocopying or internet access.

CHAPTER SUMMARY

- Without a full appreciation of the potential costs of an event, organizers risk not only the failure of the event, but also of the company, whether in terms of finances or reputation.
- Decide whether you have that capacity and capability to deliver the event using in-house resources, or whether you need to outsource.
- Ensure you have a signed-off budget from the client, and that any expenditure is accurately estimated in advance. The complexity of the event will have a direct bearing on the finances of the event.
- Ensure that you abide by financial regulations and company guidelines, as well as planning what you might do in the case of an emergency – always have a plan B and contingency funds in case things don't go to plan.
- Make sure you keep a record of financial aspects, from cash flow to ensuring you are allowed to spend budgets. If you don't manage the cash flow, you could be out of business, no matter how popular the event!
- There are detailed processes to enable you to identify and procure suppliers. We have provided a range of templates and examples that can be adapted and implemented, as well as online resources.
- Valuable models and in-depth discussion of the financial evaluation of events can be found in *Return on Investment in Meetings and Events*, by Jack J Phillips, M Theresa Breining and Patricia Pulliam Phillips.

Questions for reflection

1 What are the sources of potential income for an event?

2 Where can you find information about the regulations that affect charities for their events activities?

3 Why would some organizations choose to outsource some of their event support services and supplies?

References

Bribery Act 2010 www.legislation.gov.uk/ukpga/2010/23/contents (archived at https://perma.cc/D9UP-S27N)

Charity Commission www.gov.uk/government/organisations/charity-commission (archived at https://perma.cc/S732-2KX6)

EU procurement thresholds www.ojeu.eu/thresholds.aspx (archived at https://perma.cc/M2WW-M6CZ)

Freedom of Information Act 2000 www.legislation.gov.uk/ukpga/2000/36/contents (archived at https://perma.cc/D96T-6XRQ)

Godwin, N (2009) Meetings industry struggles to shake off the 'AIG effect', *Travel Weekly*, North Star Travel Media, NJ www.travelweekly.com/Travel-News/Corporate-Travel/Meetings-industry-struggles-to-shake-off-the-AIG-effect (archived at https://perma.cc/JE2T-EQE8)

Phillips, J J, Breining, M T and Pulliam Phillips, P (2008) *Return on Investment in Meetings and Events*, Routledge, London

www.taxpayersalliance.com/ (archived at https://perma.cc/4XW3-ZFEY)

www.tendersdirect.co.uk (archived at https://perma.cc/T8N9-6UAN)

www.thepurpleguide.co.uk/ (archived at https://perma.cc/B6KP-VRGT)

Explore further

Chartered Institute of Fundraising https://ciof.org.uk (archived at https://perma.cc/7SEH-YAZV)

10

A practical guide to managing an event on the day

FIGURE 10.1 The Dowson, Albert and Lomax Event Planning Process – managing the event on-site

PHASE 3 Managing the Event On-site
YOUR RESPONSIBILITIES
BEFORE THE EVENT
DURING THE EVENT
COMMON CHALLENGES
AFTER THE EVENT
WHAT THE SPECIALISTS SAY

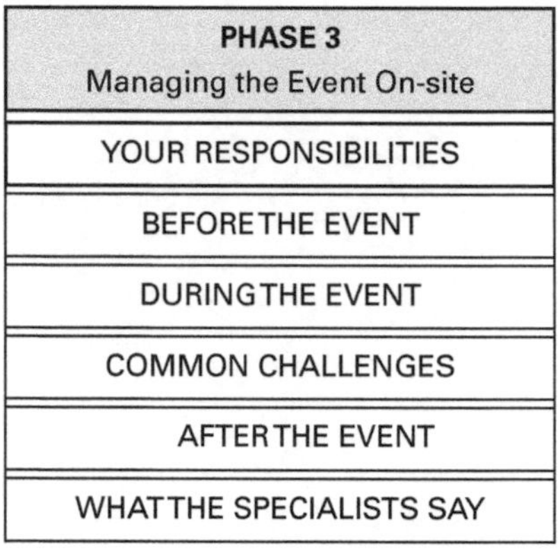

You've put lots of hard work into planning the event (as you've read about in the previous chapters) but now it's time to put your plans into action and make the event happen. This requires a different set of skills compared to when you were planning and organizing the event. Up to this point your role as event planner has benefited from a more structured approach and requires a careful eye for detail, and these are vital to the event's success. But now it's time to get out of your planning 'bubble' and start making things happen by turning your plans into something real and tangible – a necessary skill at this point is innovative and creative problem solving and being able to deal with the things that don't go according to plan!

On-site event management begins when you step onto the event site and ends when you turn out the lights and leave the building – or in some cases, the field. What happens during the delivery of your event often goes by in a flash; time really does fly by with the buzz and excitement when an event goes 'live'. Once you're on-site, even for the most organized of events professionals problems will arise. These need to be addressed in a timely and effective manner; an example could be when suppliers don't arrive in time because they're stuck in traffic, or staff call in sick, or guests have lost their luggage. As an events manager, contingency planning becomes key to your success; you need to have not only Plan A, but alternative scenarios and options for when things go wrong – as they always do, in some way. The reason why events can't be delivered using only checklists is because they are ultimately complex, and at the point where you arrive on-site, you're no longer really in control as external factors come into play and you have to respond quickly to situations as they arise. The more experienced you and your team are, the more you learn that you don't know all the answers, and that while it is vital to prepare, plan and be proactive, there will come a time when you have to use your judgement and expertise to manage a problem that has arisen.

Despite the different issues, problems, concerns and challenges, the very best on-site events managers have the capacity to make it all appear effortless – keeping track of numerous simultaneous tasks, handling several different challenges at once, dealing with a constantly changing to-do list, all the while maintaining a cool, calm, and collected demeanour. Some people call this 'the swan effect', making the analogy with the elegant bird that appears to glide effortlessly through the water, but underneath, invisible to the world, their webbed feet are frantically paddling to keep the swan moving. In reality, swans often use only one foot to paddle, with the other tucked up onto their back, so the analogy is not as accurate as people think! But, nevertheless, an on-site events manager you can trust, to ensure your event runs smoothly from start to finish, is an essential component of any successful event.

By the end of this chapter you will be able to:

- assess your responsibilities for your event;
- ensure that everyone attending your event has a seamless experience;
- identify some of the common challenges facing events managers on the day, and address the issues;
- ensure you don't overlook anything important after the event has finished;
- follow advice from event specialists.

Case study 10.1 tells the story of the complexities in planning on-site access controls, showing movements and cast flow for the prestigious opening and closing ceremonies of a major international sporting event, the Birmingham 2022 Commonwealth Games.

CASE STUDY 10.1

Air Traffic Control: How to run a global ceremony

Rob Madeley, Operations Manager – Rehearsals and Workshops Event: The Opening and Closing Ceremonies of the Birmingham 2022 Commonwealth Games; UKCEM Graduate 2012

Planning for the Birmingham 2022 Commonwealth Games ceremonies started in mid-2021. On-site planning and venue delivery commenced in earnest, and in 2022 audition sessions for up to 2,500 cast places required across both ceremonies were held off-site at Edgbaston Cricket Ground and included a wide-ranging volunteer cast of all ages and abilities.

In order to rehearse a show of this scale, a temporary rehearsal venue was required to host cast rehearsals from the beginning of June 2022, before moving into the Alexander Stadium for final dress rehearsals and the ceremonies themselves. The Operations Team secured a 32-acre site of a former car factory plant in the south of Birmingham, and building commenced at the beginning of April 2022.

A 1:1 scale outdoor rehearsal space was marked out to provide an exact replica of the field of play (FOP) in the stadium. Seven clear-span marquees of different sizes, ranging from 10×20m to 30×50m, were built and accommodated the Operations, Production, Costume, Props and Casting teams, cast check-in, cast holding and a 2:1 scale indoor rehearsal space.

Delivering a site of that scale requires detailed planning of operational processes, including scheduling, transport, access, accreditation, and security plans; welfare provisions; safety plans; weather, emergency and evacuation procedures; staffing; power and AV systems; and the provision of medical support.

In July, almost two months after first opening its doors to cast members, and having managed two to three rehearsals a day, six days a week, rehearsals finally moved to the stadium for final preparations, with almost 1,500 cast rehearsing in one session. The Operations Team then transformed the rehearsal venue to prepare for the closing ceremony. Not only did this require changing the set-up and layout of the rehearsal spaces, but due to the limited access to the stadium it required the Operations Team to facilitate all closing ceremony dress rehearsals, before moving to the stadium for the show itself.

From 10.00 am on the day of the opening ceremony, Operations, Casting, Stage Management and Costume teams prepared cast holding at the stadium to manage the 1,500-strong cast, who would arrive from 2 pm to prepare for their performance.

Doors opened at 5:00 pm and pre-show entertainment commenced at 7:15 pm as the audience started to arrive. Final technical checks were carried out to ensure all show equipment was ready, and cast members were applying the final touches to their costumes and makeup.

At 7:50 pm, as with a theatre production, cast groups were called, stacked in order, and moved from cast holding to their pre-set show positions around the stadium. What makes this production different is not only that the stage is much larger than traditional stages, but the journey between cast holding and the pre-set positions can be up to half a kilometre. A single movement of one cast group can take around 30 minutes to complete; mass cast movement on this scale requires the coordinated efforts and advanced planning of the Operations, Stage Management and Casting teams. This process is led by show control on the night to ensure all timings are met to deliver a flawless show.

Sam Hunter, Head of Production, explains:

> There are many different departments involved in putting together a ceremony, and it's vital that they all follow the rule of the 3 C's: Cooperation, Coordination and Communication. Without these, it would be impossible to implement the body of work necessary to deliver an event on a ceremonies scale.
>
> Stage Management, Operations, Costume, Casting, Props and Technical are just some of the departments that have to work together to ensure the flow of information relating to each of their functional areas interfaces with each other to allow the smooth movement of people and equipment safely and on time. The entire enterprise can be compared to air traffic control and delivering a ceremony is as complex as running an airport. Transport, catering, cast and staff arrivals, time to get into costume, security, props and scenic pre-sets, the mass movement of cast from their various holding areas to their entrance points onto the field of play (and reversing that process), plus the additional task of adding athletes who have never had the benefit of a rehearsal, is a huge operation whose complexity must fit together seamlessly. These challenges are heightened by the sheer scale of the endeavour. In London 2012 there was an opening ceremony cast of 8,500, with twice that number of costumes, over 7,000 individual pieces of scenery and a 'backstage area' that covered a footprint of over 10 miles, plus 12,500 marching athletes on the night. Over that vast area, every activity had to be conducted to split-second precision. Without cooperation, coordination and communication between all departments, this simply wouldn't have been achievable.

As 8:00 pm approached, the cast were joined in their pre-set positions by 4,500 athletes from 72 participating countries taking part in the athlete's parade, and the national television network started to broadcast the show live from the stadium.

From the start of the show until the end, Cast Holding managed a constant flow of cast leaving for their show segments and returning from stage having performed. Walking routes around the stadium had to be carefully considered to ensure cast, scenic elements and props did not obstruct one another moving to or from the stage. This had to be considered alongside stadium operations and emergency services access.

Having returned to cast holding, those cast groups performing in a second segment had to quick change into different costumes. This not only added pressure to the Costume team, but also required additional cast management and flows planning within cast holding itself.

The show concluded at 10:30 pm with a pyrotechnic display to mark the official opening of the Games. As the final cast group on stage returned, work continued in cast holding to ensure all cast were transported from the stadium safely, leaving the monumental task of clearing up to begin. Cast were encouraged to keep their costumes as a memento; however, having eaten two meals and drunk an average five bottles of water each, 1,500 cast members left the compound looking a little different to how they started around 12 hours earlier!

The following day, the Operations Team started all over again with preparations for the closing ceremony, planned just 10 days later. Adrian Bourke, Head of Operations, says:

> If Ceremonies was an airport, Operations is the Air Traffic Control Tower. We help guide the other departments (the aeroplanes) to land on the runways (the rehearsal venues/stadium spaces etc) and taxi to the terminal (the show) where they disembark. The Operations department provides the places, resources, people and support that allow the Creative and Technical divisions to get on and deliver the world-class ceremonies. We interact with every department via areas such as venue services, accreditation, volunteer organization, catering, accommodation, cleaning and waste, transport, security, health and safety, welfare and medical services. We also plan and schedule show movement away from the performance area and wrangle headline talent and cast before their arrival into the performance area alongside our stage management and casting colleagues. The Operations department also acts as the conduit between existing venue and organizing committee colleagues, working in collaboration to ensure clear communication for the event day around the stadium precinct on ceremonies day. Although often challenging, the work of the Operations department and team members forms an integral part of the ceremonies, and the collaborative nature of our work provides many rewarding opportunities and positive memories each time we do this.

Your responsibilities as an on-site events manager

Your management roles and responsibilities on-site at an event will vary for different events. You might play a significant role at some events and a smaller role at others. For example, at some events, you may be able to call on lots of team members on-site, and to allocate and delegate tasks prior to the event. But at other events, you may have only a small core team which may mean that you have to be a bit more hands-on.

In order to ensure the delivery of a successful event, there is a lot to be done, and the temptation is for you to roll up your sleeves and get stuck in. However, while a hard-work ethic is an admirable quality in an events manager, one of biggest mistakes you can make is trying to do too much yourself and failing to delegate to other members of your team. As former events managers, one of our favourite on-site roles was registration or box office duties, because you get to meet lots of people and have interesting conversations. But in these people-facing roles it is important to note that it is easy to become too embroiled in the operational roles. This is a mistake, and you risk not fulfilling your management role, which can lead to challenges with delivery as the role of overseeing all operations gets lost in the one task.

Your role as on-site manager means that you need to be able to step back and look at the bigger picture. You need to make sure that everyone and everything is where it needs to be to deliver an exceptional event. On-site event management is also about being available for others, to enable those working with you to come to you with issues or problems and then to have time to offer advice or help them to solve problems. But if you're too focused on operational tasks, you will be unable to fulfil that vital role.

EVENTS MANAGER HACK

It is important that you delegate effectively, but also that you're able to check in with team members to ensure they're not encountering any difficulties. A good on-site manager uses a strategy called Management by Walking About (MBWA), where you ensure that you are moving around the entire event site to give support to your team and ensure that they are delivering according to the plans. It also facilitates you in supporting your team dealing with any issues or challenges they may be facing. Good communication is critical at this time and whether it is verbal or using communication devices like radios, it is important that you are available to assist in a timely manner. This sort of on-site leadership also allows you to develop your team members and give them opportunities to enhance their skills with your support, increasing the capabilities of your team in an environment which is supportive and gives staff opportunities to engage in more challenging roles.

Ruth Dowson, Author

Before the event

With lots to be done even before the doors open, it can be helpful, particularly for larger events, to break the actions required down further into distinct stages. Below we have identified three key stages during this time:

1. Upon arrival at the venue
2. Lead-up to the event
3. One hour before the event.

Upon arrival at the venue

- When you first arrive on-site, it's important you get the most important people together for a meeting. For example, a conference organizer will usually hold a pre-event meeting with their venue contact to run through the programme and walk round the venue together.

- One of the first steps is establishing a base room. Conference organizers are likely to set up an office where they can meet with staff, make calls, store materials and so on. Festival organizing teams will have a central production office as well as an event control room to handle communications (more about event control shortly).
- Personally check that all essential equipment and supplies have arrived and are in good working condition. Check this yourself and do it early, while there is still time to act; failing to ensure that all your equipment and materials are on-site can lead to delays and significant challenges moving forward.

EVENTS MANAGER HACK

Always: plan to arrive earlier; over-cater; get parcels delivered in good time and check that the venue is able to receive ok; get tracking details; get crew in to do all the moving; have a runner to do errands; have a folder on your desktop on your laptop for quick access and use a tablet for even quicker access to documents!

Lori Novell, Event Project Manager, The Outlook Creative Group

Lead-up to the event

As on-site events manager, it is your responsibility to ensure that everything is going to be set up in time and to coordinate and integrate the efforts of everyone involved. Although every event has its own requirements, the checklist below includes some of the more common tasks for an indoor venue set-up.

CHECKLIST: TASKS FOR SETTING UP A VENUE

- Event branding and signage
- Sponsor branding and signage
- Directional signage
- Flags, banners, balloons and décor
- Stages, lecterns and podiums
- Microphones, amplifiers and speakers
- Lighting set-up and controls

- Air-conditioning controls
- Arrival and registration (including name badges and check-in forms)
- Information kiosks and message boards
- Catering and refreshment areas
- Setting out tables and chairs
- Table linen, centrepieces, tableware and glassware
- Venue cleaning pre-installation and post-design and décor installation
- Checking security of venue, e.g. doors
- Checking safety of venue, e.g. trip hazards, fire exit access, reviewing risk assessment
- First-aid equipment
- Checking accessibility requirements, e.g. disabled ramps and lifts, access to rooms and other conference areas, set-up of support for visual and hearing impairments/induction loops, Braille
- Reviewing your cultural, equity and inclusion risk assessment, e.g. Prayer rooms, gender-neutral toilets, baby-changing facilities

OTHER CONSIDERATIONS

- Face-to-face briefings are effective and time efficient for sharing all the vital information about the event with your team. The briefing is also the ideal forum to equip team members with anything they might need, such as uniforms and walkie-talkies. Table 10.1 provides an example of a briefing sheet. It is always a good idea to have any necessary documentation circulated to your team (including volunteers) in advance so that they have time to familiarize themselves with plans and their roles and responsibilities.
- Scheduling meetings with the wider team (running a successful event requires a 'team of teams' approach) is vital to review information about the event programme, activities and timings as well as updates on the number of guests and any special requirements they might have, prior to the event and as the event progresses. Table 10.2 provides an example of a document used in the build-up to an event, to brief participants, the client and speakers on housekeeping matters, as well as a final summary of all the requirements at the venue. It sometimes is a good idea at this point to do a walk-through with key members of your team so that they are aware of where specific things will happen and also the expectation of the quality of delivery so that all members of your team can participate in quality control activities.
- When setting up communication systems in advance of the event, make sure that everything is in working order. Testing equipment is vital, including checking the

whole event space for a signal, as there is often a dead spot for mobile phone or walkie-talkie signals and therefore it is important that your team are aware of where these spots are in the event of any issues arising, and that there are effective contingencies in place.

- Establish communication protocols so that everyone understands the lines of command. This is to ensure that during the busy event you can shortcut communication and deal with the related team members: if the events manager says 'do it', you do it, straight away, no questions asked, and no politeness needed. It is a good idea to include the mode and tone of communication in your briefing to ensure that your team are aware that brevity and action are the order of the day, and that in some instances direct and specific language ensures that challenges are dealt with as quickly as possible.
- Rehearsals take place in the lead-up to many types of events. An obvious example is musicians at concerts, but events such as weddings, awards ceremonies and after-dinner speakers all benefit from a dry run. As the events manager, you often play an important role in fixing any problems identified during rehearsals. Case study 10.1 on the opening ceremony for an international sporting event highlights the importance and complexities of rehearsals for major events.

EVENTS MANAGER HACK

Create a standard set of actions to manage the flow of your on-site logistics: these can be adapted and adjusted to suit any event. Essentials in your logistics plan include a documented chain of command, your noted back-up plans, testing AV equipment, scheduled team meetings and, of course, your sense of humour!

Selina Arnall, Event and Marketing Manager, That Event Girl; Social Traders, Australia

One hour before the event

- Final checks! Check all the different event rooms and spaces are ready to go, and review your production schedule and site plan to ensure things are where they are supposed to be. Check all equipment is in efficient working order. Check room layouts. Do a visual check for cleanliness of rooms, corridors, toilets and other public areas. Make sure to check the outdoor spaces and grounds. Check the car parks. Check food and beverage areas for readiness. Check entrances and exits. Check and check again.
- *Final chance* to reinforce any key messages you want staff to particularly focus on during the event. Meet-and-greet staff and helpers are particularly important if you

want to create a good first impression; these team members are the first point of contact so it is essential that they know where everything is and where people are going, or who to go to in the event of a question they cannot respond to. You want to make sure the guest arrival is easy and memorable for the right reasons. Remember the old adage: 'You only get one chance to make a great first impression.'

- One last walk-round to check that everything is now ready and everyone is now in place. If the event isn't completely ready, you've got a decision to make. Do you delay opening the doors or allow people in? It's a very tough call. But allowing attendees in and then trying to fix any issues when your event has gone live can often create a knock-on effect as well as increase stress levels of the team trying to mitigate the other issues which may occur as a result. If you do have to delay opening the doors, please ensure that you have your friendliest, calmest staff communicating this to the attendees and keeping them informed. Where possible, give staff an idea of the anticipated delay to support managing attendee expectations.

EVENTS MANAGER HACK

Ensure that you circulate any necessary information to your team prior to your briefing; some staff will familiarize themselves in detail but others may wait for the briefing itself. However, what this does is ensure that some team members are already well versed, particularly those who function better with having details. Having some staff who are familiar with the process will help support others who do not take in all information at the briefing. Communicating key information is essential for smooth running and minimizing questions from your team.

Bernadette Albert, Author

Table 10.1 provides an example of a briefing for volunteers working on the registration desk at an event with 500 participants.

TABLE 10.1 Event briefing sheet – example

Briefing to all Registration Team members: Diocesan Day	
Student Volunteer Coordinator:	Chris
Plus:	Ruth, Matt, Jenny
If you get any hassle or questions you don't know the answer to, call Ruth or Steve	
Set-up:	Friday from 16.00
Diocesan Day:	Saturday 08.00–18.00

(continued)

TABLE 10.1 (Continued)

Venue:	School
You will be given a room plan that shows which floor and which rooms the workshop sessions will be in. Part of your role will be to help speakers and participants to find their workshop rooms if they don't know their way around the school. You will each be given a copy of the programme, which lists all the workshops. You will have an opportunity to familiarize yourself with the layout of the school on Friday evening during event set-up.	

Set-up: Friday from 16.00

We will be setting up at the school from 16.00 on Friday. If you are unable to be there on Friday, please let Ruth know ASAP. We should be finished by 19.00 at the latest.

Tasks for Friday afternoon/evening include:

- Setting out chairs and tables around the school – for the 28 workshops (in classrooms), for children's groups, for the exhibition (in the dining room and Sixth Form Centre) and for registration (in the Main Entrance Foyer).
- Posting signage around the building – this will help you to get to know the building layout.
- Stuffing badges and arranging them correctly on the registration desk. Checking badge names against the lists to ensure all participants have a badge. As there are around 500 people coming, accuracy is **very** important.
- Speakers who wish to set up their rooms on the Friday evening will arrive sometime between 17.00 and 19.30, or from 08.00 on the Saturday morning. We put the school desks to the back of each room and will make sure that there is the required number of chairs in each room, unless otherwise specified, neatly set out in curved rows. Speakers may change the layout when they get there.

On the day – Saturday 17 April from 08.00

Ruth and Steve will be on-site from 08.00; please ensure you arrive by 08.30 latest. The registration period is due to start at 09.00 but there will inevitably be some early arrivals. The conference is due to finish around 16.00; however, we will need to clear up and return furniture to its original place, so should be done by 17.30 at the latest. If you are unable to attend for the whole time, please let Ruth know ASAP.

Tasks for Saturday include the following.

Registration Desk

- This should by staffed from 08.00 to 17.00 by at least two people all day in case of emergency, but by at least seven people during the peak morning registration period of 08.45–09.45. The Bishop will welcome people at the front door, and Ed (Stewarding Team Leader) will channel arrivals towards the registration desks to manage queueing. We will have laid out the badges in alphabetical order by surname, facing the delegates, so arrivals can find their name and take their badge. (We use badges as the basis for 'no-shows', so this is very important.) We will ask people to move away from the registration area once they have collected their badge, as there is limited space and around 500 people are expected. If someone tells you that anyone is not attending, please find their badge and give it to the Late Registration Desk. Two people are needed to work on the Late Registration Desk.

- Please **don't** let anyone take a badge for a friend as this only causes confusion.
- **Late registration:** For health and safety reasons, we need to ensure that **all** participants (this includes delegates, speakers, St John's Ambulance, children's team workers, catering team, registration team, exhibitors, musicians, singers, speakers and children) have a name badge and are booked on to the event system. Check the badges. If you cannot see a badge for the person, send them to the Late Registration Desk, where a team member will check that they aren't on the list, and they will ask them to complete a form and handwrite a name badge for them. All sections of the Late booking form **must** be completed in full.
- **Children's registration:** Forms for parents/guardians to register children attending will be on the Late Registration Desk
- As registration finishes, we will move the desks back, to make more space in the Entrance Foyer. Please use this area as a meeting point all day and note that while the main sessions are on in the Great Hall, noise levels MUST be kept to a minimum, so as not to cause a disturbance. Please ensure that exhibitors and others, e.g. St John's Ambulance, also keep quiet in this area.

Exhibition 08.00–16.00 Assisting exhibitors and speakers to set up

08:00–16:00	Two people in the exhibition until the conference starts, and to check exhibitors are ok throughout the day. Keep the exhibition area tidy in between breaks (Ed will provide black plastic bin bags). Refreshments are served in the Dining Room before the conference, at the morning break and at lunchtime.
08.30–10.30	Car park stewards: Parking is provided in the Car Park using the Main Road entrance, and shuttle buses will pick up from the Station from 08.45.
Conference Programme:	
10.00	Conference Starts, Great Hall.

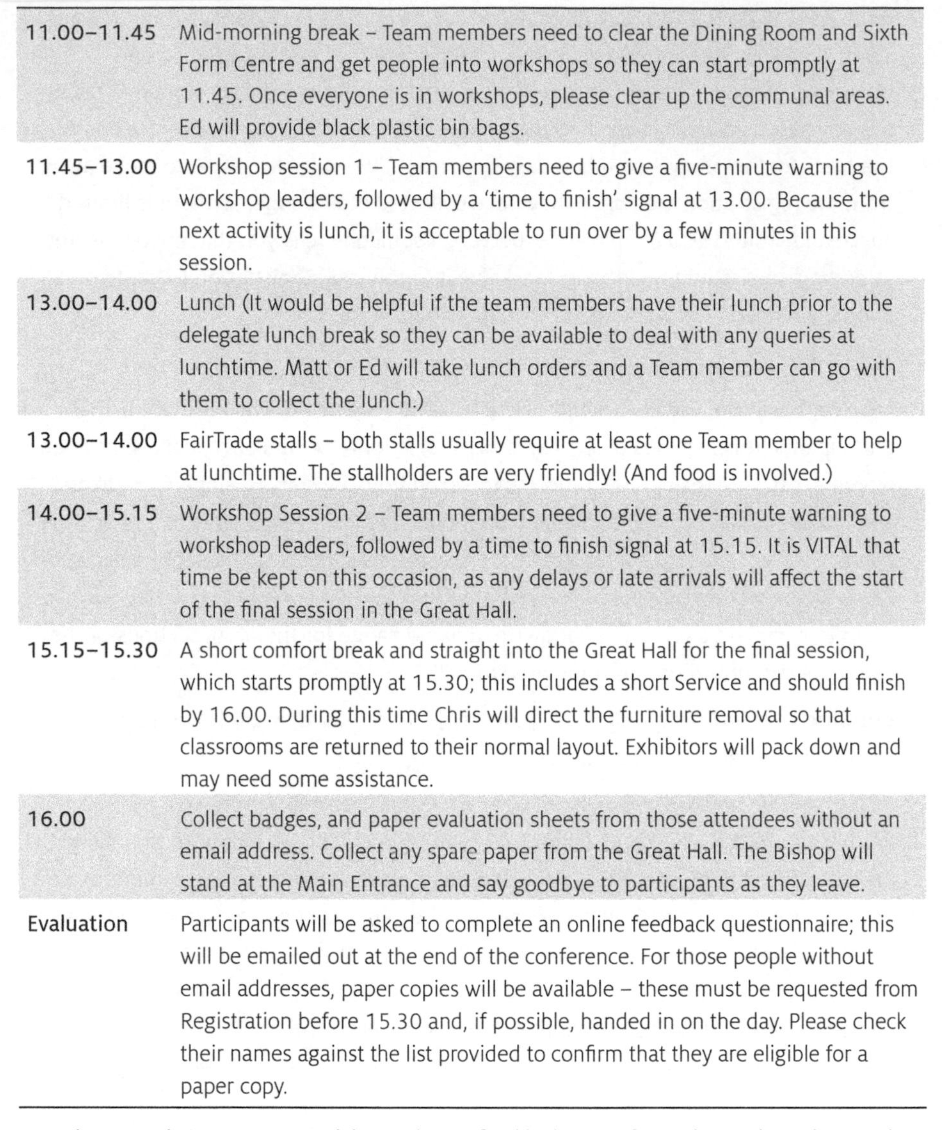

11.00–11.45	Mid-morning break – Team members need to clear the Dining Room and Sixth Form Centre and get people into workshops so they can start promptly at 11.45. Once everyone is in workshops, please clear up the communal areas. Ed will provide black plastic bin bags.
11.45–13.00	Workshop session 1 – Team members need to give a five-minute warning to workshop leaders, followed by a 'time to finish' signal at 13.00. Because the next activity is lunch, it is acceptable to run over by a few minutes in this session.
13.00–14.00	Lunch (It would be helpful if the team members have their lunch prior to the delegate lunch break so they can be available to deal with any queries at lunchtime. Matt or Ed will take lunch orders and a Team member can go with them to collect the lunch.)
13.00–14.00	FairTrade stalls – both stalls usually require at least one Team member to help at lunchtime. The stallholders are very friendly! (And food is involved.)
14.00–15.15	Workshop Session 2 – Team members need to give a five-minute warning to workshop leaders, followed by a time to finish signal at 15.15. It is VITAL that time be kept on this occasion, as any delays or late arrivals will affect the start of the final session in the Great Hall.
15.15–15.30	A short comfort break and straight into the Great Hall for the final session, which starts promptly at 15.30; this includes a short Service and should finish by 16.00. During this time Chris will direct the furniture removal so that classrooms are returned to their normal layout. Exhibitors will pack down and may need some assistance.
16.00	Collect badges, and paper evaluation sheets from those attendees without an email address. Collect any spare paper from the Great Hall. The Bishop will stand at the Main Entrance and say goodbye to participants as they leave.
Evaluation	Participants will be asked to complete an online feedback questionnaire; this will be emailed out at the end of the conference. For those people without email addresses, paper copies will be available – these must be requested from Registration before 15.30 and, if possible, handed in on the day. Please check their names against the list provided to confirm that they are eligible for a paper copy.

Most classrooms have computers and data projectors fixed in the room for use by speakers. The organizers have also arranged for a member of the school IT staff to be on hand to assist with any difficulties if speakers wish to use the school equipment.

On Saturday, lunch (fish or veggie alternative and chips) is provided for registration team members only. Refreshments are available all day at no cost. A branded events team polo shirt will be provided (which you can keep). This is to ensure that you are recognizable to delegates, exhibitors and speakers. The organizers can pay for travel expenses, either mileage or bus/train fares; please complete the claim form and give it to Steve on the day or to Ruth afterwards.

Contact

Please put the following numbers into your mobile phone in case you need them on the day.

Ruth:

Steve:

I want to take this opportunity of thanking you for what you are going to contribute to this event and also to express the thanks of Steve, the event organizer and the Bishop.

Table 10.2 provides an example of a document used in the build-up to an event to brief the client, participants and speakers on housekeeping matters, as well as a final summary of all the requirements at the venue.

TABLE 10.2 Event housekeeping – example

Event housekeeping	
(Completed by Event Registration Team on the day of the event, after briefing with the Venue Operations Manager and given to Chairperson, Event Owner and Speakers. For seminars, please ensure that every speaker has a copy of this sheet.)	
Conference information:	
Event:	To: Client/Events Team/Speakers/Registration Team/Stewards Team/Children's Team
Venue & Date:	Event Registration Team staff member on-site:
	Name:
	Mobile:
Venue Event Coordinator pre-event:	Venue Operational Manager on-site:
Name:	Name:
Mobile:	Mobile:
AV Supplier:	First Aid: St John's Ambulance
Technician Name:	Event Team Cover: on the Registration Desk/Box Office
Mobile:	Mobile:
*****To be announced at start of event sessions*****	

(continued)

TABLE 10.2 (Continued)

Fire alarm/drill instructions:	There is no fire alarm rehearsal due today, so any fire alarm is real. You should follow the green running-man signs, which indicate the exits. Please note that the way you came in is not necessarily the quickest exit route. There are signs on the walls with instructions. Please familiarize yourselves with the procedure and the location of exits in every session. Once outside the building you should make your way to the congregating area, which is: (state location, e.g. On the main lawn in front of the school). Please note that for fire and security reasons, once you are in the building, you must ensure that you have collected your badge from the Registration Desk outside the Main Hall. This is required in case of emergency evacuation of the building. This includes all delegates, speakers, exhibitors and helpers.
First aid:	In case of an accident, please contact the St John's Ambulance or the Registration Desk immediately. If there are any additional qualified first aiders attending the conference, please make yourselves known at the Registration Desk
Toilet facilities (including disabled toilets and changing rooms):	See plan of building in programme; familiarize yourself with the school layout
Rooms and locations:	Main Room: Great Hall
	Exhibition: Corridors/Dining Room/Sixth Form Centre
	Seminar Rooms as marked in the conference pack
Refreshments:	Location: Dining Room
	Time Mid-morning: 11.00–11.45
	Time Mid-afternoon: 3.15–3.30 only
Lunch: BRING YOUR OWN	Location: Dining Room/Sixth Form Centre
	Time: 1.00–2.00
Mobile phones:	Request all mobile phones are switched off/to silent mode during sessions please.
Feedback reminder:	Please remember to complete the feedback forms; these will be emailed out at the end of the conference. For those people without email addresses, paper copies will be available which must be requested at Registration before 3.30 pm – and if possible, handed in on the day.
Anything else?	

During the event

Once the event begins, you need to be proactive and solution-oriented. Being proactive means trying to anticipate a problem and acting in advance either to prepare for it or to prevent it. Being solution-oriented means that when you do encounter a problem you don't waste time thinking 'poor me' or getting frustrated by the current obstacle; instead, you accept what is going on and deal with it. Remember 'The Swan effect'.

EVENTS MANAGER HACK

As the on-site events manager, it is also important that you keep your staff calm should any issues or challenges arise. In this regard your demeanour will help to manage your teams' emotions and those of your attendees. Where possible, involve and empower your team members to find solutions for less complex problems; this supports their professional development as well as their skill set and confidence. This approach also shows trust and confidence in your team, and means you are only dealing with serious issues. Communication is key, and in the event their solution was ineffective, step in to support them in resolving it. Also, unless it is an absolute emergency, never let your attendees or staff see you running, as it means that something is out of control and can lead to attendee and staff panic, which you want to avoid at all costs.

Bernadette Albert, Author

Common challenges

Below we offer a short summary of the most common and difficult challenges that events managers routinely face during the event.

Keep your event on track

Your job is to make sure that everything is running smoothly and to time (i.e. ensuring that activities are kept to the agreed timings). At the same time, it's inevitable that things won't go to plan, and you need to respond accordingly. For instance, last-minute changes to the event programme are often necessary and it is often your decision whether to go ahead with the original plan or see what happens. There is a wide variety of tools and checklists available for events managers to help them to keep things on track. The event function sheet is widely used for business meetings and events. Table 10.3 provides a template you may wish to use.

Deliver excellent customer service

Knowing how to keep customers happy can make or break your event. Great customer service is about going the extra mile, making every single person feel like the most important one. As an events manager, it's not only paying guests but also clients, VIPs, sponsors, media and so on all require special attention. Being a successful events manager is about being visible, spending time with all the important event stakeholders and making them feel special. At a conference, for example, your keynote speaker may have travelled a long way to get to your event, perhaps even through different time zones. Find out what their favourite refreshment is and go the extra mile whenever they reach for their glass.

Be visible and available to staff

As the events manager, you are the 'figurehead', 'leader', 'role model', 'face' of the event team. An invisible events manager who hides away in a back office lacks the visibility required in such a role. That's not to say that all you do is walk around, preening like a peacock, but you need the visibility and presence to give confidence to those around you, especially in a crisis. Events require the combined efforts of different people to make them happen and, as the events manager, you need to be able to bring the team together as whole, make sure that everybody is pulling in the same direction and get the best out of every team member. There will also be times when you're the tough one, making difficult decisions, sometimes instantly, and it's in these situations that strong leadership is vital. Also, as the events manager, do not be afraid to provide physical support and assistance; this shows your staff that there is nothing that you are asking them to do that you wouldn't do yourself. This is a strong leadership skill that will support you in managing your staff.

Keep everything flowing smoothly

During the event, you play a crucial role in keeping everything running as smoothly as possible, ensuring that all the right elements are at the right place and at the right time (on-site logistics). As we discussed earlier in the book, on-site logistics entails (among other things) crowd management, transportation and communications. On a large event site, there are likely to be dedicated teams who are responsible for each of the areas, in which case your role is about making sure the different teams work together to keep everything and everyone flowing smoothly throughout the event. Ensuring that your staffing is representative of how you wish the event to be delivered is critical here. It is often a good idea to allocate a zone or area leader who takes responsibility for the team and for ensuring schedules are maintained and quality is delivered. Again, this is a good way to empower your team through delegation, but also leave room for you to manage the whole event.

Seize the opportunity to publicize your event

Your event is time-bound – maybe days, maybe weeks, maybe longer – but it is time-bound. Time can slip away incredibly quickly during the event. To fail to recognize and seize the opportunities to publicize your event is an easy mistake for a busy events manager to make. But remember you're the 'figurehead' or 'face' of the event and have an important role to play in promoting the event. Potential PR tools and tactics for 'live' events include live broadcasts, live-streaming, social media and online bloggers. Deciding where to invest your time, as an on-site events manager, isn't easy – and many fail to find time for PR and publicity. But regular PR and publicity is an essential element of any event's longevity.

Make sure your event is safe

There is nothing more important than ensuring the safety of everyone attending and working at the event. Regular site walk-rounds are the best way to identify safety concerns yourself. When you spot potential hazards, you then need to decide whether the control measures that are in place are suitable and sufficient (this practice is commonly known as a dynamic risk assessment). Holding regular staff meetings will also help you to identify safety issues and concerns. For larger events taking place over multiple days, it is especially important to schedule regular meetings with key personnel from groups such as the Health & Safety Advisory Group, Licensed Security, Traffic Management and Emergency Services. Another important way to ensure your event is safe is to actively encourage staff to communicate safety issues and concerns. Your event staff are at the 'coal face' of the event and can therefore help you to find out what is happening at all times.

EVENTS MANAGER HACK

Always have: a pen and paper; a power bank; a portable stationery box; a clipboard; a tablet for your documents; marker pens; hand sanitizer; backup name badges; a bum bag and carry pens, USB sticks, tissues, hand sanitizer and a snack; spares of everything; comfortable shoes; everyone's contact numbers handy – they will always be needed at some point.

Lori Novell, Event Project Manager, The Outlook Creative Group

Table 10.3 provides a template for an event function sheet that draws together the requirements of the overall event for the venue Operations team, whether they are from an internal or external organization.

TABLE 10.3 Event function sheet – template

EVENT FUNCTION SHEET					
<<EVENT TITLE>> <<DATE>> <<VENUE, LOCATION>>					
Pre-event contact (Events Team):			On-site contact (Events Team):		
Tel:			Mobile:		
Mobile:					
Fax:					
Email:					
Venue event coordinator pre-event:			Venue operations manager onsite:		
Tel:			Mobile:		
Mobile:					
Fax:					
Email:					
Signage required:			Meeting room name/s:		
Pre-event set-up					
Activity	Timings	Location/Room(s)	Set-up and venue responsibilities	Numbers	
				Confirmed	Set
Venue AV requirements					
Equipment	Location/ Room(s)	Set-up and venue responsibilities	Number	Agreed Cost	
Projector					
Flip chart stand					
Paper					
Screen					
Event					
Activity	Timings	Location/Room(s)	Set-up and venue responsibilities	Numbers	
				Confirmed	Set
Registration					
Morning sessions					
Mid-morning refreshments					
Sessions					
Lunch					
Sessions					

(continued)

TABLE 10.3 (Continued)

Mid-afternoon refreshments	
Sessions	
Close	
DIETARY & SPECIAL REQUIREMENTS	
Dietary requirements	
Option	Number
Vegetarian:	
Vegan:	
Halal:	
Kosher:	
Other:	
Special requirements:	Number/details
ROOMING LIST	
Name	Special requirement
Other requirements:	
Billing instructions:	
Authorized signatory for main account:	
No. of bedrooms contracted/required:	
Minimum numbers:	

After the event

After the event, there are some key things that an events manager should remember. This is often the part of the event where staff who have been on-site for the duration of the event begin to show signs of fatigue; it is important that as site manager you keep them motivated and include any specific requirements for the closing and load-out of the event in the event briefing and production schedule. After-event activities are only briefly mentioned here but are discussed at greater length in other parts of the book.

Smooth dispersal of the event attendees

The first challenge is to ensure the smooth dispersal of the event attendees, which can prove to be particularly problematic if all attendees leave *en masse* (e.g. at the end of a sporting match). Ensure that you factor this into your planning as it may require relocation of staff, stewards and security personnel, for example to parking facilities or exit routes, to facilitate smooth departure and an incident-free end to your event.

Shutting down the site

After the event attendees have dispersed, there is still a lot of work to be done. This is a good point to assemble your key staff again to take a quick break, praise the team on a well-delivered event and then brief on key aspects of shutting down the site. Remember this is the point where all your staff are probably quite exhausted, and you need to maintain the momentum to ensure that load-out is completed in a timely fashion. Equipment, supplies and materials all need to be packed up, stored away or transported away before the clean-up operation can get into full swing.

Conducting a post-event debrief

Post-event debriefs occur immediately after an event to capture any pressing problems in need of solutions. This is particularly important when it comes to health and safety issues.

Case study 10.2 highlights the benefits and challenges of student events managers running real events as part of their studies.

CASE STUDY 10.2
Teaching the impossible

Ubaldino Couto, School of Hospitality Management, Macao Institute for Tourism Studies

Like many other programmes around the world, the curriculum of the BSc Tourism Event Management at the Macao Institute for Tourism Studies (IFTM) requires third-year students to conceptualize, plan, implement, manage, operate and evaluate a public live event. Since the beginning of the programme in 2005, students have organized numerous events, typically of a charitable nature, from creating a Guinness World Record to raising awareness of social causes, and from entertainment variety shows to orienteering challenges and sports events. There are three classes of 35 students annually, each divided into project teams responsible for different functions of the event. Each class runs their own event depending on scheduling, usually two in the first and one in the second semester.

Figure 10.2 is a sample of the organization structure typically adopted in the project. Although the structure is flexible and dynamic in principle, project teams have a distinct scope of work, each headed by a department manager and team members.

- Event Directors – Overseeing the whole planning and operation of the event.
- PR and Sponsorship – Responsible for all external communications with co-organizers, partners and sponsors; also responsible for securing sponsorships.

FIGURE 10.2 Sample of organization structure

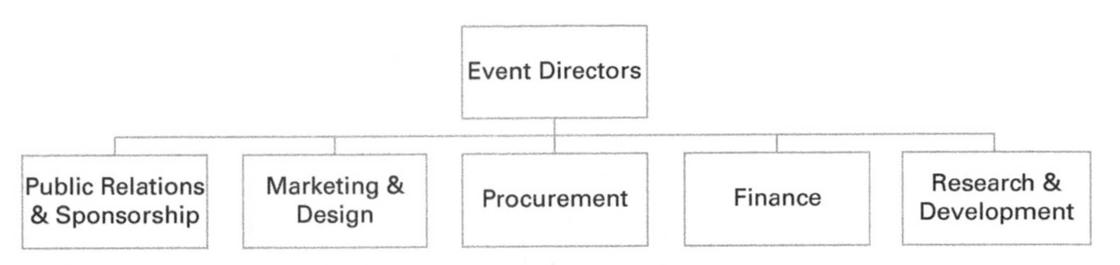

- Marketing and Design – Primarily responsible for promoting the event by devising an effective marketing plan using both traditional and social media platforms. Depending on the needs of the event, sometimes in a separate team, Design is responsible for all graphics, including marketing communications, event props and registration/ticketing systems.
- Procurement – All tasks related to the acquisition of event materials and equipment, including logistics such as purchase, delivery and installation.
- Finance – All tasks related to the finances of the event, including budgeting, control and preparing statements.
- Research and Development – Responsible for all tasks related to researching, testing, producing and training of event activities and staff.

Students are given MOP5,000 (around GBP500) as seed money which they are required to return in its entirety. Throughout these years, students have always managed to make a profit in addition to returning the seed money to IFTM. Based on observations made over the years, the formula for success appears to lie in the strategic use of side events prior to the event finale at the end of the semester, as illustrated graphically in Figure 10.3.

FIGURE 10.3 Formula of success in organizing students' events

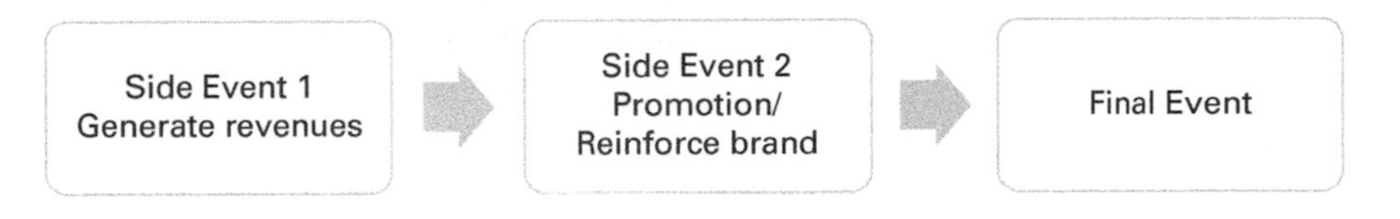

The semester starts with a selling activity dealing in handmade goods, typically to coincide with festive themes. In Macao, Semester 1 begins in August, which is close to Mid-Autumn Festival, while Semester 2 begins in January, which is near Chinese New Year. Students prepare handmade goods themed around these festivals and sell them to the public, making some profit. The objective is to generate revenues to run the final event at the end of the semester. The lead time in planning the selling activity is short, so precise planning is crucial from the start. In the middle of the semester, students typically organize workshops or parties to promote the final event and to reinforce the brand awareness of their event. This often generates a second revenue source to run the final event, and these activities range from Halloween parties to DIY workshops on a variety of goods such as leather wallets, soaps and candles, and so on. In the finale, students host the event accordingly, depending on the proposal agreed upon at the beginning of the semester.

The title of this case study is 'Teaching the impossible', but it does not actually refer to course events that are impossible to teach, but rather to an anagram of one of the students' events titled 'I'm possible'. The event was themed on encouraging people to do the impossible, to have courage in oneself and to support each other on pushing the limits. 'I'm Possible' is a series of events which began with a side event of selling personalized cookies to coincide with Valentine's Day, another side event of combat games and a variety show as the event finale showcasing guests' acceptance of different challenges on stage.

Teaching is a very rewarding experience and so is organizing course events. The diverse skills and knowledge students learn prove to be extremely useful in their future, particularly in the early years of their career. Not only are students able to put theory into practice, but they can challenge their own limits and realize their imaginations with the guidance of the course instructor and support from the university. What students typically find the most perplexing are skills related to communication and working with each other. In additional to rapid changes to global and local economic, social and political environments, the Covid-19 pandemic in recent years brings additional challenges to students organizing course events, which must adhere to guidelines operationally and fitting to the theme conceptually. The challenge, above all, is to inspire and instil a healthy learning atmosphere where students develop their creativity.

Events managers are dream makers. To play a role in guiding students 'from zero to hero' is rewarding and fulfilling. This is my reflection of teaching the impossible.

Further reading

Lei, W S and Loi, K I (2016) Explore or establish? Event graduates' early career paths, *Event Management*, **20** (1), 53–68), DOI:10.3727/152599516X14538326025071

Lei, W S C, Lam, C C C and Lourenço, F (2015) A case study on hosting an event as an experiential learning experience for event education, *Journal of Teaching in Travel & Tourism*, **15** (4), 345–61

Loi, K I and Lei, W S (2016).Graduates' perspectives of event management education, *International Journal of Event Management Research*, **11** (1), 1–11

How to be a successful events manager: what industry specialists say

1 'As the events manager, your leadership, energy, commitment to your role and ability to motivate your team are critical in delivering exceptional events. Your leadership style and how you engage with your team, service suppliers and other key stakeholders set the tone for your event and ultimately delivery of the event. In the buzz that is the lead-up to the event and event delivery it is easy to miss meals and not get enough sleep. Ensure that you are well rested so that when you arrive on-site, you have the energy to keep going and support and motivate those around you. As events manager you are also responsible for your staff's welfare, so ensure that they also take breaks and have sufficient time to eat as their energy levels and ability to deliver can also have a significant impact on your event (**Bernadette Albert**, Author/Senior Lecturer, UK Centre for Events Management, Leeds Beckett University)

2. 'Always allow for more set-up time [and budget] than your client thinks you need. Dependent on event timings and venue flexibility this may mean an ultra-early start or arranging to arrive on-site the day or night before the event set-up.' (**Rose Padmore**, Professional Conference Organizer, Director, Opening Doors & Venues)
3. 'Be proactive not reactive; don't be scared of things not going to plan. It happens more than you think. Instead, have a plan B in place and think of different situations that could go wrong and how you would deal with them. Working this way will save you time and money for when these situations occur.' (**Arron Fishwick**, Managing Director, The Event World)
4. 'Make sure all your different electronic devices are fully charged and that you have lots of spare chargers and batteries. Bring enough spares not only for you and your team, but also for contractors, suppliers, speakers and performers who are all likely to come knocking on your door.' (**Ólavur í Geil**, Managing Director, Advent Events Management, Faroe Islands)
5. 'The role of on-site events manager isn't for everyone. And if the events manager role isn't for you, then hire someone else. There are lots of freelancers and operations specialists available to hire specifically for this role, people with the skills and attributes to work in this vital front-of-house capacity. And there are lots of specialist events networking groups that can help you find someone. Try @thedelegatewranglers on Facebook for recommendations.' (**Ruth Dowson**, Author/Researcher, UK Centre for Events Management, Leeds Beckett University)
6. 'When preparing your equipment list for the base room (office) be sure to bring lots of spares.... Spares of everything! You'll need to bring enough supplies not only for you and your team, but also for contractors, suppliers, speakers or performers. They are all likely to come knocking on your door asking for extras, whether it's pens, paper or other stationery items. Or spare radios, phones and other communication devices, and these days, especially, chargers for phones, laptops and other communication devices. One of the first things is to check that all equipment has arrived and is in good working condition. Do this early, while there is still time to act; still time to rush out to the shops and buy something. Don't wait to get caught out.' (**Sharon McElhinney**, Programme Leader, Events Management, The Sino-British College, Shanghai, China)

7. 'You'll need plenty of tea, coffee, water and other refreshments to keep the troops happy! (And don't forget the decaf, as well as the caffeine!)' (**Sharon McElhinney**, Programme Leader, Events Management, The Sino-British College, Shanghai, China)
8. 'On a personal "operational" level: stay hydrated.' (**Ólavur í Geil**, Managing Director, Advent Events Management, Faroe Islands)
9. 'Put yourself in your delegates' shoes. When the programme is pretty much finalized and you're ready to prepare your on-site project management plan to include team briefings, task/role allocation lists and final signage requirements, the best thing you can do is go to the venue and "walk the walk" of your delegates with the key organizing/delivery team.' (**Rose Padmore**, Professional Conference Organizer; Director, Opening Doors & Venues)
10. 'Establish an on-site delivery team communication strategy. Experience has proved that a WhatsApp group can be very effective and reassuring, especially when it comes to dealing with simple on-site issues such as changes to refreshment timings, heating and air conditioning or speakers arriving late.' (**Rose Padmore**, Professional Conference Organizer; Director, Opening Doors & Venues)
11. 'Just before your event starts, walk in the footsteps of your attendees. Start in the car park or wherever else they arrive. Look for signage and follow the signage. Where does it take you? Are you met by a friendly smile from one of the team? Is there somewhere to hang your coat? You get the idea.' (**David Bassett**, Leadership and Management Development Consultant, Network Rail)
12. 'It's easier said than done, but try to relax and enjoy the day. Over many years of experience, I have seen too many events managers look "on edge". Your manner and behaviour will impact others. If you look nervous and worried and are waiting for something to go wrong, then others will worry too.' (**Ruth Dowson**, Author/Researcher, UK Centre for Events Management, Leeds Beckett University)
13. 'Make sure you have an environmental strategy in place for your event. Does your selected venue have an environmental policy? How can you reduce your waste output? Does your event affect the local wildlife or water sources? By considering environmental factors, you are less at risk of environmental damage and can mitigate any accidents that may occur before the event.' (**Sophia Lacey**, NSW State Fundraising Manager, The Hunger Project, Sydney, Australia)
14. 'The most important thing I have learnt is to build relationships with as many people as possible during the planning process, from venue representatives to the accountants, and from contractors to agents. Even though they are your customer, and you should be in full control, remember to treat people nicely and with respect. (**Ólavur í Geil**, Managing Director, Advent Events Management, Faroe Islands)

15 'Being a good leader means that you must be able to develop your event's human resources. This can be done through effective delegation; you cannot do it alone. Exceptional events managers give others the opportunity to develop their skills. Ensure that you empower your staff to take responsibility, problem solve when challenges are faced, in a supportive and collaborative environment. The more you develop your team the more you will be able to delegate to your upskilled team members moving forward. Who knows, one day you may be on an event site and have nothing to do. (**Bernadette Albert,** Author/Senior Lecturer, UK Centre for Event Management, Leeds Beckett University)

CHAPTER SUMMARY

- Once the behind-the-scenes, detailed event planning and organizing has taken place, it's time for the for the events manager to step up to deliver a great event.
- Working on-site can get hectic. There's no getting around it. Yet the very best events managers have the ability to step back, look at the big picture and make sure that everyone and everything is where it needs to be in order to deliver a successful event.
- As an events manager, when you first arrive on-site there are a lot of things or people to organize – lots of them. Before you become too embroiled in operational tasks, it's vital that you gather the important people together to run through the event details, walk through the venue together and check that all essential equipment and supplies have arrived.
- Shortly before the event, you need to conduct a final walk-round of the event site. If the event isn't completely ready, you've got a tough decision to make – delay opening the doors or continue as planned. The single most important factor in everything you do, and every decision you make, is safety.
- Once the event begins, you should remain visible and available to all the important event stakeholders (e.g. staff, client, contractors, VIPs, sponsors) in order to ensure everything runs as smoothly as possible for them.
- After the event, there is still a lot of hard work to be done as the clean-up operation gets under way.

Questions for reflection

1 Team leadership is critical for high-quality event delivery. What are some of the activities you would engage in with your team on the day to ensure that you have supported effective teamwork?

2. Discuss 'The Swan Effect'. Why is this a recommended approach for events managers on-site? How will it support you in actioning challenges and issues that you may face on-site during event delivery?
3. Why are event briefings and debriefs a critical part of the event delivery process? Identify some of the key areas to be noted in the briefing and debriefing.

11

Measuring event success – evaluation insights

FIGURE 11.1 The Dowson, Albert and Lomax Event Planning Process – event evaluation

PHASE 4 Evaluation and Reporting
PURPOSE OF EVALUATION
EVALUATION PLAN
WHATTO EVALUATE
ONLINE SOFTWARE
EVALUATION ISSUES
IMPACTS AND LEGACIES

Events use valuable resources, including finances, time, skills and equipment. They cost money to set up and deliver, and they take time to organize. Evaluation is essential to enable events managers to learn what works well and what doesn't work, from the inception and planning stages through the event delivery and beyond, while the information gathered can be used to plan future events. Evaluation is necessary to understand the impacts of your event – whether positive or negative. Evaluation can also be a useful way of demonstrating to others (e.g. clients, sponsors, internal event funders and other partners) that your event was a success, which can ultimately help to justify spend on future events. The days when events just happened, with no justification or clear objectives, should be long gone, and for those of us who have responsibilities for developing and delivering events, we have an obligation to understand how to measure effectiveness and outcomes for those activities.

Evaluation all too often means a scant assessment of the success of the event, but should also include evaluating the purpose of the event and the effectiveness of the teams involved. This chapter aims to present some ideas and provide examples of a range of tools and techniques for traditional evaluation, encouraging a review of the way teams work and of the relationships between event organizers, suppliers and clients, as well as participants.

By the end of this chapter you will be able to:

- explain the purpose of evaluation and what to evaluate;
- develop an evaluation plan;
- use different evaluation models and tools;
- understand what to evaluate;
- identify what works and what doesn't work within your event and the planning process;
- assess and use the findings of your evaluations;
- identify impacts and legacies of events.

One of the key characteristics of an event is that it is an activity 'with a purpose' (Bowdin et al, 2011: 14–15). Some events have the potential to have a lasting impact, or legacy, and this provides a rationale for many larger events to take place. Events may provide a catalyst for change; have an educational purpose; strengthen relationships, whether with staff, customers or other stakeholders; build a sense of community; promote goods and services: the list is seemingly endless – but it is different for each individual event. The key is to identify the purpose for your particular event – which may be simple or complex – and this will help you to plan and implement your evaluation process and content.

The purpose of evaluation

Event evaluation is important for many reasons, which can vary from one event to another. So, as the events manager, what you are evaluating should include the following aspects:

- your team, in the planning and delivery of the event
- the impacts of the event
- stakeholder satisfaction.

Rationale for evaluation

In order to be able to justify future events, events managers need to demonstrate the success of past events. Because events utilize so many resources, whether in terms of financial costs, people, or other physical assets, being able to measure the effectiveness of their use and make improvements is important. Many events agencies can suggest and shape event structures, advise on content and engagement styles, and inform on processes and locations for events. However, the initial content for an event may best come from those with an understanding of the client's objectives, clarity on the specific purpose of the event and awareness of any sensitivities around delivery. Having clear roles and identifying the scope of the contribution of the different parties involved will support your evaluation of the event planning process. For example, it may be helpful to distinguish between the teams delivering the event logistics and the development of the event content, particularly in a large or complex event. It is vital that where separate teams exist, there is frequent and effective two-way communication between them to ensure that the differences in their roles are clear, that the allocation of all activities is agreed and that both teams understand the purpose and context of the event.

Case study 11.1 evaluates the many challenging aspects of organizing a fully hybrid conference for a no-profit organization in different time zones and languages.

CASE STUDY 11.1

Hybrid events are here to stay: organizing and evaluating the conference of a non-profit Italian organization in the healthcare sector in Rome, January 2022

Serena Ferrari, Digital Event Strategist and AR Specialist; UKCEM Masters graduate 2019

The client was a non-profit organization in the healthcare sector, based in Italy. The two-day scientific conference was held in Rome in January 2022, focusing on the 50th anniversary edition of a book published in 1972 and translated into English, French and German. Due to the international nature of the event, both the pre-conference communication and the conference itself were conducted in English and Italian. Seven hundred people attended on-site and five hundred people participated remotely. The programme included six sessions, two roundtables, two workshops and one networking session.

This non-profit organization wanted to reach a much wider international audience with a fully hybrid event. Anyone remote should have been able to speak into the room with the local audience and presenters. The organization decided to implement a social media campaign with live-streaming events taking place on a regular basis on Facebook and YouTube.

We used a full-service virtual platform. The digital engagement strategy encompassed live-streaming from the venue, speakers' virtual programme, video production, online attendees' registration, on-site live-streaming and logistics, post-event video production for later views, and a social media event strategy.

A hybrid conference usually requires a larger team working both on the preparation phase and during the actual running of the event itself. This is down to a number of important factors, the main one being the larger number of elements that go into making up such a conference. It has the added wrinkle of combining two events, a cloud event and an in-person event, at the same time. A total of eight people worked on the entire event, plus a digital event strategist, a live-streaming producer, and two graphic designers who were involved in the design before the event. The implementation team was divided into three groups:

- Technical team: responsible for building the set according to the design and taking care of the interior of the conference hall. Implementation team: responsible for connecting with the keynote speakers, releasing video and content in the hall and online, video mixing, coordination of the workshops and connections and, generally speaking, the streaming. This group also included two camera operators, a sound recordist and post-event production for the on-demand videos that had just been recorded at the conference. Video switcher hardware was used to cut or fade between multiple video sources and everything in and out of the workflow was the same full-screen resolution, with an on-site AV team.
- Platform team: responsible for the platform and troubleshooting any problems that the participants had, as well as uploading new content from the client on a regular basis.
- Finally, there was the script producer, who made sure that everything happened according to the script and that each speaker knew where to stand and what to do.
- After the brief, we knew that there was a need for a full-service platform with the following requirements: enabling
    - one-to-one meetings
    - networking
    - meeting rooms
    - chat rooms
    - spaces to upload posts
    - graphics
    - creating extended profiles
    - an Expo space for partners
    - push messages from the platform
    - and the ability to embed external sites and media within the platform.

In addition, we wanted to make available on the organization website the on-demand videos for later views as in 'Netflix' style. Our research showed that not all virtual platforms are equal. Some have 3D functionalities, while others are better suited for presentations rather than collaboration, and some have unique networking and gamification functionalities but very limited capabilities of hosting online simultaneous translation. We relied on the experience of a digital event strategist to review and select the best option in terms of costs and functionalities.

The conference entailed cooperation with several international speakers at once. This meant operating on an international level, with two languages and different time zones. We created a detailed schedule of work, as well as the script and set design.

For hybrid events, it is important to keep balanced access in mind to make sure that everyone attending the event has access to the same information. This means that those guests who are present in-person at the venue should also have access to the online platform. To connect the online and offline parts we focused on a UX-friendly event app provided by the virtual platform.

The in-person and online attendees could post questions to speakers while an on-site moderator would monitor comments and work as an ambassador for the online audience and speakers. The international nature of the conference and the range of interesting topics meant that participants were more than happy to use the app and the virtual platform and share their thoughts. We used pre-recorded 'look-live' content, which is sometimes better because it can be made very dynamic through editing, and presenters are simultaneously available to comment and reply to the audience in the text chat, directly answering questions, which would not be possible if they were focused on making the presentation.

Prior to the online networking sessions, all the participants first expressed their willingness to join such meetings, and then they were able to enter a virtual room on the platform where other attendees were waiting.

Everyone can come in, look around and mingle with others at tables in the lobby where instant person-to-person, face-to-face conversations can take place. There could be two, three, five or eight people around a table. Everyone is free to move from table to table just like in a real lobby. They can read the 'Hello My Name Is' tag on whoever is at the table before they even sit down.

To encourage as many people as possible to interact, we played a short musical jingle every five minutes as the signal that it was time to change seats. If people didn't manage to fully exchange views, they could always continue their conversation behind the scenes.

The online workshops were run in groups of 10–15 people, with each group having its own moderator. The users of the platform could see a dedicated tab or 'stage' in the menu, which they would then click in order to choose a specific topic for a workshop that they had signed up for prior to the event.

The conference sponsors, partners and supporting institutions were all able to present their brands in a dedicated tab, with their logos, website links and contact details all visible. Sponsors had their own tables for face-to-face mingling, answering questions and demonstrating products. They had their own scheduled demonstrations, seminars, literature they could click and 'take home'. Seminars were single track or multi-track. They could build their own schedule or sign up for certain sessions in advance – just like an in-person event.

The feedback we received after the conference was extremely valuable. The languages, time zone and two different audiences posed no problem, and a fantastic atmosphere prevailed throughout the implementation of the project. The return on investment was leveraged by the post-event on-demand videos accessible to members throughout the year on the Foundation website.

Learning

A hybrid event is not just live-streaming a conference. It is a more complex event to organize. Success lies in an engagement strategy connecting online and offline audiences. Some of the key elements include:

- a programme delivering great content in a variety of formats, such panel discussions, videos, whitepapers;

- networking sessions around specific topics engaging both remote and on-site audiences in a co-creative way;
- workshops delivering bite-size education courses;
- Powerpoint presentations with graphic animations and videos;
- experienced moderators responsible for guiding both online and on-site attendees throughout the event;
- simultaneous translations to overcome language and cultural barriers;
- and finally, an experienced digital event strategist and live-streaming producer.

Explore further

www.serenaferrari.co.uk (archived at https://perma.cc/2QKS-S3A3)

Event objectives

A major problem for many events is that there are either no event objectives agreed, or that objectives are unclear or not measurable. Feedback from experienced events managers indicates that this continues to be the case, despite global or national economic pressures. The reasons for this lack of focus may not come from events managers themselves, but may be due to pressures of time within the client organization, for example if senior managers do not make the time to consider the event objectives because they do not see the event as an immediate priority.

Good events managers will work proactively with the client (and potentially within the client's organization) to facilitate the development of objectives that are clear and measurable. Such measures take time and effort, but the client will thank you for it, and will be more likely to commission future events. Developing a process that is applied rigorously (even if that process changes) will assist the client, and templates for taking a brief can be developed.

This is where the role of the lead events manager working with the client is important. As event expert, do you act as a consultant, leading the process to develop the event objectives? Are you an integral part of the client-supplier team where your opinion is valued? Or are you simply included in meetings with little input, if any? It has even been known for events managers to be excluded from initial planning meetings or side-lined by those who perceive themselves to be more senior but are not events experts, who will attempt to take a brief but lack the experience or expertise to ask the right questions, or might interpret incorrectly what has been said or agreed. There's no substitute for being 'in the room' and part of such discussions when they happen, keeping an accurate record of what is said and agreed, and by whom.

Audience research is not always carried out as a matter of course, but it should be, in order to test their perceptions of the proposed event and feed back their views into the content development process. There have been many occasions when an organization decides that a specific audience needs to know certain information, but when the potential audience doesn't recognize the need, such efforts are wasted. Case study 11.2 considers the financial aspects of an events organization and how important it is in evaluation.

CASE STUDY 11.2

Evaluating financial aspects of an events organization

Laura Bennett-Whiskens, Managing Director, SYLOA Ltd; UKCEM Graduate 2017

Financial management was never something I was keen on when studying for my degree, and certain financial aspects of my job are definitely my least favourite. But they are also the most important. Ultimately, everything comes back to budget. I, or the clients of SYLOA Ltd, can have the best ideas in the world, but if the budget isn't there, those plans won't become a reality. In fact, the finances are a key focal point during the beginning, middle and end of each of my project journeys. Initially, establishing what budget the SYLOA Ltd clients have to work with is key in order to ascertain what is possible – often what a client wants to produce and what their budget will allow them to produce are two very different things. By having clear outlines of the expenses involved in the planning and execution of the project, I can provide the all-important expectation management needed in order to move forward in the most effective way. Maintaining a consistent overview of finances throughout the project is also paramount – this ensures I'm not overspending/overworking, and that the client budget is being allocated effectively. It also allows me to flag any changes in scope, or requirements for budget review if unexpected costs appear or certain aspects of the project take more time/resources than initially planned. And once the project is complete, financial reconciliations and evaluations provide more than one overview for my clients, and for me as a supplier. Other than the obvious ability to provide the essential final invoices, financial evaluation is one of the Key Performance Indicators (KPIs) at SYLOA Ltd, providing a quantitative method of evaluation for the post-event client reports. It also allows me to reflect on my forecasted budget vs my actuals, the factors that impacted any differences in these figures, and how these can either be managed better next time or how I need to quote differently for similar work in the future.

My biggest mantra for successful client relationships is that communication is key – this applies to my project, events and client relations in a holistic sense, but is especially important when it comes to the finances. I never want to be in a position where I'm blind-siding my clients with unexpected or unexplained costs, and I never want to take a loss on a project because of poor financial management and/or shoddy communication. At SYLOA Ltd, my clients have access to real-time summaries of the time I have spent on projects. This is especially key when delivering services that don't necessarily provide a physical deliverable. A lot of the work

I charge my clients for is 'time', not something tangible, and they need to be able to reflect on what it is exactly they're paying for, the time they are saving by bringing me onboard and the return on investment they get from our collaboration. Communication is not the only key factor when it comes to good financial management. Financial administration and efficient financial process are also crucial. When you're busy with planning, being on-site, or just juggling your general workload, completing financial documentation can often feel like a lower-priority task; often immediate client demands or problem-solving scenarios take precedence. But having to come back and work through folders of receipts, invoices and budget sheets can be a real headache. Ensuring financial progress is monitored consistently is one of the most vital parts of the process. Implementing a clear financial process, efficient documentation and regular reporting is key (at SYLOA Ltd, Excel is our best friend, and for bigger corporations, efficient financial systems/programmes should be implemented). And it's key to remember that this doesn't just sit with the senior leaders in a team – outlining the financial boundaries of a project to the wider team is crucial to allocation of resources and the ability to understand where the limitations lie, or where additional capacity is available if required.

Overall, financial management, evaluation and consideration is one of the main foundations of each project at SYLOA Ltd; you can't build houses on poor foundations, and events and client relationships are no different.

Events need clear objectives with links to an agreed purpose that connects with the client organization's aims, that can be applied across a variety and range of events, with measurable outcomes, and that demonstrates links to the client organization.

Throughout this book, there is a range of activities involved in planning and managing an event. As such, it is vital to evaluate what has worked and what hasn't worked so well. The checklist provides a list of the most important aspects when it comes to evaluating your team's success in delivering an event.

CHECKLIST: EVALUATING YOUR TEAM'S ACTIVITIES

- Event programme and content development, advice and support
- Event programme coordination and delivery
- Procurement and management of event suppliers
- Venue search, site inspections and selection
- Venue liaison, including overnight accommodation and catering requirements
- Managing event bookings, attendee communication and registration
- Managing logistics of associated facilities and activities, such as exhibitions
- Guest liaison, including VIPs and speakers – ensuring that everyone at the event is registered, including the team delivering the event

- Event communications – sign-off by relevant parties, including the client's corporate communications and the event's logistics team
- Providing a first point of contact for all event participants via email/telephone/social media and ensuring all queries and issues are responded to immediately and resolved promptly
- Confirmation of event bookings, issuing venue and event details, and event evaluation questionnaires
- Development and production of document templates and maintaining controlled versions of documentation and communication records
- Production of event materials and collateral including signage, name badges
- On-site event support
- Developing, issuing, collating and analysing event evaluations, and sharing the results with appropriate stakeholders, including suppliers
- Completing budget and payment processes
- Collecting, uploading and maintaining event resources (online) for future access by different stakeholders

Evaluation and the events team's role

It is important to identify and then evaluate the activities allocated to each team involved in different aspects of the development and delivery of an event. Defining the scope of each event team's remit is also key to enabling a full evaluation of the resources available and in use. The importance of setting objectives prior to the start of any new event project includes listing the scope and objectives of a new or existing event team for future evaluation. Agreement on the scope of the event team's work and responsibilities feeds into the overall evaluation of the event, in terms of whether or not the team's objectives have been achieved.

What to evaluate

Some event planning models consider evaluation to be key to the first stage. This is particularly true when thinking about repeat (often annual) events, for example an annual conference or AGM, building in learning from the successes and failures of the previous event to plan and prepare fully for the following year in a cycle of continuous improvement. So where does evaluation begin? Potentially with pre-event input. And where does it end? Evaluation is an iterative process that informs future events, related or not.

We advocate a stakeholder approach that evaluates success from different perspectives – those of the client, delegates/participants/attendees, planners, suppliers, staff, any local community affected by the event, and any health and safety partners. We also recommend piloting the content of certain types of events, such as conferences, by involving and engaging potential participants in the information-gathering exercise that will inform the type of event that is appropriate for your audience. Meeting participants' needs may be more challenging than might be imagined, as such needs may not be explicit – and at times, needs may be unrecognized by the participants themselves. It is always important to demonstrate to event participants that their needs are being met, as well as those of the client. Online questionnaires are not the only form of gaining feedback for evaluation purposes – you could also include focus groups and interviews, video diaries, collecting data from social media hashtags. But there is no point in collecting data if you're not going to use it.

Evaluating procurement is a key aspect of ensuring that you have appointed the most appropriate suppliers for your event. Chapter 9 covers this procurement function, but the process begins with developing clarity about the purpose and role of each type of supplier and agreeing the criteria against which these aspects will be measured. Regular meetings with suppliers to obtain and give feedback on delivery and planning processes should include two-way feedback – to and from the supplier. Chapter 5 explains how to evaluate venue requirements using simple tools and templates. The worked example below provides ideas for the evaluation of an experiential event.

Developing an evaluation plan

In order to develop an evaluation plan, it is important to take a structured approach that includes all aspects of the event planning and delivery. The following headings suggest how such a plan might be constructed:

- Event purpose
- Background to the client and the event
- Description of the context of the event
- The overall (strategic) aims of the client organization and of the specific part of the organization procuring the event
- Identified and named roles and responsibilities
- Objectives of the event and how they relate to the overall strategy of the client organization

- Event branding, visual identity (including online) and fit with the client's brand and values
- Key audiences for the event, segmented and described (e.g. in terms of attitude)
- Key messages for the event, applied to audience segments
- Communication channels, applied to specific audience segments
- Internal (client organization) communications, including how information will be cascaded
- Activities required and their relationship to organizational objectives
- Communication dissemination plan
- Key tasks and allocated responsibilities (on the client side and for event management)
- Resources required and dependencies against a timeline
- Event timing

Once these aspects are agreed, they form the core of the event plan and evaluation against progress is possible. Any evaluation strategy or plan sits within an organizational context, so make sure that all aspects of the evaluation are appropriately developed within such a framework.

Evaluation timeline

Using the structure of your event plan, you should develop an ongoing evaluation plan that runs alongside the event plan to evaluate all actions, decisions, processes and other factors that may affect the development and delivery of your event. Figure 11.2 shows the flow of activities of an evaluation timeline for an event.

FIGURE 11.2 Evaluation timeline

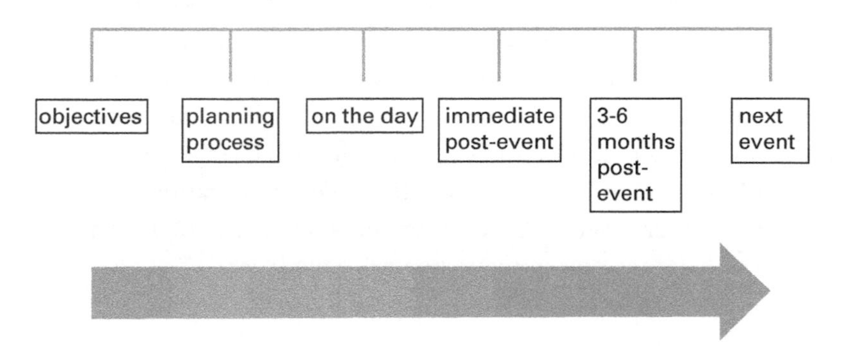

Evaluation models and tools

While there are thousands of evaluation models, Jack J Phillips' ROI model (Phillips, Breining and Pulliam Phillips, 2008) is endorsed by Meeting Professionals International (MPI) (www.eventroi.org/methodology/) and establishes six levels of assessment for any event:

Level Zero – assesses the fit between the target audience and the characteristics of actual attendees.

Level One – considers what most end-of-event questionnaires address –the participants' satisfaction with their event experience.

Level Two – focuses on measuring the learning or cognitive change achieved by participants within the event.

Level Three – addresses the extent to which learning gained at an event has been implemented, by monitoring changes in behaviour in the workplace.

Level Four – measures the impact of and benefits to the sending organization from individuals attending an event.

Level Five – compares the net financial costs against monetized benefits of a meeting or event (i.e. the required contribution to profit; for non-commercial events the fit with organizational mission often replaces financial objectives).

While this model looks more appropriate for business events such as conferences, exhibitions and meetings, the approach can be applied to any type of event in terms of measuring the experiences of participants and stakeholders. Ideally, according to the Phillips model, evaluation should demonstrate progression through each level as knowledge gained and skills learnt at an event are applied to day-to-day work practices to benefit the organization as a whole.

The underlying basis of the Phillips model is formed by the systematic Kirkpatrick model, which is derived from a commercial training environment (www.kirkpatrickpartners.com/TheKirkpatrickModel/). This theory was developed in the 1950s by Dr Don Kirkpatrick to measure individual and organizational learning from training interventions. The Kirkpatrick model covers the experience, the learning (often through tests on course or event content), the extent to which that learning is embedded on the individual's return to the workplace through changed behaviour, and the results that it brings in terms of benefits to the wider organization. For experiential, sports, music and other leisure-related events this approach is still relevant as the aim of evaluation includes measuring the customer's experience.

Online event management software

Over the past 20 years, there have been many developments in the availability of online software and apps that can facilitate the creation, organization and management of a range of events, including seminars, conferences and meetings. Such software can support teams organizing large and complex programmes of events for their own in-house organizations or for agency clients. Event software can enable the centralized management of events with their own branding and identities, and different administrator access levels. There are many different types of software that can be used for event planning, issuing online invitations and managing online bookings, as well as event evaluations and reporting of results. The use of self-service online registration provides a consistent, quality approach and improves attendees' experience, significantly reducing organizational administrative costs and workload. Software should include a reporting functionality that enables data tracking; this can provide detailed statistics for each event and each client, giving useful information to accurately measure return on investment.

For evaluation purposes, online software should include:

- a quick and easy release of template-driven evaluation questionnaires sent via an email direct to event attendees, using a set of core questions with the option to add supplementary questions, to evaluate speakers, workshops, sessions, options;
- a chase email option that can be sent only to those participants who have not already completed the online evaluation questionnaire;
- a manual completion option for users who return their evaluation separately by email or post;
- the option to communicate directly with different types of event participants, from delegates to speakers and exhibitors, suppliers and clients;
- immediate anonymized aggregated statistics and comments that save time and enable quick assessment of your event's success;
- the ability to issue a follow-up evaluation so you can measure knowledge change and the longer-term effectiveness of your event on attendees;
- the availability of reporting, from a brief summary to a detailed report.

The example shows what a summary report would look like for a specific event series for one client, using a customized online event management software system rather than some of the generic solutions that are more widely available.

EXAMPLE SUMMARY REPORT

Event X Evaluation Headlines

Jan–Feb (Year)

Four events took place, attended by a total of 274 attendees – an average of 69 per event.

The 11 speakers were rated for content, presentation and usefulness.

With an average 24.1% response rate, there were some 184 qualitative comments, grouped as follows:

- Programme structure: 2.7% (of comments received)
- Venue: 7.6%
- Support: 15.2%
- Good event: 10.9%
- Content: 31.0%
- Networking: 9.8%
- Speaker: 10.9%
- Admin: 12.0%

Some 42.4% of these comments were positive, 52.2% were negative and 5.4% were neutral.

Satisfaction ratings (Good/Excellent) were as follows:

- Overall event: 66.15%
- Administration: 85.55%
- Venues: 88.08%

For bespoke software, system users should be provided with access to ongoing web-based support, with live chat and email communication to enable issues to be resolved quickly. Table 11.1 compares the benefits of using bespoke (tailored) online event participant management software to the generic systems available online.

Evaluation issues

Having compared the differences between bespoke and generic evaluation software, there are a number of other evaluation issues to consider:

- Anonymous or named responses: anonymity often inspires respondees to be more open and honest in their responses – but they need to be able to trust that their

TABLE 11.1 Comparison of bespoke evaluation software against generic event booking systems

Area	Bespoke evaluation programme/ software	Generic online booking programme/software
General	Product tailored to meet specific needs of the client.	Product with no flexibility beyond standard configuration.
Core features	Provides all the core features needed to host, promote and manage events online, including delegate self-booking.	Provides all the core features needed to host, promote and manage events online, including delegate self-booking.
Branding and programme management	Designed for professional events managers to support the whole event marketing and management service as transparently as possible. Events are run using your own website, email domain name and branding, and operate from your own branded website (with microsites for individual events if required). Focused on your audience and your events programme rather than on one event or a series of events in isolation. Once a delegate has registered for one event, they have easy access to future events, and you have powerful reporting and communication options across the full community of delegates.	Built as a third-party service to facilitate easy set-up of ticketing for events.
Flexible payment	Flat fee for the system with no additional charges per booking or for higher activity levels. The only other charges are those levied by your payment processor (e.g. PayPal). This provides for easy budgeting and planning and offers at better value for larger events and multiple event programmes. Does not take a percentage of sales revenue. Any mainstream payment-processing service can be integrated, so you can use whichever one you prefer.	Charges percentage of the ticket value plus fixed rate per ticket; this is on top of the payment processing fee (typically 3.5% to 5% of the ticket price). Gives the option of using only PayPal or themselves as payment processor.
Post-event evaluation	Provides built-in evaluation tools to enable easy generation of feedback and measurement of effectiveness for individual events and for series of events.	Allows users to send emails to event participants to access third-party feedback tools such as SurveyMonkey.

thoughts are *really* anonymous. Some online systems will anonymize the data collected but will keep a record of who has or has not responded. It may be that you want to know who has submitted a specific response, so it can be followed up afterwards (it may also be the case that you can guess who said it). In this case it is better to include a specific question that invites respondees to add their email address if they would like a follow-up from the event organizers on a specific matter.

- Online or paper? Surprisingly, some organizations continue to use paper forms handed out at the event, often 'encouraging' completion by responding with a free gift when the form is handed in. However, a paper format requires typing up the content, an onerous and time-consuming task. While online formats are immediate, they may get lost in the attendee's email inbox or be discarded as spam mail, and response rates are never as high as those 'coerced' by free gifts. However, there are advantages, in that some people prefer to reflect on their experience and may make a more considered submission after the event. Online systems can accumulate responses automatically, providing initial analysis of anonymized data, relieving the event team of the task of manually inputting data. Some online response systems can also identify who has not responded and chase them up at a later date, as well as sending subsequent questionnaires on different topics.
- The importance of developing an ongoing picture of event delivery through consistent evaluation cannot be overestimated. Online systems provide the ability to compare and contrast evaluation and other reporting measures – such as attendance rates, no-shows, booking lead times – that can be used to improve and enhance delivery of any event as well as specific events in a series through the analysis of trends. Feedback should not only remain with the client or events team, but event participants should be informed of changes that have been made as a result of their input.

Online and social media evaluation

Online social media such as Twitter, Facebook, Instagram and LinkedIn have become a useful source of feedback about your event. You can encourage such feedback by communicating a hashtag with your event name (abbreviated) #event that is included in posts and tweets. Encouraging more followers is also useful – and this will only happen if you engage in online activity to promote your event and engage with participants online. During the event it is useful to respond to feedback, and after the event, hashtag quotes provide valuable data for evaluation purposes.

Companies such as The Live Group (2022) (www.livegroup.co.uk/) developed ground-breaking interactive software that gathers data during discussions, which is also useful for post-event analysis. An example from a conference on sexual health is shown, where pre-prepared questions were asked, discussed at each table and the

TABLE 11.2 Example of response count for issues not covered in the session.

Response	From which delegates' table
Reporting.	2
If you could cover any sites which are already live.	2
Are money and resources to be available to support deployments?	2
Can we differentiate policy for chronic conditions like HIV from sexual health?	3
Chlamydia screening and what level of sharing is acceptable between GU services and the screening programme if any.	4
Rights of underage.	5
Children's issues/parental access.	6
Need to cover partner notification issues and circumstances where sharing is done without consent.	8
What protection does use of GUM Numbers give over and above use of NHS Number?	8
How are you informing children about consent/dissent?	9

responses generated by each table were agreed and input on a tablet. Some questions may be held in reserve, while new questions may arise from the table discussions. Responses to the question 'Is there an issue not on the agenda that you would like us to cover today?' can be measured easily, as shown in Table 11.2. These topics can then be added to the agenda and included in any discussions planned for the event. Such tools are commonly used today to enable interactive sessions asking questions of the audience, whether physically present or online. In pandemic lockdown these tools provided popular quiz facilities.

Responses to the question 'Should it be possible to share identifiable clinical information, for patient care and with the patient's consent, with other same-service clinics, i.e. GUM or Reproductive Health?' give a clear picture of the opinion in the room, as shown in Figure 11.3.

Such software can provide valuable insights into the opinions of event participants but is often better managed by experienced facilitators.

Identifying what works and how to make improvements in your event planning process

There are many different methods for identifying success, failure or improvements. The 'Three Qs' process, developed in the 1970s by the Xerox Corporation, provides a simple approach that works well, consistently, and has been used in many different contexts and for many different purposes.

FIGURE 11.3 Example of question responses using software

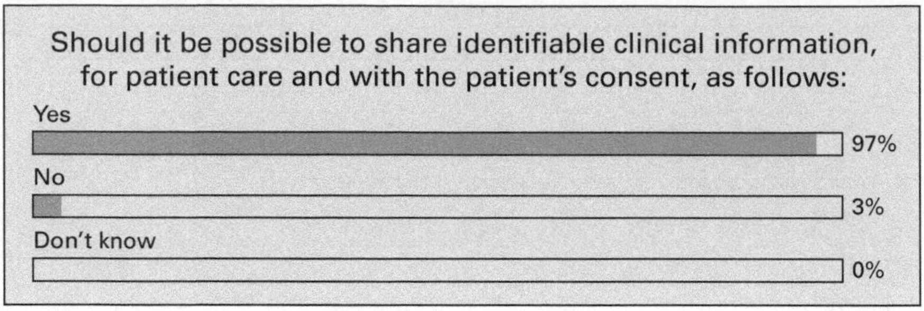

The questions can be introduced at any point in the event planning and delivery process, for example in a 'hot debrief' (immediately at the end of the event, on-site) or in a 'cold debrief' (at the end of the event process, giving time for reflection and considered input from event attendees and other stakeholders). This technique can be used to build continuous improvement and review into any part of your event management processes or content development.

The 'Three Qs' approach consists, not surprisingly, of three questions that are posed for anyone involved to respond to, informally – as ideas and thoughts and reflections arise.

The questions are:

- What has worked well? (and how can we improve it?)
- What hasn't worked well? (and how can we learn from it?)
- What issues, ideas or concerns does this raise? (and how can they be progressed?)

The most important element of these questions is not really this first part of the question (e.g. 'What has worked well?'), but what happens next. First, the responses are captured as bullet points for all to see, whether online in the chat function or even on a flipchart. Once each question has been asked and answered, a second action comes into play; this attempts to identify potential solutions or options, not casting blame, but looking for improvement at every turn. This process can be as detailed as you like (or have time for), and can be applied at any stage of the event process. The questions can be asked of different stakeholders, about any aspect of the event development or delivery, including the usual participant evaluations. And it works. But do feel free to develop your own method of asking questions and reflecting on the event. It's more important that you apply *something* for evaluation than nothing at all, but you may wish to adapt or develop your own evaluation process which becomes part of the way you 'do events'.

Evaluation may include reviewing agreed implementation and event planning processes, but it's more important to map and agree processes and ensure that they are adhered to, than not to have any processes at all and 're-create the wheel' every time you plan and deliver an event. And processes are not written in stone – they can be improved too, and should be reviewed regularly to make improvements. But these changes do need to be communicated to those who need to work to the new processes.

The event evaluation process can begin at any time – the earlier the better, and finish as late in the process as you wish. The stages of evaluation and research can include the following:

- the planning stages of the event;
- immediately pre-event;
- during the event – on-site;
- at the end of the event;
- post-event after a gap of some months.

EVENTS MANAGER HACK

The post-event evaluation, aside from rounding up your qualitative and quantitative outcomes, is also an opportunity for honesty. Ask yourself how the delivery worked, what went wrong, if goals set were met, lessons learnt and, finally, how can you maximize these learnings to keep creating successful events.

Selina Arnall, Event and Marketing Manager, That Event Girl; Social Traders, Australia

Examples of questionnaires and questions

In developing your own questionnaires and evaluation questions you might cover the following areas:

- Event participants' experience
- What they have learnt or how much
- How they will change what they do as a result; what specific action will they take?
- Relating to the specific event objectives, whether directly or indirectly
- Whether the event was memorable or worthwhile (you would have to word this question carefully to get a useful result).

Different sections of the questionnaire might cover a range of aspects, such as: the event objectives, different sessions within the event, specific issues facing the organization or its clients/customers, and the overall experience of the event. Different types of questions will provide different types of information. Quantitative questions might be Yes/No, a scale of 1–5 or 1–10 (known as a Likert scale); these give results that can be counted and measured. Qualitative responses might be sought by having an open comment box, the results of which can be analysed to identify themes, and positivity or negativity, in terms of tone.

The types of questions used in evaluation questionnaires are important, and there needs to be a balance between a quick yes/no or rating response and a considered answer with comments that add depth of understanding, and which can provide matter for qualitative analysis.

Question type:

- Yes/no
- Yes/no with don't know
- Scale 1–5
- Scale 1–10
- Rank options according to preference
- Multiple choice – single answer
- Multiple choice – multiple answers
- Free text (comment box)

Is the question mandatory?

- If a question is mandatory, this could lead to non-completion of the questionnaire.

Consider the wording of the question itself:

- Open/closed questions
- Single question not multiple
- Specific
- Measurable
- Does it relate to the event objectives (explicitly or implicitly)?

Demographics

- Consider how you want to be able to analyse your event participants

Piloting a questionnaire is always useful – and the more feedback received, the better able you will be to make improvements.

In Figure 11.4, which is a sample evaluation form, the questions were used on a consistent basis by one organization. Evaluation software provided the facility to add or delete specific questions, with a core set of questions asked every time an event was delivered.

FIGURE 11.4 Sample initial evaluation form

Please rate the following:

	Comfort of meeting rooms	Audio visual	Venue location	Car parking	Venue staff
Excellent					
Good					
Satisfactory					
Poor					
N/A					

- Do you have any other comments regarding the venue?
- Knowledge & skills: Please use the sliders below to record where you felt you were before the event and where you feel you are now. Rate between 1 and 10 as follows:

  0= I had/have no knowledge of the subjects discussed at the event and how I could use them in the future

  10= I fully understand the subjects discussed at the event and how I can use them in the future

  Before the event: 0–10

  After the event: 0–10
- What did you like best about this event?
- How could this event be improved?
- How did you find out about the event?
- How would you improve publicity and encourage participation?
- Please identify up to three actions that can be taken away today and implemented in your work/organization
- What further support would be useful to help you implement these actions?
- Where would you or your organization have accessed the information presented at this event if it had not been held?
- What further support can we offer you or your organization?
- Your evaluation entry is anonymous. If you would like to be contacted by us to discuss the event or your feedback, please leave your email details here.
- Please rate the event overall in terms of the headings below:

	Administration and event organization	Content	Venue	Event overall
Excellent				
Good				
Satisfactory				
Poor				
N/A				

- Any other comments?

TABLE 11.3 Alternative rating system

Please rate each session on a scale of 1 to 5, where 1 is poor and 5 is excellent:			
	Content	Presentation	Usefulness
Title of session			

For specific sessions, from keynote speakers to breakout sessions, a different rating structure could be used, shown in Table 11.3.

Analysing and using the findings of your evaluations

When your event is over and you have amassed lots of data, it is vital to the analyse that information and implement changes that result from your analysis. These changes could include making improvements to your event management processes, how you communicate with event participants or other stakeholders, ideas for improving content and style of future events and the way you work as an events team to deliver future activities.

The following example provides a range of data analysis that contributes to the overall evaluation reporting process. Using the evaluation findings is crucial – there's really no point in gathering data if you then don't use it, and the changes you make can improve your event success as well as help to make you more effective as an events manager.

FIGURE 11.5 Example evaluation report

Selected data from online Event Management System: Diocesan Day Conference
Attendee data: This section provides a summary of the booking statistics:
511 delegates (as registered on EMS) attended plus children, KidzKlub and Team
Total 556
Did Not Attend
22 delegates DNA; No Show Rate: 3.95% (Industry best average 10%)
Cancellations
18 delegates cancelled
(3 delegates self-cancelled; 15 cancelled by Team)
6 cancelled during the week up to the conference
6 cancelled on the day
Booking Sources
21.65% of bookings made direct to website
67.8% of bookings made by Liz (NB within two years, these figures had reversed)
10.55% of bookings made by Matt & Ruth
Email and Postal Bookings
181 participants with no email address supplied
32.55% of participants with no email address supplied
Evidence suggests that a significant proportion (possibly 50%) of these may either have an email address of their own or share an email address with their spouse. However, even with one-third of participants having postal confirmation, significant savings in stationery and postal costs achieved overall through use of internet-based bookings.

FIGURE 11.6 Workshop evaluation: example of analysis

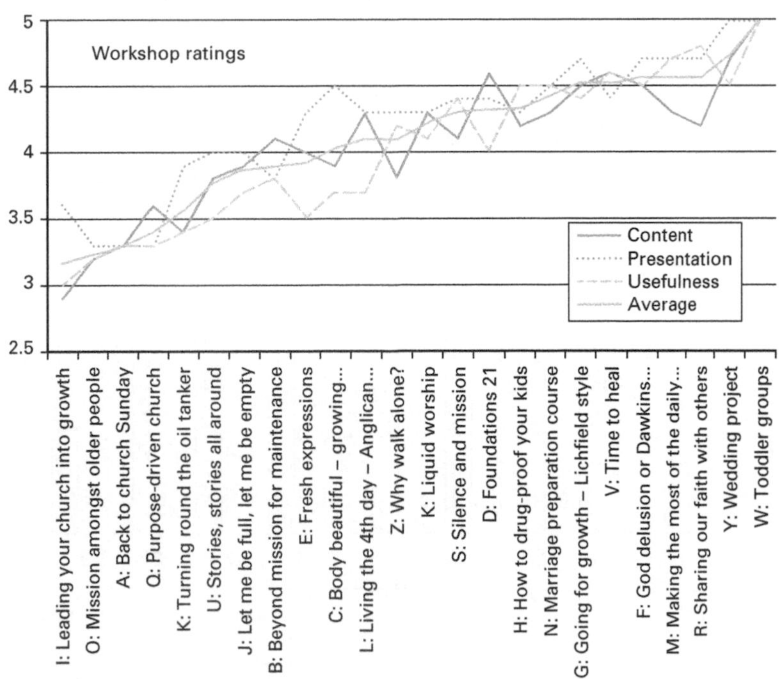

The following figures show examples of how you can present your analysis to clients or other stakeholders.

Figure 11.5 summarizes an evaluation report with key headings on attendance and bookings. These statistics are useful for event planning teams for future events, especially information about no-show rates and cancellations, along with preferences for modes of booking. The event was attended by over 550 people, mostly older – many of whom did not have access to email or online sources, so postal bookings were accepted. The savings from online bookings came partly from reduced stationery and postage costs, but also considerable savings in staff time inputting the data manually.

The event had 24 workshop options that took place several times during the day.

Figure 11.6 shows how these workshops were evaluated by participants under three criteria: for usefulness, presentation and content, on a score of 1 to 5. The first graph shows a bar chart with the three aspects rated, in alphabetical order, while the second shows the workshops in ascending order of popularity/favourable ratings. This can help to guide event planners on suitable topics for the following event.

Using a scale of 1 to 10, participants were asked to rate their skills and knowledge before and after the event. The graph in Figure 11.7 shows the accumulated averages for the before and after scores, providing a measure for the level of change as recognized by the attendees. This measurement links to Kirkpatrick's model, by inviting participants to self-assess their knowledge and experience of the event focus prior to and after the event.

FIGURE 11.7 Example of knowledge and experience ratings, before and after event

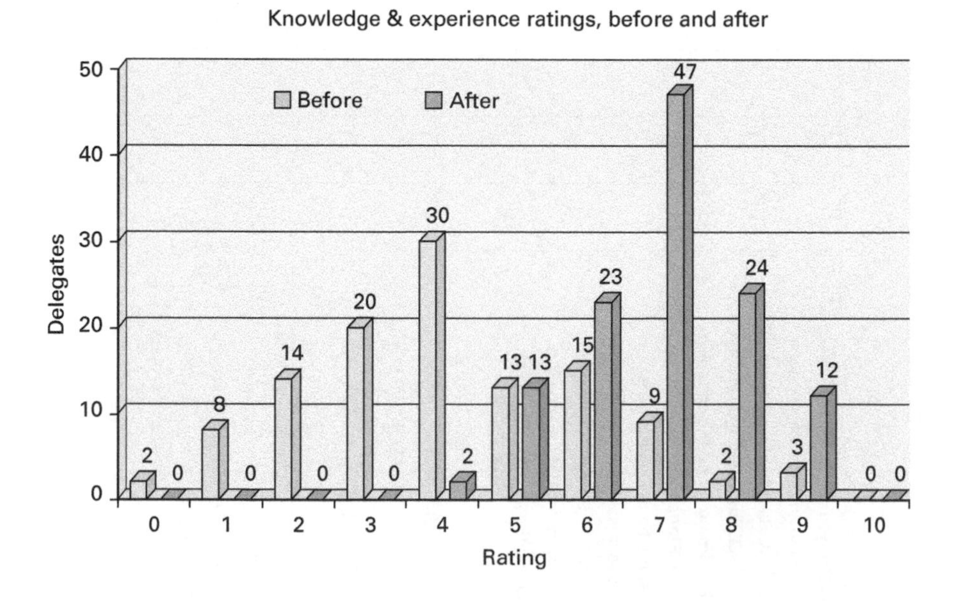

TABLE 11.4 Example of knowledge and skills averages

Knowledge and skills: averages			
Before	**After**	**Change (number)**	**Change (per cent)**
3.97	6.42	2.45	61.71%

FIGURE 11.8 Example of evaluation: question

Option	Number	Percentage
Excellent	68	51.13%
Good	53	39.85%
Satisfactory	11	8.27%
Poor	1	0.75%
Total:	133	

Table 11.4 presents a brief summary of the impact of the event, showing a 61 per cent improvement in the average self-assessment

Individual elements of the event can also be measured. The example in Figure 11.8 shows the scores for satisfaction with car parking, shown as raw data – number and percentage forms.

Participants were asked to identify their top three actions that they would prioritize as individuals, after the event. Figure 11.9 shows the grouped accumulated

FIGURE 11.9 Analysis of responses to 'What are the three priorities for you from this event?'

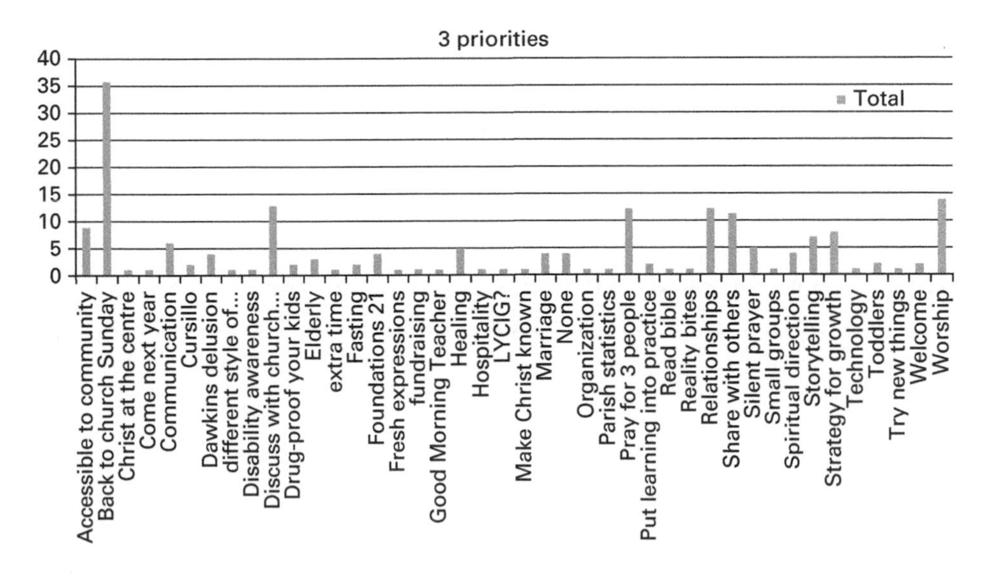

FIGURE 11.10 Analysis of comments on venue theme

Theme – Venues	Negative	Neutral	Positive
Access	1		
AV	1		
Car parking		1	2
Catering	1		
Children	1		
Exhibition	2		2
Location		2	8
Overall event			5
Signage	10	3	4
Space	5	1	2
Structure		1	
Toilets		1	
Travel	1	1	1
Venue	1		26
Worship	2		
Total	25	10	50

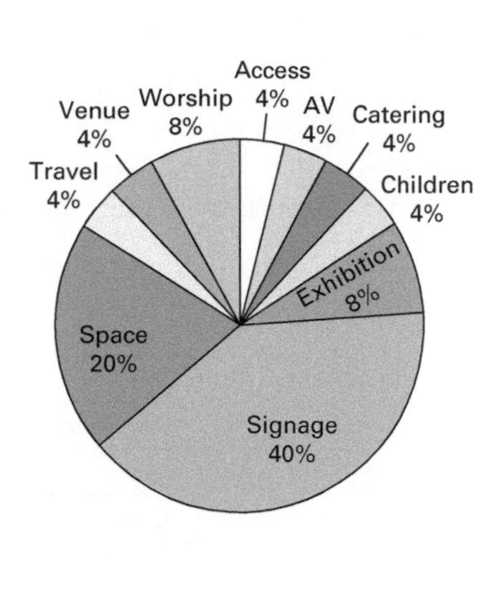

responses for prioritized personal actions post-event. Some of the groupings emerge from the workshop titles.

Questionnaire respondees were asked to provide a comment on the venue. These have been filtered and grouped according to themes, and then allocated a response rating for the tone of the comment, from 'negative' to 'neutral' to 'positive'. The table and graph in Figure 11.10 show the results. The data in the table indicates that signage was a concern that could be improved for the next event, while the most positive comments (more than half) were received about the venue. The data for the negative-tone comments is shown in a pie chart in Figure 11.10. Addressing the top three concerns would enable the event organizers to make significant improvements that would be appreciated by attendees at the following event.

Table 11.5 shows a similar tone analysis for the question 'what did you like best?' It is notable (and a regular occurrence at events) that even when a question is aimed at eliciting a positive response, there will always be some negative responses.

These examples of analysis of the evaluation responses provide a powerful set of data for improving future event planning and measuring success against objectives.

TABLE 11.5 Analysis of 'what did you like best?'

Theme	Negative	Neutral	Positive	Grand Total
Childcare			3	3
Discussion			1	1
Fellowship			58	58
Learning from others			9	9
Organization			11	11
Overall			9	9
Speakers			58	58
Worship	1	1	47	49
Grand Total	1	1	196	198

Impacts and legacies of events

For larger events (known as 'mega-events') such as the Olympics or the Football World Cup, considering the environmental, economic and social impacts of the event is key to success in the bidding process.

These three elements – environmental, economic and social, are known as the 'triple bottom line' (Elkington 1997) and they include planning for a post-event legacy. A well-known example of the triple bottom line in bidding for mega-events, such as the Olympics, would be plans for the use of buildings after the event has taken place. For the London 2012 Olympics and Paralympics, the potential for use of new buildings constructed for that purpose was emphasized within the bid. However, there are far too many images of unused and dilapidated buildings from former Olympic Games, most recently in Rio, Brazil (2016 Summer Olympics), Sochi, Russia (2014 Winter Olympics) and Beijing, China (2008 Summer Olympics).

An essential part of the bid process is outlining the intended legacy after the event has moved on, and this often makes the difference between successful and unsuccessful bids. So how does that translate into a successful event? Most of us will not be responsible for developing a bid for such a mammoth undertaking, but it is still worthwhile considering the impacts and legacy of our smaller events as part of the evaluation process. It is clear that understanding the impacts of the events we run is more important today than ever before – and that applies to planners of events of all sizes, not simply global mega-events.

The triple bottom line: environmental, social and economic sustainability

The concept of 'green' events is linked to environmental sustainability. A useful, detailed handbook and practical guide to running 'green' events is by Meegan Jones: *Sustainable Event Management* (2018). Most events involve travel of some kind, for participants as well as organizers and suppliers, perhaps only a few miles, but sometimes across the globe. Event organizers aiming to encourage participants out of their cars might follow the example of some festivals where the only way to attend is to purchase a coach ticket (one of the more sustainable forms of transport) that includes the cost of the festival ticket as well. An event might be delivered in multiple venues located in different geographical regions, with online streaming linking up the sites, and hybrid events (linking face-to-face and virtual audiences) are increasingly popular. While, in the past, exhibitions were the most wasteful events, discarding carpets after one use, it is now festivals that suffer from the plague of 'throwaway everything', from tents and sleeping bags to clothing and cutlery. Registration no longer needs to be paper based or postal, and technology today enables a variety of online registration options, from the simplicity of generic apps such as Eventbrite to more complex bespoke solutions with much broader functionality, as described earlier in this chapter.

From a social perspective, event sustainability may be related to an organization's corporate social responsibility (CSR), which includes fair pay, using Fairtrade or organic products – but also might incorporate sessions for event participants getting out and doing some good, say, working in a local school. It can be seen as an opportunity to educate attendees about making healthy lifestyle choices for healthy eating. However, this too should be viewed through the lens of whether such actions represent lived-values versus a tick-box approach. For example, former UK events agency, Universal World Events, regularly sent members of its staff team to work with African charities on projects supporting underprivileged children. PR companies and their clients might ask themselves how this appears to outside observers, as well as considering the extent to which actions and decisions are congruent with an organization's stated values.

Economic sustainability is a broad topic that encompasses the economic viability of an event, for the present and future, as well as considerations of state support and sponsorship. Australian regional government backing is vital to the success of the events sector in Sydney (www.businesseventssydney.com.au), where Business Events Sydney promotes the region and coordinates bids for new business, developing collaborative relationships between suppliers, influencers and potential clients. In a similar vein, the 'Keep Britain Meeting' campaign was developed by the British Business Visits & Events Partnership (BVEP) (www.businessvisitsandeventspartnership.com/) to encourage new events business into the British economy. Such organizations have huge resources that might be harnessed towards a specific geographic region. From another angle, economic sustainability also relates to the idea of using local suppliers for an event, generating (and keeping) cash within the local economy.

Questions relating to what should be included in evaluating the economic impact of an event to a specific locale are addressed by different methodologies developed by academics and practitioners, but it is acknowledged to be notoriously challenging to calculate an accurate gauge of the economic contribution of a specific event. The potential sources of event expenditure include: travel, including airfares, event or conference attendance fees, accommodation, catering and entertainment, as well as on-site and off-site spending by event participants, but should be measured against the cost of developing facilities for use by participants. (Remember the Brazilian demonstrations against the impact on public services and corrupt officials around the time of the 2014 Football World Cup?) (www.telegraph.co.uk/news/picturegalleries/worldnews/10133833/Brazil-World-Cup-protests-teenager-dies-as-a-million-people-take-to-the-streets.html). Sustainability in events has been measured, initially using the British Standard BS8901 (www.eco.co.uk) and ISO 20121 (www.iso20121.org/), developed as part of the London 2012 Olympics legacy. By 2018 many event-related businesses had been accredited or were working towards accreditation, so if this is important to your client, be sure to pick your venues and suppliers carefully.

Case study 11.3 describes the key benefits of implementing an evaluation plan for hybrid events, focusing on sustainability aspects.

CASE STUDY 11.3

Post-event evaluation: sustainability perspectives and hybrid events – The Aston Martin Virtual Product Showcase

Ollie Biddle, Content and Marketing Lead, Collaborate Global

Client: Aston Martin Virtual Product Showcase, July 2020

How the world changed

March 2020 shocked the world; a chain of events quite simply changed the events industry forever. Many businesses were forced to adapt and pivot as 'in-person' events were cancelled on a global scale overnight. Without the time and preparation to fully tackle the enormity of the shift, many events agencies struggled to first conceptualize what it was that they wanted to show. Clients weren't trusting of this new style of event and there was no clear path out.

We (Collaborate) had worked with Aston Martin the previous year to launch their new DBX live at an in-person event in the UK. Wanting to show the world that a virtual event can be more than just content played on a screen, we looked to replicate the same show but do it virtually. This went live in July 2020, with a view count of over 1,500 and 4 times the expected number of guests live on the day.

Virtual vs hybrid

First, let's tackle the obvious question. What is the actual difference?

The clearest way to explain the difference between the two channels is by breaking down how the content is being viewed. A virtual event has a 100% remote audience. The audience can be anywhere around the globe, but the content is being streamed and watched completely remotely. Hybrid simply means that there is a selection of the audience that is viewing the content in the room – in person.

Virtual events can have a completely remote production crew working on the show; however, both virtual and hybrid events can have large-scale in-person production crews working on them.

The difference between virtual and hybrid lies within the audience, not the content, the crew, the location or the platform.

For the Aston Martin product launch, we used a studio in Feltham and worked with a live-streaming and staging company called Anna Valley. Two stages were physically built within the warehouse in Feltham and there was a film production crew on-site capturing all of the content. The entire show was pre-recorded but edited in post to make it look as though it was being rolled out live. We did invite guests into the studio, but this was more to show the background of the event and behind the scenes. The audience was entirely based online when we hit play on the actual stream the following day, making this a virtual event and not hybrid. Had the guests been invited to watch some of the show, there could be a strong case for saying that this was a hybrid event; however, the show was not actually being pushed out live until the following day. You see how the topic can get quite confusing?

Platform

'Zoom and TEAMS have become the norm and we wanted to do things a little differently this time.' This is a direct quote from one of the senior leaders within BAE Submarines after we completed a series of virtual events for them. The key thing to think about when it comes to the platform is that, quite simply, it isn't about the platform. General consumers of virtual events have been overwhelmed with the number of platforms on offer, which leads them to get lost in the detail. The platform is there to serve the objective, whatever the event.

- Team meeting
- Product launch
- Internal sales kick-off
- Roundtable
- B2C fan event
- Virtual exhibition
- Virtual conference

All these styles of virtual events have different objectives, and therefore could live on any platform. Focus on the experience, not the platform. If in doubt, use Hopin, it can do it all.

Delivery

When you are delivering your event, there are many factors that need to be accounted for. Here is a breakdown of what to prepare for:

- Platform – get it sorted from the beginning
- Virtual vs hybrid?
- Venue
- Staging
- Film crew
- AV – live-streaming content into the platform
- Pre-recorded content or live on the day
- Guest registration
- Event moderators – where do guests go if they have a problem?
- Engagement – polls, questionnaires, breakout rooms, networking zones etc
- Bringing remote guest speakers onto 'stage'
- Exiting the event
- Collecting data and reports after completion

Innovation

Innovation should be led by the objectives of your event. There is no need to reinvent the wheel if the mode of transport is boat. When working on the virtual event showcase with Aston Martin and Randox we tackled innovation in three key parts.

LIVE STAGES

The LED stages were built to have content streamed from them, meaning that we could manipulate the set as we were presenting. This simple metric really increases the engagement for guests, as they are tuned in to what is going on around them. We quite simply had blinds that, when we pressed a fake switch on the set, would close, before rolling a VT. This added to the illusion of the set being real and it also changed the atmosphere before the VT was played.

EXTENDED-REALITY STAGES

These are a relatively complex bit of kit. In simple terms, it allows you to load up a digital version of the set (like you would on green screen) but in real life. This means that the presenter can interact with the space, rather than just pointing at some green fabric and pretending the content they are speaking about is there. It also links directly to a unique camera that tracks the movement of the speaker and the room itself, meaning that when the camera moves, the space outside the set windows moves in sync.

AUGMENTED REALITY

Finally, when presenting Randox's healthcare diagnostic kit (information that would go over most people's heads), we brought the machine to life through augmented reality, meaning that the speakers had the object floating in front of them when they were discussing it. This is an incredible way of creating depth to a story, but bear in mind that any physical guests at a hybrid event would not be able to see it.

THE FUTURE – HYBRID?

Quite simply, yes. Because why would brands not? Covid 19 has forced brands and businesses to seek out virtual events, which has in turn created global audiences, reduced carbon emissions and accelerated the growth of innovation within this space.

Physical events will never be overtaken by virtual, but adding a hybrid element that does not interfere with the live guest experience gives you the keys to a whole new, global kingdom.

Read further

www.collaborateglobal.com (archived at https://perma.cc/WV7C-E6KF)

CHAPTER SUMMARY

- Events use a huge amount of resources – financial and otherwise – and it is increasingly important for those of us involved in developing and delivering events to be able to validate the use of such resources.
- Efficiency and effectiveness in our processes and systems are vital, but planning for each event needs to start with clear objectives. As an events manager you should help your client through this process, explaining the benefits of evaluation.
- We recommend that you develop an evaluation plan that runs throughout the event planning and delivery timeframe – be creative in what you measure.
- Review a range of evaluation models and online tools that can help you to undertake useful evaluations of stakeholders and event planning processes.

- Consider how you can improve your event planning and delivery processes, how you engage with suppliers as well as their performance – and yours – by identifying what works and what improvements you can make.
- If you build in improvements and reviews as part of the way your events team works, you will find that their creativity focuses on getting better at what you do – and that will make for happy clients.
- Large events focus on evaluating the long-term benefits to the local community, the environment and the economy.

Questions for reflection

1. In events you have attended or worked at in the past, what evidence of evaluation have you seen?
2. What three things would you choose to evaluate and how would you evaluate them?
3. How would you build in evaluation to your next event project?

References

Bowdin, G et al (2011) *Events Management*, 3rd edn, Butterworth-Heinemann, London

Elkington, J (1997) *Cannibals with Forks: The triple bottom line of twenty-first century business*, Capstone, Oxford

ISO 20121 (2018) Welcome to the ISO 20121 Website www.iso20121.org (archived at https://perma.cc/DA2N-C5CJ)

Kirkpatrick Partners (2018) The Kirkpatrick Model www.kirkpatrickpartners.com/TheKirkpatrickModel/ (archived at https://perma.cc/B7H5-KB2N)

Live Group (2018) www.livegroup.co.uk/ (archived at https://perma.cc/M42Z-FYDA)

MPI (2016) Meetings Outlook http://mpiuki.org/ (archived at https://perma.cc/7XMQ-JQ64)

Phillips, J J, Breining, M T and Pulliam Phillips, P (2008) *Return on Investment in Meetings and Events: Tools and techniques to measure the success of all types of meetings and events*, Butterworth-Heinemann, Oxford

Explore further

Event ROI Institute (2016) www.eventroi.org (archived at https://perma.cc/6R5Z-WJJW)

Jones, M (2018) *Sustainable Event Management: A practical guide*, 3rd edn, Routledge, Abingdon

12

Events – the future

FIGURE 12.1 The Dowson, Albert and Lomax Event Planning Process – the future

Events The Future
SUSTAINABILITY
INCLUSIVITY
WELLBEING
CO-CREATION
BESPOKE EVENTS
INNOVATION

Since March 2020, the Covid-19 pandemic has sent multiple economic and employment shockwaves throughout the globe, impacting all industries and sectors, but few have been hit harder than the events, hospitality and tourism industries. In countries around the world, these vibrant sectors halted immediately on the imposition of the initial lockdown that was enforced to protect populations. Some events companies were able to transition to work with clients online, developing and honing new skills, creating new technologies and devising new activities, while for other events companies, the future looked bleak. By the second half of 2021, changes were beginning to emerge, as economies tentatively reopened and some on-site events began to take place, until the advent of the fourth wave as the Omicron variant flew across the globe. As a result of the pandemic, new event definitions have emerged, focused around four major formats:

On-site events – these involve attendees engaging with each other in person using a building or physical space (indoors or outdoors).

Online events – these involve attendees engaging with each other using web platforms such as Zoom, Microsoft TEAMS, Skype, and other specialist programmes.

Hybrid events – these encompass on-site and online attendees engaging together and include on-site presence with online access in parallel.

FIGURE 12.2 Post-pandemic event formats

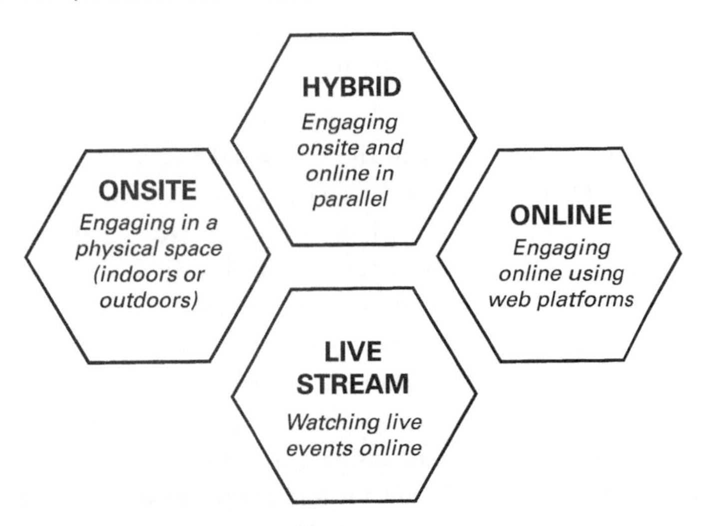

Live-Streaming – this mode uses web cams to enable participants to watch on-site events online, including through social media and YouTube channels.

Figure 12.2 shows the relationship between these event formats following the paradigm shift in events due to the pandemic.

One of the complexities that has emerged since March 2020 was triggered by the wholesale move to online events using web platforms such as Zoom, Microsoft TEAMS, Skype, and a range of specialist software programmes developed specifically to meet the new circumstances. Businesses, educational institutions and other public sector organizations, and even houses of worship, moved all engagement online, as on-site events and activities were banned by governments around the world in an effort to reduce the deadly contagious Covid-19.

So, what does the future hold for events and for the sector? First, it is important that we recognize the changes that have taken place:

- After the first 18 months of the pandemic, with limited or non-existent interaction in physical spaces, many events companies and events organizations folded, despite furlough provision in some countries, as they were unable to sustain themselves financially without adequate cash flow.
- Event business models have been subject to examination, and many that are financially unsustainable (whether in the continuing pandemic or in the post-pandemic era) are either failing or undertaking fundamental restructure.
- The 'gig economy' that was named for the events industry depended on large swathes of freelancers, many of whom were ineligible to be furloughed due to the temporary nature of their work contracts. As a result, many have chosen a different path, moving into other areas for their continuing employment.

- Many specialist, skilled events staff have found themselves more in demand as events venues reopened, with higher rates of pay for freelancers (and we would argue that these professionals were undervalued and underpaid before the pandemic).

All the future-proofing preparation in the world did not and could not possibly anticipate what would happen to the events industry in 2020. This may seem a somewhat negative perspective, but 2020–21 demonstrated what challenging times we live in. As we have seen from the experience of living through 2020–22, those companies which invest time and effort in future-proofing recognize that past successes do not mean that future success is inevitable, or even possible.

As many of the largest and most successful companies are continuously thinking about and planning for the future, they are trying to prepare themselves for what lies ahead. As event planners, we strive to ensure a bright future for the events industry by creating events that remain relevant for and appealing to participants, whether they take place online or in a physical space. We now recognize that nobody can say with certainty what the future will bring. This chapter seeks to explore new ideas and possibilities that will encourage event professionals and event management students to recognize that the future is bright and full of potential.

In writing this chapter we have undertaken research, not to provide a prophetic outlook on the future, but to contribute the thoughts and perspectives of experienced industry professionals, as well as academics who specialize in events management. We seek here to originate and present approaches that we hope will deliver practical value to our readers, proposing themes and pragmatic processes that we hope will be useful to event practitioners and students alike. Chapter 3 also includes some useful tools that can inform our decision-making processes in creating new events, and these tools are useful for thinking about the future of the events industry and considering how events might change in the future.

By the end of this chapter, you will be able to:

- adapt your approaches to fit with the future landscape of events as circumstances change;
- explore the themes that will impact on the landscape of events in the future;
- create new, bespoke and unique concepts to enhance the relevance and appeal of your events to new and existing audiences;
- identify emerging trends that could impact positively or negatively on your events, and be prepared to adapt your events to take account of these trends;
- using the tools identified in Chapter 3, find sources of information that keep you up to date with news and developments in the events industry and beyond.

Future themes

The pandemic has shown us that the future can change immeasurably, within a very short time frame. As event professionals, what we need is a set of considerations that can enable us to develop and deliver sustainable and future-proof events, and to facilitate the businesses and organizations that create, evolve, and provide these events to meet the changing needs of future event participants. These important considerations include the following.

Sustainability

This involves addressing the pressing issue of sustainability in and through every aspect of the events industry, and for every event. The November 2021 United Nations COP26 conference that took place in Glasgow brought the vital issue of climate change to the forefront of political life, raising the profile of a core aspect of events. The elephant in the room is that for an event to take place, people, goods and services need to be transported to a specific location – which may be a permanent purpose-built venue, or one that is adapted, or even temporarily created – for a limited length of time. Pre-event logistical planning also involves transport, as do post-event activities. The London 2012 Olympics provided the impetus for the UK events industry to work together to develop ISO20121. ISO, the International Organization for Standardization, published this new standard to support events organizers to integrate sustainability throughout all their activities, in order to leave behind a positive legacy, by identifying potentially negative social, economic and environmental impacts of events and mitigating their effects. While huge advances have been made over the past two decades, embedding sustainability in venues, in event organizations and in events themselves, much more progress is possible. Rather than limiting changes to improvements in packaging, or waste disposal, or focusing on 'reduce, reuse, recycle', the future events industry has the opportunity to consider how to build a new way of doing events that truly incorporates sustainable values and practice.

Inclusivity

This requires focusing on inclusivity and accessibility throughout the events industry and in events of all kinds. An obvious issue that faces business events is the lack of diversity often presented by the line-up of speakers at conferences (the accusation of 'pale, male and stale' is still all too often accurate). But achieving diversity goes well beyond assessing the impacts of failing to create culturally sensitive or culturally aware spaces and events that are able to meet ethical, moral and legal obligations for equality, diversity and inclusion. To enable the identification of excluding factors and mitigate against them, Dowson and Albert have developed a cultural risk assessment, based on research that: explores lived experience and how diverse groups navigate their own lives and spaces; creates awareness of implicit bias, stereotypes and potential prejudice; provides tools and strategies to build cultural capital, catering to diverse needs and to facilitate provision of inclusive events and event spaces; and engineers inclusivity into physical and virtual event spaces.

Case study 12.1 considers the issues around the future events industry engaging a more diverse workforce.

CASE STUDY 12.1

A more diverse future for the events industry?

Dr Kate Dashper, UK Centre for Events Management, Leeds Beckett University

The events industry serves diverse and varied audiences, offering innovative and exciting business, cultural and leisure opportunities. Yet this diversity is not reflected in the events workforce. Senior positions remain dominated by white, middle-class, able-bodied men, and people from black and minoritized ethnic communities are marginalized in many contexts. My own research has demonstrated that women feel less successful and satisfied in their careers in the events industry than do men, and black and minoritized ethnic women and men often struggle to be recognized as competent professionals, leading to issues with retention and career development. These are serious issues for the events industry that need addressing if the sector is to thrive and flourish in the coming years.

Lack of diversity in the events workforce is a problem. It limits ability to truly engage with different customers, to take maximum advantage of the range of skills and perspectives available within the labour market, and stifles innovation. It is also off-putting and limiting for those who would like to forge a successful career in the industry but do not see role models to inspire them and make them feel as if they would belong. Over the pandemic a number of industry reports, such as the Research Paper on Diversity and Inclusion produced by Fast Forward 15, or the C&IT Insight Report Achieving Racial Diversity in the Events Industry, highlighted some of the issues the sector faces in terms of diversity and proposed some practical steps towards change. It remains to be seen whether the industry will step up to the challenges and really address lack of diversity across multiple levels and sectors.

Conversations about diversity, or lack thereof, are often difficult and uncomfortable and many people shy away from them. This cannot continue, however, and I hope to see a more diverse future for the events industry. This will not happen without concerted action and a step change in how the industry recognizes and tries to address diversity issues. It is positive that diversity is a topic much more readily discussed at industry panels and forums, whether that be in relation to gender, race and ethnicity, disability, age, gender identity, religion, sexuality or any other marker of diversity. Yet for real change to happen, the industry needs to do more than just talk. Some industry initiatives are starting to make an impact, such as the

Fast Forward 15 women's mentoring programme led by Fay Sharp which has now supported many women to develop in their careers. More such initiatives are needed to enable and empower those currently on the side-lines of the industry. Companies may need to consider positive discrimination to really start to redress lack of diversity at senior levels, and education and training will have to address diversity challenges and try to equip events professionals with the tools and attributes to successfully manage diversity in their organizations.

A more diverse future for the events industry is possible and I am hopeful that new generations of events professionals will push for greater inclusion and equality across all levels and sectors of the industry. This will not necessarily be easy, as many of the barriers to inclusion are deeply entrenched and go beyond the events industry itself; however, a more diverse future is a necessity for the events industry to continue to develop and remain relevant in a globalized, interconnected world.

Find out more

www.leedsbeckett.ac.uk/staff/dr-kate-dashper/ (archived at https://perma.cc/5FXV-Y6ND)
https://fastforward15.co.uk/ (archived at https://perma.cc/Q7M5-EUPU)
www.yumpu.com/en/document/read/64348690/ff15-2020-research-paper-diversity-and-inclusion (archived at https://perma.cc/3NLA-LHLB)
www.cit-world.com/reports/achieving-racial-diversity-in-the-events-industry-2020 (archived at https://perma.cc/TL6Q-YYPQ)

Wellbeing

This involved considering and supporting mental wellbeing issues for all event stakeholders, from professional events staff, suppliers, traders, sponsors and volunteers to participants and the owners of the event. The Covid-19 pandemic has impacted on the mental health of us all, and the liminal space of an event alongside the pressures in the build stages can contribute to the release of these issues. Access to resources and information will become a threshold requirement in the future, while undertaking risk assessments could also include analysis of the psychological and emotional factors that might impact on all stakeholder groupings.

Co-creation

The trend for content co-creation, a process that engages all participants in developing the content of an event, is not new but post-pandemic it is likely to become increasingly vital, as stakeholders seek deeper authenticity in developing events as a form of community. We do not view these aspects as an excuse to avoid paying for the creation of event content, or to justify exploitation of stakeholder groupings that provide professional input in event delivery. Instead, we see this element as a recognition of the changes brought about by multiple lockdown experiences, as people express the desire for more control over their lives as well as over their work and leisure activities, valuing the creation of relationships beyond the short-term of the transient event space.

Case study 12.2 explores the future potential of events from the perspectives of industry guru Paul Cook of Planet Planit.

CASE STUDY 12.2

The future of the events industry – physical, virtual and hybrid events

Paul Cook, Planet Planit

For many years, the predominant focus of events was to bring people together in a physical setting. Whether the event was for learning, networking or socializing didn't matter. Event planners, destination management companies and numerous other suppliers benefited by having people leave their homes and attend events. And for delegates who went to in-person events it was good as well. But it was really the only option they had.

While there were virtual and hybrid events, they were very few. That was the position until Covid-19 came along and significantly impacted the events sector. The pandemic stopped events, travel and crossing borders. And it did so with effortless ease. It created other results as well, and one of the direct results was the proliferation of virtual events and the additional efforts of technology suppliers to improve their offerings.

In addition to virtual events, Covid-19 has led to a greater focus on hybrid events, which include in-person and virtual delegates.

Critical choice

Today, the event format choice is now a much bigger consideration. Events managers understand the different options available and can make considered decisions as to what will work best for them. More than in-person is now on the events menu.

Inclusivity matters

Let's add to the mix issues such as attendee inclusivity, health and wellbeing, and event anxiety and you can see there is a perfect storm brewing.

How inclusive is your event? Let's take language as a potential barrier to delegates being able to participate. This can be solved by using translation services such as subtitles or post-edited event audio. Or you could have real-time audio interpretation. Defining inclusivity is down to the individual organization.

But events cannot go back to how they were pre-Covid-19. Change is a constant. Things keep moving, but in my years as an events practitioner I have never seen such change coming from numerous directions at the same time.

Diving into data

If data is not being used to its maximum, it is effectively wasted. Data goes far beyond post-event satisfaction surveys. In the same way that scientists study the results of everything they put under the microscope, it must be the same with event practitioners. It is time to bring in specialist people, data ninjas, to help. Attempting to add this key skill to the workload of a busy planner would be madness. There is lots of data to learn from and now is the time to treat it with respect.

Honesty remains

Honesty with clients is even more of a consideration. I am not for one moment suggesting that events practitioners were not truthful before. But the income from in-person events was easier to follow and calculate. Take the simple example of an event planner being paid commission from hotels and conference centres based on how many rooms and meals were contracted. However, when a client requests a virtual event, the planner needs a different remuneration model, which requires more work. You can see how some disreputable planners could try to persuade the client that they really need an in-person event rather than a virtual one. They wouldn't last in business long, but....

The events professional is always going to look at what is best for the client and not what is best for them. And that is where the age-old challenge lies. Events professionals have a living to make as well.

A look to the future

What next for the events sector? This is tough to answer as I do not have a way of telling the future, but what I do know is that every day people expect more. They have less patience and expect more for their money. And it doesn't matter whether they are an attendee, a speaker or a stakeholder, the same basic requirements apply.

Greater expectations mean that higher levels of professionalism must be ingrained in everything that is delivered. The role that events play has to be re-evaluated. It is critical that events professionals offer the range of options available for clients, such as in-person, virtual and hybrid events. And as before, events professionals need to understand where events fit within the overall strategy of the organization.

It is crystal clear that serving up the same events as in years past will not be good enough.

However, if you combine the experience in the sector, the new entrants and the scope of event services on offer, there is no reason why events cannot be delivered to an even greater level to meet and exceed expectations.

The future for the events sector is looking brighter than ever.

Find out more

https://paulcook.co.uk (archived at https://perma.cc/7W39-JHV4); www.planetplanit.biz/ (archived at https://perma.cc/V8FV-WTP4)

Creating bespoke events

The pandemic has created a desire for people to have more freedom in what they do, not only in terms of their work but in their home and social lives, in relationships and in the communities in which they live. By the end of 2021, we saw huge numbers of people choosing to resign their jobs, changing career, moving location and even transforming their relationships. This shift is being reflected in a demand for a different type of event. No longer is it acceptable to stint on the differentiation of an event. We have thrown out past assumptions about how we dress, choosing to restyle ourselves in ways that we see fit, that make us feel comfortable – and these changes are being reflected in the events industry. In much the same way as made-to-measure suits and tailored clothes are designed to fit the customer's body, fashion preferences and tastes perfectly, bespoke events are tailored to meet the specific needs of attendees. Anybody who has ever been fortunate enough to pamper themselves with a made-to-measure clothing service will have enjoyed the satisfying moment of putting on an item of clothing that fits them perfectly. So too can event planners, who are able to design and deliver events that fit perfectly with the needs of their audiences, be able to deliver that feeling of delight among participants, guaranteeing return engagement.

Below we look at two different types of bespoke event – custom- and customer-made – that can help to deliver higher levels of audience satisfaction, which in turn will continue to draw in the crowds – future-proofing!

Custom events

Large retail stores have long been interested in the buying habits and behaviours of their customers. By understanding what their customers do and don't like, stores have been able to create the ultimate shopping experience. Online activity is tracked through the use of cookies that enable potential suppliers to pop advertising onto our Facebook feed, sponsored posts on our Instagram or Twitter feeds, all based on our search engine activity. The Bluetooth in our smartphones has helped track our movements during the health crisis, alerting us to take action when we have been in proximity to someone who has tested positive for the virus.

An example of the use of technology to track customers' movements and activity is found in Disney Theme Parks. On entry, customers receive their Disney World Magic Band which is used to gain entry to the park, to buy food and merchandise, and even to unlock their hotel room. With customers wearing their Magic Band for the duration of their visit, this makes tracking their movements and activity straightforward (e.g. how many times they went on a particular ride, where and at what time they ate, and so on).

Tracking technology is not confined to our health or to retail stores and theme parks, with Radio Frequency Identification (RFID) wristbands increasingly featuring at UK music festivals, such as Glastonbury, Radio 1's Big Weekend, the Isle of Wight Festival and T in the Park. RFID wristbands allow festival organizers to create a digital trail of festival-goers which they can then use to improve the attendee experience at future events, as well as learning about individual habits to build on the relationship with an existing event attendee. Since the pandemic began in 2020, contactless payments have aided the move away from cash and other payment mechanisms involving touch and the possibility of transferring the virus. In the UK, in October 2021 the limit for contactless payments increased to £100, reflecting the wholesale acceptance of the move – whether through a smartphone or card. These payments provide immediate access, to the organizations collecting the money, to details of customers' movements and transactions, and apply equally to events organizations as to retail shopping.

Customer-made events

We would hope that the days of business events that promote well-known speakers for attendees to sit and listen to are long gone, although evidence shows us that these events still happen. But there is a much more powerful approach –to engage with the people who are coming to the event in the process of designing what that event looks like, in terms of style, structure and content. Giving event attendees a direct input into how products and services are created is a great way to build a continued demand for them – and the same approach works for events. The more we ask for input, the more likely we are to achieve a successful event.

Asking stakeholders to contribute towards developing ideas and concepts is known as the process of co-creation. Through a process, stakeholders are invited to contribute, evaluate and refine ideas and concepts for new products and services, as well as experiences (such as events). An event planner could invite the target audience to contribute ideas for an event location or venue, suggest guest speakers or entertainers, influence food and beverage choices, and much more. This fits within a team-based approach to developing events, recognizing that the ideas of many are more effective than the ideas of one person, and even more so where that team is diverse. For example, when developing a conference or training programme, you could solicit suggestions from participants for topics for discussion, guest speakers, workshop themes and encourage those who have made suggestions to facilitate the discussions. And if an event is going to be repeated, you could pilot it with a small group of people who would be planning to attend, to identify areas for improvement. By using techniques like this, you can create events that are more tailored to the express needs of stakeholders – and therefore more likely to be successful.

Case study12.3 considers the impact of the Covid-19 pandemic on events businesses, training for events professionals in a shifting environment and the role of virtual events, by Chris Powell, The Event Expert.

CASE STUDY 12.3

Pivot my business or risk losing it

Chris Powell, The Event Expert

I had been happily running my event training and consultancy business for nearly 20 years. I had attracted some great clients, created bespoke course offerings and run open public courses. All was good at The Event Expert. I was travelling across the UK and Europe working with a range of clients, all keen to improve their event planning skills. All my courses and consultancy services were delivered face-to-face.

Enter stage left Covid-19. And you know what happened next. As for events, the super spreaders of the Covid World... they were no more.

And so, too, my events business, which quite literally ground to a halt. My last in-person training session was on 11 March 2020. For the first few weeks, as the early part of the year had been very busy, invoices were still being paid. Financially I was ok and I had cash in the bank. From mid-April, however, things were very different. I had no work, no enquiries and my business overheads were still going out. New Covid laws decreed that people were not allowed to gather and events were effectively illegal.

It was now that the word 'pandemic' was being used, and they tend to hang around for about three years. That was my 'Oh xxxx moment'. Events were not coming back any time soon and when they did, they would need to be heavily regulated. I needed to find a potential source of income and reduce my overheads. Failing all of that I needed to get a job.

On the overheads front, I got rid of any 'nice to have' expenses and focused my attention on the 'need to haves'. With a little work I'd got my overheads down to a manageable figure. Make this figure and the business remains viable.

Sorting the overheads was the easy part of the equation, trying to find something that organizations needed and would pay for was a different matter. I am self-employed: no work, no pay. At the time there was no government financial support either. The events industry had collapsed and all that remained was some wishful thinking along the lines of 'when we get back to normal...'.

Bubbling on the horizon and gaining traction were virtual events. A virtual event is an event held online with a remote audience. Many events professionals were sceptical, including me. With nothing to lose I wanted to find out what the rest of the world thought about virtual events. An online search revealed some thought leaders and with them came practical 'how to' advice. I soon became a convert.

To develop a new income stream I needed to create courses. I also needed to learn about this new virtual events world – fast. I knew that if I could learn this stuff, I could create courses based on how to run a virtual event. There is nothing like necessity being the mother of invention. I had to do something to get money coming back into my business. I watched, read and attended anything about virtual events. The result was an Essentials and Masterclass Course on 'How to plan and organize successful virtual events'.

The side issues were that I had no track record in virtual events and no money to advertise my new courses. With regard to my lack of a track record, the reality was that everyone was new to it, so any help was welcomed. In terms of advertising my new courses: if you can't afford to be seen everywhere then you'd better get busy being heard everywhere. I popped up, commented, wrote blogs and got busy getting heard. Google started to notice me.

Enquiries started to trickle in and my first booked session was in June 2020. Other bookings soon arrived and at last cash was starting to come back into the business. If I could keep the bookings coming in, I was going to be ok.

As the months and years rolled by, I have created other online courses, delivered bespoke presentations and lectures, produced virtual events and survived to fight another day. I have also published a book about virtual events, along with a podcast and expert talk.

And so to now. While I haven't delivered a course on virtual events for a while, I have been flat out helping organizations with their event Health and Safety plans and risk assessments. Meanwhile my online event planning and face-to-face bookings are also starting to creep up.

Covid-19 has dealt a fatal blow to many companies, and others left devoid of income for two years can't invest in training. Covid-19 forced my hand, which now means I actually have the largest portfolio of courses and resources I have ever had, which can be delivered in person or online. Either works for me!

I survived, I adapted, and I foresee continuing to help people deliver successful events!

Find out more

www.theeventexpert.co.uk/ (archived at https://perma.cc/RB2H-RT2L)

Innovation is key to future success

One way to know what the future holds is to create it yourself. For an event planner, this means going out and creating the events of the future. Be the first to try out new ideas. Be the first to test new ways of doing things. Put simply – become an innovator! Many university events management courses now include modules on entrepreneurship that will help to provide students with some of the skills and experience to enable them to innovate once they are working in the events industry.

Another way to introduce innovation into events is through co-creation of content, which involves inviting event participants to contribute their ideas and proposals to develop the event. Innovation can be about giving participants something unexpected, something different, something that up until now they haven't even thought of. Becoming an innovator involves striving to breathe new life into your events (whether these changes are large or small) in order to avoid stagnation, and to maintain the buzz and excitement around the event.

It is at this point that the idea of creating the events of the future through innovation can become a little daunting (it certainly does for us). Fortunately, though, it is possible to find ways to be an innovator without being wholly innovative. Admittedly, this does sound a little strange but please read on....

Below we suggest two ways to enhance creativity and innovation at your next event without being particularly innovative (at least in the purest sense of the word).

Imitate to innovate

When we imitate someone, this can have positive and negative connotations. In our studies, if we copy someone else's work, we will be penalized for doing so – and often with serious consequences. But as someone working in the events industry, we might come across a creative and innovative idea that can add something new and exciting to our own next event, and often this is something that we all do, to improve our own events – in which case, we say go right ahead and copy them. But if all you do is copy ideas from other events planners (particularly those organizing similar events to you), that is hardly going to be new and exciting for your participants (more like tried and tested). But, if you look beyond the confines of the events industry, you never know what exciting and inspirational ideas you might find.

The concept of imitating to innovate is based on the idea that many important future trends and developments for the events industry are already here, and we just need to know where to look for them. In other words, the future trends and developments that will soon be shaping and influencing the events of the future are already happening in other industry sectors. So it could be, for example, that what is happening today in the worlds of fashion, film, hospitality or music can hold the key to future success in the events industry. Perhaps the latest trend at this year's London Fashion Week will provide an event planner with their 'next big idea' for a theme and decoration of an event. Or perhaps the set for the latest blockbuster movie or a popular music video might provide inspiration for a new event location or venue. It's not always simply a case of copying exactly what others are doing, but of using their innovative ideas as a springboard to come up with your own innovations.

It is vital to look beyond the confines of the events industry for new ideas and inspiration, because only tracking the developments in your own industry (micro trends) is likely to mean that you are missing out on bigger opportunities. We have already given the examples of looking to the worlds of fashion, film, hospitality and music to provide ideas and inspirations for an event planner. These industries are often labelled creative industries and considered to be the 'trend-setters'. As such, these would seem to be obvious places to look for ideas and inspiration. But, of course, looking in the most obvious places probably means that this is exactly where everybody else is looking as well – including your competitors. It is more important to recognize that inspiration can come from anywhere, so it's worthwhile keeping your eyes open and searching in the more unlikely areas. Could it be, for example, that your next big idea will be inspired by robotic technology being developed in manufacturing, or advancements in aerospace travel? How will the pandemic influence creative changes in the events industry? Who knows? But we do know that by looking where other people aren't looking, you might just spot a great new idea that others haven't seen.

Collaborate to innovate

Collaborative working is essentially about multiple parties cooperating to create something new. This textbook, for example, is the result of the collaborative efforts of four authors, working at different times in different places – the first two editions were written by two authors, and this edition builds on that work with two new co-authors. We have all written different sections, and our work builds on our past efforts to create a better resource for the events industry and for students studying events management. There are two major benefits typically associated with collaborative working. The first is that it helps you to get the work done faster. The second is that you are able to capitalize on the strengths/talents of the other party in the collaboration. It is this second benefit that can enable an event planner to capitalize on the innovative capabilities of a partner organization to enhance the creativity and innovation of their next event. By drawing on the creative and innovative talents of their partner organization (for example, working with someone who is able to imagine or think up an idea far better than their own), together they can jointly create something new and exciting, something unique and unusual, something that will help create the buzz and excitement around the event that keeps attendees coming back time and time again (the essence of future-proofing your events).

Earlier in the book, we explained that putting on a successful event is only possible through the collaborative efforts of many different individuals and organizations. Here we suggest that choosing to collaborate with partner organizations that are particularly innovative in their approach will enable you to enhance the level of creativity and innovation at your events.

For example, a conference organizer may plan a fairly routine (some might say uninspiring) event programme, but, if they choose a venue with an award-winning chef who creates a dining experience to wow the delegates, those delegates will go away from the conference and tell others about their wonderful dining experience. While the chef clearly deserves the majority of the credit for their creative and innovative talents, the event planner too deserves credit for such a wise choice of collaborating with the particular venue and chef. So, whether you innovate through imitating others or through joining together with others to build on your shared strengths, innovation is key to a successful future in the events industry. Most innovations will be shared and spread across the industry, so you need to keep innovating to continue to be successful.

Case study 12.4 tells the story of the development of Future Event Leaders through the Event Grads® network, a community for students and graduates, and Event First Steps, helping newcomers to progress in the events industry.

CASE STUDY 12.4

Event First Steps and Event Grads® – creating graduate networks for future event professionals

Sasha Green, Naomi Hollas, Priya Narain and Gemma Gilbert, Co-Founders, Future Event Leaders, Event First Steps and Event Grads®, the community and support network for event management students and graduates

The idea for Future Event Leaders stemmed from personal experiences and research highlighting that industry newcomers were feeling disadvantaged, unmotivated and uninspired about their future careers due to the detrimental impact that Covid-19 had on the events industry. This, paired with the demand from organizations looking for engaged and proactive new talent, led us to build the Future Event Leaders platform.

Future Event Leaders is a marketplace for work experience and placement opportunities for industry newcomers across all event sectors, providing a network for growth in the industry. The industry calls for practical and first-hand experience, which is why we believe it is vital to present high-quality, high-value work experience and learning opportunities in a more accessible way to better prepare industry newcomers for entering the industry.

Our mission is to change the narrative around entry-level and placement roles and challenge the industry's reliance on unpaid work. To do this, we will only advertise roles that align with our three values:

1. Better Access
   - Industry newcomers have a dedicated marketplace for event-specific work opportunities and placements.
   - Offering companies access to an engaged talent pool (students, graduates, newcomers).
2. Better Quality
   - High-quality event-specific work experience opportunities that allow industry newcomers to demonstrate their skills and expertise while learning and developing.
   - Opportunities that better prepare industry newcomers to enter the industry.
   - Facilitated through mentorship, education, and resources.

3 Better Value

- We will only advertise paid opportunities unless the value of unpaid work is equal in other respects (training, skills, charities).
- By applying for a role on the Future Event Leaders marketplace you know the company is dedicated to supporting you and the role is suitable and relevant to an industry newcomer.
- Through an effective vetting process, only viable work and placement opportunities will be posted through the marketplace. With our feedback loop process, you can share your experiences, as we will work only with organizations that align with these values.

Future Event Leaders is driven by two community initiatives that aim to empower the next generation of events industry talent.

Event Grads®

This is a community and support network for event management students and graduates. Founded in June 2020 in response to the pandemic, Event Grads® provides community, content and events for the next generation of events professionals to bridge the gap between academia and industry.

Event First Steps

This is a not-for-profit company encouraging events industry newcomers to forge their own career path by hosting educational and social events to allow newcomers of all ages and abilities to build their networks and learn from industry heavyweights.

The team was formed after we recognized the lack of events-industry-specific placement and job opportunities that allow industry newcomers to gain work experience. Made up of students, graduates, industry newcomers and experienced events professionals, the team have a well-rounded experience and understanding of the many different routes into the industry, the demand for such a marketplace and how it will benefit future event leaders.

How does it work?

The marketplace encourages events organizations to advertise high-quality, valuable, event-specific job and placement opportunities with us. The opportunities are then shared with our engaged audience of industry newcomers who are actively seeking new prospects in the industry, via our website and mailing list as well as our social platforms.

The initial proposal was developed with the help of EMA (Event Marketing Association). Having recently received the stamp of approval from AEME (Association of Event Management Education), we are enthusiastic about the future of this project. Working with AEME allows us to connect with universities and supports our mission of improving placement opportunities and changing the narrative to reduce the reliance on unpaid internships.

We have high hopes that it will be successful in supporting events management students, graduates and industry newcomers with opportunities, enabling them to gain industry-specific experiences and help to propel their careers into the events industry. This will be achieved through the creation of relationships with events companies to address the importance and benefits of offering placement and work opportunities to new rising talent, as well as stressing the importance of believing in the new generation of future events professionals which will positively impact the development of the industry in the future.

Find out more

www.futureeventleaders.co.uk (archived at https://perma.cc/K8BX-SMHN)

@futureeventleaders on social media

EVENTS MANAGER HACKS

Hybrid events have secured their place in the event portfolio. As planners we must embrace a new way of creating event experiences, 'reinvent' rather than 'replicate', giving equal amounts of enthusiasm and attention to both in-person and online events. Attendees will be at the same event, but their experiences will differ; keep this in mind when planning.

Selina Arnall, That Event Girl; Social Traders (Australia)

CHAPTER SUMMARY

- The pandemic has taught us many lessons about planning and managing events in the future. Possibly the most important lesson is that we cannot predict what is going to happen, so what we need are tools and approaches that will help us to survive and thrive.
- Future-proofing a specific event is about making sure that it remains relevant and appealing to the target audience not only today and tomorrow, but the following day and into the distant future. Yet we shouldn't be complacent and assume that the target audience will remain constant.
- Simple economics dictates that so long as there is a demand for an event, it will most likely continue to be held. Conversely, if such a time arises that audiences no longer want to attend, the future of the event is put in doubt.
- In much the same way as a made-to-measure suit will deliver better customer satisfaction, creating bespoke events, tailored to the specific needs of the attendees, will deliver higher levels of satisfaction and are more likely to generate repeat business.

- Co-creation involves asking the target audience to contribute towards the development of ideas and concepts for an upcoming event. Social media networks such as Facebook, Twitter and LinkedIn make it easy for people to contribute, evaluate and refine ideas and concepts.
- Event planners need to spend some time understanding the emerging trends and developments that are likely to have an impact (whether positive or negative) on the events that they are arranging.
- The future trends and developments that will soon be influencing the events of the future are most likely to be already happening in other industry sectors. Stay ahead of the curve by looking beyond the confines of the events industry for new ideas and inspirations that can enhance creativity and innovation for your next event.
- Collaborating with individuals and organizations that are particularly creative and innovative in their approach will enable you to enhance the level of creativity and innovation of your event.

Questions for reflection

1. What three things could you build into your event planning process to take account of emerging trends in events?
2. Which three sources will you use to keep up to date with changes that affect the events industry?
3. Identify two possible changes that could impact on the events industry, including the Covid-19 pandemic.

Explore further

United Nations Climate Change Conference, 31 October–12 November 2021: COP26 https://ukcop26.org/ (archived at https://perma.cc/JPN7-QUR6)

United Nations Sustainable Development Goals (UN SDGs) https://SDGs.un.org (archived at https://perma.cc/A3A2-WC3V)

Albert and Dowson Cultural Inclusivity and Equity Risk Assessment 2022 (CIERA®) https://committees.parliament.uk/writtenevidence/36018/pdf/ (archived at https://perma.cc/Q7V7-7GW9); https://www.ecb.co.uk/news/2637393 (archived at https://perma.cc/6E69-9447). Venues will be subject to monitoring through the season to ensure that they are making progress against their plans and addressing the identified gaps in provision, as well as reaching ECB minimum standards. To support further work in this area, further review will be completed during the season including a Cultural Risk Assessment by Leeds Beckett University, which will look at barriers to attendance by fans from ethnically diverse communities and potential issues within cricket grounds.

INDEX

Bold page numbers indicate figures, *italic* numbers indicate tables.